Connections

Connections
A GUIDE TO THE BASICS OF WRITING

Peter Dow Adams

Essex Community College

LITTLE, BROWN AND COMPANY
Boston / Toronto

Library of Congress Cataloging-in-Publication Data
Adams, Peter Dow.
    Connections: a guide to the basics of writing.

    Includes index.
    1. English language — Rhetoric.   2. English language —
Grammar — 1950–   I. Title.
PE1408.A317   1986   808'.042   86-15239
ISBN 0-316-00950-4

Library of Congress Catalog Card No. 86-15239

ISBN 0-316-00950-4

9 8 7 6 5 4 3 2 1

MV

Published simultaneously in Canada
by Little, Brown & Company (Canada) Limited

Printed in the United States of America

Cover image: *Celtic Design Coloring Book* by Ed Sibbett, Jr. (New York: Dover
Publications, Inc., 1979).

To the Instructor

> Only connect! That was the whole of her sermon. Only connect the prose and the passion, and both will be exalted, and human love will be seen at its height. Live in fragments no longer. Only connect . . .
> — E. M. Forster

When Margaret Schlegel in E. M. Forster's *Howard's End* enjoins her husband to "live in fragments no longer," she probably had in mind a different kind of fragment than the ones discussed in this book. Nevertheless, her admonition to "only connect" is one we have embraced enthusiastically.

Writing itself is always an attempt to connect — to connect with other people and to connect with ideas. This text, too, makes a number of connections: It connects language and ideas; the various activities in the writing process; instruction in grammar and punctuation with instruction in writing; and academic writing, for instructors, with practical writing, for bosses and clients. And, most important, it connects students — it connects them with that community of people who use writing to express ideas and to get things done.

This book is founded on several principles about the teaching of writing:

1. Students should be taught the process of writing. The emphasis should be on how to write, rather than on what good writing looks like.
2. The greatest improvements in students' ability to write will result from improvements in their ability to plan and especially to revise their writing.
3. Grammar and mechanics are not the most important aspect of writing, but they *do* matter. Errors in the basic conventions of written English can seriously diminish the effectiveness of a piece of writing.
4. Grammar and mechanics are best taught inductively, incrementally, and recursively. These methods will be explained shortly.

5. Students' improved skills in grammar and mechanics must be reinforced in actual writing experiences.

These principles are incorporated into this book in the following ways:

1. **The writing process is emphasized throughout the book.** Emphasizing the writing process means that students are taught how to be effective writers instead of being taught only what effective writing is. Students are encouraged to think about the writing situation and plan what they intend to say before they begin to write. Most important, students are taught how to revise effectively. Revision is probably the area in which students can improve their effectiveness as writers most dramatically. This book deemphasizes the forms of organization traditionally taught to students of writing, as the profession in general has deemphasized them in the last ten years.

2. **This book integrates grammar and writing.** For the first twelve chapters, the chapters on writing alternate with those on grammar. The assignments in the grammar chapters reinforce the writing principles learned in the previous chapter. The assignments in the writing chapters also ask the student to attend to the grammar topic from the preceding chapter. In this way, the students learn to connect grammar with writing.

3. **The inductive approach is used throughout the book.** Most current texts use a deductive approach: The student is told a principle or rule and is then given some sentences to apply that principle to. In the inductive approach, sometimes called the discovery method, the student is given some sentences that illustrate a principle and is asked to figure out what the principle is. When the student understands the principle, he or she is asked to apply it in the exercises. The advantages of this approach are three:

   a. The student learns the principle in his or her own words and, therefore, truly understands it. Using the deductive approach, students often memorize a definition or rule without really knowing what it means.

   b. The student not only learns a principle, but also learns how to derive it. This means the student will remember the principle longer and, if he or she forgets it, will be able to derive it again at a later time.

   c. The student also learns that language is understandable, even to a basic writer.

   In *Errors and Expectations*, Mina Shaughnessy discusses the inductive approach:

   > Linguistic data are interesting to students in and of themselves. The detection of patterns, the discrimination among forms, and the application of rules to a range of situations are self-sustaining activities. Like taking machines apart or playing intricate games, they tease and challenge the brain, creating tensions and surprises that need no outside encouragement. What is needed, however, is a teacher who is prepared to expose students to linguistic data and allow them, wherever possible, to observe the phenomenon being studied and arrive through these observations at their own grammatical formulations. . . . Although it is the nature of grammar books

and handbooks to proceed deductively, with the statement of a principle or rule and then the illustrations of that rule, it is important at least at the outset of grammar study to allow time for inductive learning.

4. **The text organizes the material incrementally.** Sarah D'Eloia Fortune, in "The Uses — and Limits — of Grammar," describes the importance of incrementation: "The second strategy necessary for a successful discovery process, especially for the weaker students, is a very careful and purposeful incrementation, moving from the state of extremely simplified contrasts of bare-bones structures through the stages by which increasingly complex variables and distracting items are added, in the order which will prove most helpful to the student."

Connections begins with a discussion of the writing process. From then on, each chapter considers only one aspect of writing, and within the chapters, the topics are broken down into a series of even smaller steps, moving always from the simple to the complex.

5. *Connections* **is recursive.** This recursive organization provides that concepts, once learned, are repeated and reinforced in later exercises. This repetition is important for two reasons:
   a. Every concept a student learns is later reinforced and, therefore, not allowed to decay.
   b. Because of the incremental approach, most concepts are learned in isolation. In the exercises that follow, however, they are reinforced while other concepts are being learned, thereby encouraging students to make connections among concepts.

6. *Connections* **minimizes the amount of terminology the student has to learn.** Too often, the teaching of grammar emphasizes the learning of terminology and identification of various categories of words, phrases, clauses, and sentences. Of course, it would be nice if students could discriminate among gerunds, infinitives, and participles. If we had time, it would be wonderful to introduce students to noun absolutes and past participle expansion. However, in a basic writing course, it is essential that *all* grammar instruction be focused on the reduction of error in the students' writing. Therefore, in *Connections* the only terminology included is what is necessary for the reduction of error. As Sarah D'Eloia Fortune puts it, "grammatical instruction should proceed with a minimum of terminology and the simplest terminology possible. In practice, this seems to mean using the traditional terms which many of our students have heard and to which they are attached." When wondering whether students need to know the difference between a gerund and an infinitive, for instance, I asked myself whether the distinction was ever necessary in order to produce grammatical sentences. Since it is not, I have not included identification of gerunds and infinitives.

Some texts, recognizing that traditional terminology can be confusing or even inconsistent, have invented an entirely new set of jargon. Elegant as some of these systems of terminology are, they only place more obstacles between basic writers and the knowledge they really need: How to reduce the number and seriousness of errors in their sentences. *Connections* uses the traditional terminology, with which many students are already familiar.

Finally, a few suggestions on the use of the book. Recognizing that every writing program is distinct, the text is organized to provide maximum flexibility. Each chapter is written so it can be taught independent of others. This results in a text that can be useful in most developmental courses as well as in the tutorial settings of writing centers and writing labs.

There is more in this book than can effectively be taught to most basic writing students in one semester. If your school has two levels of developmental courses, *Connections* could be used effectively in both. If your school has only one level of remediation, you will need to select the chapters that seem most appropriate for your students.

One last piece of advice. Basic students have so many things to work on and become discouraged so easily that it is always tempting to keep things as simple as possible. When using this text, that can mean sticking to the editing exercises and avoiding the ones that require writing. After all, when asked to write, our students frequently introduce so many errors that both they and we become discouraged and confused about how to proceed. Don't give in to this temptation. Despite the difficulties, it is essential that basic writers apply what they learn in the editing exercises to their own writing. It may help both you and them if you limit your comments on their writing to the topics they have covered at that particular point in the course, but, no matter what, don't slight the writing exercises.

A number of people helped me significantly in writing this book. My students in developmental courses over the past five years have contributed a multitude of useful ideas about what they needed to learn and what worked for them in learning it. My colleagues at Essex Community College, Connie Coyle, Nancy Hume, Jean Hunter, Adelio Maccentelli, Alice O'Melia, and Al Starr, helped plan an earlier version of this text and used it in our developmental course. They suffered mightily with the typos and other mistakes and repaid me with invaluable suggestions. Barbara Fassler Walvoord at Loyola University of Baltimore provided a testing ground for my early ideas at her Institute in the Teaching of Basic Writers. The work of David Bartholomae and Glynda Hull at the University of Pittsburgh, Sarah D'Eloia Fortune at City College of New York, Linda Flower at Carnegie-Mellon University, Martha Kolln at Pennsylvania State University, and Lynn Quitman Troyka at Queens College has been especially useful to me in writing this book. The comments and suggestions of Richard Beal and Peggy F. Broder of Cleveland State University, Robert Dees and Edward Dornan of Orange Coast College, C. Jeriel Howard of Northeastern Illinois University, Michael J. Lackey of William Rainey Harper College, Cecilia Macheski of LaGuardia Community College, Mary McGann of Rhode Island College, Randall Popken of Tarleton State University, David Skwire of Cuyahoga Community College, and Harvey S. Wiener of LaGuardia Community College have resulted in many improvements in the text. Finally, my editors at Little, Brown, Joe Opiela and Victoria Keirnan, have been masterful in guiding this project to its completion.

To the Student

Writing is important. It can make a difference in your grade in almost every course you take, it can make a difference in your getting a job, and it is quite likely to be an important factor in when and how you are promoted in your career. In nearly every profession, even highly technical ones, people who move into managerial ranks must be able to write. It can also make a difference in your personal life. Being able to write about ideas is one way of making sense of them; writing can be a form of thinking. If you feel comfortable with writing, you will have one more way to grapple with the complexities that life presents to all of us. Writing is important.

Good writing makes connections. Writing can connect you with other people: When you write effectively, you inform, convince, or entertain other human beings; you enable them to understand you and the way you see the world. Writing also connects you with ideas and allows you to connect ideas with other ideas. Whether you are writing a journal, notes in class, a college paper, or a business proposal, you are connecting ideas; you compare, contrast, and synthesize what your instructor or boss has said, what you have read, what you have observed, and what you think about a complicated idea. The result of these connections is always a better understanding and is sometimes a startling insight.

This book also makes connections. It connects and integrates the different activities in the writing process. It connects work on grammar and punctuation with actual writing. It connects language and ideas. It connects school writing with business writing. And, most important, it connects you with a world in which most important communication is done in writing.

This book has only one purpose: to help you become a better writer. As you work your way through it, you will learn how an effective writer goes about the process of writing. You will learn how to get started with writing, how to analyze each writing task in terms of purpose, audience, and subject, and how to make an informal plan for your writing.

You will also learn how to become a better reviser. You will learn to revise your writing to make it better organized, better developed, more focused, and more coherent. Sometimes students who have difficulty with writing think that good writers merely hold their pens over the page and good writing pours out. The truth is that almost no one is able to produce really good writing in one draft. Even for professional writers, writing is a process that involves a lot of thinking, some writing, and a lot of revising.

While the major issues of unity, organization, development, and coherence are much more important, errors in the basics — grammar, spelling, and punctuation — do matter. They matter because they can sometimes interfere with the meaning of your writing. However, even when correct grammar doesn't influence meaning, it can make a big difference in the effect of your writing. Writing a memo, a letter, a report, or a college paper with a number of serious grammatical mistakes can have the same effect as going to a job interview with a splotch of egg on the front of your shirt. It may not be fair — having egg on your shirt may have nothing to do with the requirements for the job and you may never before have spilt egg on your shirt — nevertheless, it will probably be the one thing everyone remembers about you after your interview. Grammatical mistakes frequently have the same effect; after a reader bumps into a few serious blunders in your writing, he or she is likely to conclude that you are illiterate, that you don't care about your work, that your ideas are not worth listening to, or all of these. Now this conclusion is undoubtedly unfair and inaccurate, but, just like the egg on your shirt, it is probably the one thing people will notice first and remember longest. In this book, you will learn to avoid or correct the kind of error in grammar, punctuation, or spelling that could make your writing look bad.

There are a number of dialects of the English language in use in America. In addition, each of us uses slightly different versions of English in different situations. For example, most people speak to their friends on a Saturday night differently from the way they speak to their English teachers on Monday morning. All these dialects and versions of English are effective under the appropriate circumstances. However, there is one version of English that is usually appropriate when a writer wants to be formal and serious. We use this form of English for college papers, resumes and letters of application, and most business correspondence. It is this formal version of English, often referred to as standard written English, that this book teaches.

For many people, writing is hard work that often leaves them frustrated. We cannot promise, when you finish with this book, that writing will be an easy task. But we can promise that working your way through this book and following its suggestions will make the hard work you do when writing both more effective and more satisfying.

So, let's get started.

Contents

1 The Writing Process   3

Part A   The Writing Process   3
Part B   Getting Started   6
          What Am I Going to Write About?   6
          Who Is Going to Read This?   13
          What Is the Purpose of this Piece of Writing?   16
Part C   Revising   19

2 Subjects and Verbs   27

Part A   Identifying Verbs   27
Part B   Identifying Subjects and Verbs in Simple Sentences   43
Part C   Identifying Subjects and Verbs in Sentences
          with Verbals   54
Part D   Identifying Subjects and Verbs in Sentences with More Than
          One Clause   61
          Review   64

3 Writing Paragraphs   68

Part A   The Topic Sentence   68
Part B   Paragraph Unity   76
Part C   Other Kinds of Paragraphs   79

4 Subject-Verb Agreement   81

Part A   Simple Subject-Verb Agreement   81
Part B   Agreement with Irregular Verbs   90
Part C   Agreement with Prepositional Phrases, Compound Subjects, and Inverted Word Order   100
          Review   107

5 Using Concrete Language   110

Part A   Concrete Details   110
Part B   Telling Details   116

6 Sentences   120

Part A   Identifying Independent Clauses   120
Part B   Identifying Fragments   131
Part C   Correcting Fragments   135
          Review   151

7 Thesis and Unity in Longer Pieces of Writing   157

Part A   The Thesis   157
Part B   Unity   167

8 Punctuating Independent Clauses 173

Part A Avoiding Run-On Sentences and Comma Splices 173
Part B Commas with Coordinating Conjunctions 179
Part C Semicolons with Independent Clauses 185
Part D Semicolons with Conjunctive Adverbs 191
Review 198

9 Organizing Longer Pieces of Writing 205

Part A Making a List 205
Part B Revising for Organization 216

10 Punctuating Introductory Elements 227

Part A Commas with Introductory Phrases 227
Part B Commas with Introductory Clauses 234
Review 239

11 Developing Ideas 248

Part A Assertions and Evidence 248
Part B Asking What Needs to Be Proved 263

12 Coherence 267

Part A Transitions 267
Part B Consistent Point of View 272
Part C Consistent Tense 275

13 Noun Use   282

Part A   Singular and Plural of Regular Nouns   282
Part B   Singular and Plural of Irregular Nouns   285
Part C   Capitalization   289
         Review   296

14 Future Tense and Perfect Tenses   300

Part A   Future Tense   300
Part B   Perfect Tenses   302
Part C   Irregular Verbs   314
         Review   327

15 Pronoun Reference and Agreement   330

Part A   Identifying Pronouns   330
Part B   Identifying Antecedents   338
Part C   Pronoun Reference   339
Part D   Pronoun Agreement   342
         Review   350

16 Commas with Series, Places, and Dates   354

Part A   Items in a Series   354
Part B   Commas with Places   356
Part C   Commas with Dates   357
         Review   358

17 The Apostrophe   362

Part A   Recognizing Possessive Situations   362
Part B   Forming Possessives   367

Part C   Using Contractions   374
Part D   Contractions versus Possessives   375
         Review   379

18 Confusing Words   382

Part A   Words That Are Confused Because They Sound Alike   382
Part B   Words That Are Confused Because They
         Sound Similar   385
Part C   A, An, and And   389
Part D   Words That Are Confused with Incorrect Words   393
Part E   Contractions and Possessive Pronouns   395
         Review   397

19 Wordiness   400

Part A   Wordiness   400
Part B   False Humility   403
         Review   404

20 Awkwardness   409

Part A   Parallelism   409
Part B   Misplaced Modifiers   417
         Review   422

21 Spelling   426

Part A   Correct Spelling as a State of Mind   426
Part B   Some Spelling Rules   435

Index   439

Connections

1

The Writing Process

Part A   The Writing Process
Part B   Getting Started
Part C   Revising

Part A · The Writing Process

For the last ten years, English teachers have been watching people write.

We've put people in rooms and told them to write, and then we've videotaped everything they've done, sometimes from several angles. We've asked them to "think out loud" as they write, that is, to say out loud every thought that goes through their heads while writing. And we've recorded everything they've said. Sometimes, every ten minutes while they were writing, we've given them a pen with a different color ink so that later we could tell what was written when. And when they have finished writing, we have interviewed them. We've asked them every question we could think of about how they went about writing.

And whom did we do this to? We did it to every kind of writer we could find. We did it to people who make their living writing—journalists, authors, and public relations people. We did it to lawyers and economists and nurses. We did it to college students—graduate students in English and students in developmental writing courses. We even did it to each other—to English teachers.

When we got through and studied the results of all these observations, we were quite surprised. At first it looked as if each person had a different approach to writing; sometimes the same person even seemed to use different approaches on different days.

But gradually a pattern began to appear. No matter how people went about writing, the process seemed to boil down to some combination of three basic activities:

| they planned what they were going to write | they wrote | they revised what they had written |

At one time we thought the writing process could be represented by a diagram like this:

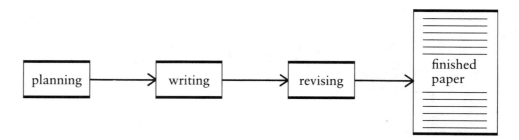

But our observations of people actually writing revealed that this model of the writing process was much too simple. Writers don't first do all their planning, then all their writing, and then all their revising; they mix the three activities together. Take a look at a simulation of one student, Karen, getting started on a writing assignment. As we join her, she has already decided what she is going to write about. The following are the words that Karen thinks as she starts writing; the words that she actually writes on paper as she is thinking them are underlined.

Let's see . . . I want to prove that grades aren't fair. I think I'll limit myself . . . limit the paper . . . to grades in college, not high school or other levels . . . So, I'll start . . . <u>Grades are the bottom line in college education</u> . . . No I don't like that expression "bottom line." Too slangy. How about . . . <u>At the end of the semester, after all the chapters have been read, all the classroom discussion is over, all the papers are written, and all the tests are taken, the entire semester's work is summed up in one letter grade. For the rest of the student's life, those fifteen weeks of thinking, of listening, and of writing are summed up by the letter "B."</u> Now, how does that sound? Oops, I used the expression "summed up" twice in a row. How can I fix that? Ah . . . those fifteen weeks . . . <u>will be represented by the letter "B."</u> That's better. Now what's wrong with that? What's wrong with a grade representing a semester's work? Hmmm. Is there anything wrong with it? Well, I know the grade I got in math last fall wasn't fair. But why not? Why aren't grades fair? This will take some thinking . . .

If you look closely at this representation of a student getting started on a paper, you will find that she begins in the planning stage—thinking about what she wants to prove, "grades are unfair," and narrowing it down to grades at the college level. Then she moves into the writing stage and writes her first sentence. As soon as she has written her opening sentence, she jumps into the revising stage; she changes the phrase "bottom line." Then she returns to the writing stage and gets two sentences written before she again moves into revision—changing the second "summed up" to "represented." Then she returns to the planning stage. She starts thinking about her main point and what will be necessary to prove it. In fact, as we leave her, she seems to be wondering whether her main point is really something she can prove.

Karen's process is similar to that of most writers: it involves a constant moving back and forth among the three basic activities involved in writing. Instead of three neat little boxes or stages of planning, then writing, then revising, the writing process for most of us involves this kind of weaving back and forth among the three activities. Therefore, a diagram that represents this complicated (English teachers sometimes call it "recursive") pattern would have to look more like this:

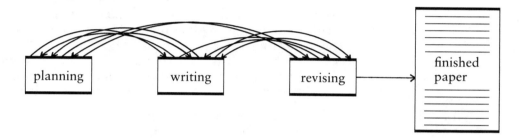

Once we figured out that this process of writing could be classified into these three parts, we were ready to examine the differences among the ways in which different people wrote. It seemed logical to assume, for example, that people who made their living by writing and the honors students in English were fairly good writers, that average students in freshman composition classes were average writers, and that students in developmental English classes were having trouble with their writing.

We then looked for differences among the writing processes of these groups of writers. What we found has revolutionized the teaching of writing. All three groups spent some time doing each of the three activities; however, there were startling differences in the percentage of time the different goups spent in the different activities.

These differences all added up to one fact: The more competent the writer was, the more time he or she spent planning and revising. This discovery has made considerable difference in the way English teachers across the country are teaching writing. We have come to recognize that we cannot just explain what a good paper consists of and then expect you to go home and write one. We've got to teach you how to go about writing in a way that will produce better writing. We cannot any longer merely focus on the final product; we've got to help you with the entire process of writing.

And what do you need to do? At first glance it would seem fairly simple: You need to increase the percentage of time you spend planning your writing and the percentage you spend revising what you have written. Unfortunately, it's not that simple. If you have no idea how to come up with a good idea for a paper, spending several hours planning is unlikely to result in a better paper than if you just wrote about the first idea that popped into your head. If you don't know how to improve the organization of your writing, doubling the amount of time you spend checking the organization will not improve it at all. If you don't know how to fix a fragment, spending an extra ten minutes proofreading for fragments is not likely to help.

So what English teachers and this book are trying to do is, yes, to urge you to spend more time planning what you are going to say and more time reviewing and revising what you have written. But more important, we want to teach you how to plan and to revise more effectively. We want to help you to improve the effectiveness of the time you do spend both planning and revising.

Part B · Getting Started

Even though, as you learned in Part A, the writing process does not consist of three distinct phases, it is still true that almost every writer begins almost every writing task with some kind of planning. This planning may consist of no more than a few minutes thinking about what it was the boss asked you to put in a memo, or it might consist of the entire weekend spent writing the formal outline that your history professor requires as the first step in writing a research paper.

Whether it is a few minutes or a few days, almost everyone spends some time planning before they actually begin writing. During this preliminary planning stage, there are three questions you must answer:

1.   What am I going to write about?
2.   Who is going to read this writing?
3.   What is the purpose of this writing?

Many writing problems can be traced to the writer's failure ever to answer these questions. Too often writers rush into writing without really thinking about these basic questions. It's not always possible to answer them completely before you start writing, but it is always possible to give them some thought. In the remainder of this section we will discuss each of these questions in detail.

What Am I Going to Write About?

Many people feel that getting started—finding something to write about—is the hardest part, and often it is. It is particularly difficult in academic writing when the instructor gives only general suggestions, but it can be almost as hard when the instructor or the boss at work gives you a more specific assignment, especially if that specific assignment is something you are not interested in or know nothing about.

In any case, the place to start is with the assignment itself. Make sure you understand it. If you've been given an assignment in writing, read it over during the planning stage. Look, for example, at the following assignment, which was actually used in one English course on the first day of class:

> Think about the best book you have read in the past two years. Write a paper in which you explain what the fact that you liked that book best reveals about the kind of person you are. Be sure to provide concrete details to support your ideas. The audience for this assignment will be your instructor, who will use it to get to know you.

What book would you write about if this were your assignment? What would your paper say?

If you picked a book and then wrote a "book review" about it, you would be making the same mistake as many of the students who actually received this assignment. If your paper focused on the book's strengths and weaknesses, you would not have been writing on the assigned topic. Go back and reread the assignment. Notice that it does not ask for a review of the book; in fact, the main focus of your paper is not to be on the book but on you. You are asked to explain what your reading preference reveals *about the kind of person you are.* Your paper is mainly to focus on *you* and not on the book. Admittedly, this assignment is a little complicated, but assignments often are complicated. That is why it is crucial that you read the assignment carefully before you do any planning or writing.

But what if there is no written assignment? What, for example, if you work for a kitchen remodeling company and your boss, Ms. Meyer, calls you in one morning and says, "By three o'clock today, I want a proposal on my desk for a new procedure for handling customer cancellations." What do you do first? Head for the typewriter? Head for the policy manual on customer relations? Head for the aspirin bottle?

Wait a minute. Before you head for anything, make sure you understand the assignment. Ask the boss a few questions. What does she mean by "customer cancellations"—when the customer cancels an order or when the company cancels a customer's order (perhaps because an item is out of stock)? Or does she mean both? And why does she want a new policy? Is there something wrong with the old policy? What? Or has something just happened that requires a change in policy? What? Just as in academic writing, make sure you correctly understand the assignment before you do anything else.

Sometimes merely reviewing the assignment will be all it takes to come up with a subject to write about, but often you won't be so lucky. It sometimes takes some work to find something that satisfies the assignment and that you actually want to write about. No one technique will work for everyone all the time, but some of the following may work for you:

1. Brainstorm, that is, just make a list of every possibility. Don't do any censoring. Write down every idea that pops into your head. If you seem to run out of possibilities after a while, keep working at it; often the best ideas come only after you've gotten the easy ones out of the way (of course, sometimes the best ideas *are* the easy ones, but you'll have them on your list too). Finally, read over your list looking for the right subject to write about this for assignment.

    Below is one student's brainstorming about the following assignment:

    > Think about an opinion you once held that has now changed. Write a paper to your instructor in which you explain why your opinion changed.

school	voting
education	my parents
religion	honesty
drinking	(friends)
women	popularity
love	competition
politics	success

This student ended up writing a paper about friends. In it he explained that, in high school, he had tried to be friends with people who were popular and would help him to be more popular and successful. In college, he had found that his friends were people he really liked, and popularity didn't seem to have much to do with it.

2. Freewrite. Just start writing. Don't worry about anything—grammar, spelling, whether it makes any sense, where it is going—just keep writing. Don't let your pencil stop. If you can't think of what to write about next, just write about what it feels like to be stuck. Just keep that pencil moving. Then, when you've got a couple of pages of writing, go back over it looking for ideas. You will probably have to throw out 95 percent of what you have written, but somewhere in it all you may find just the right idea to use as the start of a great paper.

The following is the beginning of some freewriting in response to the same assignment as we used for the previous example:

> Opinions. I have lots of them—but I need one that has changed. How about "school"? I've sure changed my opinion about that—I used to hate it—missed as much as I could in high school. Now, ten years later, I'm back of my own free will. But I don't want to write about that—it would sound too much like I'm trying to butter up the professor. How about my parents. I used to think they knew everything—then I decided they knew nothing—now I know they know some things. I know my father is very idealistic and romantic and is good to talk to about "lofty ideas." I also know that his advice about cars is unreliable. And my mother—she's very sharp about money, about finances. Her advice about budget has been very helpful—her advice about men has been disastrous. Yea. I'll write about my opinion of my parents.

3. Keep a notebook. This is a technique that you have to start before you actually have an assignment to write. Just keep a notebook handy at all times when an idea for a paper might occur to you. Some people get their best ideas while doing their reading for a course. Others get them while driving to school or riding on the bus. Still others get them during class discussions. Some even get their best ideas as they are falling asleep at night. Wherever you get yours, make sure you don't

lose them; write them down—preferably in a notebook that you keep for that purpose. Then, when you actually do get ready to write a paper, you'll have a list of possible ideas to start from.

The following is an excerpt from one student's notebook:

Sep 15 — I'm furious. Men are unreliable. I'm giving up on men for at least six months. They don't know what they want.

Sep 16 — psych is boring. I wonder why. Dr. Gregoravich is a great instructor, but I'm bored in the class.

Sep 17 — The mass of men lead lives of quiet desperation. Very true. I wonder who said it.

Sep 18 — In psych, Dr. G. said that we are all bisexual. Now that's interesting... but it's not true. At least, I don't think so. I wonder what she means by "bisexual."

Sep 19 — Time and money are the two big forces in my life. I never have enough of either one. If I increase my hours at work, I'll have more money but less time. I need more of both!

Sep 19 — Men are frustrating. I'm going to take a six months' vacation from them.

Sep 20 — Another terrorist attack in the Near East today. These things don't really even bother me any more. Am I becoming bored with terrorism? It used to make me very upset.

4. Start an argument with a friend. Arguing will often not only lead to a good idea for a paper, it will force you to come up with good arguments that may later make your paper more convincing. This one can be a little hard on friendships, especially if, right at the height of the argument, you say, "Hey. That's a great idea for my political science paper. Excuse me, but I've got to go write it now." But what's really important—friendship or good writing? Well, maybe you can have both, but try to hang on to those good ideas for when you actually write the paper.

Ultimately, everyone develops his or her own techniques, but one of the above or some variation on one of them may help you over that point when you just don't know what to write about.

 ## EXERCISE 1-1

Here is an assignment for a piece of writing:

> Here it is early in the semester, and your instructor is trying to figure out how to help a classroom full of students become more effective writers. And, he or she hardly even knows your names. To help your instructor get to know you, write a paper telling him or her what the hardest part of writing is for you. This paper should be fairly brief, no more than two or three paragraphs.

For this exercise, *don't write the assignment;* instead, use one of the four techniques you've just learned to arrive at a subject for this paper if you were going to write it.

If you choose the first technique, brainstorming, then turn in the results of your brainstorming. If you choose method two, keeping a notebook, turn in the notebook (you may not have had enough time to use this technique for this assignment). If you choose method three, freewriting, turn in that freewriting (don't worry; your instructor knows that freewriting is very "free" and will have a lot of "junk" in it). If you choose the fourth technique, having an argument with a friend, write a paragraph or two in which you describe how that technique worked for you.

 ## EXERCISE 1-2

For this exercise, repeat Exercise 1-1 and try a different technique for getting started.

Once you have a subject to write about, you will need to ask some questions to make sure your subject will result in a good piece of writing:

1. **Will this subject really satisfy the assignment?**   Have you found a subject that will allow you to satisfy the assignment? Go back and reread the assignment to make sure.

2. **Is this subject something I can write a good paper about?**   Sometimes the subject you have arrived at does satisfy the assignment, but it is not right for *you*. It is something you have no interest in or know

nothing about. Of course, if the subject is specified in the assignment, you may have no choice; you may have to write about it whether you are interested or not. And, if you don't know anything about it, you may have to learn. But when *you* can choose the subject, try to find something that you can write effectively about.

3. **Is the subject narrow enough for the paper I am going to write?**   This is the one that causes the most trouble for the most people.

You've probably been told by one teacher or another, "Your subject needs to be narrowed down." Why are teachers always writing this on student's papers? Because it is one of the most common problems in student writing. Most writers worry that they will not have enough to say, and so the temptation is to choose a very broad subject, one that is sure to produce "five hundred words" or "three typed, double-spaced pages." Don't give in to this temptation. A subject that is too broad will produce the necessary number of words, but it won't produce effective writing. Instead, it will produce writing that is overly general and doesn't convince the reader because it doesn't develop its ideas with enough details.

Ask yourself if your subject is too broad. Is it something you can really write about effectively in the time and length you have for this piece of writing? If not, narrow it down to something you can write about.

One student who had to write about an opinion of hers that had changed had arrived at three possible subjects: religion, politics, and health foods. She then evaluated them to see if they were too broad.

She had been raised as a Catholic, but had not been to mass in three years. In fact, she now felt fairly hostile toward her religion and religion in general. She didn't like the attitude of most religions toward women. She also didn't agree with the attitude of most religions toward sex. Further, she no longer found the religious explanations of things—of creation, for example—to be convincing. She also had decided that religious services—she had tried several after giving up on the Catholic mass—only depressed her. She got more inspiration out of reading a good book. She soon realized, however, that all this was much too broad for a five-hundred-word essay. She could write five hundred words about her first reason for leaving the church—its attitude toward women.

Then she thought about that as a possible subject for a paper; the problem was she really wasn't sure what the church's attitude toward women was. She knew women couldn't be priests, but beyond that, she didn't know a lot. So she decided not to write about religion.

Next she thought about politics. She was very interested in politics and had joined the Greenpeace organization on her campus. It was immediately clear, however, that "politics" was far too broad for five hundred words. Then she thought about narrowing her subject to environmental politics, but she just didn't know enough about it. She had just joined Greenpeace a few weeks before, and she had not yet attended any meetings or read any of their literature. Politics didn't seem like a very promising subject.

How about health food? Actually, she had been eating health foods since she was in the ninth grade. She knew a lot about health foods—too much for a five-hundred-word essay, but perhaps she could narrow it down. She considered doing the paper on vitamins, but decided that would be too technical and factual for her English teacher. Besides her opinion had not really changed about vitamins. Then she thought about vegetarianism. She had been avoiding eating meat for years because she just didn't like it very much; the thought had been repugnant to her for years. Lately, however, she had developed a more serious objection to meat—a political one. She had learned that meat is a very inefficient way to feed the world. It requires a lot more nutrients from the soil to feed a cow long enough for it to grow to maturity. The same soil, if used to produce soybeans, could feed three times as many people as the beef would.

Now there was a subject she could write about in about five hundred words. She could discuss the inefficiency of feeding people with meat in a convincing manner in a short paper. She did and she wrote an excellent paper. Even though her instructor continued to eat beef, she got an "A" on the assignment.

 EXERCISE 1-3 _____

Here are some possible subjects for a five-hundred-word essay. Read over the list and mark each subject as "too broad" or "about right." Then select three of those you marked as "too broad' and narrow them down to something that would be appropriate for a five-hundred-word paper.

TOO   ABOUT
BROAD   RIGHT

_____ _____   1. World War II

_____ _____   2. nuclear power

_____ _____   3. computers

_____ _____   4. the whooping crane's struggle for survival

_____ _____   5. pollution

_____ _____   6. the difficulties of living in a one-parent family

_____ _____   7. technology

_____ _____   8. honesty

_____ _____   9. marriage

_____ _____ 10. getting a job

Now narrow three of the ones you marked as "too broad" to subjects that would be "about right" for a five-hundred-word paper.

1. _____

    _____

2. _____

    _____

3. _____

    _____

EXERCISE 1-4 _____

Here is the paper assignment from Exercise 1-1 again:

> Here it is early in the semester, and your instructor is trying to figure out how to help a classroom full of students become more effective writers. And, he or she hardly even knows your names. To help your instructor get to know you, write a paper telling him or her what the hardest part of writing is for you. This paper should be fairly brief, no more than two or three paragraphs.

For this exercise, again you are not going actually to write the paper. Instead, return to the subject that you arrived at in Exercise 1-1 or 1-2 and answer the following three questions about it. If you discover problems with the subject you chose, of course, you should revise it. Use this form to evaluate your subject:

Subject _____

1. Will this subject really satisfy the assignment?

    ☐ Yes

    ☐ No   Revised Subject _____

2. Is this subject something I can write a good paper about?

    ☐ Yes

    ☐ No   Revised Subject _____

3. Is the subject narrow enough for the paper I am going to write?

    ☐ Yes

    ☐ No   Revised Subject _____

Who Is Going to Read This?

Read over these two passages and try to decide which is the better piece of writing:

Version 1

Dear Doctor Henley:

For the past thirteen years, you have been treating my cat, Jimmie. You may remember that last summer Jimmie was hit by a car and required major surgery to his hip and a three-week stay in your animal hospital. The total bill was $650.

You may also remember that in October you had to operate on Jimmie again because of an infection that apparently resulted from the previous accident and surgery. The bill for this second operation was $280.

Now Jimmie's hip is apparently infected again; he is limping badly, seems to be in considerable pain, and is constantly scratching the area that you operated on.

Please understand that I am not questioning the quality of the treatment Jimmie received in the slightest; however, because of the expense, the obvious pain Jimmie is suffering, and the apparent likelihood that the infection will recur yet again, I am asking that you agree to put Jimmie to sleep. I know that your philosophy is to do this only as a last resort, but I think, in this case, we have reached the last resort.

If you agree, I will bring Jimmie in at 5:00 on Friday.

Sincerely,

Maria Ramirez

Version 2

Dear Tina,

You won't believe this, but Jimmie's hip is infected again. Yes, it's the same one that Dr. Henley operated on last summer.

I'm quite upset because Jimmie is in an awful lot of pain. He can barely walk, and he is constantly clawing at the incision. Also, I've had to come up with $930 to pay for the two operations. I don't really think Doctor Henley has done anything wrong, although sometimes I'm not so sure, but I don't want to have to go through another operation. I can't afford it, and I don't think it will do any good anyhow. I just can't see spending more than $1,000 to keep a thirteen-year-old cat alive for another year or two.

I'm afraid that once I get Jimmie in there, Dr. Henley will try to pressure me into having another operation, so I've written to ask him to agree to put Jimmie to sleep. Do you think I'm being too cruel?

Your friend,

Maria

Sometimes students feel that version 1 is better written than version 2. But is it? How would you describe the differences between the two? They both contain the same basic facts, but somehow those facts sound different in version 2. The first passage is more formal, less emotional, and more objective sounding. The second document is a personal letter to a friend, and in it Maria sounds more personal, less sure of herself, and much more emotional.

We probably agree on the differences between the two, but what about the original question: Which is better writing?

Well. That is an impossible question to answer. A more reasonable question is "Which is a better letter to a veterinarian?" or "Which is a better letter to a friend?" And the answers to those questions are easy. If Maria had written the second letter to the vet, he probably would have reported her to the Society for the Prevention of Cruelty to Animals. If she had sent the first letter to her friend, Tina probably would have called up to see if something was wrong. Phrases like "Please understand that I am not questioning" sound cold and distant in a letter to a friend.

The point is that neither style of writing is more "correct" than the other; each of them is appropriate for the audience it is addressed to. And that is the point: Before you start writing you should think about the audience for the writing. You should ask yourself, "Who is going to read this?" If you write without awareness of whom you are writing for, at best, you will write in a bland style that is appropriate for everyone; at worst, you will write in a style that is not appropriate for the actual person who will be reading what you have written.

EXERCISE 1-5

Here is the paper assignment from Exercise 1-1 again:

> Here it is early in the semester and your instructor is trying to figure out how to help a classroom full of students become more effective writers. And, he or she hardly even knows your names. To help your instructor get to know you, write a paper telling him or her what the hardest part of writing is for you. This paper should be fairly brief, no more than two or three paragraphs.

Once again you are not going actually to write the paper assigned. Instead, write a paragraph or two in which you describe the *audience* for the assignment above. This piece of writing (that is, the piece you are going to write about the audience) is to be directed to your instructor, and in it you should demonstrate that you understand what the audience for a piece of writing is and that you are capable of "figuring out" a few things about a particular audience.

The following questions may help you think about your instructor as an audience for your writing. You do not have to answer all of them, nor do you have to discuss them in the order presented. Also, feel free to add ideas of your own that are not suggested by these questions.

1. Who is the intended audience?
2. How much does this person seem to know about writing? Will he or she understand any technical terms or jargon I might use in the piece of writing?
3. Would he or she seem to prefer an informal style of writing or a more formal one?
4. Is he or she the kind of person who would appreciate a little humor in my writing?
5. Will this person be very interested in what I have to say or will he or she be reading this because he or she has to?
6. Will this person have plenty of time to read this or will he or she be more likely to be in a hurry?
7. Has this person revealed anything that he or she is particularly bothered by? Are there any subjects or problems I should probably avoid?
8. Is there anything this person has said about writing that I could use in this paper?

What Is the Purpose of this Piece of Writing?

Now that you have an idea what you are going to write about and who your audience is, you need to think about the purpose of the writing. Are you trying to get your money back for a lawn mower that never worked? Are you trying to demonstrate to your economics professor that you understand the results of increasing the amount of money in circulation? Are you trying to convince the manager of the House of Beef that you should be allowed to serve those slabs of prime rib to his customers this summer? Or are you trying to convince the zoning board that you should be allowed to add a deck onto your house? What is the purpose of the piece of writing? What do you want it to accomplish?

Quite often, just to make things a little more complicated, a piece of writing has more than one purpose. It may have an obvious purpose and, underneath that, a more subtle purpose. The letter you write to your parents about the new love in your life may have any or all of the following purposes:

- to alert them to the fact that you are "getting serious" about someone
- to see if they are going to have any bad reactions to this new relationship
- to begin to break the news that you will be spending the summer wherever this person lives rather than at home
- to divert their attention from your low grades for the fall semester by giving them something different to worry about

And why should you worry about the purpose? Basically, for the same reason that you worried about your audience: because the purpose makes a difference in how you write. It changes the tone that you use. It influences the organization of the writing. It even makes a difference in the content of the writing. Being conscious of the purpose you are trying to accomplish makes subtle differences in the way you express yourself.

Here, for example, is a letter to a garden store named the Garden Shop about a lawn mower they sold you that has never worked. What do you think the purpose of this piece of writing is?

Version 1

Dear Garden Shop:

Last May I made the mistake of purchasing a power lawn mower (T3000) from you. I should have known a store with stupid employees like the man who sold me the mower would not sell quality merchandise. The piece of junk has never worked. I have cranked it till my arm was ready to fall off, and the damn thing has never even kicked over. Furthermore, while I was cranking away, the cranking rope broke. Also three of the bolts to fasten the handle on were missing when I opened the box.

I have written a number of letters about this piece of junk and about your lousy service, and I've gotten nothing but grief in return. I have concluded that your store is a rip-off and you are all a bunch of crooks.

Sincerely,

Kimberly Klein

You may have decided the letter has no useful purpose, but perhaps it does. It has allowed the writer to blow off steam. Perhaps it has made her feel better about all the trouble she has had. If so, the letter has served as therapy, and that is fine. However, if Kimberly's purpose was to get her money back, then the letter is a disaster. No one at the Garden Shop is likely to respond favorably to such an outburst of rage.

Now take a look at another version of the same letter. What seems to be the purpose this time? What is the purpose of version 3? How is the purpose of version 2 different from that of version 3?

Version 2

Dear Garden Shop:

Last May I purchased a power lawn mower, model T3000, from your store. That mower has never worked.

I have tried repeatedly to get it to start, but have been unsuccessful. I have cleaned the fuel line and replaced the spark plug, to no avail. I believe that the motor itself is defective.

I have written your service department several times in the last month and have received no reply, so I am now writing to you as the manager.

Please advise me as to what steps I should take to rectify this situation. I would be happy to talk the problem over with you on the phone; my number is 522-1436. I can be reached any day during business hours.

Sincerely,

Kimberly Klein

Version 3

Dear Garden Shop:

I am writing to inform you of the steps it will be necessary for me to take if you do not correct the situation by August 15.

I bought the mower, model T3000, from you on May 28. To this date, despite numerous efforts on my part, it has not yet started. The steps I have taken have included cleaning the fuel line and replacing the spark plug.

I have written your service department on June 12, June 30, and July 15, but have received no reply. This will be my last correspondence with your store.

If you do not agree to replace the mower or refund the $238 I paid for it by August 15, I will advise my lawyer to file the suit he has prepared. In addition, he will notify your parent company in Des Moines of all the particulars and recommend that they revoke your franchise.

I should also mention that I am the owner of Klein's Landscaping Service. Not only is my company a potential customer for a considerable amount of equipment in future years, but also hundreds of my customers ask my advice about the purchase of lawn and garden equipment. If I have not received satisfaction by August 15, not only will I never buy another piece of equipment from your firm, but also I will advise all of my customers to avoid your store.

Sincerely,

Kimberly Klein

It seems clear that the main purposes of versions 2 and 3 are the same: Ms. Klein wants to convince the Garden Shop to give her a new machine or her money back. However, each of these has a secondary purpose, and these are slightly different. In version 2, her secondary purpose is to convince the manager at the Garden Shop that she is a reasonable person with whom he can discuss the matter rationally. She goes out of her way to demonstrate her reasonableness by including details about the machine and her purchase of it, by listing the steps she has taken to try to fix the mower herself, and by telling him how to reach her by phone. It would be hard for the manager to find an excuse to avoid responding to this letter.

In version 3, Kimberly has a completely different secondary purpose. She doesn't care whether the manager thinks she is reasonable or not; she wants him scared. She uses several different approaches to convince him that she will make considerable trouble if she does not get satisfaction and soon. She threatens to sue him, to try to get his franchise revoked (the fact that she knows about franchises and that they can be revoked is included to make her seem more threatening), and to cost him customers. The letter has the tone of a legal document to make it seem more threatening.

These three letters demonstrate how much the purpose of a piece of writing can influence the style and content. It is impossible to say which of these is the best letter, but it is clear that differences in purpose make a big difference in the way one writes.

Therefore, it is important that you think about the purpose of your writing before you start and that you remain conscious of that purpose as you are writing and revising.

EXERCISE 1-6

For each of the following writing situations, write a statement in which you explain what the purpose or purposes of the piece of writing might be. Remember that these purposes may not be completely obvious. In addition, there could be more than one right answer for each of these. Try to think of purposes that might be less than obvious. The first one has been done for you.

1. A memo to your boss in which you suggest several improvements in the way the office does business.

   ① to make my job easier
   ② to impress the boss

2. A cover letter to go with your résumé to the personnel office of a company where you would like to work.

3. A note to the owner of a parked car which you have just backed into, denting the fender.

4. A letter to your parents letting them know that you have a summer job in New York City that starts June 3. Therefore you will be visiting them from May 25 to June 1.

5. A paper for your psychology teacher discussing a major revision in Freud's theories in which you propose the existence of a "superid" to parallel the superego.

6. Instructions to be posted near the office copying machine explaining how to operate it.

Part C · Revising

For most people, revising is the worst part of writing. Sometimes they imagine enviously what it would be like to be a "really good writer." They would merely hold their pens over a piece of paper, and "good writing" would drip onto the page. Or, they would merely have to poise their fingers over the keys of the typewriter and "good writing" would almost leap onto the paper.

Needless to say, it doesn't happen like that. Even very good writers have to work hard in order to produce good writing. It doesn't come easily for anyone. In fact, most good writers only produce good writing by revising their first drafts several times. Good writing is a process of writing and then reworking and reworking until the writing is powerfully effective.

Perhaps this would be a good place to make sure that what we mean by "revising" is completely clear. Revising is *not* just reading over a paper and correcting the mistakes—that is proofreading. Revising is a much more elaborate process of which proofreading is just one part, usually the last. Revising is the careful reviewing and, where necessary, changing of a piece of writing to see that it is unified and effectively organized, that it includes satisfactory support for all of its assertions, that it is coherent and graceful, that its language is as powerful as possible, and, finally, that it doesn't violate any of the conventions of grammar or punctuation. To accomplish all this normally requires several revisions.

Of course, planning your writing and the actual writing are very important skills to master if you want to be a proficient writer. However, it is a basic assumption of this book that the part of the writing process that can be most improved is revision. This book assumes that you can learn to revise much more effectively and that to do so will greatly improve your writing.

To illustrate just how complicated revision truly is, on the following pages we have included four successive versions of the same essay.

Version 1

In the early days of television, people had great expectations that it would develop into a powerful force for education. Instead, it has grown into a threat to the younger generation. Television in the eighties, a danger from which children must be protected. Somehow, our expectations got derailed in the fifties.

One problem with television is that it is exciting—too exciting. The world of television, weather in police shows, or soap operas, or game shows, or even on the news, is deliberately crafted to keep the attention of viewers by providing excitement. By comparison, real life seems boring and plodding. Television makes us dissatisfied with our own lives, it makes reality look too pale. It raises the expectations of our children to the point that they are bound to be disappointed with what life really has to offer.

And life has a lot to offer if we are only open to it. There is the spendor of nature. Is anything on television as beautiful as a sunset? There is the warmth of friendship. Can television give us the affection and compassion of a close friend? There is the excitement of travel. We can both have fun and learn about the world by traveling to exciting places like Rome or Tokyo.

OMIT

Another major problem with television is that watching it is a completely passive activity. The viewers just sit there (or in the case of most teenagers, just lie there) and let entertainment "flow over them." And it eats up enormous amounts of time. Defenders of television might respond, "What is wrong with that?" They might ask, "Would you complain if they spent that same amount of time at the theater or reading a book?" The answer of course is "No, I would not complain." Watching good theater or reading a decent book are *not* a passive activity like watching television. They require that we make our minds work to understand what is going on and to think about our reactions to the play or the novel. Television is designed to minimize thinking. The plots are always so simple that one can follow what is going on without thinking at all. That's the third major problem with television: it discourages thinking.

Add a paragraph on sex and violence on TV

OMIT

Television is completely controlled by big business. The corporations that buy advertising time are able to dictate what we see. Because corporations are only interested in making money, decisions about programming only consider how to attract the largest possible audience. The networks never consider the artistic or educational values of the programs they offer.

Revise to agree with opening

Television has become a crass, commercial activity with only one point: to make money. The profit motive has completely corrupted any artistic or cultural value it once had.

In reading over this first draft of the essay, the writer was looking for major problems. She asked herself, "Is the point of the paper clear? Do all sections of the paper support that point? Are there any new ideas I can think of that would support my main point?"

She discovered that the main point of the paper was not completely clear. In the first paragraph, the point seemed to be that too much television can be harmful to children; in the concluding paragraph, the main point seemed to be that television has sold out its artistic values for the profit motive. She decided to change the concluding paragraph so that it restates the main point from the first paragraph.

She next discovered that the third, fifth, and sixth paragraphs do not support the main idea, so she took them out of the paper. Then the paper looked a little thin; it seemed to need a least one more reason that TV is dangerous to children. She then thought of the "sex and violence" argument and decided to include it.

Version 2 includes these changes.

Version 2

be more specific

give example

In the early days of television, people had great expectations that it would develop into a powerful force for education. Instead, it has grown into a threat to the younger generation. Television in the eighties, a danger from which children must be protected. Somehow, our expectations got derailed in the fifties.

give examples

add examples

One effect of television that is harmful to young people, even those who never commit a crime. Television is exciting—too exciting. The world of television, weather in police shows, or soap operas, or game shows, or even on the news, is deliberately crafted to keep the attention of viewers by providing excitement. By comparison, real life *give examples* seems boring and plodding. Television makes us dissatisfied with our own lives, it makes reality look too pale. It raises the expectations of our children to the point that they are bound to be disappointed with what life really has to offer.

be specific

The other major problem with television is that watching it is a completely passive activity. The viewers just sit there (or in the case of most teenagers, just lie there) and let entertainment "flow over them." And it eats up enormous amounts of time. Defenders of television might respond, "What is wrong with that?" They might ask, "Would you complain if they spent that same amount of time at the theater or reading a book?" The answer of course is "No, I would not complain." Watching good theater or reading a decent book are *not* a passive activity like watching television. They require that we make our minds work to understand what is going on and to think about our reactions to the play or the novel. Television is designed to *tell how — in detail* minimize thinking. The plots are always so simple that one can follow what is going on without thinking at all. That's the third major problem with television: it discourages thinking.

make this first body paragraph We all know that one of the problem's with contemporary TV is too much sex and violence. There has been plenty of publicity about the dangers of children being exposed to all this blatant sexuality and violent activity. It may be, as some have proposed, that increases in crime are the result of exposure to television. It is certain that exposure to blatant sex and violence has a negative affect on young children.

Since children are particularly effected by sex and violence, are particularly excited by the hype of TV, and are particularly in need of exercise for their thinking ability, it is crucial that parents severely restrict their childrens television watching.

This time the writer found a number of places where she needed to add more examples, more concrete details to support her argument. She also decided that the most obvious argument, the one concerning sex and violence, should come first in the essay. These changes are included in version 3.

Version 3

In the early days of television, people had great expectations that it would develop into a powerful force for education. It would

~~send~~ *bring the drama of* Shakespeare into every living room in the country. It would provide a constant flow of "good English" which would help all children develop proficiency with ~~English~~ *the language*. It would keep all of us informed of current events and the great issues of the day. Instead, it has grown into a threat to the literacy, the morality, and perhaps the sanity of the younger generation. Television in the eighties *is* a danger from which children must be protected.

Somehow, our expectations ~~got~~ *were* derailed in the fifties. How much Shakespeare or other serious drama ~~are~~ *is* scheduled in an average TV week? What is the language like on most television shows these days? When was the last time you saw children ~~watching the news~~ *settled down in front of Dan Rather or David Brinkley*? In place of the high culture we expected, television gives us "Dallas," "Miami Vice," and "Kate and Allie."

We all know that one of the problem's with contemporary TV is too much sex and violence. There has been plenty of publicity about the dangers of children being exposed to all this blatant sexuality and violent activity. It may be, as some have proposed, that increases in crime are the result of exposure to television. It is certain that exposure to blatant sex and violence has a negative *e*ffect on young children.

However, there is another effect of television that is also harmful to young people, even those who never commit a crime. Television is exciting—too exciting. The world of television, ~~weather~~ *whether* in police shows, or soap operas, or game shows, or even on the news, is deliberately crafted to keep the attention of viewers by providing excitement. Television ~~has~~ *throbs with* the excitement of the high speed chase, of the torrid romance, of the sudden winning of wealth, or of natural disasters and terrorist hijacking*s*. By comparison, real life seems boring and plodding. Receiving a ticket for running a stop sign is nothing like the arrests every Thursday on "Hill Street Blues." Our own marriages are pale reflections of the marriages and divorces on "Dynasty." The small pay raise we get each year on our jobs is considerably less exciting than the hundreds of thousands that can be won on "Wheel of Fortune." And, the minor catastrophes of our lives—the washing machine overflowing or the electricity going off—are quite pale beside the earthquakes and bombings of airports on the evening news. Television makes us dissatisfied with our own lives. It makes reality look too pale. It raises the expectations of our children to the point that they are bound to be disappointed with what life really has to offer.

The other major problem with television is that watching it is a completely passive activity. The viewers just sit there (or in the case of most teenagers, just lie there) and let entertainment "flow over them." And it eats up enormous *chunks* ~~amounts~~ of time. Children often watch as much as thirty or forty hours of TV each week. Defenders of television might respond, "What is wrong with that?" They might ask, "Would you complain if they spent the same amount of time at the theater or reading a book?" The answer of course is "No, I would not complain." Watching good theater or reading a decent book *is* ~~are~~ not a passive activity like watching television. They require that we make our minds work to understand what is going on and to think about our reactions to the play or the novel. Television *minimizes* ~~is designed to minimize~~ thinking. There are "laugh tracks" that tell us how to react. There is background music that swells with emotion when we are suppose*d* to feel strong emotion. And the plots are always so simple that one can follow what is going on without thinking at all. That's the third major problem with television: it discourages thinking.

Since children are particularly *a*ffected by sex and violence, are particularly excited by the hype of TV, and are particularly in need of exercise for their thinking abilit*ies*, it is crucial that parents severely restrict their childrens television watching.

Now the writer is satisfied with the major structure of the paper. So she reads version 3 over to look for places to improve the grammar, the choice of words, the spelling, and the punctuation. Version 4 includes these changes.

Version 4

In the early days of television, people had great expectations that it would develop into a powerful force for education. It would bring the drama of Shakespeare into every living room in the country. It would provide a constant flow of "good English" which would help all children develop proficiency with the language. It would keep all of us informed of current events and the great issues of the day. Instead, it has grown into a threat to the literacy, the morality, and perhaps the sanity of the younger generation. Television in the eighties is a danger from which children must be protected.

Somehow, our expectations were derailed in the fifties. How much Shakespeare or other serious drama is scheduled in an average TV week? What is the language like on most television shows these days? When was the last time you saw children settled down in front of Dan Rather or David Brinkley? In place of the high culture we expected, television gives us "Dallas," "Miami Vice," and "Kate and Allie."

We all know that one of the problems with contemporary TV is too much sex and violence. There has been plenty of publicity about the dangers of children being exposed to all this blatant sexuality and violent activity. It may be, as some have proposed, that increases in crime are the result of exposure to television. It is certain that exposure to blatant sex and violence has a negative effect on young children.

However, there is another effect of television that is also harmful to young people, even those who never commit a crime. Television is exciting—too exciting. The world of television, whether in police shows, or soap operas, or game shows, or even on the news, is deliberately crafted to keep the attention of viewers by providing excitement. Television throbs with the excitement of the high speed chase, of the torrid romance, of the sudden winning of wealth, or of natural disasters and terrorist hijackings. By comparison, real life seems boring and plodding. Receiving a ticket for running a stop sign is nothing like the arrests every Thursday on "Hill Street Blues." Our own marriages are pale reflections of the marriages and divorces on "Dynasty." The small pay raise we get each year on our jobs is considerably less exciting than the hundreds of thousands that can be won on "Wheel of Fortune." And, the minor catastrophes of our lives —the washing machine overflowing or the electricity going off—are quite pale beside the earthquakes and bombings of airports on the evening news. Television makes us dissatisfied with our own lives. It makes reality look too pale. It raises the expectations of our children to the point that they are bound to be disappointed with what life really has to offer.

The other major problem with television is that watching it is a completely passive activity. The viewers just sit there (or in the case of most teenagers, just lie there) and let entertainment "flow over them." And it eats up enormous chunks of time. Children often watch as much as thirty or forty hours of TV each week. Defenders of television might respond, "What is wrong with that?" They might ask, "Would you complain if they spent that same amount of time at the theater or reading a book?" The answer of course is "No, I would not complain." Watching good theater or reading a decent book is *not* a passive activity like watching television. They require that we make our minds work to understand what is going on and to think about our reactions to the play or the novel. Television minimizes thinking. There are "laugh tracks" that tell us how to react. There is background music that swells with emotion when we are supposed to feel strong emotion. And the plots are always so simple that one can follow what is going on without thinking at all. That's the third major problem with television: it discourages thinking.

Since children are particularly affected by sex and violence, are particularly excited by the hype of TV, and are particularly in need of exercise for their thinking abilities, it is crucial that parents severely restrict their children's television watching.

Notice that revision is much more than just correcting errors. It involves major changes in the content of the paper—adding and deleting whole paragraphs, shifting sections of the paper, and adding examples to support arguments. During these major changes, little attention is paid to matters of grammar, spelling, or punctuation. Only when the major structure of the paper is settled does the writer proofread to correct these minor errors.

This book will help you become more effective at planning and at writing. But more than anything else, it is designed to improve your ability to revise your writing effectively.

2

Subjects
and Verbs

Part A   Identifying Verbs

Part B   Identifying Subjects and Verbs
         in Simple Sentences

Part C   Identifying Subjects and Verbs
         in Sentences with Verbals

Part D   Identifying Subjects and Verbs
         in Sentences with More than One Clause

In Chapter 1 you learned about the writing process, including the fact that an important part of the writing process is revision. The final step in revision is proofreading—checking for errors in grammar, punctuation, and spelling. We believe that grammar is important, but that it must be seen as part of the complete writing process. Therefore, this book alternates between chapters on writing and chapters on grammar and punctuation. This is the first of the chapters on grammar.

A large number of the rules of grammar depend on your ability to find the subject and the verb in a sentence. Indeed, this is an important step in figuring out whether or not you even have a complete sentence. It is also crucial in checking subject-verb agreement (that is, whether you need to put an "s" ending on the verb or not). Finding the subject and verb also is important in punctuating introductory elements and in pronoun case. Although it is true that in your actual writing you may not need to identify subjects and verbs, being able to do so is so important to so many other grammar skills that we have chosen to make it the first grammar topic in this book.

Part A · Identifying Verbs

The first step in finding the subject and verb in a sentence is to find the verb. In this section you will focus completely on this first step: identifying verbs.

EXERCISE 2A-1

Study the underlined words in the following sentences very carefully. All these words are verbs. Try to figure out what makes them verbs. What is the same about all of them? What do they have in common?

1. My parents run every morning.
2. These puppies eat all day.
3. Many of my friends drive to school.
4. Most of the players hit the ball very well.
5. They swim every afternoon.

NOTE: A discussion of the answers to this exercise can be found on page 39.

EXERCISE 2A-2

In the following sentences, underline all verbs twice.

1. Mark and Larry run five miles every day.
2. My cat eats only oatmeal.
3. Joan's dog chases cars.
4. My math teacher always collects our homework.
5. Jennifer drives more than twenty miles to her office.
6. My daughter often cries during her baths.
7. Today Kevin opens his birthday presents.
8. Nancy sometimes walks to school.
9. I feed my fish every morning.
10. Rhoda drives my children to school on Thursdays.

EXERCISE 2A-3

Study the underlined words in the following sentences very carefully. All of these words are also verbs. What is the same about all of them? When did the action they express take place?

1. Yesterday Craig and Helen walked to the campsite.
2. Last summer I worked in Ocean City.
3. Larry threw the book across the room.
4. My sister went to her interview.
5. Fred and Greg saw their instructor.

NOTE: A discussion of the answers to this exercise can be found on page 39.

EXERCISE 2A-4

In the following sentences, underline all verbs twice.

1. My horse jumped over the fence.
2. Kathy looked for her lost earring.
3. My father always called me "Bud."
4. Karen ran after the bus.
5. Dow threw the cat out the window.
6. My neighbor mows his grass every Saturday.
7. Some people waited for three hours.
8. My psych teacher always begins the class five minutes late.
9. The dentist found one cavity.
10. Maria washed her clothes early this morning.

EXERCISE 2A-5

Study the underlined words in the following sentences very carefully. All of these words are verbs. Try to figure out what makes them verbs. What is the same about all of them? What do they have in common? Do they express actions?

1. My dog sleeps in the kitchen.
2. Mark thinks about basketball all the time.
3. I sit in the front of the classroom.
4. Connie has the keys to the car.
5. Avery had a cold last week.

NOTE: A discussion of the answers to this exercise can be found on page 40.

EXERCISE 2A-6

In the following sentences, underline all verbs twice.

1. My brother sleeps late on Saturdays.
2. Marcy usually sits too close to the television.
3. I often listen to folk music.
4. Karen has a cold and a headache.
5. Hank guessed the name of the song.
6. My daughter suspected something.
7. I think about verbs a lot on weekends.
8. The settlers had a difficult time the first winter.

9. Ms. Pierce cancelled my vacation.

10. The ladder rested against the wall in the bedroom.

EXERCISE 2A-7

Study the underlined words in the following sentences very carefully. All of these words are verbs. What is the same about all of them? Why are they a little confusing? Are these words always verbs? Could they be used as something else in another sentence? What?

1. I <u>telephone</u> my mother every Sunday.

2. The cowboy <u>roped</u> the calf.

3. Karen <u>mothers</u> her children too much.

4. Eastern Air Lines <u>bussed</u> the passengers to Kennedy Airport.

5. Marcy <u>shelves</u> books in the library on Mondays.

NOTE: A discussion of the answers to this exercise can be found on page 40.

EXERCISE 2A-8

Study the underlined words in the following sentences very carefully. Are they verbs? Are they expressing actions *in these sentences?*

1. Diane had a <u>run</u> in her stocking.

2. Laurie's <u>jump</u> was a school record.

3. Steve made a good <u>try</u> on the exam.

4. The <u>drive</u> to Tulsa is very pleasant.

5. Vic gave Maria a <u>drink</u> from his thermos.

NOTE: A discussion of the answers to this exercise can be found on page 40.

EXERCISE 2A-9

In the following sentences, underline all verbs twice.

1. Steve boxed the glasses very carefully.

2. They bus children to our high school from all over the city.

3. Kelly's jump broke the record.

4. I heard a laugh from the basement.

5. We nursed our cat back to health.

6. Ms. Stein has a record of our scores on all her tests.

7. Mickey salts everything too much for my taste.

8. We booked a reservation on a cruise ship for our twenty-fifth anniversary.

9. Our team scored a run in the ninth inning.

10. Hilda and Anne vacation together every summer.

 ## EXERCISE 2A-10 ————————————

Study the following sentences very carefully. The verbs have been underlined. What do these *sentences* have in common? Notice, this time we are asking what the *sentences* have in common, not what the verbs have in common.

1. Last night I tossed and turned for hours.

2. The driver of the Cadillac honked his horn and flashed his lights.

3. Grandpa leaned forward and whispered to me.

4. Every Saturday I cook waffles and serve them to my family.

5. My grandmother speaks softly and carries a big stick.

NOTE: A discussion of the answers to this exercise can be found on page 40.

 ## EXERCISE 2A-11 ————————————

In the following sentences, underline all verbs twice.

1. Judy tripped and fell in front of the entire class.

2. My boss called me in and talked to me about my lateness.

3. We wrapped and mailed three hundred packages on Friday.

4. I scratch my head and crack my knuckles a lot during English.

5. The radio only crackled and buzzed.

6. Donald shelved all the books by two o'clock.

7. Ed coughed and sneezed during the entire movie.

8. Mike refused my offer in a cruel and offensive manner.

9. I smile and giggle frequently during my math class.

10. The secretary typed and mailed forty letters by ten o'clock.

 ## EXERCISE 2A-12 ————————————

Study the underlined words in the following sentences very carefully. Even though they look quite different from the verbs we have been looking at so far, these words are all verbs. Try to figure out what makes them verbs. What do they "do" in these sentences?

1. My uncles are volunteer fire fighters.

2. The apple was green.

3. Monday is the first day of spring.

4. I <u>am</u> a Scorpio.

5. Friday <u>will be</u> my parents' anniversary.

NOTE: A discussion of the answers to this exercise can be found on page 41.

 EXERCISE 2A-13 _____

In the following sentences, underline all verbs twice.

1. My mother was a Democrat.

2. These verbs are fascinating.

3. This bag is very heavy.

4. The name of my first cat was Grey.

5. Two of her children were blondes.

6. The movie was very sad and was very long.

7. Donna boxed the clothes and gave them to the Salvation Army.

8. In her childhood, she was very sick and spent two years in the hospital.

9. I am now an expert on linking verbs.

10. This is the last sentence in this set.

 EXERCISE 2A-14 _____

Study the underlined words in the following sentences very carefully. All of these words are verbs. Try to figure out what makes them verbs. What is the same about all of them? What do they have in common?

1. The cake <u>looks</u> delicious.

2. The gerbil's cage <u>smelled</u> terrible.

3. This record <u>sounds</u> wonderful.

4. The soup <u>tastes</u> too salty.

5. Jerry <u>seems</u> sad.

NOTE: A discussion of the answers to this exercise can be found on pages 41–42.

 EXERCISE 2A-15 _____

In the following sentences, underline all verbs twice.

1. I felt sick at breakfast this morning.

2. The president appeared angry at his news conference.

3. This salad tastes too salty.

4. The locker room smells awful.

5. This sentence looks very simple.

6. My appointment is at nine o'clock this morning.

7. The algebra course seems harder each week.

8. My grandmother sounded very lively on the phone last night.

9. Francine's aunt arranged the entire concert by herself.

10. The rice at the banquet tasted awful.

 EXERCISE 2A-16

Study the underlined words in the following sentences very carefully. These words are also all verbs, but they are different in one fairly obvious way from any of the verbs you have studied up till now. Try to figure out how these verbs are different.

1. I <u>will be jogging</u> at eight o'clock on Saturday morning.

2. That bird <u>has been coming</u> to my feeder for the entire winter.

3. We <u>will be</u> late for the movie.

4. The dogs <u>have been fed</u> already tonight.

5. Tom <u>does take</u> good care of his motorcycle.

6. Susan <u>should have opened</u> the letter.

7. Genghis Khan <u>may have slept</u> here.

8. Boris <u>might be</u> late to the meeting.

NOTE: A discussion of the answers to this exercise can be found on page 42.

 EXERCISE 2A-17

In the following sentences, underline all verbs twice. Be sure to include the helping verbs.

1. Bruce had been swimming for two hours.

2. My parents should have been more strict with my sister.

3. Max might be living in New York.

4. I have looked everywhere for my earring.

5. Susan will be sending you an application.

6. I had wrapped the picture very carefully.

7. At nine o'clock, Julio had been studying for four hours.

8. I did read the homework last night.

9. You could have given me a ride home last night.

10. Alice was singing in the shower.

 EXERCISE 2A-18

Now study the underlined verbs in the following sentences. Try to figure out why, in some sentences, the verb includes the word following the "be" verb while, in other sentences, it does not. For example, in sentence 1, why does the verb include the word "studying," while in 2, the word "angry" is not a part of the verb?

1. By eight o'clock, Denise <u>was studying</u>.

2. By eight o'clock, Denise <u>was</u> angry.

3. Janet <u>is leaving</u> now.

4. Janet <u>is</u> twenty-one now.

5. In the morning, Frank <u>was sleeping</u>.

6. In the morning, Frank <u>was</u> sorry.

7. I thought I <u>had answered</u> all her questions.

8. I thought I <u>had</u> the answer to her question.

NOTE: A discussion of the answers to this exercise can be found on page 42.

EXERCISE 2A-19 _____

In the following sentences, underline all verbs twice.

1. Marcy was sleepy this morning.

2. Marcy was sleeping this morning.

3. Jessie is lazy.

4. My sister will be singing in the concert.

5. People are unpredictable about their preferences for movies.

6. The nurse was careless with my medicine.

7. Our neighbors will be moving next week.

8. Tommy Wilhelm will be mowing their grass for them.

9. John Clayton has been patient with me.

10. I am sick of your foolishness.

EXERCISE 2A-20 _____

Study the underlined words in the following sentences very carefully. All of these words are verbs. See what else you can learn about what is and what is not a verb from these sentences.

1. My mother <u>is</u> not <u>playing</u> bridge tonight.

2. We <u>will</u> not <u>miss</u> much of the movie.

3. Lou <u>is</u> not the right man for that job.

4. Sherry <u>should</u> not <u>be using</u> that drill.

5. My sister <u>is</u> not <u>running</u> in the marathon.

NOTE: A discussion of the answers to this exercise can be found on page 43.

EXERCISE 2A-21

In the following sentences, underline all verbs twice.

1. I did not go to the movie last night.

2. Stacy will not be attending the convention.

3. My father is not a police officer.

4. Business people are not supporting Henry Marcello for mayor.

5. These sentences are not very hard.

6. I have not finished the homework.

7. The movie had not started at eight-thirty.

8. My son did not return my iron yet.

9. This coffee is not strong enough for me.

10. Sam is not joining us for lunch.

EXERCISE 2A-22

Now study the following sentences very carefully. The underlined words are verbs. First try to figure out what these *sentences* have in common. Then, figure out how these verbs are different from others you have studied.

1. Is your car running well these days?

2. Did your sister write a note to her teacher?

3. Are your feet wet?

4. Will you remember your lunch tomorrow?

5. Did Mike get a date for this Saturday?

NOTE: A discussion of the answers to this exercise can be found on page 43.

EXERCISE 2A-23

Rewrite each of the following sentences as a question.

1. Your car is parked behind the office.

2. Kevin's brother was elected chair of the committee.

3. Li has received a letter from her grandparents in China.

4. Frank's tulips are blooming already.

5. Ms. Rodriguez was sleeping when I called.

EXERCISE 2A-24

Now consider the next set of sentences. What can you learn about verbs from these?

1. What <u>is</u> your brother <u>making</u> for the picnic?
2. Where <u>is</u> your office <u>located</u>?
3. Why <u>is</u> your car <u>running</u>?
4. What <u>was</u> Gretchen <u>saying</u> about me?
5. When <u>does</u> your father <u>arrive</u> home from work?

NOTE: A discussion of the answers to this exercise can be found on page 43.

EXERCISE 2A-25

In the following sentences, underline all verbs twice.

1. Is Francis wearing your sweater?
2. Have you seen the play at Center Stage?
3. Why is your mother wearing a miniskirt?
4. Where does this bus stop?
5. Are you going to Scarborough Fair?
6. Will your boss give you the day off next Wednesday?
7. My cat is having kittens very soon.
8. Did you see the hat in Ginny's closet?
9. Sally did not receive an invitation to the reception.
10. Where did you get that wonderful costume?

Now you have considered most of the kinds of verbs that you will find in the English language. Review all the sentences you have worked on up to now and write your definition of a verb in the space below.

_____

_____

_____

_____

Below is our definition of a verb. Compare yours with ours.

• **verb**   A verb is a word that expresses an action or links the subject with words at the end of the sentence.

Although they are not really a necessary part of the definition of a verb, there are some other facts you should have learned about verbs in this section. You may have included some of these in your definition:

a. A verb can be expressed in present or past tense.
b. A sentence can have more than one verb.

   c. A verb can include helping verbs.

   d. The word following a helping verb may or may not be a verb. You have to check it carefully.

   e. The word "not" is never a verb.

   f. In questions, the first word in the verb may be moved to the beginning of the sentence.

EXERCISE 2A-26 ———————————————————

This exercise is a review of everything you have learned about verbs. Underline all the verbs in the following sentences twice.

1. Gwen booked a reservation at the Hilton.

2. My favorite meal is lasagna.

3. Cherryl was laughing very loudly.

4. The car exploded and burned after the accident.

5. The driver felt terrible about his mistake.

6. In July, my parents will have been married for thirty years.

7. What is Fred bringing to the potluck supper?

8. My typewriter is not working correctly.

9. Doug will be thirty on Sunday.

10. Have you hugged your kid today?

11. Rebecca chaired the meeting.

12. My car did not start this morning.

13. Bobby jumped up and made a speech at the student government meeting last night.

14. Did you know my sister in high school?

15. Randy became very quiet at the dinner.

16. I had not studied German before this year.

17. The cake tasted wonderful.

18. Emily is writing a letter to the president.

19. When are you taking your makeup exam?

20. Verbs will be the death of me yet.

EXERCISE 2A-27 ———————————————————

In the following paragraph, underline all the verbs twice.

On my first job, I learned that hard work is not the key to success. My parents always had told me that if I would work hard, in the long run I would be successful. When I was in high school, I worked very hard, and my teachers always rewarded me with high

grades. Then I took my first job, in a grocery store. I worked
extremely hard. If we were busy, I did not take my breaks. I always
came to work when they called me, even on my days off. And I always
worked overtime if the store needed me. As time went by, I noticed
that the other employees seemed angry at me. None of them ever
invited me out for a beer after work. In fact, no one even ate lunch
with me. Then I found out that someone had told the manager that I
was stealing from the store. As I left work one day, I noticed a strange
package in the back seat of my car. Just as I picked it up, someone
shouted my name. It was the manager. He grabbed the package out of
my hands and unwrapped it. I stared in shock as he unwrapped a
large roast beef. I had no idea how it had gotten into my car.
Nevertheless, things looked very bad. I still remember his words.
"Leave this store and never come back." After I had thought about it,
I realized that a person can work too hard for his own good.

 EXERCISE 2A-28 _____

Imagine that you are applying for financial aid, and the application asks you
to describe what you did last summer to earn money. Before you start
writing your response, think about the planning techniques you learned in
Chapter 1. The questions you learned there are repeated below; write your
answers in the space provided.

1.   What subject are you going to write about?_____

     _____

2.   What do you know or what can you guess about the audience for this

     piece of writing?_____

     _____

3.   What is the purpose of this piece of writing? What do you want it to

     accomplish?_____

     _____

In the space below write your response. Then, underline all the verbs twice.

_____

_____

_____

_____

_____

_____

_____

_____

_____

_____

_____

_____

_____

_____

_____

_____

_____

_____

_____

_____

_____

_____

_____

DISCUSSION OF INDUCTIVE EXERCISES

EXERCISE 2A-1

What these five words have in common is that they all express actions. They all express something you can "do." You can "run." You can "eat." You can "drive." You can "hit," and you can "swim." Therefore, all the underlined words are verbs.

This kind of verb is the easiest to find. It is a word that expresses a clear action, something you can "do."

EXERCISE 2A-3

What these words have in common is the following:

a. All the underlined words express actions, something you can "do."
b. The action expressed by all the underlined words took place in the past.

Since all the underlined words express actions, they are all verbs. Notice that they all have changed their forms somewhat to show they are expressing actions that took place in the past.

You will learn much more about verbs whose action takes place in the past when you get to Chapter 14. For now, all you are working on is finding verbs, so all you need to remember is that a word that expresses an action is a verb, whether that action takes place in the present or in the past.

EXERCISE 2A-5

You may have had a little more trouble with these. They all do express actions; however, the actions they express don't have much activity in them. You would not see much action if you watched my dog "sleeping," Mark "thinking," me "sitting," Connie "having," or Avery "having." Nevertheless, each of these words does express action, but that action is not very visible. Perhaps it will be clearer if you think of each of the underlined words as expressing something you can "do." You can "sleep," you can "think," you can "sit," you can "have," or you could have "had" in the past. Since each of these words expresses something you can "do," each of them expresses an action. Therefore, each of them is a verb.

Look especially closely at the underlined verbs in sentences 4 and 5. The words "has" and "had" in these sentences are both forms of the verb "have." All three forms of this verb are always verbs. In addition, even though it is hard to see, the words "have," "has," and "had" express actions. They each express something you can "do." For example, if you have five dollars, you are doing something. You are "having" the five dollars; you are possessing it. If you find this idea impossible to grasp, you may just want to remember that any time "have," "has," or "had" is used alone as a verb, it is expressing an action.

EXERCISE 2A-7

You probably figured out that each of these underlined words expresses an action, and that is correct. Did you also realize that each is a word that is usually a noun? "Telephone," "rope," "mother," "bus," and "shelf" are usually nouns. Like many nouns, however, they are sometimes used as verbs. In these sentences, they are clearly expressing actions, so they are verbs. You need to be aware that words which are usually used as nouns may sometimes be used as verbs.

EXERCISE 2A-8

All these words are *nouns,* but they have something else in common too. Each of them is a word that is usually a verb. In these sentences, however, they are used as nouns. You have to be careful, when you are asked to identify verbs, that you do not get confused by words like these.

To know whether a particular word is a noun or a verb, you need only ask yourself, "Is this word standing for a thing, or is it expressing an action?" If it is a thing, it is a noun; if it expresses an action, it is a verb.

EXERCISE 2A-10

Each of the preceding sentences has this in common: it has two verbs. Not only are two verbs all right, but it is possible for sentences to have even more than two, as in this example:

George <u>did</u> the laundry, <u>made</u> the beds, and <u>took</u> out the garbage.

This sentence has three verbs. As long as you are aware that a sentence can have more than one verb, these sentences should cause you no trouble.

EXERCISE 2A-12

You may be having a little trouble with these. They certainly are not express-ing any action, yet they are verbs. They are known as linking verbs. Instead of expressing an action, they merely "link" the subject with whatever fol-lows the verb. For example, in sentence 1, the subject, "uncles," is being linked with the phrase "volunteer fire fighters." In 2, the subject, "apple," is being linked to the word "green." In 3, the subject, "Monday," is being linked to the phrase "first day of spring." In 4, "I" is being liked to "Scor-pio," and in 5, "Friday" is being linked to "my parents' anniversary."

1. My uncles are volunteer fire fighters.

2. The apple was green.

3. Monday is the first day of spring.

4. I am a Scorpio.

5. Friday will be my parents' anniversary.

All the verbs in these sentences are different forms of the same word, "be." The verb "be" is the most unpredictable word in the English language; it appears in many forms. Yet, it is also the most frequently used verb in the language. It would be a good idea for you to become familiar with all the forms of this verb, so we have listed them below.

am	was
is	were
are	will be
have been	had been
has been	will have been

Later in this part, you will learn that the verb "be" can also be used with an action verb. When it is used in this way, it is called a "helping" or "auxiliary" verb. For now, we will use the verb "be" only as a linking verb.

EXERCISE 2A-14

You may have figured out that none of these verbs express actions. The cake didn't do anything; it didn't open its eyes and "look" at anything. The gerbil's cage didn't do anything; it didn't sniff anything with its nose. In fact, a cage doesn't even have a nose. The record didn't sound anything, the soup didn't taste anything, and even Jerry didn't really do anything. He just "seemed sad."

So none of the underlined words express actions, yet each of them is a verb. What they are is linking verbs, just like the verb "be." This linking can be seen below:

1. The cake looks delicious.

2. The gerbil's cage smelled terrible.

3. This record sounds wonderful.

4.　The soup tastes too salty.

5.　Jerry seems sad.

　　Besides the verb "be," the other words that can be linking verbs are listed below. Can you figure out anything these seven verbs have in common?

look	seem
sound	appear
smell	taste
feel	

　　What these linking verbs have in common is that they all involve the senses. Remember that your five senses are sight, hearing, taste, smell, and touch. Each of these seven linking verbs is related to one of your senses, so they are called sensory verbs.

EXERCISE 2A-16

The way in which these verbs are different from any you have worked with until now is that each is made up of more than one word. In each sentence, the verb consists of a main verb (usually an action verb) preceded by one or more other verbs. These "other" verbs are known as helping or auxiliary verbs. Notice that many of these helping verbs are some form of the verb "be."

　　The following list includes most of the words that can be used as helping verbs. Do not attempt to memorize this list, but you should be able to recognize these words when they are used as helping verbs.

is	has been	have
are	have been	had
am	had been	could
was	do	should
were	does	must
will be	did	may
will have been	has	might

EXERCISE 2A-18

Some people have trouble deciding whether the word after a "be" verb is part of the verb or not. To figure this out, you need only look closely at the word in question. If that word is something you can "do," it is a verb. If it is not something you can "do," it is not a verb.

　　In sentence 1, for example, the word in question is "studying." Just ask yourself if "studying" is a verb. Is "studying" something you can do? Since the answer is yes, then "studying" must be included as a part of the verb.

　　Now look at sentence 2. Ask yourself whether "angry" is a verb. Is "angry" something you can do? Since the answer is no, then "angry" is not a part of the verb. Notice that you can "be" angry, but that doesn't make "angry" a verb; to be a verb, the word must be something you can "do," not just something you can "be."

　　Apply this technique in Exercise 2A-19.

EXERCISE 2A-20

This set of sentences shows that the word "not" is never a part of the verb.

EXERCISE 2A-22

The first thing you should have noticed about these sentences is that they are all questions. Then you should have noticed that in each sentence, the first word in the verb has been moved to the front of the sentence.

If sentence 1 were not a question, for example, it would look like this:

a. Your car <u>is running</u> well these days.

To change it into a question, the helping verb "is" was moved to the front of the sentence.

b. <u>Is</u> your car <u>running</u> well these days?

In each of the sentences in Exercise 2A-22, the first word in the verb has been moved to the front of the sentence to form a question.

EXERCISE 2A-24

Again, all these sentences are questions. Further, they all begin with a "wh" word (what, where, why, when). Finally, the first word in the verb has been moved to the position immediately after the "wh" word in the sentence.

From these two sets of sentences (Exercises 2A-22 and 2A-24), you should be able to see that, when a sentence is a question, one word from the verb is likely to be separated from the rest of the verb and moved to a position near the beginning of the sentence.

Part B · Identifying Subjects and Verbs in Simple Sentences

At the heart of every sentence are the subject and verb. In fact, the basic meaning of the sentence is usually expressed by the subject and verb. To understand the basic structure of sentences, and even to know whether a group of words is a sentence or not, you will need to be able to identify the subject and verb.

EXERCISE 2B-1

In Part A of this chapter, you learned to identify verbs. As a review of that skill, underline the verbs in the following sentences twice. Remember that every sentence must have at least one verb and may have more than one.

1. Al opened the package in front of us.

2. Vicky took forty-five dollars out of her checking account.

3. The doctor wondered about Debbie.

4. Boston always fascinates and irritates me.

5. A deer was grazing in the back yard.

6. My car is sitting in the school parking lot.

7. Marvin opened the bottle and took two aspirin.

8. The third problem gave me a hard time.

9. The movie starts at seven fifteen.

10. Elephants eat only grasses and leaves.

 EXERCISE 2B-2 _____

The sentences from Exercise 2B-1 have been repeated below, but this time the verbs have been underlined twice and the subjects once. Study the words that are subjects and try to figure out from them just what a subject is. What is the relationship between the subject and the verb?

1. Al opened the package in front of us.

2. Vicky took forty-five dollars out of her checking account.

3. The doctor wondered about Debbie.

4. Boston always fascinates and irritates me.

5. A deer was grazing in the back yard.

6. My car is sitting in the school parking lot.

7. Marvin opened the bottle and took two aspirin.

8. The third problem gave me a hard time.

9. The movie starts at seven fifteen.

10. Elephants eat only grasses and leaves.

If you are familiar with the term, you may have noticed that all the subjects in these sentences are nouns. More important, you can see that the subject is the "do-er" of the verb. In each sentence the subject is the person, place, or thing that is "doing" the verb:

1. "Al" did the "opening."
2. "Vicky" did the "taking."
3. The "doctor" did the "wondering."
4. "Boston" does the "fascinating" and the "irritating."
5. The "deer" did the "grazing."
6. The "car" is doing the "sitting."
7. "Marvin" did the "opening" and the "taking."
8. The "problem" did the "giving."
9. The "movie" is doing the "starting."
10. "Elephants" do the "eating."

For most people, it is easier to find the verb in a sentence than to find the subject. Therefore, unless you are quite different from most people, you should follow the following procedure to identify the subject and verb in a sentence:

1. Find the verb.
2. Ask yourself one of the following two questions. Where the blank line is, you should fill in the verb.
   a. Who ___(the verb)___ ?
   b. What ___(the verb)___ ?

The answer to one of these two questions (depending on whether the subject is human or nonhuman) will be the subject of the sentence. Consider the following sentence:

Jerry was chasing a dog down the alley.

Applying step 1, you would identify "was chasing" as the verb. Next, you would ask yourself, "Who was chasing?" The answer, of course, is "Jerry." To check your answer, you might ask yourself if the sentence says that "Jerry was chasing." Since the answer is yes, you would know that you had correctly identified the subject and verb.

Use these two steps in Exercise 2B-3.

EXERCISE 2B-3 ———————————————

In the following sentences, underline all verbs twice and all subjects once.

1. My sister works for a dentist.
2. Mr. Bladgett gave me a ride to work.
3. Hawaii really attracts a lot of tourists each year.
4. This little stream flows all the way to the Gulf of Mexico.
5. A bright red Toyota was parked in my driveway.
6. Anna Maria told Eric about my mistake.
7. Deborah Kent was born in Little Rock.
8. A lightning bolt struck the tree outside my window.
9. Ms. Kufel was injured in an accident last night.
10. The library opens at noon on Sundays.

EXERCISE 2B-4 ———————————————

Study the underlined subjects and verbs in the following sentences. Try to figure out something new about subjects or verbs from these examples. In particular, look at the subjects. What do they all have in common? How are they different from the subjects in Exercise 2B-2?

1. We decided on a name for the dog.
2. You should not drive on a day like this.
3. Someone donated fifty dollars to the scholarship fund.

4. No one <u>asked</u> me about the missing money.

5. <u>I</u> <u><u>called</u></u> my grandmother on her birthday.

NOTE: A discussion of the answers to this exercise can be found on page 51.

EXERCISE 2B-5

In the following sentences, underline all verbs twice and all subjects once. The subjects may be nouns or pronouns.

1. They asked me for a suggestion about the menu.

2. Everyone did a good job on fund raising last year.

3. Bruce suggested a friend of his as master of ceremonies.

4. I do not believe in Santa Claus.

5. You should buy yourself a new vacuum cleaner.

6. She looks a lot like her mother.

7. Ricky loaned me his car for the night.

8. He goes to the same school as my brother.

9. Spinach gives me a stomachache.

10. Anyone can enter this contest.

EXERCISE 2B-6

Study the underlined subjects and verbs in the following sentences. Look particularly at the verbs. How are they different from the verbs you have been working with?

1. <u>Mr. McCaskill</u> <u><u>is</u></u> an accountant.

2. <u>We</u> <u><u>were</u></u> late for the meeting.

3. <u>Christeen</u> <u><u>was</u></u> sick on the day of the party.

4. The <u>picnic</u> <u><u>was</u></u> a disaster from the very beginning.

5. My <u>room</u> <u><u>is</u></u> my only refuge from my brother.

NOTE: A discussion of the answers to this exercise can be found on page 51.

EXERCISE 2B-7

In the following sentences, underline all verbs twice and all subjects once. These sentences include both action and linking verbs.

1. Nobody is angry at Katrina.

2. Mr. Parker was absent from the board meeting.

3. We asked the boss for an explanation.

4. Mary Beth will be the maid of honor at my wedding.

5. Tom shocked everyone with his answer.

6.   Walter appeared exhausted in the morning.

7.   The park was quiet last night.

8.   The interstate is too crowded this time of day.

9.   Someone was asleep in my bed.

10.   Ms. Zandt is my best friend.

EXERCISE 2B-8

Study the underlined subjects and verbs in the following sentences. Look particularly at the subjects. In each sentence do you see another word that could be confused with the subject? What do all these words that could be confused with the subject have in common?

1.   The cover of the book was wet.

2.   The fender of my car is damaged.

3.   Some of the children were sleeping.

4.   Many of the flowers were damaged by the frost.

5.   Each of the new glasses is chipped.

NOTE: A discussion of the answers to this exercise can be found on pages 52–53.

EXERCISE 2B-9

In the following sentences, underline all verbs twice and all subjects once.

1.   The front of my dress was wet.

2.   Most of the snow had melted by noon.

3.   All of the records were by Stevie Wonder.

4.   One of the lambs is sick.

5.   The attic of my house is very hot.

6.   Some of the birds were juncos.

7.   Of the two sisters, Tuyet speaks English better.

8.   A friend of my sister is visiting for the weekend.

9.   Much of the work was a waste of time.

10.   The top of my refrigerator is quite dirty.

EXERCISE 2B-10

These sentences are similar to those in Exercises 2B-8 and 2B-9. Study these closely. If you can, place brackets around the prepositional phrases. Instead of the preposition "of," these prepositional phrases begin with other prepositions. Make sure you can recognize the subjects in this kind of sentence.

1.   The man with the pipe is my psychology teacher.

2.   The woman in the blue sweater is losing her touch.

3. The <u>pot</u> on the stove <u><u>contains</u></u> tomato soup.

4. The <u>flag</u> over the high school <u><u>was flying</u></u> at half mast.

5. The <u>road</u> to Wayne <u><u>is</u></u> very busy.

NOTE: A discussion of the answers to this exercise can be found on page 53.

EXERCISE 2B-11 _____

In the following sentences, underline all verbs twice and all subjects once.

1. A kick in the pants is a good motivator for someone like him.

2. The package under the table is ready for the mail.

3. The man with lipstick on his cheek was kissed by Meryl Streep.

4. The bottom of my closet is a mess.

5. The weather in the spring here is delightful.

6. The desk in the corner belongs to my grandfather.

7. The restaurant near the post office has gone out of business.

8. Veal with a tomato sauce is my favorite meal.

9. A lamb among wolves was safer than I.

10. Sunshine in the morning always gives me a good feeling.

EXERCISE 2B-12 _____

Study the underlined subjects and verbs in the following sentences. What can you learn about subjects or verbs from these examples? Again, look especially at the subjects.

1. <u>George</u> and <u>Kris</u> <u><u>had</u></u> a terrible fight at the party.

2. <u>She</u> and her <u>sister</u> <u><u>are leaving</u></u> for California this Monday.

3. The <u>television</u> or the <u>radio</u> <u><u>was</u></u> on all night.

4. <u>Baltimore</u> or <u>Richmond</u> <u><u>will get</u></u> the federal grant.

5. My <u>umbrella</u> and my <u>raincoat</u> <u><u>are</u></u> at home.

NOTE: A discussion of the answers to this exercise can be found on page 53.

EXERCISE 2B-13 _____

In the following sentences, underline all verbs twice and all subjects once. Some of the subjects may consist of more than one word joined by an "and" or an "or."

1. The Giant and the A&P are closing at the end of this month.

2. Ms. Burkart and her husband are moving to Colorado.

3. The Orioles or the Tigers will probably win the pennant this year.

4. My mother or my father will give me a ride to your house.

5. Some of the cookies were baked by my father.

6. Marc and Karl are swimming at the "Y."

7. Statistics and English are my two hardest courses.

8. Many of the sea gulls will die from the oil spill.

9. I cleaned the bathroom and the bedroom.

10. Some of the tomatoes and many of the peaches have gone bad.

EXERCISE 2B-14

Study the underlined subjects and verbs in the following sentences. What can you learn about subjects and verbs from these examples? Look particularly at the position of the subject in relation to the verb in numbers 1 through 7. Also, compare the position of the subject in 8, 9, and 10 with that in 5, 6, and 7.

1. There was a small kitten in my garage.

2. There were three mistakes in my paper.

3. There are six shoe stores in this mall.

4. There have been three accidents at that intersection this year.

5. In the closet was an old stovepipe hat.

6. Under my bed is my collection of baseball cards.

7. Next to my car stood a smiling police officer.

8. In the closet I found an old stovepipe hat.

9. Under my bed I store my collection of baseball cards.

10. Next to my car a smiling police officer was waiting for me.

NOTE: A discussion of the answers to this exercise can be found on pages 53–54.

EXERCISE 2B-15

In the following sentences, underline all verbs twice and all subjects once. Some of these sentences will have inverted word order.

1. There are three problems with Harriet's plan.

2. In the morning, I had a terrible headache.

3. After the lecture came a question-and-answer period.

4. There were no absences from this morning's class.

5. There will be twenty questions on the quiz.

6. In my shoe was a tiny stone.

7. Under Nancy's doormat was the key to her front door.

8. There must be a simple explanation for his behavior.

9. There are no tests in Mr. Greenfelder's course.

10. Next to the bank is a Burger King.

EXERCISE 2B-16

In the following sentences, the verbs have been underlined twice. Unless you have learned about this kind of sentence before, you will probably have some trouble identifying the subject. Therefore, instead of finding the subjects, try answering the following questions:

a. What do all five sentences have in common? What kind of sentences are they?
b. Can you say anything about the person who is going to "do" the verb in each of these sentences? Can you identify him or her?

  1. <u>Hand</u> me that screwdriver.

  2. <u>Meet</u> me at the Hilton.

  3. <u>Park</u> your car at the end of the street.

  4. <u>Stand</u> up.

  5. <u>Close</u> your books.

NOTE: A discussion of the answers to this exercise can be found on page 54.

EXERCISE 2B-17

In the following sentences, underline all verbs twice and all subjects once.

  1. Give me a hand with this couch, please.

  2. Write me a letter from San Francisco.

  3. Go to the Safeway and buy us some eggs.

  4. Be quiet.

  5. Do not smoke in this restaurant.

  6. Eat your spinach.

  7. Write me a letter from college.

  8. Remember your parents on their anniversary.

  9. Hold this dog for me.

 10. Stand up and look for the top to this bottle.

EXERCISE 2B-18

This exercise reviews everything you have learned about identifying subjects and verbs. Underline all verbs twice and all subjects once.

  1. My typewriter has been cleaned.

  2. Joanne and her husband took a trip to Wyoming and saw grizzly bears.

  3. Some of your answers were wrong.

  4. There were two reasons for her anger.

  5. Send your order to the following address.

  6. A friend of my sister is the president of CBS.

7. One of the boys was selected for the show.

8. Jim and Cathy will not be coming to the meeting.

9. In my bed was a grey-striped furry animal.

10. Helen and a neighbor of hers will be waiting for us at the station.

11. Monique has booked a reservation for the whole group.

12. The man in the checked suit and the string tie is my uncle.

13. One section of the roof of my new house is tile.

14. My little sister and her friend stayed up late and watched TV.

15. In a few minutes, we should leave for the movie.

16. The cover of my typewriter was left on the floor.

17. Get a firm grip on yourself.

18. The handle of the lawn mower was broken.

19. There are always exceptions to grammar rules.

20. One of the boys and none of the girls remembered to bring a notebook.

 EXERCISE 2B-19

In the paragraph below, underline all verbs twice and all subjects once.

I love baseball. Every summer I go to about a dozen games. Each of these games is different from every other one. Some of them are pitchers' duels with very few hits. These games are very tense and exciting. Most years, there are also several high-scoring games with lots of action. However, my favorite games are the boring ones. During these boring games, I can go to the booths for hot dogs and beer. My kids and I can talk about past games. Also, I can watch the people around me. Other people may like the exciting games. But the boring ones are my favorites.

DISCUSSION OF INDUCTIVE EXERCISES

EXERCISE 2B-4

The subjects in Exercise 2B-4 were all a little different from those in the preceding exercises. They were little words that took the place of nouns—words like "we," "you," "someone," "no one," and "I." These words are known as pronouns. Just like nouns, they can be used as the subjects of sentences.

EXERCISE 2B-6

In these sentences the verbs were all linking verbs. Until now, all the verbs in this section have been action verbs. If you don't remember linking verbs, you may want to refer back to page 41 to refresh your memory.

Finding linking verbs is really no different from finding action verbs. You merely ask yourself one of the same two questions you used for action verbs. Where the blank line is, you merely fill in the verb.

a. Who _____(the verb)_____ ?

b. What _____(the verb)_____ ?

Here, for example, are the first two sentences from this exercise:

1. Mr. McCaskill is an accountant.
2. We were late for the meeting.

To find the subject in number 1, you would ask yourself "Who is (an accountant)?" In number 2, you would ask, "Who was (late for the meeting)?" So, you see, the process is basically the same with linking verbs as it was with action verbs.

EXERCISE 2B-8

The sentences in this exercise are reproduced below:

1. The <u>cover</u> of the (book) <u>was</u> wet.
2. The <u>fender</u> of my (car) <u>is</u> damaged.
3. <u>Some</u> of the (children) <u>were sleeping</u>.
4. <u>Many</u> of the (flowers) <u>were damaged</u> by the frost.
5. <u>Each</u> of the new (glasses) <u>is</u> chipped.

You probably noticed that in each of these sentences there is a second word that might be mistakenly identified as the subject. These words are placed in parentheses above. You may also have recognized that each of these words is part of a phrase that begins with the word "of":

1. of the book
2. of my car
3. of the children
4. of the flowers
5. of the new glasses

These phrases are part of a large group known as prepositional phrases. However, 99 percent of the problems with identifying subjects are caused by prepositional phrases that begin with "of," so that is the only kind we will worry about in this exercise.

There are two ways to find the correct subject in sentences with prepositional phrases; you need to be familiar with both of them. First, the two questions you learned earlier, if carefully applied, will usually locate the correct subject. Second, you should remember that *the subject will never be in a prepositional phrase.*

Let's apply both these techniques to sentence 1. First, if you ask yourself "What was wet?" you will correctly identify the subject as "cover." The sentence does not say that the book was wet, only that the *cover* was wet. Second, you should recognize that "book" is in a prepositional phrase and, therefore, cannot be the subject.

The subjects in each of the other sentences could be identified in the same way.

EXERCISE 2B-10

The sentences from this exercise are reproduced below with parentheses around the prepositional phrases.

1. The <u>man</u> (with a pipe) <u>is</u> my psychology teacher.

2. The <u>woman</u> (in the blue sweater) <u>is losing</u> her touch.

3. The <u>pot</u> (on the stove) <u>contains</u> tomato soup.

4. The <u>flag</u> (over the high school) <u>was flying</u> at half mast.

5. The <u>road</u> (to Wayne) <u>is</u> very busy.

These prepositional phrases begin with words other than "of." Here is a list of the words most commonly used as prepositions:

above	by	near	to
among	during	of	toward
around	for	off	under
at	from	on	until
behind	in	out of	up
below	in front of	since	upon
beside	into	since	with
between	like	through	

Although each of these words can be used as a preposition, many of them can also be used in other ways. When they are prepositions, they will begin a phrase that will end with a noun or pronoun, as in the sentences above.

The important thing here is not to recognize prepositions, but to make sure that you not confuse the subject in a sentence with the noun in the prepositional phrase.

EXERCISE 2B-12

The subject in each of the sentences in Exercise 2B-12 consists of two words joined by "and" or "or." In fact, any number of words can be joined by "and" or "or" and used as the suject of a sentence, although three or four is about as many as can usually be used gracefully. The following examples show three and four words as subjects:

1. <u>Strawberries</u>, <u>raspberries</u>, and <u>peaches</u> <u>are</u> in season.

2. <u>Kris</u>, <u>Bernie</u>, <u>John</u>, and <u>Annetta</u> <u>got</u> A's in biology.

EXERCISE 2B-14

In most sentences in English, the subject comes near the beginning of the sentence and the verb follows. The sentences in Exercise 2B-14 show that this is not always the case. In sentences that begin with the word "there," the subject is found after the verb. Also, in sentences beginning with a prepositional phrase, the subject *may* be found after the verb, but it also may be in its normal location in front of the verb. Sentences in which the subject follows the verb are known as sentences with inverted word order.

EXERCISE 2B-16

The answers to the two questions preceding this exercise are as follows:

a. Each of the five sentences is telling someone to do something. Each of them gives a command. You may have learned somewhere earlier that these are called imperative sentences.
b. The person who will "do" the verb in each of these sentences is the person being spoken to. For example, take a look at sentence 1:

Hand me that screwdriver.

Whomever the speaker is speaking to is going to "hand (me that screwdriver)." The pronoun that we use for the person being spoken to is always "you." Therefore, in a sentence that gives a command, the subject is said to be "you understood." "Understood" means that anyone who hears or reads the sentence will understand that the subject is "you" even though it is not spoken or written. In an exercise, when asked what the subject is in a sentence that gives a command, you can indicate "you understood" the way we have below.

(you)   1.   Hand me that screwdriver.

(you)   2.   Meet me at the Hilton.

(you)   3.   Park your car at the end of the street.

(you)   4.   Stand up.

(you)   5.   Close your books.

Part C · Identifying Subjects and Verbs in Sentences with Verbals

In this part you will learn how to identify subjects and verbs in sentences that are more complicated because they contain verbals. You may be wondering about that word "verbal." No, it's not a mistake. A verbal is something quite different from a verb. In this part, you will learn about that difference, about how to tell verbs and verbals apart, and about what a verbal can do.

EXERCISE 2C-1 _____

We have underlined all the verbals in the following sentences. Study these sentences and see what you can figure out about this kind of verbal. In particular, try to figure out what this kind of verbal consists of.

1. Margaret wanted to go to the movies.

2. To buy a new car was foolish.

3. I offered to give Robin a ride home.

4. Carville hoped <u>to get</u> an A on the final.

5. Ms. Singleton expected me <u>to forget</u> her birthday.

NOTE: A discussion of the answers to this exercise can be found on page 59.

EXERCISE 2C-2 _____

Underline all the verbals in the following sentences. Each sentence may contain no verbals, one verbal, or more than one verbal.

1. Steve liked to swim in the quarry.

2. I lent my book to Nick for the weekend.

3. Mike and Holly are going to build a house together.

4. We planned to drive to Toledo on Monday.

5. To write a poem was a great challenge for Bonnie.

7. I drove my father's car to town.

8. Mr. Lutz was afraid to drive in the snow.

9. Cynthia expects to get a present from me.

10. Sophie gave Gene a ticket to the dance.

EXERCISE 2C-3 _____

In this exercise you will be introduced to a second kind of verbal. Study the underlined words in the following sentences. These are all verbals. See if you can describe this form of verbal.

1. Al enjoys <u>singing</u>, but he can't carry a tune.

2. <u>Studying</u> her verbals, Karen forgot our date.

3. <u>Choosing</u> a career is not always easy.

4. I hate <u>waiting</u> in lines.

5. <u>Chopping</u> wood is very relaxing for most people.

NOTE: A discussion of the answers to this exercise can be found on page 59.

EXERCISE 2C-4 _____

Underline all the verbals in the following sentences. Both "to" + verb and verb + "ing" forms are included. Each sentence may contain no verbals, one verbal, or more than one verbal.

1. I enjoy dancing even though I am not much good at it.

2. Studying never helps me with tests.

3. Julie is afraid of falling through the ice.

4. Last summer I learned to program in Cobol.

5. Feeling a little nervous, Alex went to school.

6. To get into the movie, we had to be there by five o'clock.

7. Saving aluminum foil will never make you rich.

8. The purpose of this class is to teach you CPR.

9. Barry worried about making a speech.

10. Delivering this box to Betsy will not be any trouble for me.

EXERCISE 2C-5

To make matters a little more confusing, verbs with "ing" endings are *not always* verbals. In the following sentences, some of the verb + "ing" words are verbals, and some are not. The *verbals* have been placed in parentheses. The subjects are underlined once, and the verbs are underlined twice. Study these sentences very closely and try to determine when a verb + "ing" is a verbal and when it is not.

If you have trouble with this distinction, here is one more clue. Look closely at the word preceding the verb + "ing" words that are not verbals. What are all these words?

1. Rafael does not approve of (smoking).

2. Rafael was smoking at Linda's party.

3. Nadia is tired of (seeing) Bruce every weekend.

4. Nadia is seeing nobody but Bruce these days.

5. I am tired of (doing) grammar exercises.

6. I am doing grammar exercises in my sleep these days.

NOTE: A discussion of the answers to this exercise can be found on pages 59–61.

EXERCISE 2C-6

What you have learned about verbals should help you in this exercise, but you are *not* being asked to identify verbals. Instead, in the following sentences, underline all verbs twice and all subjects once. Do *not* mark the verbals. The first one is done for you.

1. Carol was staying with her aunt for the summer.

2. Professor Stivaletta is famous for assigning a lot of homework.

3. They were working on my car at six o'clock.

4. Mark wanted to see a doctor.

5. I paid eight dollars to see this movie in New York.

6. Nancy or David will call you next week about fixing the roof.

7. Diane appeared to forget the purpose of her visit.

8. Ms. Carlton invited us to her office for the reading of the will.

9. Henry is trying to remember the name of his first grade teacher.

10. Dick was attempting to convince me to go out drinking with him.

EXERCISE 2C-7

We have underlined the subjects once and the verbs twice in the following sentences. Study these sentences closely and try to determine a use for verbals that you had not seen until now.

1. To open this package requires a pair of pliers.

2. To open this package, I used a pair of pliers.

3. Driving on a day like this is very dangerous.

4. Driving on a day like this, I get nervous.

5. To laugh in the face of danger is a sign of insanity.

6. To laugh in the face of danger, he had to be crazy.

7. Swimming every day keeps my weight down.

8. Swimming every day, I have lost fifteen pounds.

9. To take this course costs eighty-four dollars.

10. To take this course, I paid eighty-four dollars.

NOTE: A discussion of the answers to this exercise can be found on page 61.

EXERCISE 2C-8

Now use the same procedure to underline the verbs twice and the subjects once in the following sentences. Be careful not to confuse verbs and verbals.

1. To get into the dance required a ticket.

2. Finding a key in my purse is not easy.

3. Hoping for a miracle, I turned in my test.

4. To get a job, Paul mailed over 100 résumés.

5. Greg was working on a degree in engineering.

6. Looking to his left, Kent did not notice the approaching truck.

7. To get to Kay's house is easy.

8. To mail that letter will require four stamps.

9. Cleaning the bathroom, Tom found his wallet.

10. To raise tomatoes, one must have lots of sun.

11. Running several miles a day is good for your heart.

12. Sitting at my typewriter, I found peace of mind.

13. Steven wanted to finish his paper by Friday's class.

14. To reach the ocean by noon was our plan.

15. Forcing the lock, Robin broke her key.

16. Holding my head made my headache a lot better.

17. To fix my zipper, I needed three hands.

18. To teach her cat a lesson, Helene tied his paws together.

19.   Telling Jackie about the death of her mother was not easy.

20.   To cover his mistake, Jeff had to tell several lies.

EXERCISE 2C-9 _____

Underline the verbs twice and the subjects once in the following sentences. Be careful not to confuse verbs and verbals.

1.   Joking about Sammy's grade was not a good idea.

2.   Leading off in the third inning, Eddie Murray hit a double.

3.   To get to heaven, you have to know your verbals.

4.   Floyd and Tippy were talking about you last night.

5.   Raising his eyebrows, Ron looked puzzled.

6.   Telling Jean about Bob got me into a lot of trouble.

7.   To open this jar, you need two hands.

8.   Reading the Sunday paper takes me about three hours.

9.   To drive with bald tires is very dangerous.

10.   To give up so soon was not a good idea.

11.   Katherine hoped to graduate next year.

12.   The front of my car was damaged in the accident.

13.   To drive to Houston takes about five hours.

14.   Listening to the radio, I heard the news about the fire.

15.   To pay for her trip, Lucille took a second job.

16.   Turning off the lights, Mr. Washburn settled down for the night.

17.   Spotting my brother in the crowd was very lucky.

18.   Forgetting about our date, Joleen was studying for her finals.

19.   Taking the mustard out of the refrigerator, Vinnie noticed a beer on the back shelf.

20.   To forget her mother's birthday was very thoughtless.

EXERCISE 2C-10 _____

Underline all verbs twice and all subjects once in the following paragraph.

You should think about taking up bird watching. It is very enjoyable and not too expensive. To get out into the wild is therapeutic. Breathing all that fresh air and getting all that exercise are good for your health. Furthermore, you will not need to spend a lot of money. To go bird watching requires only a pair of binoculars, a bird book, and a little free time. Keeping a list of all your birds adds to the excitement. Seeing a new bird for the first time is extremely satisfying. To relax your nerves, you should think about going bird watching.

DISCUSSION OF INDUCTIVE EXERCISES

EXERCISE 2C-1

Each of the verbals in Exercise 2C-1 consisted of two words. The first word was always "to," and the second word was always a verb.

This combination of "to" + verb is *always* a verbal. This form of verbal is known as an infinitive, but the terminology is not important. It is important that you recognize that "to" + verb is always a verbal.

Also, you need to remember that "to" + noun is a prepositional phrase. Look, for example, at the following sentence.

I hoped to send my children to college.

"To send" is "to" + verb and, therefore, is a verbal, but what about "to college"? Is "college" a verb? Can you "college"? Of course not, and so "to college" is not a verbal. It is a prepositional phrase.

Don't get these two confused. Only "to" + verb is a verbal. "To" + noun is *never* a verbal; it is always a prepositional phrase.

EXERCISE 2C-3

All the verbals in this exercise are composed of a verb with an "ing" ending. Verb + "ing" is the second form that verbals may take in English.

Although this kind of verbal is usually referred to as either a gerund or a participle, in this book we will just use the term "verbal" to refer to this type as well as the "to" + verb type which you learned earlier.

EXERCISE 2C-5

The pairs of sentences in this exercise demonstrate that a verb + "ing" can either be a verbal or a part of the verb. Further, whenever it is a part of the verb, it *always* has a helping verb (like "was," "is," or "am") in front of it. If it doesn't have a helping verb in front of it, it cannot be a verb; it must be a verbal.

What you have learned about verbals is summarized below:

1. "To" + verb is always a verbal. This means a verb with a "to" in front of it can never be a part of the verb.
2. A verb + "ing" is a verbal unless it has a helping verb in front of it. This means that a verb + "ing" cannot be a verb in a sentence unless it has a helping verb.

If you are the kind of person who likes diagrams, and especially if you like flow charts, you may find the diagram on the following page helpful in distinguishing verbs from verbals. If you are only confused by complicated diagrams, just disregard this chart.

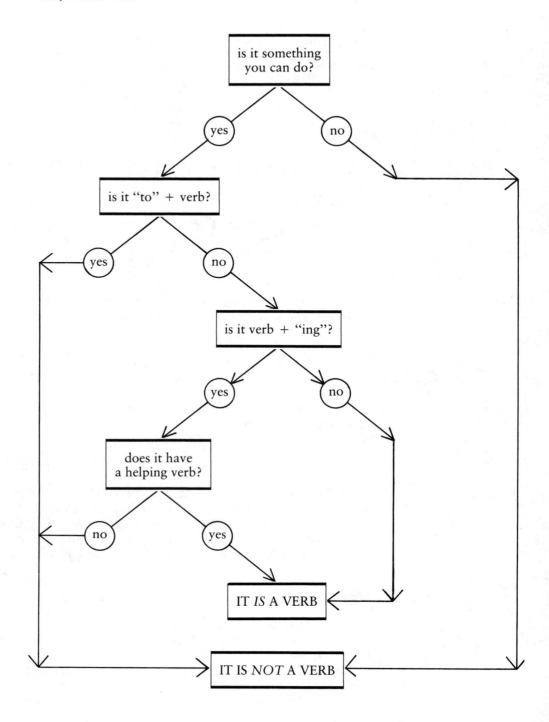

Of course, the point of all this is not to help you find verbals, but rather to help you find subjects and verbs. Recognizing verbals, however, will make finding subjects and verbs easier. If you can't recognize verbals, you may confuse them with verbs. From here on, the exercises are going to ask you to identify *subjects* and *verbs,* not verbals.

EXERCISE 2C-7

The sentences in this exercise reveal the startling fact that verbals may be used as subjects. Of course, they are not always subjects, but they may be. In other words, a verbal may or may not be the subject in a sentence, but it can never be the verb.

Remember the procedure you learned for finding subjects in Part B:

1. Find the verb.
2. Ask yourself one of the following two questions:

    a. Who ___(the verb)___ ?

    b. What ___(the verb)___ ?

Well, the same procedure will work in sentences that have verbals. You just need to remember that a verbal *may* be the subject, but it can never be the verb. Let's apply that procedure to the first two sentences from the preceding page.

1. To open this package requires a pair of pliers.

The verb is "requires." The answer to the question, "What requires (a pair of pliers)?" is "To open." "To open (this package)" is what "requires (a pair of pliers.)" So, the subject is the verbal "To open."

Now let's look at number 2:

2. To open this package, I used a pair of pliers.

The verb is "used." The answer to the question "Who used (a pair of pliers)?" is "I." "I" is who "used (a pair of pliers)." So, the subject of the sentence is "I."

Part D · Identifying Subjects and Verbs in Sentences with More Than One Clause

 EXERCISE 2D-1 _____

In the following sentences, the verbs have been underlined twice and the subjects once. What can you learn about subjects and verbs from these examples?

1. Anita gave a party, and Kim went to it.
2. I wanted to take History 201, but it is not offered this semester.
3. I bought an Apple computer, and then they went on sale.
4. Pam jacked the car up, and Mike loosened the lug nuts.
5. Bill will give me a ride, or I will take the bus.

NOTE: A discussion of the answers to this exercise can be found on page 64

EXERCISE 2D-2

In the following sentences, underline all verbs twice and all subjects once. Some of these sentences will contain more than one pair of subjects and verbs.

1. Don did the dishes, and I emptied the garbage.

2. English is not easy for me, but math is much harder.

3. Jerry hopes to get a B in this class, but he will settle for a C.

4. Laurie bought tickets for the symphony, and Jamie made us a reservation for dinner at the Hilton.

5. Janice failed statistics, so she is taking it again this spring.

6. Anita planted a lot of tomatoes, but she forgot to water them.

7. I saw my high school principal, but he did not remember my name.

8. Rick wanted to be an accountant, but he was terrible at math.

9. I bought the right size jeans, but they shrank.

10. The name of the woman in the purple blouse is Emily, but I cannot remember her last name.

EXERCISE 2D-3

In the following sentences, the verbs have been underlined twice and the subjects once. These sentences also contain more than one pair of subjects and verbs because they contain more than one clause. These clauses are somewhat different from the ones in Exercise 2D-1, however. Don't worry about the different kinds of clauses; we'll work on them in Chapter 6. For now, just make sure you can find all the subjects and verbs in sentences like these.

1. When Cynthia arrived at work, she remembered her glasses.

2. Evelyn sold her house because it was too big.

3. If Peter is late tonight, I will be furious.

4. The man whom I was talking to is Mark's brother.

5. The dog that the bus hit died a few minutes later.

EXERCISE 2D-4

In the following sentences, underline all verbs twice and all subjects once. Some of these sentences will contain more than one pair of subjects and verbs.

1. When the rain started, Lenny was riding his bike.

2. Because I was in the army, I know something about map reading.

3. The course that I am worried about is Anatomy and Physiology.

4. Gloria opened her purse, so I started reading the paper.

5. My husband likes to talk when he is at the movies.

6. While the salesclerk was talking on the phone, someone stole a leather coat.

7. Give this note to the woman whom you ride with to work.

8. I broke the pen that you gave me for my birthday.

9. If you want to go bowling, give me a call.

10. Ben hoped to buy a new TV, but they were too expensive.

EXERCISE 2D-5

In the following sentences, underline all verbs twice and all subjects once. Some of these sentences will contain more than one pair of subjects and verbs.

1. Whenever I jog, my knees swell.

2. Agnes was late because she missed her bus.

3. I did not buy that refrigerator because it only came in white.

4. I saw the man whom my mother used to date.

5. Rick opened the champagne, but it exploded all over the floor.

6. If you need a place to swim, you should join the "Y."

7. My sister was asleep, and my brother was watching TV.

8. We drove to the ocean, but Jenny took the train.

9. I left a large tip because the waitress had been very pleasant.

10. When I had my checkup, the doctor said that I was in perfect health.

11. Liza pays all the house bills, and Dan buys the groceries.

12. Edith bought a car, but it was a real lemon.

13. The teacher whom I like best is Mr. Brandt.

14. Diana has medical insurance, so this operation will not cost her very much.

15. Even though Mike was late with his return, the IRS did not charge him a penalty.

16. My basement is flooded, and my roof is leaking.

17. The suit that Reed bought was much too small for him.

18. If I am hired, I hope to start working next week.

19. I am not going to the party because my cat is quite sick.

20. I am quite fond of verbs, but I adore subjects.

DISCUSSION OF INDUCTIVE EXERCISE

EXERCISE 2D-1

The sentences in Exercise 2D-1 show that a single sentence can contain more than one pair of subjects and verbs. For example, sentence 1 is repeated below:

  1. Anita gave a party, and Kim went to it.

The first verb is "gave," and the first subject is "Anita"; the second verb is "went," and the second subject is "Kim."

    You will learn in future chapters that these sentences contain two clauses. In fact, a sentence can contain even more than two clauses; in these cases, it will contain more than two pairs of subjects and verbs.

    For now, however, you should not worry about clauses. All you need to do is identify subjects and verbs. You must be aware, though, that sentences can contain more than one pair of subjects and verbs.

R E V I E W

 EXERCISE 2-REVIEW-1 _____

In the following sentences, underline all verbs twice and all subjects once. These sentences include all the types you have studied in this chapter.

1. Lou and Helen are starting their own business.

2. When Bob graduated from high school, he did not intend to go to college.

3. To be considered for that job was a great honor.

4. Nancy ran out the door, and her dog ran right after her.

5. As Hank's plane arrived in Washington, he remembered his briefcase.

6. While the rice is cooking, prepare the tomato sauce for the veal.

7. Scanning the chapter is not the same as reading it.

8. To buy a house was impossible, but we did it anyway.

9. The book that I read was about the Civil War.

10. Seeing my college roommate after ten years was really surprising.

11. The bottom of the desk was covered with chewing gum.

12. I want to apologize to whomever my mistake has affected.

13. Until you hear from your lawyer, do not talk to your ex-husband.

14. I answered the phone, but no one was there.

15. When I received an overdraft notice from the bank, I called them immediately.

16. The front of my car was badly damaged, but the back was untouched.

17.   I would like to scream at whomever this car belongs to.

18.   To get an appointment with my dentist has become quite difficult.

19.   To locate the subject in a sentence is not very difficult.

20.   Washing the dishes, he lost his ring.

EXERCISE 2-REVIEW-2 _____

In the following sentences, underline all verbs twice and all subjects once. These sentences include all the types you have studied in this chapter.

1.   A friend of my sister gave me a ride to Philadelphia.

2.   To memorize this poem, I will need about three hours.

3.   While we were at the ocean, the sun never appeared.

4.   A black cat and a spotted dog were fighting in the back yard.

5.   Kicking your bicycle will never fix it.

6.   Mark noticed that his notebook was missing.

7.   Open the garage door for Lou.

8.   Turning on the typewriter, Paul began to work on his paper.

9.   Until I receive your payment, I will keep your bicycle.

10.   I missed the first question.

11.   To see that movie, we will have to wait in a long line.

12.   The shirt that Luke bought was made in Hong Kong.

13.   Jazz and gospel are both American musical forms.

14.   To forget an appointment with the president of the company is hard to live down.

15.   Before I had read any science fiction, I thought of it as kids' stories.

16.   In the morning, close the window.

17.   Finishing the test early, Leslie had time to check her answers.

18.   Jan screamed when she received the letter about her scholarship.

19.   One of Polly's jumps broke the school record.

20.   Starting his own business was Craig's goal.

EXERCISE 2-REVIEW-3 _____

In the following essay, underline all verbs twice and all subjects once. The essay includes all the types of sentences you studied in this chapter.

Millions of Americans are jogging to keep in shape. At the same time, walking for exercise is not at all popular. This fact reveals several things about our national character.

Although few of us would admit to bring puritans, we are all influenced by puritan attitudes. This influence can be seen in our preference for jogging. An important puritan attitude is the idea that hard work is better for us than easy work. Walking is very pleasant, so we think that it could not be good for us. To jog is hard work. While jogging, we sweat and breathe hard. Therefore, we think it must be good for us. These ways of thinking are a direct result of puritan attitudes.

In addition to being puritans, Americans also are strong-willed. This attitude sometimes means that we hold on to our beliefs even when the facts prove them wrong. Our preference for jogging demonstrates this trait very clearly. A growing number of medical studies have shown the dangers of jogging. Knee problems are quite common among joggers. A number of joggers have suffered heart attacks from overexertion. Finally, the damage to internal organs from the constant jarring during jogging is being studied. Despite this medical evidence, Americans continue to assume that jogging is good for them. We are a strong-willed people.

A third trait of Americans is the way that we worship youth. Anything that we associate with aging is automatically avoided. For some reason, walking has become associated with older people. As a result, the majority of Americans are never going to become dedicated walkers.

The character traits of Americans make a major contribution to our country's greatness. Nevertheless, I wish we could overcome our puritanism, our strong will, and our fascination with youth long enough to try walking as exercise.

 EXERCISE 2-REVIEW-4 _____

Your English instructor has asked you for a short piece of writing in which you tell what your high school English teachers did that helped or hurt you most in your efforts to become a better writer.

Before you start writing your response, think about the planning techniques you learned in Chapter 1. The questions you learned there are repeated below; write your answers in the space provided.

1.   What subject are you going to write about? _____

   _____

2. What do you know or what can you guess about the audience for this piece of writing? _____

_____

3. What is the purpose of this piece of writing? What do you want it to accomplish? _____

_____

Now, on a separate piece of paper, write the assignment your English teacher asked for.

 **EXERCISE 2-REVIEW-5** _____

Now, using what you learned in Chapter 1, you are going to work on revising the piece of writing you produced for Exercise 2-Review-4. First, answer each of the following questions about that piece of writing:

1. What is the subject? _____

_____

2. Is there only one subject? _____

3. Can I change the piece of writing in any way that will make the subject clearer? _____

4. Is the subject too broad for this short piece of writing? _____

5. Does the piece of writing really do what the assignment asked me to do? _____

6. Who is the audience for this piece of writing? _____

_____

7. Is it written in a way that is appropriate for this audience? _____

_____

Based on your responses to the questions above, revise the paper on another sheet of paper.

8. After you have finished revising the paper, proofread it carefully and correct any errors, such as spelling, word endings, words omitted, or punctuation.
9. Finally, go back over your writing and underline all verbs twice and all subjects once.

C H A P T E R

3

Writing Paragraphs

Part A   The Topic Sentence
Part B   Paragraph Unity
Part C   Other Kinds of Paragraphs

Part A · The Topic Sentence

In this chapter you will learn the basic ingredients of a well-unified paragraph. In this section, you will learn about the topic sentence. But first, an overview of the paragraph.

EXERCISE 3A-1 ———————————————

The following diagram represents an essay. How many paragraphs does this essay include? How do you know? There are *two* clues that tell you when one paragraph ends and another begins. Do you see both of them?

_____
_____
_____
_____
_____
_____
_____
_____
_____
_____
_____

_____

There are six paragraphs in the diagram of the essay. You can tell where each paragraph begins because the first line of each paragraph is indented (moved over) about eight spaces. You can also tell where each of the paragraphs ends because a blank space follows the final word. The length of this blank depends on how much space the last sentence takes up on the last line. Every once in a while, the last sentence of a paragraph will happen to end right at the end of the last line, but this arrangement is quite unusual. These blank spaces, one at the beginning and one at the end of a paragraph, are important. They help the reader to see the organization of the piece of writing. They signal the reader when one point has been completed and another is beginning.

There is another style for paragraphing, called the block style. In block style, the first line is not indented; instead, there is double spacing between paragraphs. For most of the writing you will do as a student, the indented style is more appropriate.

Now that you know what a paragraph looks like, it's time to find out what goes into a well-written paragraph.

EXERCISE 3A-2 _____

Study the following two paragraphs and decide which one you like better. Then, figure out why you like it better. What is wrong with the other one?

Paragraph 1

Last week I went to visit my mother, who is in her sixties. She lives in the middle of downtown Washington, D.C. Besides being the center of the federal government, Washington is a city of museums. It has art galleries, space museums, industrial museums, and the world-famous Smithsonian Institution. The Smithsonian also sponsors many musical concerts. My favorites are those which include baroque music. My favorite baroque composer is Antonio Vivaldi. Vivaldi was known as the "red priest" because he was an ordained priest and had a bright red beard. His best-known work, and my favorite, is the The Four Seasons.

Paragraph 2

Washington, D.C., is an exciting city to visit. There is always the possibility of catching a glance of a politician or two; on my last visit, I saw Gary Hart talking intensely with Teddy Kennedy. But even if you don't enjoy politician watching, there is an awesome collection of museums. My favorite is the old-fashioned Smithsonian, but my children like the Space Museum best. The National Gallery is just one of several art collections; my favorite is the Freer Gallery, which specializes in Oriental art. The Natural History Museum has wonderful exhibits of animals, fish, birds, insects, and gems. In the evening, the Kennedy Center for the Performing Arts offers a range of concerts and plays. But, perhaps the best part of Washington is its beauty; I love to ride around and look at the monuments and statues clustered along the Potomac River.

These two paragraphs illustrate one important ingredient of a well-written paragraph: It must focus on a single subject.

If you made diagrams of paragraphs 1 and 2, they might look like the following:

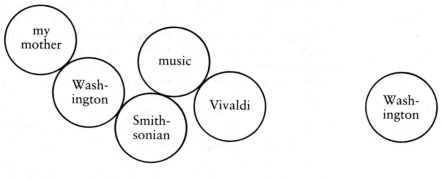

Paragraph 1   **Paragraph 2**

Paragraph 1 can hardly be called a paragraph at all. It is just a group of sentences that jump from one subject to another. For example, the fact that my mother is sixty has nothing to do with Vivaldi; the fact that I like *The Four Seasons* is unrelated to the fact that Washington is a city of museums. A paragraph must have a single clear subject, and this one doesn't.

Of course, paragraph 2 also discusses a number of subjects: politicians, the Smithsonian, other museums, the Kennedy Center, and the beauty of Washington. The reason this paragraph is better unified is that each of these subjects relates back to the central subject: Washington. Each of them makes a point about Washington.

And so, in a well-unified paragraph, every sentence will make a statement about a single subject. It takes more than just a single subject to make a good paragraph, however.

EXERCISE 3A-3

Take a look at the paragraphs 3 and 4 and decide which you like better.

Paragraph 3

Brazil is the largest nation in South America. It is about 90 percent of the size of the United States with just over 50 percent of the population. Its capital is Brasilia, which is a city less than twenty years old. The climate is temperate, and, since Brazil is located in the southern hemisphere, the seasons are the reverse of ours. The national language is Portuguese, and the majority of Brazilians are Roman Catholics. The largest city is Rio de Janeiro, a beautiful and modern city on the Atlantic Ocean. The economy of Brazil is growing and is no longer dependent completely on the success of its coffee crop. The military in Brazil is quite strong and well equipped.

Paragraph 4

Brazil is a great place for a winter vacation. Most important, the climate in the winter there is delightful. Since Brazil is in the southern hemisphere, it is summer there in December, January, and February. Also, a vacation in Brazil is fairly inexpensive. Even in Rio, a decent hotel room costs no more than twenty-five dollars a night, and the fanciest dinner in town can be had for about fifteen dollars. There is also plenty to do in Brazil. The beaches are beautiful and not too crowded. If one gets tired of swimming and sun-bathing, shopping in Rio is fun and rewarding. After fifteen minutes of haggling, I bought a beautiful leather briefcase for just twenty dollars. In addition, tours of the rest of Brazil are fascinating. I visited Brasilia, the modern capital that was carved out of the jungle, and I took a boat trip up the Amazon. I highly recommend a winter's trip to South America's largest country.

You may have had a little more trouble deciding which of these you liked better, and you probably had even more trouble deciding why. Let's take a closer look at them.

Do these two paragraphs each have a single subject? Yes. They both are about Brazil. So there is no trouble with subject.

Now let's look more closely at paragraph 3. If someone read number 3 and then said to the writer, "So what? What's the point? What is this paragraph getting at? What does it *prove* about Brazil?" how would the writer respond? What is the point? Is there one? Or, does paragraph 3 just include a collection of facts "about" Brazil? Do those facts add up to anything?

How about paragraph 4? If someone asked the writer of paragraph 4, "What's the point?" he or she would have an answer. The point is that Brazil is a good place for a winter vacation. In other words, paragraph 4 doesn't just talk "about" Brazil; it has a point to make. It proves something. All the facts add up to a conclusion about Brazil, and that makes it a more focused and, therefore, a better piece of writing.

Diagrams of paragraphs 3 and 4 would look like the following:

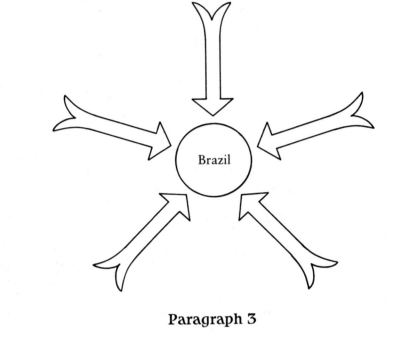

Paragraph 3

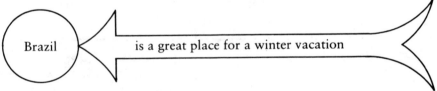

Paragraph 4

When you write a paragraph, you should make sure it both has a subject and makes some point about that subject. Furthermore, it must be clear to the reader what the subject and the point about the subject are. The following diagram represents these two essential components of a good paragraph:

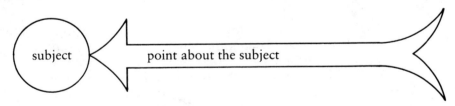

Often, these two components are combined into one sentence, which is called the topic sentence. If you have trouble writing paragraphs that have a clear subject and point about the subject, it may be a good idea to place them in a topic sentence and to make it the first sentence in the paragraph. If you do so, the reader will never have any trouble figuring out what the "point" is. When you are a more experienced and more confident writer, you may want to experiment with other ways of expressing your subject and point about the subject. You may want to place the topic sentence some-where else in the paragraph, perhaps in the middle or at the end. You may want to split the topic sentence into two sentences, one for the subject and one for the point. All these are possibilities; the crucial thing is that it be clear to the reader what the subject is and what point you are making about that subject.

 ## EXERCISE 3A-4 _____

Read each of the following paragraphs and underline the topic sentence. Then write the subject and the point about that subject in the diagram underneath the paragraph.

Paragraph 5

My father has a double standard about honesty. He always tells me that I shouldn't lie. In fact, he has punished me more severely for lying than for anything else. When he found out that I had met my boyfriend on a night when I said I was going to be studying with my girlfriend, he grounded me for six weeks. I could understand his attitude if I didn't see him lying all the time. Just last weekend I heard him tell my grandmother that we couldn't come over for Sunday dinner because he had to work. Then, on Sunday, he played golf all day. Another time, he told the manager at Sears that a toaster we bought was defective, when I knew that he had dropped it when he took it out of the box. His double standard really makes me angry.

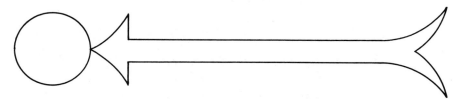

Subject   **Point about the Subject**

Paragraph 6

Greg's car is extremely well organized. He has little plastic tapes on the dashboard that say, "Please buckle your seat belt." Fastened to the dashboard is a chrome change holder that is always stocked with quarters, dimes, and nickels. Under the dashboard he has fastened a bright red fire extinguisher. On the shelf behind the back seat is an umbrella. And, when you open the trunk, you find highway flares, jumper cables, and a small tool kit. I'm surprised Greg hasn't found a way to install a refrigerator and stock it with sandwiches and beer.

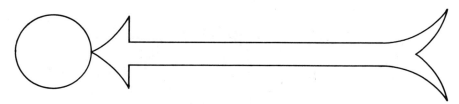

Subject   **Point about the Subject**

Paragraph 7

Yesterday morning, as I was leaving for work, I heard a terrible noise from the intersection in front of my house. There was a horn beeping frantically, then a terrible screeching of tires on pavement, and then a sickening crash. A station wagon with a woman and three small kids had been hit by a city bus. One of the kids had flown through the windshield and landed on the grass on the far side of the street. I ran to the car, and, in a few seconds, determined that miraculously no one was seriously injured. Even the little girl who flew out of the car received only scratches and bruises. But they were very lucky. Just a few months ago a woman was killed in a similar accident at this same corner. In fact, during the three years that I have lived here, there have been four serious accidents at this corner. My intersection desperately needs a traffic light.

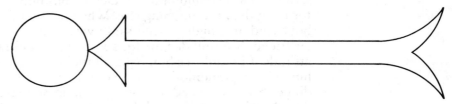

Subject   Point about the Subject

Paragraph 8

Every time I go to Chincoteague, I see great birds. One day last summer, I saw five different herons, a glossy ibis, three different egrets, a least bittern, black skimmers, and an oystercatcher. Chincoteague Island, Virginia, is one of the greatest spots for bird watching on the East Coast. One reason it has so many birds is that it is a national seashore, protected by the federal government. A variety of birds flock there because it includes both salt water and fresh water ponds. Also, it is directly on the East Coast flyway, along which millions of birds migrate. Finally, it is great for bird-watchers because it is just a few hours' drive from Washington, Baltimore, and Philadelphia.

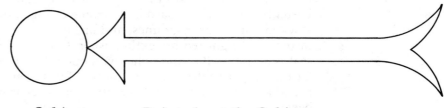

Subject   Point about the Subject

 EXERCISE 3A-5 _____

Listed below are ten possible topics to write papers about. Most of them need to be narrowed considerably before they will be appropriate for a five-hundred-word essay. Select five of these, narrow them down if necessary, and write topic sentences for them.

the medical system   unemployment
divorce   finding a job
child raising   education
computers   taking tests
dreams   fears

1. _____

_____

2. _____

_____

3. _____

_____

4. _____

_____

5. _____

_____

EXERCISE 3A-6

A couple of months ago, a cousin of yours named Jason came to town for a few days and stayed with you. While he was visiting, you introduced him to your friend Theresa. Now he has written that he is coming back to see Theresa and he wants to take her out to dinner. He wants you to recommend a restaurant. Write a paragraph in which you recommend a restaurant to your cousin. You can imagine that this paragraph is part of a longer letter, so you don't need to write any greetings or other small talk. Just write the paragraph about the restaurant.

Before you start writing, spend some time thinking about the purpose of the paragraph, the audience, and the subject.

When you have finished the paragraph, underline the topic sentence and write the subject and the point in the diagram on the following page.

_____

_____

_____

_____

_____

_____

_____

_____

_____

_____

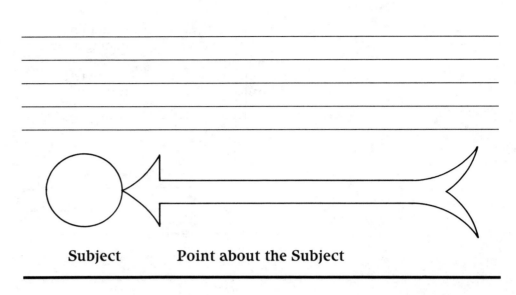

Subject   Point about the Subject

Part B · Paragraph Unity

In Part A you learned how to write the topic sentence of a paragraph. In this section you will learn how to make sure the rest of the paragraph is unified with that topic sentence.

EXERCISE 3B-1 _____

Study the following paragraph and see if there are any sentences that don't seem to belong.

Paragraph 8

Ocean City is overpriced. A room no bigger than a large closet costs as much as seventy-five dollars a night. A simple hamburger, which would cost little more than a dollar anywhere else, can cost as much as three dollars in Ocean City. This year I went to Myrtle Beach, and it was just as bad. Gasoline in Ocean City is about twenty cents a gallon more than anywhere else. And, the beach there is not kept very clean; last summer I cut my foot on a broken beer bottle that was buried in the sand. Ocean City is no bargain.

If you are having trouble, identify the topic sentence. Then read each of the other sentences and ask yourself if it supports the topic sentence. If a sentence doesn't support the topic sentence, then it doesn't belong in the paragraph.

First, the topic sentence is "Ocean City is overpriced." The first sentence that didn't support the topic sentence was "This year I went to Myrtle Beach, and it was just as bad." This sentence clearly doesn't belong in this paragraph. It doesn't even discuss the subject, Ocean City. If the writer wants to discuss Myrtle Beach, he or she should do that in another paragraph.

The next sentence that doesn't belong is not quite as obvious: "And, the beach there is not kept very clean; last summer I cut my foot on a broken beer bottle that was buried in the sand." This sentence *does* discuss the subject, Ocean City. It still doesn't belong in this paragraph, however, because it doesn't support the point about the subject. It doesn't say anything about Ocean City's being overpriced. In a well-unified paragraph, every sentence should support, not only the subject, but the point about that subject as well.

When those two sentences are removed, the paragraph is much better unified:

Paragraph 9

Ocean City is overpriced. A room no bigger than a large closet costs as much as seventy-five dollars a night. A simple hamburger, which would cost little more than a dollar anywhere else, can cost as much as three dollars in Ocean City. Gasoline in Ocean City is about twenty cents a gallon more than anywhere else. Ocean City is no bargain.

EXERCISE 3B-2

Proofread the following paragraphs and cross out any sentences that do not support the topic sentence.

Paragraph 10

Making vegetarian tacos is easy if you follow my recipe. First, you empty a pint of cottage cheese into a mixing bowl. Next, pour in two tablespoons of anise seeds; then, add a cup of raisins. Finally, chop up about two cups of green onions and add half to the cottage cheese mixture. I first ate green onions when I was in the army. Stir the mixture and use it to stuff six taco shells. Place the shells in a large, flat bowl and cover with grated Swiss cheese, taco sauce, and the remaining green onions. Bake the tacos at 350 degrees for about fifteen minutes.

Paragraph 11

Buying a present for someone always leaves me feeling guilty. I worry about what the present I buy will mean to the person I give it to. For example, my sister has always had an inferiority complex because she didn't go to college. If I buy her something for the kitchen, will she get the idea that I think of her main interest as cooking? Instead, if I buy her a book of T. S. Eliot's poetry, will she think I am trying to educate her? Eliot wrote poetry in which he described modern society as a wasteland. And my mother is just as bad as my sister, only her touchy point is her age. If I buy her a tennis racket, I'll worry that it's too young for her. If I get her a pair of Isotoner gloves, I'll be concerned that only "senior citizens" wear Isotoners. Because I worry so much over every gift, it usually takes me a full weekend to buy anything.

Paragraph 12

You are probably aware that, for most trips, it is cheaper to go by train than it is to fly. Did you also know that it can be faster? If you count the time spent getting to the airport and waiting for the plane, trips under five hundred miles can be quicker by train. In addition, train travel is the safest means of transportation. Even when train accidents do occur, seldom are passengers injured. Many people also find traveling by train to be psychologically more satisfying. Of course, psychologists sometimes have fairly "far out" ideas about things; everyone has heard of Freud's theories about boys wanting to kill their fathers and make love with their mothers. But on this matter of flying, I think they're right. If you've watched miles of countryside go by your window, you really feel more satisfaction with the trip; somehow, flying above the clouds makes it hard to believe you've really traveled. Further, most people find riding a train more pleasant. Every time I've ever taken the train, I've found myself meeting people whom I enjoy talking with. That never happens to me on a plane. And finally, have you ever heard of a train being hijacked? So, all things considered, there are many advantages to traveling by train.

A lot more can be said about writing effective paragraphs, but this is enough to get you started. From here on make sure you proofread your paragraphs for topic sentences and unity.

 EXERCISE 3B-3

Imagine that your school doesn't have a smoking policy. Your class is going to vote on what the class's policy will be about smoking in the classroom. Write a paragraph in which you state what the policy on smoking should be. Then give some reasons why the policy should be what you propose.

Before you write this assignment, answer the following questions:

1. Who will be the audience for this paragraph?_____
   _____

2. What is the purpose of this paragraph? What are you trying to accomplish?_____
   _____

3. What will be the subject of the paragraph?_____
   _____

4. What point will you make about that subject?_____
   _____
   _____

(The combination of 3 and 4 will be the topic sentence.)

On a separate sheet of paper, write this paragraph.

EXERCISE 3B-4

Now you are going to revise the paragraph you wrote for Exercise 3B-3. Ask yourself each of the following questions about the paragraph. If the answers to any of these reveal weaknesses in the paragraph, revise it to correct those weaknesses.

1. Does the paragraph do what the assignment asked you to do?
2. Are the language and content appropriate for the audience?
3. Is it clear what the topic sentence is? What is it?
4. What is the subject of the paragraph?
5. Is the point you are making about the subject clear?
6. Does every sentence in the paragraph support the topic sentence?

Now revise the paragraph to correct any weaknesses you may have discovered. After you have revised the paragraph, check it carefully for mistakes in spelling, grammar, and punctuation.

Finally, to review what you learned in Chapter 2, underline all verbs twice and all subjects once.

Part C · Other Kinds of Paragraphs

It would be a mistake if you left this chapter with the impression that all paragraphs should look just like the ones you have been working with. In fact, paragraphs are a lot more flexible than that.

The type of paragraph you have been working with—the paragraph with a topic sentence and all the other sentences supporting that topic sentence—is often referred to as a "body paragraph" because it is commonly used in the "body," that is, the middle portion of the essay.

Although many, even most, of the paragraphs you will write will be body paragraphs, in longer pieces of writing, you will also write a number of paragraphs that do not fit this model. These other kinds of paragraphs usually fall into one of three categories:

1. **Introductory paragraphs.** Sometimes called "opening paragraphs," these come at the beginning of a longer piece of writing like an essay or a business report. They can do any number of very useful things like provide background information, announce the main point (thesis), outline the argument, explain the assumptions, or just attract the reader's attention. Most introductory paragraphs accomplish a combination of these.

   The following example of an introductory paragraph is taken from a five-hundred-word essay written for a history class.

   Even though we have come to see the American Revolution as a triumph of justice over tyranny, many Americans in the years after the war came to think they had just substituted one tyranny for another. These middle- and working-class Americans felt that democracy was limited to the wealthy, that tax laws made it difficult for the small farmers to maintain their farms, and that banking practices made it likely that only the very rich would be able to keep their property.

2. **Closing paragraphs.**   These come at the end of the essay and also serve a number of purposes. They can restate the main idea, summarize the arguments, suggest an action, leave the reader thinking, or point to additional areas of concern.

The following example of a closing paragraph comes from the end of the same history paper as the last example.

> It does appear that America in the years immediately after the Revolutionary War was a democracy only for wealthy, white men. The desperate acts of men like Daniel Shays were necessary to start America on the road to true democracy. We're still traveling down that road today.

3. **Transition paragraphs.**   Frequently, one body paragraph completes one line of thought, and the next body paragraph starts on a different idea. If you just go straight from the one to the other, the reader may have a little trouble following your argument. What you need between the two ideas is a little "transition paragraph." This is a paragraph that has no topic sentence; all it does is help the reader make the transition from the first idea to the second without feeling confused or jarred. It says, "Reader, now we have finished that part of the discussion, and we are going on to a new point." A transition paragraph is often quite short.

The following example of a transition paragraph is taken from the same essay as the first two examples.

> Virginia was not the only state experiencing disruptions in the decade following the American Revolution. In Massachusetts, Daniel Shays was the center of another group of disillusioned Americans.

The point of all this is not to teach you how to write all these other types of paragraphs, but rather, to alert you to the fact that they are also perfectly correct when used appropriately.

CHAPTER

4

Subject-Verb Agreement

Part A   Simple Subject-Verb Agreement
Part B   Agreement with Irregular Verbs
Part C   Agreement with Prepositional Phrases,
           Compound Subjects, and Inverted Word Order

Part A · Simple Subject-Verb Agreement

In Chapter 2, you learned how to locate the subject and verb in a sentence. In this chapter you will learn how to change the form of verbs so that they agree with their subjects.

 EXERCISE 4A-1 —————————————————————

To review your skill at identifying verbs, underline twice all the verbs in the following sentences. If you have any trouble, review Chapter 2.

1. The Red River is nearly at flood stage.

2. My watch is about five minutes fast.

3. My husband has the car.

4. Rose is in the swimming pool.

5. Lynn has a great idea.

Now, try to figure out *when* each of the sentences above is taking place. For example, according to sentence 1, when is the Red River nearly at flood stage? Yesterday? Tomorrow? Last year? Now?

How about the other sentences? When does each of them take place?

NOTE: A discussion of the answers to this exercise can be found on pages 88–89.

EXERCISE 4A-2

The following sentences illustrate another use of the present tense. Study these examples carefully and try to figure out when these sentences take place. How would you describe the time when these sentences are true? When is each of them true?

1. *Moby-Dick* is a novel about whaling.
2. Rome is the capital of Italy.
3. Mr. Curran takes the 7:28 train to work.
4. The Congo River flows into the Atlantic Ocean.
5. The Chinese alphabet consists of thousands of characters.

NOTE: A discussion of the answers to this exercise can be found on page 89.

EXERCISE 4A-3

Now that you know what the present tense can be used for, let's take a look at how it is formed.

  The verbs in the following sentences are all in the present tense.

1. One student hopes to graduate in August.
2. Two students hope to graduate in August.

3. That dog barks every morning at six.
4. Those dogs bark every morning at six.

5. My uncle talks with a southern accent.
6. My uncles talk with a southern accent.

7. A child lives in the apartment next door.
8. Two children live in the apartment next door.

9. A man delivers the computer printout every Friday.
10. Two men deliver the computer printout every Friday.

Write the subject and verb of each of the sentences above on the corresponding numbered line below. The first one is done for you.

	A SUBJECT	B VERB		C SUBJECT	D VERB
1.	*student*	*hopes*	2.	_____	_____
3.	_____	_____	4.	_____	_____
5.	_____	_____	6.	_____	_____
7.	_____	_____	8.	_____	_____
9.	_____	_____	10.	_____	_____

How are the subjects in column A different from the subjects in column C? How are the verbs in column B different from the verbs in column D?

  Can you state the rule for forming present tense verbs? When do you put an "s" ending on the verb?

_____

_____

_____

_____

NOTE: A discussion of the answers to this exercise can be found on pages 89–90.

EXERCISE 4A-4 _____

Use the four-step procedure (see pages 89–90) to correct any errors in the following. All errors involve subject-verb agreement. Each sentence may contain no errors, one error, or more than one error.

1. My dog always chase cars.
2. My sisters gives me a lot of help with my homework.
3. Marie gives me a ride to work on Wednesdays.
4. Larry call me up every night.
5. My typewriter often break.
6. This expressway leads right into the business district.
7. These folders contains the mailing list for our fund drive.
8. Only one problem stand in our way.
9. My father gives everyone advice.
10. A gremlin sometimes hide in my computer.
11. Four students always sits in the back row.
12. The roof leak when it rains.
13. My car uses a lot of gas.
14. The mailman deliver the mail early on Saturdays.
15. My daughter sometimes sleeps until eight.
16. Often, the Wilson kids visits their grandmother.
17. Leroy play his stereo very quietly.
18. This gas station opens at seven o'clock in the morning.
19. That song remind me of my high school days.
20. Grammar rules sometimes scares people.

EXERCISE 4A-5 _____

A small group of verbs requires a slight modification in the procedure you have learned for making verbs agree with their subjects. The verbs in the following sentences illustrate this modification.

1. Ms. Bottecelli kisses her husband good-bye every morning.
2. Most wives kiss their husbands good-bye every morning.

3. Julie passes this sign on her way to work.
4. Many people pass this sign on their way to work.

5.   My father rushes to the sales immediately after Christmas.
6.   People rush to the sales immediately after Christmas.
7.   This earthworm pushes little piles of dirt out of its tunnels.
8.   Earthworms push little piles of dirt out of their tunnels.
9.   Mr. Garcia lunches at the Homewood Deli every Friday.
10. Mr. and Ms. Garcia lunch at the Homewood Deli every Friday.
11. A hunter poaches on our farm every fall.
12. Hunters poach on our farm every fall.

Write the subject and verb of each of the sentences above on the corresponding numbered line below. The first one is done for you.

	A SUBJECT	B VERB		C SUBJECT	D VERB
1.	*Ms. Bottecelli*	*kisses*	2.	_____	_____
3.	_____	_____	4.	_____	_____
5.	_____	_____	6.	_____	_____
7.	_____	_____	8.	_____	_____
9.	_____	_____	10.	_____	_____
11.	_____	_____	12.	_____	_____

How are the subjects in column A different from the subjects in column C? How are the verbs in column B different from the verbs in column D? What do the verbs in column D have in common? What about their endings?

        Can you state the rule for forming present tense verbs with this group of verbs? What ending do you add to the singular verb?

_____

_____

_____

_____

NOTE: A discussion of this exercise can be found on page 90.

EXERCISE 4A-6

Use the four-step procedure (see pages 89–90) to correct any errors in the following. All errors involve subject-verb agreement. Each sentence may contain no errors, one error, or more than one error.

1.   My parents fusses too much over my little sister.

2.   Joe always kiss his crucifix before a football game.

3.   My car sit in my driveway with a broken axle.

4.   Katrina crushes her beer cans and throws them into the trash.

5.   Two young boys punches holes in our tickets as we go into the theater.

6.   The teachers wishes for an end to the dance.

7. Lou miss his sister very much.

8. Every Monday, the customers push their way into the store.

9. George shut his garage door every night.

10. Students often loses their registration forms before the first day of classes.

 EXERCISE 4A-7

The following sentences illustrate a slight modification to the rule for subject-verb agreement. Study these examples carefully and try to figure out what this modification is.

1. One student comes to class late on Fridays.
2. Two students come to class late on Fridays.
3. I come to class late on Fridays.
4. You come to class late on Fridays.

5. Karen Williams walks from her house to school every day.
6. The Williams girls walk from their house to school every day.
7. I walk from my house to school every day.
8. You walk from your house to school every day.

9. He talks with a southern accent.
10. We talk with a southern accent.
11. I talk with a southern accent.
12. You talk with a southern accent.

If you are having trouble figuring this one out, look closely at the endings on the verbs when the subject is "I" or "you."

NOTE: A discussion of the answers to this exercise can be found on page 90.

 EXERCISE 4A-8

Correct any errors in the following. All errors involve subject-verb agreement. Each sentence may contain no errors, one error, or more than one error.

1. To get to my house, you takes the number two bus.

2. I always eats breakfast before going to work.

3. That disc jockey play only hard rock.

4. I take a shower every night.

5. If the phone rings while I am cooking, sometimes I ignores it.

6. You know how to change the oil, don't you?

7. My son laugh when he spills his food.

8. When you arrives in Honolulu, my cousin will pick you up.

9. If I sends you a check, will you sends me the ring?

10. I hope that you feel better now.

EXERCISE 4A-9 _____

Sometimes people leave the "s" ending off verbs with singular subjects because they don't pronounce the "s." For example, the "s" on the end of "asks" or "costs" is extremely hard to pronounce. Most people just pronounce these words "ask" and "cost," omitting the "s" sound. This omission is less noticeable when you are speaking, but when you write these words, you must include the "s" ending when the subject is singular.

Correct any errors in the following. All errors involve subject-verb agreement. Each sentence may contain no errors, one error, or more than one error.

1. A new Honda Prelude cost more than ten thousand dollars.

2. When Tom ask you to go out, what are you going to say?

3. If a bargain exist, my mother will find it.

4. The candidates boasts about their qualifications for the position.

5. If you asks me, there is nothing to worry about.

6. I hope this car last as long as my first one.

7. If a suspect resists, the police officer may use force.

8. This brochure list the many attractions at the aquarium.

9. A fire fighter risk his or her life every day.

10. My Pontiac waste a lot of fuel.

EXERCISE 4A-10 _____

Now you have learned the basics of subject-verb agreement. This exercise reviews everything you have learned in this section.

Correct any errors in the following. All errors involve subject-verb agreement. Each sentence may contain no errors, one error, or more than one error.

1. I gives as much to charity as I can afford.

2. This bus takes us right past the museum.

3. The library close at 4:30 on Fridays.

4. The movie only cost $2.50 if we go before six o'clock.

5. The placement test take more than thirty minutes.

6. The groceries costs more every week.

7. Luanne always ask the dumbest questions.

8. If you want to go on vacation, you should submit your request now.

9. Brian's father often rushes out of the house to catch the bus.

10. Doris calls me almost every night and ask about you.

11. When my parents try to talk me into getting married, I resists, but I will probably give in.

12. The schedule list a six o'clock train, but I think it is wrong.

13. This course meet on Tuesday nights from seven to nine.

14. The IRS take about one third of my paycheck every month.

15. Timothy boast about his tennis, but Brenda usually beat him.

16. Phil kiss his dog every night before going to bed.

17. Unless Laurie waste her money, she should have enough for next semester.

18. I hope that Phuoc like it here in America.

19. When the mail arrives, check to see if I got a letter from Karen.

20. If you asks me, subject-verb agreement is easy.

EXERCISE 4A-11 _____

Rewrite each of the following sentences in the space provided. If the subject is now singular, change it to plural; if the subject is now plural, change it to singular. Change the verb to agree with the subject. The first one is done for you.

1. Two men walk past my house every morning at 6:00.

    A man walks past my house every morning at 6:00.

2. A friend of mine runs the movie theater on weekends.

3. Several teachers lunch at the diner across the street.

4. These books cost twenty dollars.

5. My course is on Tuesday nights.

6. The teachers ask too many questions.

7. This car is made of aluminum.

8. Our cat chews on the telephone cord.

9. The teachers wish you would come back to school.

10. My sisters waste a lot of time.

EXERCISE 4A-12 _____

This exercise reviews everything you have learned about subject-verb agreement in the present tense.

The following paragraph is written in the past tense. Rewrite the paragraph in the space below, changing it to the present tense. To help you get started, the first sentence has been done for you.

Last year my job caused me lots of headaches. I drove forty-five minutes to get there and then spent twenty minutes looking for a parking space. My desk sat right next to the coffee machine, so people always stopped to talk to me while they took their coffee break. This wasted my time and kept me from getting my work done. In addition, my boss gave me more work than anyone could do in forty hours a week. I suggested frequently that we hire another person, but he always resisted my suggestion. When I asked for a raise, he insisted that I already made more than anyone else. My job made my life miserable.

These days my job causes me lots of headaches.

_____

_____

_____

_____

_____

_____

_____

_____

_____

_____

_____

DISCUSSION OF INDUCTIVE EXERCISES

EXERCISE 4A-1

The five sentences in Exercise 4A-1 are listed below:

1. The Red River is nearly at flood stage.

2. My watch is about five minutes fast.

3. My husband has the car.

4. Rose is in the swimming pool.

5. Lynn has a great idea.

Each of these sentences is describing or reporting something that is taking place right *now*, in the present. The Red River is nearly at flood stage *right now*. My watch is five minutes fast right now—at this very moment. When does my husband have the car? Now. When is Rose in the pool? Right now. And, when does Lynn have her great idea? At the present time.

The word in each of these sentences that tells the reader when the sentence is taking place is the verb. Notice that if we change the verb slightly in sentence 1, the time when the Red River was nearly overflowing its banks changes:

6.   The Red River was nearly at flood stage.

In this form the sentence indicates only that the river was near flood stage some time in the past; we don't know, from sentence 6, whether it is still near flooding or not. The sentence only indicates that, in the past, the river *was* near flooding.

Of course, it is possible to indicate when the sentence takes place in other ways, for example, by including expressions like "when I was young" or "in the future," but the most common way to indicate when a sentence took place is by changing the form of the verb.

This characteristic of verbs, that they indicate the time when the sentence is taking place, is known as their tense. The verbs in the sentences in Exercise 4A-1 all indicate that the sentences are taking place in the present, so these verbs are said to be in the *present tense*. The most common use of present tense is to show that a sentence is taking place at the present time, but there are other uses, as you will see in the following exercise.

EXERCISE 4A-2

If you answered "now" to this question, you are only partially correct. For example, it is true that right now *Moby-Dick* is a novel about whaling, but it was also true last week, last year, and fifty years ago. It will still be true tomorrow, next year, and fifty years from now. In other words, the present tense of the verb can also be used to describe or report things that are always true, continually true, or repeatedly true—things that are true now, as well as in the past and the future.

Thus, the present tense has two uses in the English language:

1.   to express events that are going on right now, in the present
2.   to express events that are true always, continually, or repeatedly—in the past, present, and future

EXERCISE 4A-3

You should have noticed that all the subjects in column A were singular, and all the subjects in column C were plural. Also, all the verbs in column B ended in an "s," and none of the verbs in column D had "s" endings. So, the rule is as follows:

1.   If the subject is singular, the verb must have an "s" ending.
2.   If the subject is plural, the verb must not have the "s" ending.

Subject-verb agreement is the term for having the ending on the verb that "agrees" with the subject as indicated in the two rules above. One way to help make your verbs agree with your subjects is to remember that, for *verbs,* an "s" ending stands for singular. Of course, for *nouns* just the opposite is true; an "s" ending on a *noun* means it is plural.

The most foolproof way to ensure that you have subject-verb agreement is to follow this procedure:

1.   Locate the verb in the sentence.
2.   Locate the subject that goes with that verb.

3. Determine whether the subject is singular or plural.
4. Make the verb "agree" with the subject (it should have an "s" ending if the subject is singular, no "s" ending if the subject is plural).

EXERCISE 4A-5

The subjects in column A are all singular, and those in column C are plural. The verbs in column B all have "es" endings added to the forms in column D. The verbs in column D all end in an "s," a "sh," or a "ch" sound. The rule for this group of verbs is as follows: When the verb ends in an "s," a "sh," or a "ch" sound, add an "es" ending to the verb when the subject is singular.

EXERCISE 4A-7

What the sentences in Exercise 4A-7 illustrate is that, when "I" or "you" is used as the subject, the verb does not need an "s" ending. In other words, for purposes of subject-verb agreement, "I" and "you" are treated the same as plural subjects.

Part B · Agreement with Irregular Verbs

In Part A, you learned about subject-verb agreement with present tense verbs. All the verbs you worked with in that part followed the same rule: if the subject was singular, you added an "s" ending; if the subject was plural or was "I" or "you," you did not add an "s." Because they all follow the rule exactly, they are called "regular" verbs. Unfortunately, not all verbs are regular. In fact, some of the most frequently used verbs are very irregular. In this part you will learn about subject-verb agreement with irregular verbs in the present tense.

EXERCISE 4B-1

The most common verb in the English language is the verb "be." Unfortunately it is also the most irregular. The following sentences illustrate various forms of the verb "be."

1. I am too sick to go to work.
2. I am the best person for this job.

3. You are too late to get in to the first show.
4. You are my favorite dancing partner.

5. He is a little crazy on the subject of baseball.
6. She is the winner of the Caldecott Award.
7. It is a very boring movie.

8. The concert is three hours long.
9. Jan is a Scorpio.

10. We are sick and tired of her arrogance.
11. We are computer fanatics.

12. You are my favorite students.
13. You are the last people to arrive.

14. They are my good friends.
15. They are nurses at Sinai Hospital.
16. These roses are very beautiful.
17. The answers are in the back of the book.
18. Flies are a terrible nuisance.

Write the subjects and verbs from the sentences in Exercise 4B-1 on the appropriate lines below. The first one has been done for you.

SUBJECT	VERB	SUBJECT	VERB
A	**B**	**C**	**D**
1. _I_	_am_	10. ___	___
2. ___	___	11. ___	___
E	**F**		
3. ___	___	12. ___	___
4. ___	___	13. ___	___
G	**H**		
5. ___	___	14. ___	___
6. ___	___	15. ___	___
7. ___	___	16. ___	___
8. ___	___	17. ___	___
9. ___	___	18. ___	___

1. What do the subjects in box A have in common? How about the verbs in box B?
2. What do the subjects in box C have in common? How about the verbs in box D?
3. What do the subjects in box E have in common? How about the verbs in box F? What do the verbs in box F have in common with the verbs in box D?
4. What do the subjects in box G have in common? How about the verbs in box H?

In the space below, write the rules for subject-verb agreement in the present tense with the verb "be."

_____

_____

_____

_____

_____

_____

_____

NOTE: A discussion of the answers to this exercise can be found on page 99.

EXERCISE 4B-2

The following sentences are all written in the past tense. Rewrite them in the present tense.

Example:

a. Annie was absent this morning.

Annie is absent this morning.

1. My answer was just a guess.

2. The suspect's car was a late model Buick.

3. They were my best cuff links.

4. Tickets to the play cost three dollars.

5. Terry was my best friend, but I was angry at her.

6. You were not welcome here.

7. Neal risked his life when he jumped from the plane.

8. I was surprised at the ending of the novel.

9. We were pleased with his work.

10. The students were angry with the dean.

EXERCISE 4B-3

Another irregular verb that causes some people trouble is the verb "have." The following examples illustrate the rules for subject-verb agreement with the verb "have."

1. I have two tickets to the game.
2. You have two tickets to the game.
3. He has two tickets to the game.
4. Barb has two tickets to the game.
5. My sister has two tickets to the game.
6. We have two tickets to the game.
7. They have two tickets to the game.
8. My sisters have two tickets to the game.

Write the subjects and verbs from the sentences above on the appropriate lines below. The first one has been done for you.

	SUBJECT	VERB		SUBJECT	VERB
1.	*I*	*have*	6.	_____	_____
2.	_____	_____	7.	_____	_____
3.	_____	_____	8.	_____	_____
4.	_____	_____			
5.	_____	_____			

Study the subjects and verbs above, and then, in the space below, write the rule for subject-verb agreement in present tense for the verb "have."

_____

_____

_____

_____

_____

_____

_____

_____

NOTE: A discussion of the answers to this exercise can be found on page 99.

EXERCISE 4B-4

The following paragraph is written in the past tense. Rewrite it in the present tense, making sure that all your verbs agree with their subjects. To get you started, the first sentence is done for you.

My high school friends had their eccentricities. For example, my best friend, Yvonne, had a problem with her hair, so she always wore a hat. Donald had a pet monkey, which he took everywhere with him. The Culligan sisters had a habit of constantly whispering between themselves. This behavior was no problem for me because I knew them well, but it bothered some people. Around the school, we had a pretty weird reputation.

My high school friends have their eccentricities.

_____

_____

_____

_____

_____

_____

_____

_____

_____

_____

_____

_____

_____

_____

_____

_____

EXERCISE 4B-5

The following sentences illustrate the rules for subject-verb agreement with the verb "do."

1. I do fairly well in math.
2. You do fairly well in math.

3. He does fairly well in math.
4. Fran does fairly well in math.
5. My brother does fairly well in math.

6. We do fairly well in math.
7. They do fairly well in math.
8. My brothers do fairly well in math.

Write the subjects and verbs of the sentences above on the appropriate lines below.

	SUBJECT	VERB		SUBJECT	VERB
1.	_____	_____	6.	_____	_____
2.	_____	_____	7.	_____	_____
3.	_____	_____	8.	_____	_____
4.	_____	_____			
5.	_____	_____			

Study the subjects and verbs on the list above, and then, in the space below, write a statement of the rule for subject-verb agreement with the verb "do" in the present tense.

_____

_____

_____

_____

_____

NOTE: A discussion of the answers to this exercise can be found on page 99.

EXERCISE 4B-6

The following paragraph is written in the past tense. Rewrite it in the present tense, being careful that your verbs agree with their subjects. The first sentence has been done for you.

  Last year, my computer did many valuable services for me. It did my tax return almost all by itself. All I did was feed in a few figures. I also did all my school papers on the computer. The computer allowed me to correct mistakes very easily. After I did my taxes, my homework, and any other work that I had to do, I entertained myself by playing computer games.

These days, my computer does many valuable services for me.

_____

_____

_____

_____

_____

_____

_____

_____

_____

_____

_____

_____

_____

_____

EXERCISE 4B-7

The following pairs of sentences illustrate an exception to what you have learned about subject-verb agreement. Study these sentences and figure out what this exception is.

1. Kathleen is talking to the math instructor.
2. Kathleen and Gary are talking to the math instructor.
3. Kathleen will talk to the math instructor.
4. Kathleen and Gary will talk to the math instructor.

  You might be wondering whether there are other exceptions. To help you find out here are two test sentences:

5. My brother _____ call (or called or calling) me every Friday night.

6. My brothers _____ call (or called or calling) me every Friday night.

Here is a list of helping verbs:

can	must
could	shall
does	should
has	was
is	will
may	would
might	

Try out each of these helping verbs by placing them on the blank line in the test sentences to see which ones are exceptions to the rule requiring that you add an "s" ending when the subject is singular. Write the helping verbs that are exceptions, that is, the ones that do *not* add an "s" when the subject is singular, in the space below:

NOTE: A discussion of the answers to this exercise and a list of the helping verbs that do not add an "s" when the subject is singular can be found on pages 99–100.

 EXERCISE 4B-8 _____

The following sentences have plural subjects. Rewrite each of them in the space provided with the singular subject indicated. Make sure to check for subject-verb agreement. The first one is done for you.

1. Jim and Jean can give me a ride to school tomorrow.

   Jim *can give me a ride to school tomorrow.*

2. My parents must worry a lot about my little sister.

   My mother _____

3. The teachers are hoping that we have a snow day soon.

   The teacher _____

4. Those dogs may be lost.

   That dog _____

5. My friends will lend me the money.

   My friend _____

6. Mr. and Ms. Caprio have opened a store.

   Ms. Caprio _____

7. Gayle and her sister should be here soon.

   Gayle _____

8. Ford and Chrysler are bringing out new models in January.

   Ford _____

9. The mayor and his staff can influence the vote.

   The mayor _____

10. My enemies would love to find out my plans.

    My enemy _____

 EXERCISE 4B-9 _____

Now you understand the rules for subject-verb agreement in the present tense for regular and irregular verbs. This exercise reviews all these rules.

   Correct any errors in the following sentences. All errors involve subject-verb agreement. Each sentence may contain no errors, one error, or more than one error.

1. Ralph be sick a lot.

2. Walter have a hard time with anatomy and physiology.

3. These waiters is very friendly.

4. That woman musts be April's aunt.

5. I is not sure that I wants to go to Florida.

6. We does aerobics every Monday and Wednesday afternoon.

7. The students are afraid of your midterm exam.

8. Fred have a bad attitude.

9. Cocker spaniels has a reputation for being good house dogs.

10. Chris cans open the door for you.

11. My mother be a student at this college also.

12. She am studying to be a nurse.

13. David ask a lot of questions in algebra.

14. The police officer have to fill out a report on the accident.

15. My history book have a lot of charts.

16. My cat can do a few tricks.

17. That car cost less than six thousand dollars.

18. He is the best swimmer on the team.

19. Tina does her homework on weekends.

20. George have a good chance of winning the contest.

EXERCISE 4B-10 _____

The following sentences are written in the past tense. Rewrite them in the present tense, being careful of subject-verb agreement.

Example:

a. I had a hunch that you were depressed about something.
    I have a hunch that you are depressed about something.

1. The music was very loud.

2. Glen was the captain of the lacrosse team.

3. Kris did her arguing in private.

4. Zinnia had a crush on Larry.

5. My friends were afraid to drive in the snow.

6. We could do the dishes by hand.

7. Bridget was one of fifty applicants for the two jobs.

8. Barbara did her hair in the sink every morning.

9. I had only fifty cents in my account.

10. Mike had a sprained ankle.

11. Pat did very well when the pressure was on.

12. Joanna was upset when she was doing badly in school.

13. They were silent during the singing of the national anthem.

14. My shoes only cost $19.95.

15. Charles was an enemy of all bicyclists.

16. Paul did crossword puzzles on the train.

17. Elaine asked too much of her friends.

18. I thought Marc might win the tournament.

19.   She was a friend of my boss.

20.   They had two good reasons for their response.

DISCUSSION OF INDUCTIVE EXERCISES

EXERCISE 4B-1

We probably have worded the rules a little differently from the way you did, but yours should look something like ours:

1.   If the subject is singular and not "I" or "you," then the verb should be "is."
2.   If the subject is plural or "you," the verb should be "are."
3.   If the subject is "I," the verb should be "am."
4.   The word "be" is never used as a present tense verb.

EXERCISE 4B-3

Our version of the rules is listed below. Yours was probably worded a little differently, but it should mean the same thing as ours.

1.   For singular subjects other than "I" or "you," the verb should be "has."
2.   For plural subjects or for "I" or "you," the verb should be "have."

EXERCISE 4B-5

Here is our version of the rules for subject-verb agreement in the present tense for the verb "do." Yours, of course, is in your own words, but it should say roughly the same thing.

1.   When the subject is singular, other than "I" or "you," the verb should be "does."
2.   When the subject is plural or is "I" or "you," the verb should be "do."

EXERCISE 4B-7

Part 1

In sentence 4, the subject is "Kathleen and Gary," which is plural, and the verb is "will talk." In sentence 3, the subject is "Kathleen," but the verb is "will talk" instead of "wills talk." Apparently, the helping verb "will" is an exception to the rule about adding an "s" ending to verbs when the subject is singular.

Part 2

The following helping verbs do not add an "s" when their subjects are singular:

will	could	may
would	shall	might
can	should	must

Part C · Agreement with Prepositional Phrases, Compound Subjects, and Inverted Word Order

In Part A of this chapter you learned a four-step procedure for ensuring that your verbs agree with your subjects:

1. Locate the verb.
2. Locate the subject that goes with that verb.
3. Determine whether that subject is singular or plural.
4. Make the verb agree with the subject.

In Part B you primarily focused on step 4 of this procedure: making the verb agree with the subject. The other steps in the procedure were fairly easy. Sometimes, however, it is step 2, finding the subject, which causes some difficulty. In some types of sentences finding the subject can be a little tricky. Also, once you have found the subject, step 3, deciding whether it is singular or plural, can occasionally be slightly complicated. In this part you will learn how to find the subject and determine whether it is singular or plural in several of these more difficult types of sentences.

 EXERCISE 4C-1 ─────────────

The following sentences illustrate one complication that makes subject-verb agreement a little more difficult. To see why these are complicated, perform steps 1 and 2 from the four-step procedure on them; that is, underline the verbs twice and the subjects once.

1. The knives in this drawer belong to my mother.

2. A friend of my parents calls them every weekend.

3. A group of children sells Girl Scout cookies in this neighborhood.

4. Tourists from Japan often visit Washington.

5. The sound of trains puts me to sleep when I visit my grandparents.

NOTE: A discussion of the answers to this exercise can be found on pages 105–106.

 EXERCISE 4C-2 ─────────────

The following sentences contain errors in subject-verb agreement. Use the four-step procedure to correct any errors. Be careful when you apply step 2 to make sure you don't confuse the subject with a noun in a prepositional phrase. Each sentence may have no errors, one error, or more than one error.

1. The lights on the ocean liner is visible for miles.
2. The papers in this box belongs to my grandmother.
3. A friend of my parents sends them oranges from Florida every winter.
4. The color of her eyes are a deep blue.
5. A list of these items is located on the desk at the front of the room.
6. A group of democrats are trying to raise money with a bake sale.
7. Directions for this test is printed on the cover.
8. The danger in these waters are that you might hit your head on a rock.
9. The players in this orchestra is very well trained.
10. The explanation for his mistakes are that he worked too fast.

 ## EXERCISE 4C-3

The following sentences illustrate another difficulty in applying step 2. Underline the verbs twice and the subjects once in these.

1. There is a cat stuck in this tree.
2. There are two causes of her disease.
3. Under the bed is my collection of baseball cards.
4. On the bottom shelf are the history books.
5. Next to the post office is a delightful coffee shop.

NOTE: A discussion of the answers to this exercise can be found on page 106.

 ## EXERCISE 4C-4

The following sentences contain errors in subject-verb agreement. Read each sentence carefully and correct any errors. Each sentence may have no errors, one error, or more than one error.

1. There is three choices for dessert.
2. In this closet are my winter clothes.
3. Val's problem with languages is that she cannot remember vocabulary.
4. There are a good reason for Jay's decision.
5. In that box is my good shoes.
6. There is two movies that we could see tonight.
7. The blouses on this rack needs no ironing.
8. In my hand is the tickets for the concert.
9. There is a crack in Helen's mirror.
10. There is several reasons why I can't go with you.

EXERCISE 4C-5

The sentences in this exercise all have compound subjects, that is, a subject made up of two words or phrases joined by "and" or "or." In these sentences, step 2 is no problem, but step 3 sometimes is. Sometimes it is a little difficult to determine whether compound subjects are singular or plural.

The following examples illustrate one rule for determining whether they are singular or plural.

1. David and Karen are going to the beach this afternoon.
2. David or Karen is going to the beach this afternoon.

3. Lettuce and spinach are delicious in a salad.
4. Lettuce or spinach is delicious in a salad.

5. Checks and credit cards are accepted here.
6. Checks or credit cards are accepted here.

7. Leg raises and sit-ups are good for your stomach.
8. Leg raises or sit-ups are good for your stomach.

Write the subjects and verbs from these sentences on the appropriate lines below. The first one has been done for you.

	SUBJECT	VERB
1.	*David and Karen*	*are going*
2.		
3.		
4.		
5.		
6.		
7.		
8.		

Study these subjects and verbs and write, in the space below, the rule for subject-verb agreement in this kind of sentence.

_____

_____

_____

_____

_____

_____

_____

NOTE: A discussion of the answers to this exercise can be found on page 106.

EXERCISE 4C-6

There is one more possibility for compound subjects that we didn't cover in the last exercise. Study the following pairs of sentences and try to figure out this addition to the rules for determining whether a compound subject is singular or plural.

1. The judge or the lawyers are wrong about the law in this case.
2. The lawyers or the judge is wrong about the law in this case.

3. Mr. Keller or the children are going to pay for my broken window.
4. The children or Mr. Keller is going to pay for my broken window.

Write the subjects and verbs from these four sentences on the appropriate lines below.

	SUBJECT	VERB
1.	_____	_____
2.	_____	_____
3.	_____	_____
4.	_____	_____

Study the subjects and verbs above and write, in the space below, the rule for subject-verb agreement in this kind of sentence.

_____

_____

_____

_____

_____

NOTE: A discussion of the answers to this exercise can be found on page 106.

 EXERCISE 4C-7 _____

Correct any errors in the following. All errors involve subject-verb agreement with compound subjects. Each sentence may contain no errors, one error, or more than one error.

1. John and his dog is running in the park.

2. A mouse or a rat is chewing the boxes in the basement.

3. Val or her brothers gives me a tennis lesson every weekend.

4. The teacher or the students in this class is going to apologize.

5. The players and the coach are angry at the newspaper.

6. The politicians or the public is responsible for this pollution.

7. My sisters and my mother agree with your decision.

8. Jean or Barbara weed the garden once a week.

9. The conductor or the players has the wrong score.

10. Raisins or cinnamon is delicious in oatmeal.

EXERCISE 4C-8

The kinds of sentences that you've worked with in this section are a little trickier. They do not, however, require any change in the four-step procedure for subject-verb agreement. They require only that you be more careful when applying steps 2 and 3.

This exercise reviews everything you have learned thus far about subject-verb agreement. Correct any errors in the following sentences. Each sentence may contain no errors, one error, or more than one error.

1.   The swimmers or the lifeguard are to blame for the accident.

2.   There is three reasons why I cannot go camping with you.

3.   A group of students wait for the bus in front of my house every morning.

4.   The color in these photographs does not look right to me.

5.   Fran or George have your gloves.

6.   In this bag is two sandwiches and an apple.

7.   A pair of cats is more than I can tolerate.

8.   The twins or Reggie Yost have your books.

9.   In between those two police officers is my friend Mark.

10.   Several pages in my favorite childhood story book is stained.

11.   A group of rabbits is eating my lettuce.

12.   There is no reason for your depression.

13.   Inside these little bottles are the biggest scientific discovery of this century.

14.   My parents and their dog is coming to spend the weekend with me.

15.   The writer of these letters have to be crazy.

16.   There have to be an explanation for Rhoda's erratic behavior.

17.   The mother of these kittens is a grey tabby.

18.   A group of students gather in the cafeteria at two every day.

19.   The price of those pants are not too high.

20.   There is a delicate beauty that only comes from subject-verb agreement.

EXERCISE 4C-9

The following paragraph is written in the past tense. Rewrite it in the present tense, being especially careful with subject-verb agreement. The first sentence has been done for you.

There were many shops in the new mall. Shoe stores or jewelry stores were the most numerous, but the dress shops interested me the most. There were five dress shops to choose from. In the record store were many kinds of records. The best-smelling store in the mall was the coffee shop, where they roasted their own beans. The healthiest store was the vitamin store, where they were giving away free samples of vitamin C. But my favorite part of the mall wasn't a store at all. At the center of all these shops was a beautiful open area with a fountain, tropical plants, and chairs and couches. There people sat relaxing and talking in a way that is not possible in most malls. The combination of stores and open area impressed me greatly.

There are many shops in the new mall.

DISCUSSION OF INDUCTIVE EXERCISES

EXERCISE 4C-1

The sentences from Exercise 4C-1 are repeated below with the subjects and verbs underlined.

1. The knives in this drawer belong to my mother.
2. A friend of my parents calls them every weekend.
3. A group of children sells Girl Scout cookies in this neighborhood.
4. Tourists from Japan often visit Washington.
5. The sound of trains puts me to sleep when I visit my grandparents.

Notice that each of these sentences has a prepositional phrase following the subject. If you aren't careful, you might think the nouns in these prepositional phrases are the subjects. If you made this mistake, it could lead you into an error in subject-verb agreement.

In sentence 1, for example, you might incorrectly think the subject is "drawer." Since "drawer" is singular, this choice would lead you to change the verb to "belongs." In other words, if you make a mistake in step 2 of the procedure, you can get the subject-verb agreement completely wrong. In sentences with prepositional phrases, then, it is important that you correctly identify the subject of the sentence.

EXERCISE 4C-3

The sentences from this exercise are repeated below with their subjects and verbs underlined.

1. There is a cat in this tree.
2. There are two causes of her disease.
3. Under the bed is my collection of baseball cards.
4. On the bottom shelf are the history books.
5. Next to the post office is a delightful coffee shop.

Notice that each of these sentences begins with either the word "there" or a prepositional phrase. Also, notice that the subjects occur following the verbs.

When applying step 2 to this kind of sentence, you must be careful to look for the subject after the verb.

EXERCISE 4C-5

The rule for subject-verb agreement in sentences like those in this exercise is as follows. Of course, yours was probably worded a little differently, but it should have covered the same three points.

1. Compound subjects joined by "and" are always plural.
2. Singular compound subjects joined by "or" are singular.
3. Plural compound subjects joined by "or" are plural.

EXERCISE 4C-6

The subjects of the sentences in this exercise consist of two nouns, one singular and one plural, joined by the conjunction "or." Since, in these cases, it is impossible to say whether the verb will be done by one person or by more than one, the rule for determining whether the subject is singular or plural is very arbitrary. The subject that is nearer the verb determines whether the verb is singular or plural. The complete rules for compound subjects are as follows:

1. Compound subjects joined by "and" are always plural.
2. Singular compound subjects joined by "or" are singular.
3. Plural compound subjects joined by "or" are plural.
4. When one singular and one plural subject are joined by "or," the verb should agree with the subject nearer to it.

R E V I E W

EXERCISE 4-REVIEW-1 _____

Proofread the following sentences carefully and correct any errors. All errors will involve verb use. Each sentence may contain no errors, one error, or more than one error.

1. Mr. Sabiston waste a lot of money on his yard.
2. Your car do not have enough room for me and my pet hippo.
3. The best approach to these problems are to make a list.
4. There are a book of recipes in the back seat of Kostis's car.
5. The students and the teacher is waiting in the library.
6. The color of her eyes are very unusual.
7. This book list three hundred names for dogs.
8. This be the best party I have ever gone to.
9. The driver or the passengers are lying about the speed of the bus.
10. In the paper this morning is several articles about cholesterol.
11. Beth and her boyfriend are working at the deli this summer.
12. The author of these stories are extremely imaginative.
13. Francis give me a ride to work on Saturdays.
14. Barry do a lot of odd jobs, but he never has any money.
15. Betsy or her parents is taking pictures at the party.
16. Cal resist his parents' suggestions most of the time.
17. In this book, General Motors cars gets a higher rating than any others.
18. This washer waste a lot of water.
19. The seam in these trousers are not straight.
20. The president or his advisers is wrong about the amount of opposition this proposal will stir up.

EXERCISE 4-REVIEW-2 _____

Proofread the following essay and correct any errors. All errors involve subject-verb agreement.

It seems obvious that work is something human beings are not fond of. We knows how hard some people will try to avoid work. We knows how great it feel when work is unexpectedly called off because of a power failure or a big snow storm. From all the evidence, it seem clear that human beings do not like to work.

However, it also appears to be true that, at least in some ways, human beings like to work. In fact, in some circumstances we will fight to be allowed to work. Think about the person who is laid off. Does he or she think of being laid off as a blessing? Of course not. How many people are ready to retire when the company say they should? Even if their retirement benefits and social security is as much as their salary, many people would do anything to keep working.

Now you may be thinking, "Not me, baby. Try offering me retirement at full pay and see how fast I accept." But how long would you be happy? All of us would welcome a week or a month or even a year without working. But how many people would be willing never to work again? Not too many, I'll bet.

What is it about work that makes us want it, even though, on a day-to-day basis, we would do anything to get out of it? I think there is several answers to this question. Of course, there is the money. But there is several other factors as well.

Work is one important way that we give meaning to our lives. Work, at least if we are lucky, allows us to feel we are making some contribution to society. It is at work that we gains a sense of success. Being able to do something useful in the workplace makes us feel needed.

Also, work provides a social outlet. Our bosses might not approve, but a large reason we come to work is to interact with other people. There is a lot of satisfaction to be gained from day-to-day contact with our fellow workers. We laugh and cry at work. We has fights, and we make up. In some ways the workplace has replaced the extended family as our social arena.

Finally, we goes to work because we would feel strange if we didn't. Going to work is what adults do in this society. This used to be true only for men, but lately it has became somewhat true for women too. If we stay home on weekdays and sit out in a lawn chair, the mailman will think we has come down with some disease. This feeling that it is necessary to go to work is understandable since five mornings a week we have been getting up, getting dressed, and going off somewhere ever since kindergarten. It just feels wrong to stay home.

Thus, no matter how much we complain about work and no matter how good it feels to take a day off, there is still some powerful forces in our personalities that make us want to work.

EXERCISE 4-REVIEW-3

Imagine that you have an appointment with a college counselor next week to discuss your educational and career plans. To help you prepare for this session, the counselor has sent you the following request:

> For our counseling session next week, please bring a one-paragraph discussion of the career that sounds most appealing to you at this time. Don't worry about whether such a career is feasible or not. Just explain why it sounds appealing to you. I will use this paragraph to learn something about your interests and ambitions. It will give us a place to get the discussion started.

Before you write this assignment, answer the following questions:

1. Who will be the audience for this paragraph? _____

    _____

2. What is the purpose of this paragraph? What are you trying to accomplish? _____

    _____

3. What will be the subject of the paragraph? _____

    _____

4. What point will you make about that subject? _____

    _____

    _____

(The combination of 3 and 4 will be the topic sentence.)

On a separate sheet of paper, write the paragraph the counselor has requested.

EXERCISE 4-REVIEW-4

Now you are going to revise the paragraph you wrote for Exercise 4-Review-3. Ask yourself each of the following questions about the paragraph. If the answers to any of these reveal weaknesses in the paragraph, revise it to correct those weaknesses.

1. Does the paragraph do what the counselor asked you to do?
2. Are the language and content appropriate for the audience?
3. Is it clear what the topic sentence is? What is it?
4. What is the subject of the paragraph?
5. Is the point you are making about the subject clear?
6. Does every sentence in the paragraph support the topic sentence?

After you have revised the paragraph, check it carefully for mistakes in subject-verb agreement. Also, correct any other errors you can find in spelling, grammar, or punctuation.

5

Using Concrete Language

Part A   Concrete Details
Part B   Telling Details

Part A · Concrete Details

In this chapter you will learn how to make your writing more effective by making it more concrete.

 EXERCISE 5A-1 _____

Take a look at these two paragraphs and decide which one you like better and why.

Paragraph 1

My family knows that it is possible to have a great vacation even though we don't have much money. Early one morning last summer, we loaded all our things into the car and left for our vacation. When we arrived at the campsite, we set up the tent, unloaded everything out of the car, and headed off for our first swim. Three days later, after lots of swimming, boating, and just plain relaxing, we headed home. The entire three days had been very inexpensive.

Paragraph 2

My family knows that it is possible to have a great vacation even though we don't have much money. At seven o'clock one morning last summer, we loaded our borrowed tent, two duffle bags full of clothes, a footlocker of cooking equipment, five sleeping bags, and one small cocker spaniel into our rusty old Ford station wagon and headed off for Assateague National Seashore. When we arrived at the campsite, we set up the bright green tent, stowed all our equipment in it, and walked down to the ocean for the first of many delightful swims in the Atlantic. Three days later, after lots of swimming in the surf, an afternoon canoeing on the nearby Pokomoke River, about twenty games of Trivial Pursuit, and some great talks around the campfire, we headed home. The total expense for the vacation had been $18 for the campsite, $11 for one tank of gas, $6 rental for the canoes, about $32 for food, and $1.89 for suntan lotion.

After you decide which of the two paragraphs you like best, try to figure out why. What is the difference between them?

NOTE: A discussion of the answers to this exercise can be found on pages 115–116.

The following is a conversation that illustrates another aspect of the distinction between concrete and abstract.

HELEN: Laura, will you step across the hall and get that thing off the desk in my office?

(Laura goes across the hall but returns a few minutes later.)

LAURA: Helen, what "thing" do you mean? There are lots of things on your desk.

HELEN: I'm sorry, Laura. I meant the book on my desk.

(Laura leaves and returns again a few minutes later.)

LAURA: Helen, there are a dozen books on your desk. Which one do you mean?

HELEN: For heaven's sake, Laura. What a fool I am. I mean the red book on my desk.

(Laura leaves and returns empty-handed again.)

LAURA: Helen, do you know there are three red books on your desk?

HELEN: Oh no. The red dictionary, please.

This dialogue could continue for some time. The red Random House dictionary. The red Random House dictionary, third edition. The red Random House dictionary, third edition, with the coffee stain. This, however, is enough to demonstrate the point—there is a continuum of ways of expressing an idea, from the very vague "thing" to the very specific "the red Random House dictionary, third edition, with the coffee stain." This continuum is represented by the following diagram:

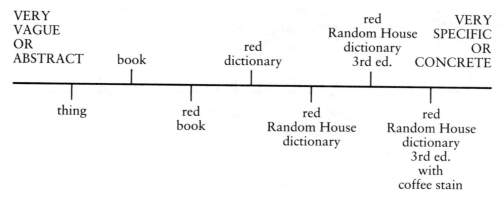

This diagram shows that any idea can be expressed by a range of words from the very vague to the very specific. This fact leads us to the point of all this: Most writing can be improved by moving it toward the concrete end of the spectrum. It is possible for writing to be too concrete, but that is very unusual. It is far more common for writing to be too vague.

You can take a number of steps to make your writing more concrete. When planning your writing, you can make lists of concrete examples to support your ideas. When revising, you can read your paper through once looking only for expressions that can be made more concrete.

EXERCISE 5A-2 _____

Let's work on the planning stage first. Think about the first time you registered for classes at college. In the space below, list *concrete* details that you remember from that experience. These details might include things like "a line of students stretching down the hall," "the hum of fans set up because the air conditioning was broken," or "the buff, goldenrod, and pink copies of every form." Or, they might include "the woman with the southern accent" who helped you select classes, "the emptiness of the building" because you registered very early, or "the coffee and bagels" that were available.

Write whatever *concrete* details you can remember from this experience in the space below. Just write words and phrases; don't worry about complete sentences.

If you prefer, you may use the experience of your first class or your first visit to the bookstore instead of registration.

Now you have worked on one way to make your writing more concrete—making a list of concrete details while you are planning the writing. Next you are going to work on a second way—during revision, replacing vague or abstract expressions with more concrete or specific ones.

EXERCISE 5A-3 _____

In the following sentences, the underlined expressions are too vague or abstract. Revise each of these to make it more concrete or specific.

1. The furious secretary <u>went</u> into the boss's office and <u>requested</u> an explanation.

2. Don placed the flowers in a beautiful Chinese <u>container</u>.

3. My father <u>placed</u> the books on the table with such violence that the noise woke the baby.

4. The bird-watcher <u>saw</u> a blue-grey gnatcatcher outside the school.

5. Someone was <u>eating</u> hard candy in the row behind us and making a lot of noise.

6. Karl's new <u>car</u> was parked in front of my house.

7. Joy's <u>dog</u> is extremely beautiful and well behaved.

8. Julio opened the refrigerator and took out a <u>container</u> of <u>fruit</u>.

9. Ms. Friedlander's leg was <u>injured</u> in the accident.

10. Mr. Morucci sits at a <u>machine</u> all day with only a <u>short</u> break for lunch.

 EXERCISE 5A-4 _____

Revise the following sentences to make them more concrete.

1. The investigator saw bloodstains in the bedroom.

2. A bird landed in the tree in our back yard.

3. Teddy fixed Marcy a drink and then started yelling at her.

4. The lawyer parked his car in a no-parking zone.

5. Because we were late for the movie, we went from the parking lot directly to the theater.

6.   Alex took some reading material with him on the bus.

7.   Wayne took a container of strawberries out of the refrigerator.

8.   Ralph returned the appliance to the dealer and demanded his money back.

9.   Mr. Hernandez hurt his ankle when he tried playing racquetball.

10.   Lenny ate a snack before he telephoned his parents.

 EXERCISE 5A-5

A friend of yours from out of town is going to attend your school next year. You are writing that friend a letter about the school, and you want to include a paragraph in which you describe what it was like to register for classes for the first time. Use the concrete details you listed in Exercise 5A-2 to help you make this piece of writing concrete, but don't feel you have to use all of them.

In Exercise 5A-2, if you chose to list details about your first class or your first visit to the bookstore instead of registration, you should write this paragraph about that experience instead.

Don't write the whole letter, just the paragraph on registration. You don't need to include any of the pleasantries that would be included in other parts of such a letter.

Before you write this assignment, answer the following questions:

1.   Who will be the audience for this paragraph? _____
_____

2.   What is the purpose of this paragraph? What are you trying to accomplish? _____
_____

3.   What will be the subject of the paragraph? _____
_____

4.   What point will you make about that subject? _____
_____
_____

(The combination of 3 and 4 will be the topic sentence.)

On a separate sheet, write this paragraph. Include as many concrete details from the list you made for Exercise 5A-2 as seem effective

EXERCISE 5A-6 _____

Now you are going to revise the paragraph you wrote for Exercise 5A-5. Ask yourself each of the following questions about the paragraph. If the answers reveal weaknesses in the paragraph, revise it to correct those weaknesses.

1. Does the paragraph do what the assignment asked you to do?
2. Are the language and content appropriate for the audience?
3. Is it clear what the topic sentence is? What is it?
4. What is the subject of the paragraph?
5. Is the point you are making about the subject clear?
6. Does every sentence in the paragraph support the topic sentence?

Next, read the paragraph carefully looking for expressions that can be made more concrete or specific. Revise them.

After you have revised the paragraph, check it carefully for mistakes in spelling, grammar, or punctuation. Look especially for errors in subject-verb agreement.

DISCUSSION OF INDUCTIVE EXERCISE

EXERCISE 5A-1

Most people agree that paragraph 2 is the more effective piece of writing. Let's take a look at the two paragraphs and see what the differences are.

The first sentences are identical. The second sentences, however, are quite different and illustrate very well why paragraph 2 is more effective. These two sentences are repeated below with their differences italicized.

Paragraph 1	Paragraph 2
Early one morning last summer,	*At seven o'clock* one morning last summer,
we loaded all our *things*	we loaded our *borrowed tent, two duffle bags full of clothes, a footlocker of cooking equipment, five sleeping bags, and one small cocker spaniel*
into the *car*	into our *rusty old Ford station wagon*
and left for our *vacation.*	and headed off for *Assateague National Seashore.*

The basic difference between these two sentences is that the vague or abstract expressions in the paragraph 1 sentence have been replaced with much more concrete or specific expressions in the paragraph 2 version.

The very first word, "early," is a little vague; for example, what is early to some people might be late to others. To some people, leaving for vacation at seven o'clock would be very late. In the second version, this vague expression has been replaced with the much more specific "at seven o'clock."

In the next section, the extremely vague "things" is replaced by a list of concrete items.

Next, the abstraction "car" is replaced with the much more concrete "rusty old Ford station wagon."

Finally, the vague "vacation" becomes "Assateague National Seashore."

In every case, a vague or abstract expression has been replaced with a more concrete or specific one. And, these sentences are typical of the remainder of the paragraphs. The result is that paragraph 2 is clearer, more convincing, more powerful, more believable, and more entertaining.

Part B · Telling Details

EXERCISE 5B-1 ⎯⎯⎯⎯⎯⎯⎯⎯⎯⎯⎯⎯⎯⎯⎯⎯

Read the following two paragraphs and decide which one you like better.

Paragraph 1

I took the little green plastic basket of strawberries out of the refrigerator and dumped them on the counter. Most were perfect—a deep red with little greenish seeds all over them. A few had light green tips. I picked up each one, grasped the stem and leaves between my fingers, and tried to pull out the stem and core. Most of the time, the stem snapped off, and I had to slice off the top portion with a paring knife. Next I sliced all the strawberries in half, exposing their whitish inner parts. I placed them in a bowl, poured milk over them, and set them on the table. On the countertop, I left behind a gory pile of green and red debris.

Paragraph 2

I took the package of strawberries out of the almond-toned G.E. refrigerator, which we had purchased just a few months earlier, and dumped them on the beige formica counter. Most were perfect— red and plump and delicious. A few were less ripe. I cleaned the berries using a plastic-handled paring knife with a serrated blade. Then I sliced each berry in half with the same knife, placed them in a white cereal bowl with a blue stripe around it, poured 2 percent low-fat milk from Greenfield Dairy over them, and set them on our maple drop-leaf table. On the countertop I left behind the leaves and stems, a puddle of juice, the container they had come in, and the plastic-handled knife.

After you have decided which of these you think is more effective, try to figure out why.

NOTE: A discussion of the answers to this exercise can be found on pages 118–119.

To increase the number of telling details in your writing, you can do several things:

1. Become more observant—really look at things. When you are going to describe something in your writing, try to actually look at that thing as you write. I actually cut up some strawberries right before I wrote the two paragraphs we have been examining; until I forced myself to really look at those strawberries, I had never realized that the center of a strawberry is white, not red.

2. When you are writing, push yourself to remember telling details and don't settle for stale or obvious ones.

3. Keep your details focused on the subject you are writing about; don't go into a lot of detail about unrelated ideas.

4. In Part A of this chapter you learned two techniques for making your writing more concrete:
   a. Make lists of details while planning your writing.
   b. Proofread your writing one time looking for expressions that can be made more concrete.

Use these same two techniques, but push yourself to come up with *telling* details.

EXERCISE 5B-2

Choose one of the following and make a list of concrete details that would help you describe it:

1. the cafeteria or dining room at your school when it's extremely crowded
2. your school on a rainy day
3. a men's or women's room
4. a fast food restaurant on a crowded night

EXERCISE 5B-3

Write about the assignment below that corresponds to the topic you chose for Exercise 5B-2.

1. In a letter to a dean of your school, you are complaining about the eating arrangements your school provides. Write a paragraph from that letter in which you describe the cafeteria or dining room when it's extremely crowded.

2. You are writing an article for your school paper about the day your team (in whatever sport you want) lost a crucial game. As part of this report, you want to describe how the campus looked as the team arrived back from its defeat. It happened that, on that day, there was a heavy rainstorm. Write the paragraph in which you describe your school in the rain, but don't mention anything about the team. Just describe the campus.

3. You are writing a lighthearted article that you hope will be published in the school paper. The article discusses the differences between men and women. As part of the article, write a paragraph describing the inside of a men's or a women's room—or describe how they are different.

4. In a statement for the police, you are trying to explain how someone snatched your purse in a crowded fast food restaurant on a Friday night. You were not able to see who it was. Don't write the entire

statement—just the paragraph in which you describe how crowded it was.

Before you write this assignment, answer the following questions:

1. Who will be the audience for this paragraph?_____

_____

2. What is the purpose of this paragraph? What are you trying to accomplish?_____

_____

3. What will be the subject of the paragraph?_____

_____

4. What point will you make about that subject?_____

_____

_____

(The combination of 3 and 4 will be the topic sentence.)

Once you have answered these questions, write the paragraph on a separate sheet of paper.

EXERCISE 5B-4

Now you are going to revise the paragraph you wrote for Exercise 5B-3. Ask yourself each of the following questions about the paragraph. If the answers reveal weaknesses in the paragraph, revise it to correct those weaknesses.

1. Does the paragraph do what the assignment asked you to do?
2. Are the language and content appropriate for the audience?
3. Is it clear what the topic sentence is? What is it?
4. What is the subject of the paragraph?
5. Is the point you are making about the subject clear?
6. Does every sentence in the paragraph support the topic sentence?

After you have checked these questions, proofread the paragraph carefully, looking for places where you can strengthen it with telling details. Make these improvements.

Finally, correct any errors you can find in spelling, grammar, or punctuation. Look especially for errors in subject-verb agreement.

DISCUSSION OF INDUCTIVE EXERCISE

EXERCISE 5B-1

This time the differences between the two paragraphs are a little more subtle; nevertheless, most people prefer paragraph 1.

You probably noticed that both paragraphs have plenty of concrete details, yet for some reason the details in the first paragraph are more effective. Let's look more closely at the differences. The chart below lists the details from the two paragraphs.

Paragraph 1	Paragraph 2
little green plastic basket	package
deep red with little greenish seeds	red and plump and delicious
light green tips	beige formica counter
the stem and core	almond-toned G.E. refrigerator
stem snapped off	plastic-handled paring knife with a serrated blade
whitish inner parts	a white cereal bowl with a blue stripe
a gory pile of green and red debris	2 percent low-fat milk from Greenfield Dairy
	maple drop-leaf table

Examination of these lists of details reveals two important differences.

1. The concrete details in the first paragraph all are closely related to the subject of the paragraph—strawberries. In the second paragraph almost all the details are related to objects other than the strawberries—the refrigerator, counter, knife, bowl, milk, and table.
2. Where the paragraphs include corresponding details, those from the first paragraph seem much more perceptive and descriptive. For example, in paragraph 1 the strawberries are described as being in a "little green plastic basket." In paragraph 2, the container is merely described as a "package." In paragraph 1, the strawberries are "deep red with little greenish seeds" while in paragraph 2 they are "red and plump and delicious." Now, both of these descriptions are correct, but the ones from the first paragraph are the result of careful observation and thorough recall. The adjectives used in paragraph 2, "red and plump and delicious," are unimaginative and unconvincing. For one thing, they are not very distinctive descriptions of strawberries; they could just as easily be applied to cherries, tomatoes, or plums. Further, the last adjective, delicious, is illogical in this paragraph at this time. How would the writer know that the strawberries were "delicious" when he or she had just taken them out of the refrigerator? A strictly visual description makes more sense here.

In summary, both paragraphs include concrete details but those in the first paragraph are consistently more accurate, more observant, and more focused on the subject. As a result, paragraph 1 is more effective. Time after time, it makes you say, "That's right. Strawberries do have little greenish seeds, and they are whitish in the middle. This person really knows his or her strawberries."

The kind of details that really make a difference, like those in paragraph 1, were referred to as "telling details" by a very influential teacher and writer named Ken McCrorie.

C H A P T E R

6

Sentences

Part A   Identifying Independent Clauses
Part B   Identifying Fragments
Part C   Correcting Fragments

Part A · Identifying Independent Clauses

Many of the errors of unskilled writers involve sentences. These writers sometimes write groups of words that are not sentences and punctuate them as if they were. At other times, they run two or more sentences together with incorrect punctuation or none at all. These kinds of errors cause severe problems for the reader and make the writing appear to be badly flawed. In this chapter and the next, you will learn to avoid such errors. To avoid them, however, you will have to understand the major building block of the grammatical sentence, the independent clause. In this part you will learn to identify independent clauses.

 EXERCISE 6A-1 _____

The following pairs will show you one basic ingredient of an independent clause. Study these pairs closely and see if you can figure out why the b versions are not independent clauses. What is missing in the b version of each of these?

1. **a.** Independent clause: The television in the corner is broken.
    b. Not independent clause: The television in the corner.

2. **a.** Independent clause: The tall man with the red hair teaches English.
    b. Not independent clause: The tall man with the red hair.

3. a. Independent clause: The old-fashioned grocery store on the corner is going out of business.
    b. Not independent clause: The old-fashioned grocery store on the corner.

4. a. Independent clause: My teacher and his wife bought a house.
    b. Not independent clause: My teacher and his wife.

5. a. Independent clause: Some of the clothes in my suitcase were damaged.
    b. Not independent clause: Some of the clothes in my suitcase.

NOTE: A discussion of the answers to this exercise may be found on page 129.

EXERCISE 6A-2 _____

Read each item below carefully. If it is an independent clause, place brackets around it; if it is not, leave it alone. The first one is done for you.

1. ⎡My dog barked.⎤
2. The woman in the trench coat and green hat.
3. Prices are going up.
4. Some of the names on the list of candidates.
5. Most of the people at my office.
6. My next door neighbor and her young child.
7. The radio was blaring.
8. The soup is ready.
9. Most of the men in my class.
10. The chipped cup is an antique.

EXERCISE 6A-3 _____

The following pairs will allow you to discover another essential ingredient in an independent clause. Study these pairs closely and see if you can figure out why the b versions are not independent clauses. What are they missing?

1. a. Independent clause: I opened the store at eight o'clock.
    b. Not independent clause: Opened the store at eight o'clock.

2. a. Independent clause: My best friend was injured in a three-car accident last night.
    b. Not independent clause: Was injured in a three-car accident last night.

3. a. Independent clause: William Casey has decided not to apply for this job.
    b. Not independent clause: Has decided not to apply for this job.

4. a. Independent clause: Peggy forced me to take her to the dance.
    b. Not independent clause: Forced me to take her to the dance.

5. a. Independent clause: A few skiers actually made their way to the lodge.
    b. Not independent clause: Actually made their way to the lodge.

NOTE: A discussion of the answers to this exercise can be found on page 129.

EXERCISE 6A-4 _____

Read each item below carefully. If it is an independent clause, place brackets around it. If it is not an independent clause, leave it alone. The first one has been done for you.

1. [I never expected to win the whole thing.]

2. Some of the schools opened two hours late.

3. Received a lovely gift from Uncle Brian.

4. Slowly hid the evidence under her bed.

5. My car overheated.

6. Reggie believes in himself.

7. Listed the names of all the students in my class.

8. Edward and three of his children.

9. Were rowing a small boat across the lake.

10. Had a wonderful time at the ocean.

EXERCISE 6A-5 _____

The following pairs will allow you to discover an additional requirement for an independent clause. Study these pairs closely and see if you can figure out why the second versions are not independent clauses.

1. a. Independent clause: I arrived at the clinic.
    b. Not independent clause: When I arrived at the clinic.

2. a. Independent clause: Nancy was born in Hawaii.
    b. Not independent clause: Because Nancy was born in Hawaii.

3. a. Independent clause: My trial is scheduled for next week.
    b. Not independent clause: Since my trial is scheduled for next week.

4. a. Independent clause: Pam had no formal training.
    b. Not independent clause: Although Pam had no formal training.

5. a. Independent clause: We dug Mr. Barnes's car out of the snow.
    b. Not independent clause: After we dug Mr. Barnes's car out of the snow.

NOTE: A discussion of the answers to this exercise can be found on pages 129–130.

EXERCISE 6A-6

Read each item below carefully. If it is an independent clause, place brackets around it. If it is not an independent clause, leave it alone.

1. Terry did not see the truck parked in his driveway.
2. When we finally took a break.
3. If you see Frank in the next few days.
4. Marriage is a lifetime commitment.
5. Before you decide to get married.
6. Although she went to law school for four years.
7. Until your textbooks arrive.
8. Lee and Kim are looking for a car pool.
9. Because Lori does not have a shovel or a hoe.
10. Dang has lived in this country for five years.

EXERCISE 6A-7

The following are all independent clauses. Sometimes students feel that sentences like these are not complete thoughts, but in the grammar of the English language, they are considered complete. Study them closely, and see if you can figure out what word in each sentence might make someone feel that it is not complete. What do all these words have in common?

1. She received a letter from Japan.
2. They did not have a jumper cable.
3. It was cracked.
4. He spilled chili on the floor.
5. Someone scratched the side of my car.

NOTE: A discussion of the answers to this exercise can be found on page 130.

EXERCISE 6A-8

Read each item below carefully. If it is an independent clause, place brackets around it. If it is not an independent clause, leave it alone.

1. She invited everyone for dinner at seven.
2. While he made the crust for the pie.
3. They did not have enough money to pay the cabdriver.
4. Someone wrote poetry all over the bathroom walls.
5. It surprised everyone in the room.
6. If you believe in astrology.
7. Because he took aerobics classes and also loved to dance.
8. When we heard the explanation for the layoffs.

9. She lay on her back with her feet on a pillow.

10. Although it was advertised in the Sunday paper as having three bed-rooms.

EXERCISE 6A-9

The following are all independent clauses. What can you learn about independent clauses from these? In particular, look at the subject of each clause.

1. Get me a beer from the refrigerator.
2. Meet me in St. Louis.
3. Fold this form on the dotted line and place it in the envelope.
4. Do not make any marks in the test booklet.
5. Give me a few more minutes to get ready.

NOTE: A discussion of the answers to this exercise can be found on page 130.

EXERCISE 6A-10

Read each of the following items carefully. If it is an independent clause, place brackets around it. If it is not an independent clause, leave it alone.

1. Turn that stereo off.

2. Hand me the sugar, please.

3. She opened the letter very cautiously.

4. When you take out the trash.

5. If Sid shows up for the meeting.

6. Screw the lid on very tightly.

7. Because she always tried to help other people.

8. Sit down.

9. Until Maxine gets here.

10. Look at that fool.

EXERCISE 6A-11

The following sentences demonstrate something about independent clauses that you haven't seen up to this point. In these sentences, each independent clause is bracketed. See if you can figure out anything new about independent clauses from these examples.

1. [Elaine brought a casserole,] and [Carl brought some popovers.]
2. [My car is broken,] so [I rode to school with Paul.]
3. [Eastern is offering discount flights,] but [Piedmont is even cheaper.]
4. [My mother has gone to work,] but [she forgot her briefcase.]
5. [Debbie took a nap,] and [her husband went shopping.]

NOTE: A discussion of the answers to this exercise can be found on page 131.

EXERCISE 6A-12

In the following, place brackets around each independent clause. Some items may contain no independent clauses, some may contain one, and some may contain more than one.

1. The snow is melting, and the days are getting longer.

2. We came in first, and Parkville came in second.

3. I walked into the kitchen and started making dinner.

4. Don't forget your lunch tomorrow.

5. Her dog ran to the back of the yard and started barking.

6. Jerre expected an A, but she got a B.

7. The garbage was overturned, the bag was ripped open, and chicken bones were spread all over the kitchen floor.

8. I am going to the library, and Anita is going to meet me there.

9. She has the notes from our biology class, and I have the study questions for psych.

10. The manager picked up the phone and started swearing at the customer on the other end.

 EXERCISE 6A-13

In the following sentences, brackets have been placed around the independent clauses. See if you can figure out something new about independent clauses from these.

1. When the curtain went up, [Diane was alone on the stage.]
2. If you have any money, [we can go out to dinner.]
3. Even though I have taken French, [I cannot understand Monique.]
4. [My cat cries] whenever I use the can opener.
5. [Rhonda always reads the paper] before she comes to work.

NOTE: A discussion of the answers to this exercise can be found on page 131.

 EXERCISE 6A-14

In the following, place brackets around all independent clauses. Each item may contain no independent clauses, one independent clause, or more than one.

1. When you get to Dallas, Denise will pick you up at the airport.

2. My begonia has not developed any flowers, because I overwatered it.

3. Turn out the lights before you come to bed.

4. As I walked into the store, I saw Shirley at the cash register.

5. While I was trying to get dressed in the dark.

6.   While Herbert was in Chicago, we painted his house.

7.   Virgil called me, and Donna came by to see me.

8.   As I drove into the parking lot, Marge came out of Penny's.

9.   When I was a teenager, Elvis was king.

10. If it starts to rain, Ann will close the windows, and I will bring in the laundry.

EXERCISE 6A-15

In the following sentences, brackets have been placed around the independent clauses. These sentences also contain other groups of words that interrupt the independent clauses. These other groups of words themselves include subjects and verbs, but do not express complete thoughts. Therefore we have indicated by dotted lines just what is included in the independent clauses. Study these examples carefully so that you understand this kind of sentence.

1.   [The coat that I bought had a rip in the lining.]
2.   [The woman whom you called last week returned your call.]
3.   [Animals that nurse their young are called mammals.]
4.   [That portrait, which was painted by my grandfather, is really ugly.]
5.   [My bathroom, which is quite small, is my favorite spot for reading.]

EXERCISE 6A-16

In the following sentences, place brackets around all independent clauses. Use dotted lines to indicate groups of words that interrupt the independent clauses.

1.   The box that this lamp came in is in the basement.

2.   The tall man who is wearing a plaid shirt looks like Uncle Frank.

3.   I would like to order the chicken that is marinated in soy sauce, but I don't see it on the menu.

4.   David broke the record that his brother had set.

5.   The road that I took was not the quickest way to get here, but it is very scenic.

6.   Before you order a new raincoat from that catalog, let me show you something.

7.   The movie that we saw was filmed in Baltimore.

8.   My mother, who organized an antinuclear rally, had never been involved in politics before.

9.   People who live in glass houses should not throw rocks.

10. Henry, who is a poodle, lives with my mother.

EXERCISE 6A-17

In the following, place brackets around all independent clauses. Each item may contain no independent clauses, one independent clause, or more than one independent clause.

1. I forgot my keys, but an extra set is hidden under the flowerpot.

2. The asparagus fern which Paul gave me is not doing very well.

3. Birds fly, and snakes crawl.

4. If it rains on Saturday or Sunday.

5. He sent me a package by UPS.

6. My uncle and his new wife.

7. The bus stopped, and the driver got off.

8. When the play ended, she rushed up to the stage.

9. The paper that Elaine turned in is not very good.

10. Since I learned Chinese, I have not found anyone else to talk to.

11. Bob Hartzog is running for delegate, Jeanne Hartzog is conducting his direct mail campaign, and their children are delivering flyers.

12. Karen showed me a shortcut, so now I can get to work in twenty minutes.

13. Until I get a raise, I cannot afford a new car.

14. Donald gave blood when the bloodmobile visited his school.

15. Open the door.

16. After the game is over, Roseann will meet us at the Pizza Pub.

17. If this sweater goes on sale, I am going to buy it.

18. Bonnie hates to swim, but she loves to go to the ocean.

19. The only question that I missed on the midterm was the one about relative humidity.

20. Whenever the final paper is due in Ms. Bonomo's class.

EXERCISE 6A-18

In the following paragraph, place brackets around all independent clauses.

The SPCA is a great place to get a cat. When we picked up our cat there, the only cost was twenty dollars to cover his shots. There were about thirty cats to choose from, and they were all adorable. My daughter particularly liked a grey tabby who was named Jimmie, but I liked a calico named Elsie. The choice was going to be very difficult. After we had debated for about ten minutes, the decision was taken out of our hands. When Jimmie touched my daughter's arm by sticking his paw through the bars of his cage, we didn't have a chance. Jimmie had chosen us.

EXERCISE 6A-19

Imagine that you are experiencing a financial emergency and need to raise some cash quickly. You have decided to sell something that you own. As part of the ad for this possession, you are going to write a paragraph in which you physically describe it. You do not need to write the entire ad—just the paragraph describing what you want to sell.

    Before you write this assignment, answer the following questions:

1.   Who will be the audience for this paragraph?_____

_____

2.   What is the purpose of this paragraph? What are you trying to accomplish?_____

_____

3.   What will be the subject of the paragraph?_____

_____

4.   What point will you make about that subject?_____

_____

_____

(The combination of 3 and 4 will be the topic sentence.)

    In the space below, list telling details that describe the item you want to sell.

    Once you have answered these questions, write the paragraph on a separate sheet of paper.

EXERCISE 6A-20

Now you are going to revise the paragraph you wrote for Exercise 6A-19. Ask yourself each of the following questions about the paragraph. If the answers reveal weaknesses in the paragraph, revise it to correct those weaknesses.

1. Does the paragraph do what the assignment asked you to do?
2. Are the language and content appropriate for the audience?
3. Is it clear what the topic sentence is? What is it?
4. What is the subject of the paragraph?
5. Is the point you are making about the subject clear?
6. Does every sentence in the paragraph support the topic sentence?

After you have checked these questions, proofread the paragraph carefully, looking for places where you can strengthen it with telling details. Make these improvements.

Next, correct any errors you can find in spelling, grammar, or punctuation.

Finally, to review what you have learned in this section, place brackets around each independent clause in your paragraph.

DISCUSSION OF INDUCTIVE EXERCISES

EXERCISE 6A-1

In Exercise 6A-1, the b versions were all missing verbs. Thus, an independent clause must apparently include a verb.

EXERCISE 6A-3

These examples show that an independent clause must include a subject. The b versions of the items in Exercise 6A-3 are not independent clauses because they have no subjects. Now you know that an independent clause must include both a subject and a verb.

EXERCISE 6A-5

The reason why the second versions of these items are not independent clauses is a little trickier but, nevertheless, is very important. Each of the second versions does include a subject and a verb. What keeps them from being independent clauses is that they do not express complete thoughts. Look, for example, at number 1:

When I arrived at the clinic.

This is not an independent clause because it is incomplete; it is lacking something. It makes you want to say, "When I arrived at the clinic, what?" It leaves you hanging.

If you compare this group of words with the independent clause, you will see something interesting:

I arrived at the clinic.

What makes the incomplete version feel incomplete is the *addition* of the word "when." It is strange but true: Sometimes the addition of a word, usually at the beginning, makes an independent clause incomplete.

There is a fairly small group of words that, when placed at the beginning of an independent clause, make it incomplete. These words are subordinate conjunctions, but some people call them "busters." They include the following:

after	if	than
although	in case that	though
as	in order that	unless
as if	like	until
as long as	no matter how	when
as soon as	now that	whenever
as though	once	where
because	provided that	whereas
before	since	whether
even if	so long as	while
even though	so that	

Whatever the cause of the incompleteness, these incomplete thoughts are not independent clauses, even though they have subjects and verbs. Now you know that an independent clause must include a subject and a verb and must express a complete thought.

EXERCISE 6A-7

The underlined words in the following sentences are the ones that make them seem a little incomplete to some people.

1. <u>She</u> received a letter from Japan.

2. <u>They</u> did not have a jumper cable.

3. <u>It</u> was cracked.

4. <u>He</u> spilled chili on the floor.

5. <u>Someone</u> scratched the side of my car.

Each of these words is a pronoun, a word that takes the place of a noun and its modifiers. It is certainly true that pronouns add a slight sense of incompleteness to sentences. It is also true that, in number 1, we don't know who "she" is, and in number 2, we don't know who "they" were. However, this kind of incompleteness doesn't count when you are trying to determine whether a group of words is or is not an independent clause. If a group of words feels incomplete to you, ask yourself whether the incompleteness comes from a pronoun. If it does, then that group of words is still a grammatically complete thought. Your common sense may tell you it is incomplete, but grammatically it is complete.

This is an area where the grammar of the English language seems a little illogical to many students. But after you get used to the difference between incompleteness due to a pronoun (which doesn't count as incompleteness) and the other kinds of incompleteness, it will not seem complicated at all.

EXERCISE 6A-9

Each of the sentences in this exercise is a command; each of them tells someone to do something. In sentences that are commands, the subject is always understood to be "you." If you don't remember about "you understood," look back at Exercise 2B-16 on page 54 of Chapter 2.

What this exercise shows, then, is that sentences that give commands *are* independent clauses even though the subject is "understood."

EXERCISE 6A-11

From these sentences, you can see that a sentence can include more than one independent clause. Nevertheless, each independent clause *could* be a sentence all by itself. Take a look at sentence 1 again:

   1.   Elaine brought a casserole, and Carl brought some popovers.

This is all one sentence, and it contains two independent clauses. However, each of the clauses could be written as a sentence by itself:

   a. Elaine brought a casserole.
   b. Carl brought some popovers.

Notice also that the word "and," which joins the two independent clauses, is not a part of either one. There are seven words, known as coordinate conjunctions, which can be used this way to join independent clauses. When these words are used to join independent clauses, they are *not* a part of either clause. These coordinate conjunctions can also be used to join smaller grammatical units like phrases or words. The seven coordinate conjunctions are "and," "but," "or," "for," "so," "yet," and "nor." Try to remember these seven words; you will be working with them frequently in future chapters.

Now you know that a sentence can contain more than one independent clause and that each independent clause has to be capable of being a sentence by itself.

So far the sentences you have seen contain no more than two independent clauses. Occasionally, sentences have three or even, on rare occasions, more independent clauses:

   c. I like dogs, and I like cats, but I love hamsters.
   d. I heard that Madonna was in *Playboy,* so I wanted to buy the magazine, but I have never really approved of it, so I didn't.

EXERCISE 6A-13

The sentences in this exercise show that an independent clause can be combined with other groups of words that are not independent clauses. In a sentence like number 1, you might be tempted to call "the curtain went up" an independent clause. It has a subject and a verb and expresses a complete thought. There is one problem with analyzing the sentence in this way, however; you have ignored the word "when." Remember that the only words you can ignore at the beginning of a clause are "and," "but," "or," "for," "so," "yet," and "nor." You cannot ignore "when"; when you do include it, the clause becomes the following:

               When the curtain went up.

Clearly this is not an independent clause because it does not express a complete thought.

Part B · Identifying Fragments

In Part A, you learned to recognize independent clauses. In this part, you will use that knowledge to tell the difference between sentences and fragments. You probably already have a sense that fragments are something to be avoided, and you are quite right. They almost always make your writing appear ungrammatical and even illiterate. Some very good writers occasionally use fragments effectively, but this use requires a sophisticated ear for language and should probably not be attempted by the beginning writer. It is much simpler just to avoid fragments altogether.

Since fragments may occasionally slip into your rough drafts by mistake, however, it is important that you be able to recognize them. Later, in Part C of this chapter, you will learn how to correct fragments. But for now, all you need to worry about is recognizing them.

EXERCISE 6B-1 _____

The following examples are identified as sentences or fragments. In these examples, place brackets around all independent clauses. Be careful: Many have no independent clauses.

1. Sentence: Opening a store in the new shopping center is a large gamble.

2. Fragment: Opening a store in the new shopping center.

3. Sentence: To speak to me about your problem was a good idea.

4. Fragment: To speak to me about your problem.

5. Sentence: Mr. Franklin was trying to catch his dog.

6. Fragment: Was trying to catch his dog.

7. Sentence: The man with a mustache and a straw hat is my boss.

8. Fragment: The man with a mustache and a straw hat.

9. Sentence: Gregor has a big test on Monday.

10. Fragment: Because Gregor has a big test on Monday.

Look back over these examples. What is necessary before a group of words is a sentence? What is the relationship between sentences and independent clauses?

NOTE: A discussion of the answers to this exercise can be found on page 134.

EXERCISE 6B-2 _____

Using the four rules you discovered in Exercise 6B-1 (see p. 134), decide if each of the following is a sentence or a fragment. On the line in front of the number, write an S if the item is a sentence and an F if it is a fragment.

_____ 1. Understanding two languages other than English.

_____ 2. To think of a topic for a five-hundred-word essay.

_____ 3. Has worked in a sporting goods store for the past year.

_____ 4. Ms. Ambrose held the answer in her hand.

_____ 5. When Neal started looking in his pockets.

———— 6. Laughing right out loud, Tina ran from the room.

———— 7. To reach my career goal, I must have a full-time job this year.

———— 8. Since we moved to the center of the city.

———— 9. The horse with a white spot on his back.

————10. To solve a quadratic equation requires concentration.

✎ EXERCISE 6B-3 _____

In Exercise 6B-2, each item consisted of just one sentence or fragment. In real writing, however, you are not likely to be writing a series of separate sentences numbered from 1 to 10. Instead, you normally write groups of sentences organized into paragraphs.

To make this exercise more realistic, each numbered item contains several sentences or fragments. If the item contains only sentences, write an S on the line in front of the number. If the item contains even one fragment, write an F. Underline all fragments.

———— 1. At that point, my car hit a guardrail. Causing it to spin out of control. I came to rest in the median strip.

———— 2. I came to college to find the right career for me. I don't expect to learn a lot of specifics about a job. Just help in deciding on a career.

———— 3. To get a parking place at the new shopping center. You have to be very aggressive.

———— 4. Driving to work this morning, I saw a deer crossing the road. It was beautiful. I pulled onto the shoulder and watched it for five minutes.

———— 5. To work a jigsaw puzzle is a good way to spend a rainy day. Four or five people can work on the puzzle at once.

———— 6. People work hard to get ahead. Then, something happens that they had no reason to expect. Wiping out their savings overnight.

———— 7. To buy a new car this year. Bruce will have to take a second job in the evenings. I hope he keeps his old Chevy for one more year.

———— 8. There was only one person in the room when I arrived. A man with a scar on his cheek and a sinister grin on his face.

———— 9. Taking fifteen credits, Glen doesn't have much time for social life. He also works twenty hours each week. He should take some time off this summer.

———10.   A woman was standing in the shadows. Watched every move I
made. She was writing something in a little notebook.

 EXERCISE 6B-4_____

Read the following paragraph carefully and underline any fragments.

Being in the army was certainly unpleasant for me. I hated
everything I did for those two years. Physical training every morning
at a quarter past six and inspections almost every Saturday. The
boredom was even worse. I spent about five hours a day just waiting.
Doing nothing constructive. To make matters worse, my first sergeant
hated me. When I first arrived at Fort Bragg. I dropped my rifle on his
shoe. Making him my enemy for the next year. He put me on KP
every weekend. Now, six years later, I still have nightmares about
being in the army.

DISCUSSION OF INDUCTIVE EXERCISE

EXERCISE 6B-1

The sentences from this exercise are repeated below with brackets around
the independent clauses.

1.   Sentence: [Opening a store in the new shopping center is a large
     gamble.]
2.   Fragment: Opening a store in the new shopping center.
3.   Sentence: [To speak to me about your problem was a good idea.]
4.   Fragment: To speak to me about your problem.
5.   Sentence: [Mr. Franklin was trying to catch his dog.]
6.   Fragment: Was trying to catch his dog.
7.   Sentence: [The man with a mustache and a straw hat is my boss.]
8.   Fragment: The man with a mustache and a straw hat.
9.   Sentence: [Gregor has a big test on Monday.]
10. Fragment: Because Gregor has a big test on Monday.

From the preceding examples, you can conclude the following about sentences:

1.   Sentences must contain at least one independent clause.
2.   Therefore, sentences must include at least one subject and verb and
     must express a complete thought.
3.   Sentences may contain more than one independent clause.
4.   A group of words that does not include at least one independent clause
     but that begins with a capital and ends with a period is a fragment.

Part C · Correcting Fragments

So far in this chapter, you have learned only to *recognize* fragments. Recognizing them is important, but once you have recognized them, you have to be able to correct them. Correcting fragments is what you will learn in this section.

In the first exercise, we will teach you how to correct the types of fragments that you worked with in the last section. Then we will gradually add more complicated types until, at the end of this section, you will be able to correct all the kinds of fragments that you are likely to encounter.

EXERCISE 6C-1

The following pairs illustrate one way to correct fragments. First, underline the fragments. Then study the corrections until you understand this method for correcting fragments.

1. Fragment: A car was double-parked in the street. Blocking me into my parking place. I was furious.

    Corrected: A car was double-parked in the street, blocking me into my parking place. I was furious.

2. Fragment: My whole purpose for going to school was related to my ambition. To become a C.P.A. Now I've changed my mind.

    Corrected: My whole purpose for going to school was related to my ambition to become a C.P.A. Now I've changed my mind.

3. Fragment: My mother only knows one person at this party. The woman in the green dress.

    Corrected: My mother only knows one person at this party, the woman in the green dress.

4. Fragment: I could not go to the ocean with Jennie. Because I had to work.

    Corrected: I could not go to the ocean with Jennie because I had to work.

5. Fragment: My brother played in the waves. While I read my book under the umbrella. It was a perfect afternoon.

    Corrected: My brother played in the waves while I read my book under the umbrella. It was a perfect afternoon.

NOTE: A discussion of the answers to this exercise can be found on page 148.

EXERCISE 6C-2

Correct any fragments in the following. If there is no fragment, then don't change anything; just write the words "no fragment" at the end of the item.

1. The bridge was completely covered by ice. Causing my car to spin out of control.

2. There is one good reason for buying a personal computer. It is extremely beneficial to your kids' education.

3. I will loan you the money you need for this semester's tuition. Because I know you will pay me back.

4. There are many reasons why people become alcoholics. Some people are under a lot of stress at work. Others are depressed about their family situations.

5. The federal government needs to do something. To control the rising cost of medical care.

6. I really enjoy a small party with just two or three couples. Talking with a few good friends is very rewarding.

7. I no longer subscribe to the morning paper. Since I don't ever have time to read it. I do take the evening paper, however.

8. Last year Karen and Barbara spent a week at Sea Island. Swimming in the Atlantic was lots of fun. They both are going back this year.

9. I completely stripped the gears on my car. As a result, it will be in the shop for a week. Making me dependent on my friends for rides to work.

10. Annette makes me furious. When she forgets to do her homework.

 ## EXERCISE 6C-3

The following pairs illustrate a second way to correct fragments. First, underline the fragments. Then study the corrections until you understand this technique.

1. Fragment: Teaching himself to use a word processor. Hafez really impressed his boss. The next week he was promoted.

    Corrected: Teaching himself to use a word processor, Hafez really impressed his boss. The next week he was promoted.

2. Fragment: To achieve what I want in life. I will have to be willing to work hard. I will also need a little luck.

    Corrected: To achieve what I want in life, I will have to be willing to work hard. I will also need a little luck.

3. Fragment: To get to work by eight in the morning. I have to leave home by a quarter past seven. This means I have to get up at six.

Corrected: To get to work by eight in the morning, I have to leave home by a quarter past seven. This means I have to get up at six.

4.   Fragment: After all the legal procedures were finished. He changed his mind about the divorce. I think he is crazy.

   Corrected: After all the legal procedures were finished, he changed his mind about the divorce. I think he is crazy.

5.   Fragment: When Marty makes up his mind to do something. There is no stopping him. Sometimes he is a little hard to take.

   Corrected: When Marty makes up his mind to do something, there is no stopping him. Sometimes he is a little hard to take.

NOTE: A discussion of the answers to this exercise can be found on page 148.

EXERCISE 6C-4 _____

Correct any fragments in the following. If there is no fragment, then don't change anything; just write the words "no fragment" at the end of the item.

1.   To get a job at any of the television stations in this town. You must have some experience on television. That is why working at the college station is such a good idea.

2.   When Debbie fell, she bruised her hip. Therefore, she is not going running with us today.

3.   After all the trouble she made. She did not get her money back. As a result, she doesn't shop at Hutzler's any more. I really don't blame her.

4.   To swim in the college's pool. You must be registered for a swimming class. However, they hardly ever check.

5.   Looking in the basement for a box to wrap your gift in. I came across a stack of old *National Geographic* magazines. So, I decided to send them to you.

6.   While Brian was trying to remember the name of the restaurant. I was looking in the yellow pages, trying to find a Chinese restaurant that was open on Monday nights.

7.   To finish my paper by class tomorrow. I will need to stay up all night. It's my own fault for putting it off so long.

8.   Driving with the top down, Sonja looks very glamorous. When she gets wherever she is going. Her hair is always a mess.

9.   If this pancake is too burned, just throw it away. We have plenty of batter.

10.   To buy a new car this year. I will need to sell my Horizon for more than three thousand dollars. This is not very likely because it has seventy thousand miles on it.

EXERCISE 6C-5

The following pairs illustrate a third way to correct fragments. First, underline the fragments. Then study the corrections until you understand this technique.

1.   Fragment: When I first bought a house, I was very naive. Thinking that my mortgage would be my only monthly expense. I didn't think about utilities, insurance, or maintenance.

       Corrected: When I first bought a house, I was very naive. I thought that my mortgage would be my only monthly expense. I didn't think about utilities, insurance, or maintenance.

2.   Fragment: When I first came to college, it was just like the first day of school back in kindergarten. The thought of new faces, new surroundings, and a new life-style. But after a little while, I felt right at home here.

       Corrected: When I first came to college, it was just like the first day of school back in kindergarten. The thought of new faces, new surroundings, and a new life-style made me very nervous. But after a little while, I felt right at home here.

3.   Fragment: The man's eyes had that hush-puppy look about them. His face full of wrinkles and scars. He wore a shabby old brown coat.

       Corrected: The man's eyes had that hush-puppy look about them. His face was full of wrinkles and scars. He wore a shabby old brown coat.

4.   Fragment: When I come for a nine o'clock class, I am lucky if I find a parking place on the highway. Although I realize there is nothing I can do about the situation. I am just going to have to get here by eight-thirty.

       Corrected: When I come for a nine o'clock class, I am lucky if I find a parking place on the highway. Although I realize there is nothing I can do about the situation, it still makes me mad. I am just going to have to get here by eight-thirty.

NOTE: A discussion of the answers to this exercise can be found on page 148.

EXERCISE 6C-6

Correct any fragments in the following. In some cases, you may be able to make your corrections by crossing out or adding punctuation; in other cases, you may need to rewrite the entire sentence. If there is no fragment, then don't change anything; just write the words "no fragment" at the end.

1. When I first was laid off, I was extremely depressed. The thought of looking for a new job. Now I'm getting a little more optimistic about the future.

2. Marriage has not been anything like what I expected it to be. Just a whole lot of arguments. I suppose I'll get used to it after a while.

3. I could speak very little English when I first came from Vietnam. Just a few phrases. Now, I'm much better at it.

4. Everyone in my neighborhood has agreed to a project. We are going to clear all the weeds and trash out of a vacant lot. When it's cleared, we will turn it into a Little League baseball field.

5. Jim's parents are awfully strict with him. Lots of arguments and punishments. Nevertheless, he gets into more trouble than anyone else I know.

6. For Neal to get into the stadium and see a game, he has to call a week in advance and make arrangements. The stadium was not designed to be accessible to wheelchairs. No ramps or spaces for wheelchairs.

7. My basement is a complete mess. Boxes of mildewed clothes. This weekend, I'm going to clean the place up.

8. When I had my first baby, I was very scared. I was afraid that I was going to go through a lot of pain that I couldn't control. Now that my daughter is four, I hardly remember the pain. Just the joy of bringing another person into the world.

9. Even though I took a course in statistics, I still don't understand much about it. For example, I never could figure out the difference between permutations and combinations. All I did was memorize a bunch of formulas.

10. My current job is very rewarding. Taking care of the elderly in a nursing home. I only wish the pay was better.

 EXERCISE 6C-7 _____

Now you have learned the three ways to correct fragments. This exercise reviews all three methods.

Correct any fragments in the following items. In some cases, you may be able to make your corrections by crossing out or adding punctuation; in other cases, you may need to rewrite the entire sentence. If there is no fragment, then don't change anything; just write the words "no fragment" at the end.

1. When I started back to school, I was not sure I would be able to do it. The thought of studying every night. Now I am really enjoying college.

2. Now that I have children of my own, Christmas is nothing like I remember it being when I was a child. Just a lot of worrying about how I am going to pay for everything. I suppose it was the same for my parents, but they never let me know it.

3. When I got my first Apple II. I spent about ten hours a day working on it. Now I only spend about four hours each day.

4. Everyone who attends my temple has agreed to a big project for this year. We are going to raise money for the poorer members of our community. We will use this money to provide low-rent housing.

5. Nathan worked very hard for four years. To pay off the mortgage on his farm. He will need to work just as hard for another six years.

6. To get me to pay this outrageous bill. You will have to convince me that I really used this much electricity. In the meantime, I will just pay half of what you say I owe.

7. The paper Sheila turned in was a real mess. A lot of crossed-out mistakes. There was even a Rice Krispie stuck to the back.

8. When Katy arrived in Mexico City, she was a little scared. The idea of being alone in a foreign country. After about two days, she relaxed completely and really enjoyed herself.

9. Even though I speak French, I always dread going to a French movie. Because I have to read the subtitles. I never can relax and enjoy the movie.

10. After I had worked for this company for ten years. I got a large raise and an extra two weeks of vacation. The fact that they have treated me right has made me want always to work hard for them.

EXERCISE 6C-8

In the following items, place brackets around all independent clauses and write "fragment" after each item that is not a sentence. Be careful. Do not expect many independent clauses.

1. Running down the stairs and slamming the front door.

2. To get an A on one of Ms. Starr's quizzes and to get an A on a reading test in the same day.

3. Opened the refrigerator and took out a package of Lebanon bologna.

4. The woman in the car and the man on the bicycle.

5.   When the sun comes up or when the alarm goes off.

NOTE: A discussion of the answers to this exercise can be found on pages 148–149.

EXERCISE 6C-9

Correct any fragments in the following items. In some cases, you may be able to make your corrections by crossing out or adding punctuation; in other cases, you may need to rewrite the entire sentence. If there is no fragment, then don't change anything; just write the words "no fragment" at the end.

1.   When I saw the room and heard the price. I decided that I would sleep in the park for the night.

2.   There are two people at this party that I want you to meet. The man in the raincoat and the woman with a pigeon on her head. They used to live in my apartment building.

3.   To confess to everything and throw yourself on the mercy of the court. You have to be very naive. This court has no mercy.

4.   Since Vivian lives in a trailer and has very little room, we cannot stay with her. We will have to stay in a motel.

5.   Walking during the night and sleeping during the day, the escaped prisoner avoided being recaptured. Until he reached his girlfriend's house.

6.   The man in the black cape and the dog with the long fangs. This can't be the right party. Did you write down Ruth's address?

7.   There are many reasons why people drop out of school. Some for financial reasons and some for personal reasons. My sister dropped out for no reason at all.

8.   Wearing a nightgown and screaming at the top of her lungs, Sharon ran out of the burning building. Her screams woke several of her neighbors and saved their lives.

9.   Pat had one goal in life. To win the lottery and take a trip around the world. He bought a ticket every week.

10.   Brian walked into the library and spotted Barry. He appeared to be very involved in studying. Reading a book and taking a lot of notes.

EXERCISE 6C-10

Study the following examples of a kind of fragment that you haven't seen until now and determine why the a and b versions are fragments but the c and d versions are sentences.

1. a. Fragment: Running after the bus.
   b. Fragment: The man running after the bus.
   c. Corrected: The man was running after the bus.
   d. Corrected: The man running after the bus is my father.

2. a. Fragment: Watching television.
   b. Fragment: The little girl watching television.
   c. Corrected: The little girl was watching television.
   d. Corrected: The little girl watching television is avoiding her home-work.

3. a. Fragment: Eating a big plate of spaghetti.
   b. Fragment: That jerk eating a big plate of spaghetti.
   c. Corrected: That jerk is eating a big plate of spaghetti.
   d. Corrected: That jerk eating a big plate of spaghetti is supposed to be on a diet.

NOTE: A discussion of the answers to this exercise can be found on pages 149–150.

EXERCISE 6C-11 _____

Correct any fragments in the following items. In some cases, you may be able to make your corrections by crossing out or adding punctuation; in other cases, you may need to rewrite the entire sentence. You may also need to cross out some words. If there is no fragment, then don't change anything; just write "no fragment" at the end.

1. The car sitting in front of the fire hydrant. Belongs to the mayor. I don't think he should be allowed to break the law just because he is mayor.

2. The officer, thinking about the shoot-out the week before. Made a tactical mistake. He entered the building without any backup.

3. The baby-sitter, thinking the child was asleep, went into the kitchen. As soon as she left the bedroom. The child climbed out of the crib.

4. I have great sympathy for one person. The woman dating Leroy. She is going to have a lot of trouble with him.

5. A weed in my garden has a 90 percent chance of surviving. I just don't have any time for weeding. I hate it anyhow.

6. To understand how a computer works and to know how to fix one. Are Belinda's goals. She plans to work as a computer repair person.

7. I envy one person in this company. The man sitting behind that desk. He has more freedom to make decisions than anyone else.

8. Before you try white-water canoeing and get yourself in a dangerous situation. You had better take some lessons. I have a friend who was nearly drowned canoeing on the Delaware River last summer.

9. The clerk standing arrogantly behind her register and chewing gum

fiercely. She announced loudly that my credit card was "refused." I was humiliated.

10.   Until your check clears the bank and I know there is no problem. I cannot mail you the tickets. This should take about seven working days.

 EXERCISE 6C-12

This exercise introduces another type of fragment that you haven't worked with until now.

1.   Fragment: I always eat ice cream too fast. Which means I get a head-ache.
      Corrected: I always eat ice cream too fast, which means I get a head-ache.

2.   Fragment: Mr. Zielinski likes students who talk a lot in class. Which means I did well in his course.
      Corrected: Mr. Zielinski likes students who talk a lot in class, which means I did well in his course.

3.   Fragment: The deli tries to hire reliable workers. Who will always get to work on time.
      Corrected: The deli tries to hire reliable workers who will always get to work on time.

4.   Fragment: I love a concert by energetic musicians. Who dance all over the stage while they are playing.
      Corrected: I love a concert by energetic musicians who dance all over the stage while they are playing.

5.   Fragment: The teacher who helped me the most. Ms. O'Melia deserves a lot of praise.
      Corrected: Ms. O'Melia, the teacher who helped me the most, deserves a lot of praise.
      Corrected: The teacher who helped me the most was Ms. O'Melia, and she deserves a lot of praise.

6.   Fragment: There is one thing that keeps me in college. The fact that I don't know what else I would do.
      Corrected: There is one thing that keeps me in college, the fact that I don't know what else I would do.
      Corrected: The fact that I don't know what else I would do is the one thing that keeps me in college.

When you understand this type of fragment and how to correct it, go on to the next exercise.

 EXERCISE 6C-13

Correct any fragments in the following items. In some cases, you may be able to make your corrections by crossing out or adding punctuation; in other cases, you may need to rewrite the entire sentence. You may also need to cross out some words. If there is no fragment, then don't change anything; just write the words "no fragment" at the end.

1. When I was in college, I was very dependent on one person. The man who typed all my papers for me.

2. Gerald had one advantage over the other candidates for the position. The fact that he had good writing skills.

3. I studied biology until three o'clock last night. Which meant I overslept and missed the exam.

4. Max is looking for a reliable man to share his apartment. A man who will be able to pay his share of the rent every month.

5. I now have seven points on my driving record. Which means I cannot get another ticket for the next three years. If I do get a ticket, I will lose my license.

6. Luis asked me to help him with his psychology homework. Which means I won't have time to do my English or to do my laundry. I don't know why I said I would.

7. There is one reason why I don't accept her offer. The fact that she is a liar. To agree to work with such a woman. I would have to be a complete fool.

8. When Tyrone heard about the opening and called for an interview. He was told that the position had already been filled.

9. When I drove up to Maxine's house and saw that no one else was there. I knew something was wrong. It turned out that the party was the next Saturday.

10. There was only one person who could back me up in court. The woman who was waiting for a bus when the accident occurred. Unfortunately, I have no idea who she was.

EXERCISE 6C-14 _____

Another type of fragment that causes some people a little trouble is illustrated below:

1.   a. Fragment: The message that she gave to the teacher.
         b. Fragment: The message she gave to the teacher.
         c. Corrected: The message that she gave to the teacher was from Lauren.
         d. Corrected: The message she gave to the teacher was from Lauren.

2.   a. Fragment: The book that Ginny left in my car. It was *Great Expectations*.

    b. Fragment: The book Ginny left in my car. It was *Great Expectations.*

    c. Corrected: The book that Ginny left in my car was *Great Expectations.*

    d. Corrected: The book Ginny left in my car was *Great Expectations.*

    What do these sets of sentences reveal about the word "that"? What happened to the "that" in the b and d versions of these sentences? Does the "that" in these sentences remind you of another kind of sentence you learned much earlier?

NOTE: A discussion of the answers to this exercise can be found on page 150.

EXERCISE 6C-15

Correct any fragments in the following items. In some cases, you may be able to make your corrections by crossing out or adding punctuation; in other cases, you may need to rewrite the entire sentence. You may also need to cross out some words. If there is no fragment, then don't change anything; just write the words "no fragment" at the end.

1. When I learned Liz was going to be late. I was furious. She has not been on time for a single meeting this year.

2. The fact that Judith was promoted. Made me determined to work even harder this year. I am going to get the same kind of promotion if I can.

3. The woman who rode to work on her bike and changed clothes in the women's room. She turned out to be a friend of Carolyn's. Now she drives a BMW to work every day.

4. I have saved money out of my check every week for two years. Meaning I now can afford a vacation in Europe. When I return in three weeks. I expect to have some money left over.

5. The teacher in the red blouse and the grey skirt. She is the one who gave me an A in physical education. There was only one reason I got an A. The fact that I was never absent or late.

6. The car Sylvester was driving. It used to belong to Karen. He does not know that it was badly damaged in an accident.

7. The binoculars I borrowed from Ms. Williams and then lost on my camping trip. They cost more than a hundred dollars. I will have to pay her back over the next six months.

8. Until Joyce learns I won't be pushed around. I will continue to refuse to work with her. She is just too bossy.

9. To hunt for a cat for three weeks and not find him. That was almost

more than I could bear. I had given up looking for him, and he just walked into the back yard.

10. The doctor whom Linda has been going to and who also treated my mother. He has an office on Pratt Street. I have an appointment with him next week.

EXERCISE 6C-16

The following examples are identified as sentences or fragments. Look closely at the first word or phrase in each example. These words or phrases, usually called transitional expressions, are frequently used incorrectly to begin a fragment. Make sure you can see the difference between the sentences and the fragments in these examples.

1. Sentence: For example, Luanne is studying animal science.
2. Fragment: For example, raising geese and studying their habits.

3. Sentence: In addition, my accounting teacher expects our projects on Friday.
4. Fragment: In addition, a twenty-page accounting project.

5. Sentence: Therefore, Tim will not be coming to Thanksgiving dinner.
6. Fragment: Therefore, ruining everyone else's plans.

7. Sentence: Also, Phil is calling me three times a week.
8. Fragment: Also, calling me three times a week.

9. Sentence: Thus, the party ended about two hours early.
10. Fragment: Thus, an early ending to the party.

NOTE: A discussion of the answers to this exercise can be found on page 151.

EXERCISE 6C-17

Correct any fragments in the following items. In some cases, you may be able to make your corrections by crossing out or adding punctuation; in other cases, you may need to rewrite the entire sentence. You may also need to cross out some words. If there is no fragment, then don't change anything; just write the words "no fragment" at the end.

1. I am developing some physical problems as I reach my forties. For example, my knees are bothering me a lot. In addition, a shortness of breath when I try to work out.

2. AAA is great when you have minor problems. Such as, a flat tire, a dead battery, or an overheated engine. I recommend that you become a member.

3. Brenda has ignored me at the last three meetings. Also, she didn't invite me to her wedding. Now, I am going to get even with her.

4. I drove my car without any water in the radiator. As a result, cracking the engine block. The bill will be more than five hundred dollars.

5. My company paid my claim within two weeks of the accident. Plus, they rented a car for me while mine was being repaired. I highly recommend them.

6. The plane was thirty minutes late. Therefore, we missed our connecting flight in Chicago. As a result, we didn't get home until three in the morning.

7. My brother has done a lot of foolish things. Such as, getting married four times. Also, he has quit at least seven jobs.

8. Several people have helped Janice get where she is today. For instance, the teacher who encouraged her to play the piano. Also, she was greatly assisted by her brother, who is a fine musician himself.

9. The management at my apartment building really takes care of things. Such as, the time that my furnace quit in the middle of a snowstorm. They were there fifteen minutes after I called and had it fixed an hour later.

10. My life these days is filled with unpleasant tasks. For example, my alarm goes off at six every morning. Also, on Thursdays, I have to go grocery shopping after a full day at work.

 EXERCISE 6C-18

Correct any fragments in the following paragraph. In some cases, you may be able to make your corrections by crossing out or adding punctuation; in other cases, you may need to rewrite the entire sentence. You may also need to cross out some words.

There are plenty of ways to get exercise and still enjoy yourself. Such as, playing tennis or riding a bicycle. I get angry at people who are exercise puritans. People who think exercise doesn't do any good unless it hurts. They always seem to be around when I am going for a swim or taking a relaxing walk. For example, my next-door neighbor teases me constantly because I won't go jogging with him. When he jogs past me, he yells that I will never lose any weight by walking. However, I walk an average of ten miles a day. While he jogs only once or twice a week. If exercise is going to do a person any good, only one thing is absolutely necessary. The fact that they do it regularly.

DISCUSSION OF INDUCTIVE EXERCISES

EXERCISE 6C-1

The pairs of sentences in this exercise demonstrate that fragments can be corrected by joining the fragment to the preceding sentence. This is the solution that works most often with fragments. For now, don't worry about the comma when you join them; in Chapter 10, you will learn when you need this comma. Now you have learned option 1 for correcting fragments:

Option 1: Join the fragment to the preceding sentence.

EXERCISE 6C-3

In these sentences the fragment was corrected by joining it to the following sentence. Again, don't worry about the comma when you join them; in Chapter 10, you will learn when you need a comma. This is a second option for correcting fragments:

Option 2: Join the fragment to the following sentence.

EXERCISE 6C-5

In these sentences, it was impossible to correct the fragments by joining them to the preceding or the following sentences. Instead, it was necessary to rewrite them so that they were complete sentences. To do this involves figuring out what the fragment was intended to say and then finding the words to express that meaning in a complete sentence. This, then, is the third option for correcting fragments:

Option 3: Rewrite the fragment as a complete sentence.

EXERCISE 6C-8

Sometimes the various kinds of fragments you have been working with are made more complicated because they are joined with each other using one of the coordinate conjunctions ("and," "but," "or," "for," "so," "yet," or "nor," but most often "and"). This makes the situation a little harder to figure out, but it will help if you just remember that adding two fragments together just makes one longer fragment, not a complete sentence.

Take a look, for example, at sentence 1:

1.   Running down the stairs and slamming the front door.

It is easy to see that "Running down the stairs" is a fragment. Similarly, "slamming the front door" is obviously a fragment. When these two fragments are added together with the conjunction "and," they are merely a long fragment. Two fragments do not add up to a sentence unless they contain a subject and a verb and express a complete thought.

Now take a look at sentence 2:

2.   To get an A on one of Ms. Starr's quizzes and to get an A on a reading test in the same day.

This item is also made up of two fragments joined with an "and." "To get an A on one of Ms. Starr's quizzes" is clearly a fragment and so is "to get an A on a reading test in the same day." Two fragments do not add up to a complete sentence.

The other three sentences are similarly composed of two fragments joined with a conjunction:

3. Opened the refrigerator and took out a package of Lebanon bologna.
4. The woman in the car and the man on the bicycle.
5. When the sun comes up or when the alarm goes off.

Sometimes, when two fragments are joined with a conjunction, the first word or two of the first fragment are omitted in the second fragment. An example should make this clearer:

6. Because I kept up with the readings and because I studied very hard for the exam.

This can just as correctly be written as the following:

7. Because I kept up with the readings and studied very hard for the exam.

Another example:

8. To swim across the lake and to rescue the puppy.

This can just as correctly be written as the following:

9. To swim across the lake and rescue the puppy.

Notice that, in each of these cases, the item is still a fragment, even when the first word or two are omitted in the second half. Two fragments do not add up to a sentence.

EXERCISE 6C-10

Here are the a versions of each of the items:

1. a. Fragment: Running after the bus.
2. a. Fragment: Watching television.
3. a. Fragment: Eating a big plate of spaghetti.

The a versions of each of these are just like the fragments you have already worked with. They are fragments because they

1. do not have verbs (remember from Chapter 2 [page 59] that the verbs with "ing" endings are not verbs unless they have helping verbs, which these don't)
2. do not have subjects
3. do not express complete thoughts

Any one of these three conditions would make each of these a fragment; they meet all three conditions.

Here are the b versions:

1. b. Fragment: The man running after the bus.
2. b. Fragment: The little girl watching television.
3. b. Fragment: That jerk eating a big plate of spaghetti.

In the b versions, a noun, which could be considered the subject, has been added at the beginning of each item. This would only take care of the lack of subject, however. The items still have no verbs (remember that the "ing" ending makes these words verbals unless they have helping verbs, which they don't) and still do not express complete thoughts. Therefore, they are still fragments. It is this kind of fragment that you are seeing for the first time in this exercise.

Here are the c versions:

1. c. Corrected: The man was running after the bus.
2. c. Corrected: The little girl was watching television.
3. c. Corrected: That jerk is eating a big plate of spaghetti.

In the c versions, the verbals have all been turned into verbs by the addition of helping verbs. This change also makes them into complete thoughts. Therefore, the c versions are all sentences. This is one way to correct the kind of fragments represented by the b versions.

Here are the d versions:

1. d. Corrected: The man running after the bus is my father.
2. d. Corrected: The little girl watching television is avoiding her home-work.
3. d. Corrected: That jerk eating a big plate of spaghetti is supposed to be on a diet.

The d versions demonstrate another way to correct the fragments. The verbals are left as verbals, and a different verb is added at the end of the sentence. Now each item has a subject and verb and expresses a complete thought, so each is a sentence.

EXERCISE 6C-14

Do you remember what the subject was in sentences like this?

Bring me a cold beer from the refrigerator.

If you don't remember, you might want to check back to Chapter 2 (page 54). This sentence gives a command, so the subject is "you." However, "you" doesn't actually appear in the sentence; it is "understood" to be the subject.

This concept of words being "understood" is used in several other situations in English. One of these is the word "that" when it is used to introduce a subordinate clause. This is what's going on in the sentences in this exercise:

1. a. Fragment: The message that she gave to the teacher.
   b. Fragment: The message she gave to the teacher.

2. a. Fragment: The book that Ginny left in my car. It was *Great Expectations.*
   b. Fragment: The book Ginny left in my car. It was *Great Expectations.*

In the b versions (and in the d versions, for that matter), the "that" is still present, but it is "understood." It is not written, but all users of English understand the sentence as if it were. We can show that in the following way:

1. b. Fragment: The message (that) she gave to the teacher.
2. b. Fragment: The book (that) Ginny left in my car. It was *Great Expectations.*

Most of the time when "that" is used in this way, it can be "understood." As long as you are aware of this option, you should not have any trouble with fragments of this type.

EXERCISE 6C-16

In each of the examples in this exercise, a word or expression at the beginning is set off by commas. These expressions are known as transitional expressions because they help the reader make the transition from the preceding sentence to this one.

   For some reason, when one of these transitional expressions appears at the beginning of a fragment, it makes it look like a sentence to many people. Actually, it is fairly easy to tell the difference between the sentences and the fragments in these cases. All you have to do is disregard the transitional expression and look at what is left. For example, look at numbers 1 and 2:

1. Sentence: For example, Luanne is studying animal science.
2. Fragment: For example, raising geese and studying their habits.

If you disregard the transitional expression, you are left the following:

1. Sentence: Luanne is studying animal science.
2. Fragment: Raising geese and studying their habits.

It is obvious now that number 1 is a sentence and number 2 is a fragment. Most sentences of this type are equally easy. Just don't let the transitional expression distract you.

   Here are the most common of these transitional expressions: "also," "consequently," "for example," "plus," "such as," "thus," "thereby," "therefore," and "well."

R E V I E W

 EXERCISE 6-REVIEW-1 ━━━━━━━━━━━━━━━

Correct any fragments in the following items. In some cases, you may be able to make your corrections by crossing out or adding punctuation; in other cases, you may need to rewrite the entire sentence. You may also need to cross out some words. If there is no fragment, then don't change anything; just write the words "no fragment" at the end.

1. I want to prove that I am capable of handling college-level work. Which means studying a lot harder than I ever have before. Even my own parents doubt that I will succeed.

2. The Orioles defeated the Giants in four straight games. Proving decisively why they are the national champions again.

3. Although my husband gets along well with his parents, he doesn't see them very often. I see more of them than he does.

4. Nancy has made several mistakes since she came to college. For example, she took too many courses during her first semester. Also, the math course which she meant to sign up for. It was cancelled.

5. Although I realize there is nothing I can do about the parking situa-

tion. It still makes me mad. I need to blow off steam somehow, so I am writing this letter.

6. Mark has pulled a muscle in his leg. Which means he will miss two weeks of practice. The team will really miss him.

7. I studied all day Saturday and Sunday. Therefore, the math test that I had been nervous about. It was easy.

8. This winter has been extremely hard. We have had over thirty inches of snow. Plus, the temperature has been below ten degrees for thirty-one out of forty days.

9. The president has appointed a new Supreme Court justice. A man who agrees with most of the president's political views. I'm worried about the Constitution.

10. I have mastered several grammar problems in the Writing Center. For example, I now understand apostrophes. Also, I have gotten much better at correcting fragments.

11. There is only one thing that saved my life. The fact that I had chains on my car. Otherwise, I wouldn't be here today.

12. I hate most green vegetables. Such as, broccoli, Brussels sprouts, and asparagus. I even hate lettuce.

13. When you have mastered fragments and conquered subject-verb agreement. You are ready for the easy stuff. Like run-ons and comma splices.

14. There is one person who knows what I am capable of. The man who coached me in high school and taught me everything about basketball.

15. Wearing a pair of shorts and a tee shirt, Tracey walked into the bank and announced she wanted to borrow ten thousand dollars. An hour later, she walked out with a check.

16. Gene knew very well what he wanted in life. To be a dancer with a world-wide reputation. He is having a hard time settling for anything less.

17. I am good at lots of very practical things. For example, fixing broken garbage disposals and changing storm windows. However, I'm not much good at balancing my checkbook.

18. There is one man I would love to locate after all these years. The guy who took me to my senior prom fifteen years ago. I've never been happier than I was that night.

19.   I've never been very good at math. For example, in high school I took algebra three times. I never did pass it.

20.   There are two things about camping that I really don't like. Getting all the equipment loaded into the car and then unpacking it all when we get back.

EXERCISE 6-REVIEW-2 _____

Correct any fragments in the following items. In some cases, you may be able to make your corrections by crossing out and adding things; in other cases, you may need to rewrite the entire sentence. If there is no fragment, then don't change anything; just write the words "no fragment" at the end.

1.   College can be the greatest time of your life or the toughest. Depending on how you look at it and what kind of experience you have. I'm finding it very tough.

2.   Because my last name starts with an "A," I was always asked to go first on things in school. Meaning I gained a lot of self-confidence that people whose names start with "Z" don't have.

3.   Paula was placed in Freshman English. Thus surprising her and her parents. She had assumed she would need a remedial course.

4.   I really enjoy the time I get to spend with my children. Such as the day we went canoeing on the Red River. I'll remember that day long after they're grown up and living on their own.

5.   When I first moved to Oklahoma, I really missed the East. I just didn't fit in. Now I love it here, and you would never know I haven't lived here all my life.

6.   An abused child usually feels terribly alone. He or she is often filled with anxiety. For example, fears that he or she has done something wrong. Or, fears that the abuse is really his or her fault.

7.   I found learning to drive to be extremely difficult. Shifting gears and steering at the same time seemed impossible. In addition, the idea that a small mistake could wreck the car and seriously hurt someone.

8.   When Lennette found her dog after it had been missing for three days. She was extremely happy and very relieved. From that day on, she has allowed him to sleep on the end of her bed.

9.   When I meet a woman in a bar or at a party, I always say the stupidest things. For example, I told a woman that I wanted to marry her, and I didn't even know her name.

10. After all the studying is over. The time arrives when one has to face the music. It is time for final exams.

11. I accidentally left my typewriter on when I went away for a weekend. Causing it to overheat and blow a fuse. It could have been a lot worse.

12. Nancy was late for work this morning for the third time this week. Proving beyond a doubt that she cannot be depended on to open the store. I don't understand why Ms. Rodriguez puts up with her.

13. Along the beach, there were lots of signs that there had been a storm. Such as broken tree limbs and an unusual amount of seaweed and kelp that had washed up on the sand. The ocean was still very rough.

14. I guess I deserve the D that I got on my term paper. It was only six pages long including the footnotes. Plus, the fact that it was a week late when I turned it in.

15. When the boss is away, we all work a lot better. For example, the pressure lets up, and we don't make as many mistakes. Also, we are more productive because he isn't there interrupting us.

16. The car that stopped to pick me up was already extremely full. With the man driving, four kids, and a dozen balloons floating around. I just squeezed my way into the back seat. Trying not to take up much room.

17. When the ice storm hit this city, there were a number of traffic accidents. The largest of which involved fourteen cars on the expressway. I had a close call myself when I skidded through an intersection.

18. Grace is just not going to work out as a district manager. She makes entirely too many mistakes and irritates many of the customers. With the best of intentions and a sincere desire to be helpful.

19. The bar where we met after the conference was extremely shabby. Tables with cigarette burns on them and a floor that felt very sticky when we walked on it.

20. Jeff had a cold that was really making him cranky. Plus, he was worried about finishing all of his courses. I knew we would have to be careful not to give him a hard time.

 EXERCISE 6-REVIEW-3 _____

Proofread the following essay carefully and correct all fragments.

There are just two things that I need more of, and they are time and money. Now, when I say I need more of these two things.

I'm not talking about a whole lot more. I just need enough money to make my family comfortable. For example, to be able to afford an apartment with three bedrooms. Right now, I am working a forty-hour week, working overtime on Saturdays, and going to college two nights a week. Thus, hardly ever getting to spend time with my family. If I could cut out either the overtime or the school, I would feel a lot better about my kids.

The problem is that time is money, and money is time. This results in a vicious circle that keeps me from having enough of either one. If I could make more money, I wouldn't need to work the overtime. The result being more time with my family. But to get a raise in the kind of high-pressure business I work in. I have to be willing to work on weekends. Also, the need for more education to make me qualified for management. The problem is that the education itself costs me a lot of money. Tuition is almost $175 per semester. Plus over $60 a semester for books and supplies.

It seems like all I want is a little more time and a little more money. However, to get any more of either one, I need to put up with less of both. At least, until I get where I want to be. There is one question, though, that is really starting to bother me. Will I ever get caught up?

 ## EXERCISE 6-REVIEW-4

A friend has asked you for advice about managing her time when she goes to college. You write her a letter about how you try to get everything done when there is never enough time to do it all. For this assignment, write one paragraph from that letter. In this paragraph, tell your friend about one thing you do to manage your time, one trick or technique for getting things done when there is too much to do and too little time to do it in.

As an alternative, imagine that your friend has asked for advice about how to live on a reduced budget while going to school. Write a paragraph in which you tell her about one thing you do to keep your expenses down.

Whichever option you choose, do not write the entire letter; just write the one paragraph. Imagine, however, that your paragraph is part of a longer letter in which you have included all the usual pleasantries; your paragraph will only need to discuss the option you select from the two we have described.

Before you write this assignment, answer the following questions:

1.   Who will be the audience for this paragraph?_____

_____

_____

2.   What is the purpose of this paragraph? What are you trying to accomplish? _____

_____

3.   What will be the subject of the paragraph? _____

_____

4.   What point will you make about that subject? _____

_____

_____

(The combination of 3 and 4 will be the topic sentence.)

5.   On a separate sheet of paper, make a list of telling details.

Once you have answered these questions, write the paragraph on a separate sheet of paper.

EXERCISE 6-REVIEW-5 _____

Now you are going to revise the paragraph you wrote for Exercise 6-Review-4. Ask yourself each of the following questions about the paragraph. If the answers reveal weaknesses in the paragraph, revise it to correct them.

1.   Does the paragraph do what the assignment asked you to do?
2.   Are the language and content appropriate for the audience?
3.   Is it clear what the topic sentence is? What is it?
4.   What is the subject of the paragraph?
5.   Is the point you are making about the subject clear?
6.   Does every sentence in the paragraph support the topic sentence?
7.   Could the paragraph be strengthened by the inclusion of more concrete details?

Next, carefully proofread the paragraph, once looking for errors with subject-verb agreement and then a second time looking only for fragments. Finally, correct any errors you can find in spelling, punctuation, or other grammar.

7

Thesis and Unity in Longer Pieces of Writing

Part A   The Thesis
Part B   Unity

Up to this point, all the writing we have worked on has been paragraph length. In this chapter you will begin work on longer pieces of writing. Whether you are writing college essays, letters to the editor of your local paper, letters of application for jobs, or business memos, the principles you will learn in this chapter will be very useful.

Part A · The Thesis

When we talked about getting started on a piece of writing in Chapter 1, we came up with three questions that need to be answered about every piece of writing:

1. What am I going to write about?
2. Who is going to read this?
3. What is the purpose of this piece of writing?

Usually these three questions should be answered before you start writing, although sometimes answers to one or more may develop out of a first tentative draft.

This section will depend very heavily on what you learned in Chapter 1. We will expand slightly on many of the concepts that were discussed there. For example, we will now add a fourth question to the above list:

4. What is the thesis?

You may want to answer this question too, at least tentatively, before you start writing. For some writers, however, it is sometimes easier to start writing without a clearly stated thesis and "see what happens." Either way, by the time you are ready to start revising your first draft, you should know very clearly and definitely what the thesis is.

But what is a thesis? Perhaps a diagram will help:

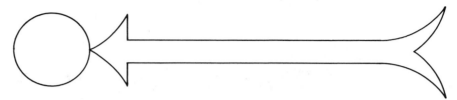

Does this diagram look familiar? It should. It is exactly the same as the diagrams we used back in Chapter 3 to represent topic sentences. The similarity is no accident: Thesis statements strongly resemble topic sentences. In fact, a thesis is to a longer piece of writing what a topic sentence is to a paragraph.

EXERCISE 7A-1

Listed below is a series of possible thesis statements. In each pair, one is labeled "a good thesis" and the other "not a thesis." Study these pairs and figure out what a good thesis must include.

1. Not a thesis: The American space shuttle program.
2. A good thesis: The space shuttle is an expensive luxury.

3. Not a thesis: Flex-time.
4. A good thesis: This company should allow flex-time.

5. Not a thesis: Owning your own home.
6. A good thesis: Owning your own home is the American nightmare.

What can you conclude about a good thesis from these first three pairs?

_____

_____

NOTE: A discussion of the answers to this exercise can be found on page 166.

EXERCISE 7A-2

Now look at these pairs:

1. A good thesis: Computers can make human beings more powerful.
2. Not a thesis: In this paper I will discuss computers.

3. A good thesis: Every pet should be inoculated against rabies.
4. Not a thesis: Rabies will be the subject of this essay.

5. A good thesis: Nuclear energy is too dangerous to be used as a source of electrical energy.

6. Not a thesis: There are a number of pros and cons to nuclear energy.

7. A good thesis: All drivers should be required by law to wear seat belts.

8. Not a thesis: The proposal for a mandatory seat belt law is very controversial.

What can you conclude about a good thesis statement from these examples?

_____

_____

NOTE: A discussion of the answers to this exercise can be found on pages 166–167.

EXERCISE 7A-3 _____

Here are some more examples of theses:

1. Not a thesis: Is Alfred Hitchcock's movie, *Vertigo*, a perfect thriller?

2. A good thesis: Alfred Hitchcock's movie, *Vertigo*, is a perfect thriller.

3. Not a thesis: Is it possible to have a perfectly good marriage without love?

4. A good thesis: It is possible to have a perfectly good marriage without love.

What can you conclude about a good thesis statement from these examples?

_____

_____

_____

NOTE: A discussion of the answers to this exercise can be found on page 167.

EXERCISE 7A-4 _____

The following groups of theses reveal something else about good theses:

1. A weak thesis: The Palestinians do not have a homeland.
2. A good thesis: A homeland must be created for the Palestinians.
3. A weak thesis: Something should be done about the Palestinians.

4. A weak thesis: Harry Truman was the only president to use nuclear weapons.
5. A good thesis: The nuclear bombs we exploded on Hiroshima and Nagasaki were a crime against the human race.
6. A weak thesis: Nuclear weapons are a powerful force in the world today.

7. A weak thesis: Burning coal with a high sulphur content contributes to acid rain.

8. A good thesis: It should be made illegal to burn high-sulphur coal.
9. A weak thesis: The federal government should take a stand on acid rain.

What can you conclude about a good thesis statement from these examples? Why are numbers 1, 4, and 7 weak thesis statements?

_____

_____

_____

_____

Why are numbers 3, 6, and 9 weak thesis statements?

_____

_____

_____

_____

NOTE: A discussion of the answers to this exercise can be found on page 167.

EXERCISE 7A-5

Use what you have learned about thesis statements to evaluate each of the following. If it is a good thesis, leave it alone. If it is weak, revise it to make it effective.

1. Religion in America will be the focus of this paper.

2. Lyndon Johnson was the president who first committed American troops in Vietnam.

3. Required courses are opposed by many.

4. Who really assassinated President Kennedy?

5. Violence on TV provides a harmless outlet for the natural violence we all sometimes feel.

6. Something must be done about the divorce rate in this country.

7. People disagree about the wisdom of leaving children in day-care centers.

8. The causes of the Civil War.

9. The dangers of genetic engineering.

10. The average doctor's salary is greater than $80,000 per year.

 EXERCISE 7A-6

In the last exercise, you revised our theses. In this exercise you will write some of your own.

Write a thesis statement for each of the following topics.

1. teachers' salaries

2. smoking in public places

3. the replacement of human workers by robots

4. the 55-miles-per-hour speed limit

5. ambition

If you look back at the three questions from Chapter 1, you may feel that there is some confusion between the third question, "What is the purpose of this piece of writing?" and the topic we are discussing in this chapter, the thesis.

The purpose and the thesis are sometimes similar, but often they are not. In a letter demanding that a company reimburse you for a faulty product, the purpose and the thesis are probably identical: The company should refund your money. In a paper for an economics course, however, the purpose may be to demonstrate that you understand macroeconomics; the thesis, on the other hand, might be something like "An increase in the supply of money in circulation will result in a decrease in interest rates." In a case like this, the purpose is quite different from the thesis. The purpose is what you hope will happen as a result of the paper; the thesis is the point you are trying to prove in the paper.

Now you know what a good thesis looks like, but we haven't talked at all about how, in an actual writing situation, you are supposed to come up with a thesis.

Of course, the answer to that question depends on the writing situation. Sometimes, the thesis is given to you, either by an instructor or by someone you work for. Your biology instructor says, "Write a paper in which you explain why the 'big bang' theory is not compatible with Darwinian evolutionary theory." Or, your boss greets you one morning with the news that by three o'clock he wants a report on his desk justifying the purchase of a new word processor. In these cases, the thesis is dictated by someone else.

At the other extreme is the situation in which you have total responsibility for developing a thesis. Your psychology professor requires that each student write a ten-page research paper on some aspect of human psychology.

Most writing situations lie somewhere in between these two extremes. Life presents us with a general situation, and we develop a specific thesis within the limits prescribed. A teacher asks us to write a paper on pornography and the First Amendment. Our neighborhood organization asks us to investigate and report on the proposal for a new shopping center. The boss asks us to investigate the parking situation and make a recommendation for improving it. In each of these cases, someone has given us a general situation, and we have to arrive at a specific thesis.

In all these situations except the most restrictive, we must develop a thesis. There are several methods for doing this.

Sometimes the best approach is to gather information before formulating a thesis. As you read in the library about the First Amendment or interview the developer who is planning the new shopping center or investigate the parking situation at the office, you may naturally form an opinion that can be used as a thesis. Then you need only to check it against the criteria we have been discussing to ensure that it is an effective thesis, and you are ready to write.

At other times, you have all the information you need, and the time has arrived to come up with the thesis. For some people, this means it is time for staring at a wall. The only way they can come up with a thesis is to stare and think until they have wrestled it into existence. If this technique works for you, then stick with it. For lots of writers, however, this is a very painful and frustrating way to try to get started. If you feel this way, you may want to try some of the methods discussed below.

You may find brainstorming or list making to be a helpful technique. The idea is to free your mind to think in a looser, less inhibited fashion. You just write down every idea that pops into your head on a sheet of paper, without any censoring or judging. If you had to write a paper on some aspect of human relationships, for example, you might want to start by making a list of ideas. Such a list might look like this:

love
hate
(divorce)
friends

old age
(being alone)
clinging
(breaking up)

good times
rejection
fear
loneliness
togetherness
growing apart

independence
courtship
role playing
being popular

Sometimes the mere process of making such a list will jog loose just the right idea to serve as a thesis. At other times a little more work on the list will be necessary.

In the list, you might notice that a number of your thoughts (the ones that are circled) have to do with loneliness and the fear of being alone. You know that, for a long time in your life you used to worry about being alone, especially about being alone in your old age. This fear made you really hang on to friendships—perhaps too much. Your friends sometimes complained that you didn't give them enough space. You seemed to demand too much of them for fear that they might stop being your friends. Finally, you found yourself all alone for a while, and it wasn't so bad. In fact, you remember that you actually enjoyed that period of loneliness quite a bit. And so you stopped hanging on to your friends; you discovered you didn't need them as desperately as you had always thought. The funny thing was that once you stopped needing friends so much, you had plenty of them. It seemed that they had been pulling away from you because you seemed to be grasping at them too hard. Now that you knew that you could get along just fine alone, you had plenty of friends.

Now you have thought your way to an excellent thesis: The best way to have friends is to be able to live without them. Making a brainstorming list allowed you to get all your thoughts out on paper so you could locate just the right one to write a paper about.

Notice that most of the items on the list will now be discarded. You made the list, not so you could put everything into your paper, but so you could locate the one idea that would make a good focus for your writing.

Another good technique for generating a thesis is to discuss the general subject with a friend, classmate, or co-worker. Out of this kind of discussion, very often, will emerge an excellent idea for the thesis of a piece of writing.

In Chapter 1, we talked about keeping a notebook of ideas as you study, sit in class, ride the bus, or lie in bed—wherever ideas are likely to occur to you. Another fruitful way to come up with a thesis is to browse around in that notebook. The thesis itself may not be written in the notebook, but as you read through it, something may trigger a thought that will develop into a thesis.

Finally, some writers find that the only way to arrive at a thesis is to start writing and see what happens. This is often a very useful technique, but it requires one important realization. This is a very different kind of writing from what you are used to doing; it is exploratory writing, which is less inhibited and less organized. Its purpose is to discover what you have to say. You have to be prepared, once you have arrived at a thesis, to discard large portions of what you have written. As you explored your thinking through writing, you undoubtedly touched on many areas that will have no relevance to your final thesis; these sections, although they may contain some very good ideas, must be eliminated because they don't support the thesis. Discarding chunks of good ideas is always hard, but you must be ruthless with yourself on this point, or you will never be able to produce well-organized papers.

Once you have developed a thesis, you should make a series of checks before you start writing the paper. In Chapter 1, these questions were posed about the *subject* of the writing. Now we are going to expand them to cover the entire *thesis*.

1. Will this thesis really satisfy the assignment?
2. Is this thesis really something I can write a good paper about? (Am I interested in it? Do I know enough about it?)
3. Is the thesis narrow enough to be thoroughly discussed in a paper of the length I am going to write?

One matter remains to be discussed. You have developed an effective thesis and made sure it will work for the assignment, but now what do you do with it? Where does it go in the paper? The first sentence? The last sentence of the first paragraph? Somewhere in the first paragraph? The last paragraph? All of these are possibilities. In fact there is no hard-and-fast rule about where the thesis should be located. The only "rule" is that, when the reader finishes reading your paper, he or she must have absolutely no doubt about what the thesis was. If you have any difficulty with this, you may want to play it safe and put your thesis in the first paragraph. This will guarantee that you have a thesis and that the reader will have no difficulty identifying it; however, it sometimes leads to a paper that is not very creative.

Later, when you are more confident of your writing ability, you may want to experiment with placing a paragraph or two of lead-in or background information or attention-catching material in front of the paragraph that contains the thesis. You might even want to try withholding the thesis until near the end of the paper. For now, the crucial point is that your writing *must* have a thesis and that the thesis *must* be absolutely clear to the reader. To accomplish this you will probably want to locate the thesis in the first paragraph.

It is undoubtedly true that every rule concerning writing can occasionally be violated without harming the writing. It takes a skillful writer to know when and how to break the rules, however. Most of the time, when writers break the rules, the result is writing that is less effective than it could have been. Like other rules, the rule about having a single thesis is sometimes successfully violated, but to do so is always running a risk. Unless you have a good reason for doing otherwise, you should make sure that everything you write has a single clear thesis.

Everything we have said about the thesis so far has been about the planning stage of writing—what to do about the thesis before you actually start writing. In the Part B of this chapter you will learn about the thesis in the writing and revising stages of the writing process.

EXERCISE 7A-7

Even though it is no longer the beginning of the semester, imagine that it is and that your instructor is trying to get to know his or her students a little better. He or she has asked you to write an essay in which you tell one thing about the kind of person you are. Don't try to tell everything—just focus on one aspect of yourself.

This time you are writing a longer piece of writing than you have been in earlier chapters. Nevertheless, the process you have been using will still work very well. First answer the following questions about this writing situation.

1. Who will be the audience for this essay?_____

_____

2. What is the purpose of this essay? What are you trying to accomplish?_____

_____

Because this essay is about a subject you know very well, yourself, this is a perfect time to try the list-making method for arriving at a thesis. On a separate piece of paper, brainstorm about possible ideas for the essay.

EXERCISE 7A-8

In the preceding exercise, you thoroughly brainstormed a topic for an essay. Now, write a thesis for the same essay in the space below. Do not write the essay at this time.

Thesis: _____

_____

Now you are going to check the thesis to insure that it will be effective:

1. Is the thesis a complete sentence?

   ☐ yes ☐ no   revised thesis_____

_____

2. Does the thesis include a subject and a point about that subject?

   ☐ yes ☐ no   revised thesis_____

_____

3. Is the thesis a statement rather than a question?

   ☐ yes ☐ no   revised thesis_____

_____

4. Does the thesis make a point that needs to be proved rather than merely state a fact?

   ☐ yes ☐ no   revised thesis_____

_____

5. Is the thesis appropriately focused (not too broad or vague)?

   ☐ yes ☐ no   revised thesis_____

_____

6. Will this thesis really satisfy the assignment?

    ☐ yes ☐ no   revised thesis_____

    _____

7. Is this thesis really something I can write a good paper about? (Am I interested in it? Do I know enough about it?)

    ☐ yes ☐ no   revised thesis_____

    _____

8. Is the thesis narrow enough for the paper I am going to write?

    ☐ yes ☐ no   revised thesis_____

    _____

For now, this is all you will do with this thesis; later you will use it to write a paper.

DISCUSSION OF INDUCTIVE EXERCISES

EXERCISE 7A-1

In items 1 though 6, all the good theses ("theses" is the plural form of "thesis") are complete sentences; all the items that are not theses are just single words or short phrases. So, one can conclude the following:

1. A thesis must be a complete sentence.

EXERCISE 7A-2

In these pairs, all the good theses consisted of two parts—a subject and a point to be made about that subject. The same diagram we used for topic sentences can be used to represent these two parts:

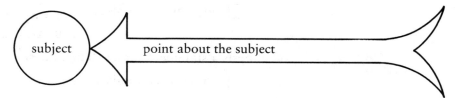

Number 1, for example, could be represented as follows:

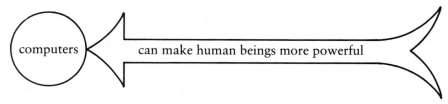

When we try to identify the two parts of number 2, we run into a problem:

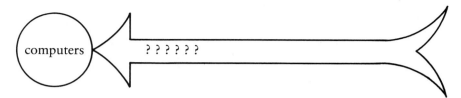

It is clear that thesis number 2 is about computers, but there is no indication of what point will be made about them. This is why number 2 is not a thesis.

An examination of the other pairs will illustrate the same point. From these examples, we can conclude the following:

  2. A thesis must include a subject and a point about that subject.

EXERCISE 7A-3

These examples reveal the following:

  3. A thesis must be a statement and not a question.

EXERCISE 7A-4

To see why the weak theses in this exercise are, in fact, weak, let's take a detailed look at the first threesome:

  1. A weak thesis: The Palestinians do not have a homeland.
  2. A good thesis: A homeland must be created for the Palestinians.
  3. A weak thesis: Something should be done about the Palestinians.

All three have subjects and points to make about those subjects. They are all sentences, and none is a question. Number 1, however, is a very narrow statement; it really just states a fact about the Palestinians. It would be hard to use this as a thesis because it is so factual that there is hardly anything left to say about it. Numbers 4 and 7 have the same weakness. From these we can conclude the following:

  4. A thesis should not merely state a fact.

Number 3 has the opposite problem: It is too broad. In fact, number 3 is so broad that it is difficult to figure out what it means. What kind of a "something" should be done? Does it mean that we should help the Palestinians acquire a homeland? Or, does it mean we should do something to control the Palestinians militarily? There is not even an indication of who should do this "something."

Numbers 6 and 9 are equally vague and are, therefore, also weak theses. From these examples, we can conclude the following:

  5. A thesis should not be too broad or vague.

Part B · Unity

In the first section of this chapter, you learned that a piece of writing will be more effective if it has a clear thesis. Most of the discussion was about what you could do *before* you started writing to make sure you had an effective thesis.

In this section, you will learn how to check a draft *when you have finished it* to make sure it doesn't have any thesis problems. Most thesis problems fit into one of three categories:

1. The paper doesn't have a clear and effective thesis.
2. The paper's thesis changes at one or more points.
3. Parts of the paper do not support the thesis.

EXERCISE 7B-1

Read the following essay and then answer the questions at the end. The bracketed numbers identify each paragraph.

[1] This weekend a drunk driver struck again. This time a middle-aged businessman, on his way home from a party, swerved across the center line and struck an oncoming car head-on. The woman driving the car and one of her children were killed; a second child is still in a coma. This tragic situation on our highways has gone on too long. It is time this state enacted a really tough law to punish drunk drivers.

[2] The number of persons killed by drunk drivers in this state has increased dramatically in the past twenty years. In 1967, there were 43 deaths directly caused by persons driving under the influence of alcohol. By 1977 that number had increased to 71. In 1982 the death toll had risen to 98, and last year, for the first time, the figure passed 100. The total number of deaths last year was 114.

[3] Speeding on our highways is also increasing. The State Highway Department estimates that ten years ago, 43 percent of the drivers on the road were exceeding the speed limit. In 1982 that figure had risen to 51 percent, and last year the figure was estimated at 58 percent. Speeding also contributes to many deaths on the highways.

[4] The major reason that drunk driving is increasing is that the penalties allowed by law are too lenient. Under the existing law, the maximum sentence for a first-time conviction for drunk driving is one year in prison. However, the precedent is for first-time offenders to have the entire sentence suspended. Even second-time offenders can only receive a maximum sentence of eighteen months, and they usually avoid serving any time at all by agreeing to join a program like Alcoholics Anonymous. Only third-time offenders are likely to spend any time in jail, and on the average they spend only about thirty days actually behind bars. No wonder people are not afraid of getting caught driving under the influence.

[5] Also, the current law makes it very difficult to take a drunk driver's license away. Only on the third offense can it be cancelled for a year. On earlier offenses, it can merely be suspended for thirty days. In fact, because judges know how difficult it is to survive in our society without driving, they are reluctant to suspend or cancel a license, except in the most severe cases.

[6] Before a judge ever sees a drunk driver, the driver has to be detected and arrested by a police officer. Unfortunately, too many officers are soft-hearted. My boss, for example, was stopped twice in a six-week period for drunk driving. Both times, he failed the Breathalyzer test. The second time he was so drunk that the officer had to drive him home. Nevertheless, because he looked respectable in his business suit, both officers just warned him and let him go.

[7] This attitude on the part of the police is far too common. They too often don't charge middle-class offenders because they don't want to embarrass them or ruin their careers. However, a person killed by a drunk driver is just as dead whether the drunk is a laid-off coal miner or the president of a bank.

[8] One of the ironies of this whole situation is that when a drunk driver hits someone, the drunk is usually not injured; it seems that they are so relaxed that they just roll around in their cars. Meanwhile, innocent people, more than 100 per year in this state alone, are being slaughtered. We've got to insist that the police get tough and start enforcing the law.

Now answer the following questions about this essay.

1. Reread the final paragraph. Based on that paragraph, what is the thesis of this essay?

_____

_____

2. Reread the first paragraph. Based on that paragraph, what is the thesis?

_____

_____

3. Do you see any conflict between these two statements of the thesis?
4. Rewrite the final sentence of the essay to correct the problem with the thesis.

_____

_____

_____

NOTE: A discussion of the answers to this exercise can be found on pages 171–172.

Once you have a clear and effective thesis and you have made sure that it doesn't change at any point in the paper, there is one more problem to check: the unity of the essay. Back in Chapter 3, you learned that a paragraph needed to be unified. If it was unified, every sentence in the paragraph would support the topic sentence. Unity for an essay is very similar. If an essay is well unified, every paragraph will support the thesis. If some paragraphs don't support the thesis, they should be removed.

The best technique for checking unity is backward outlining. At some point in your education, you have probably had to make an outline before you started writing a paper. Actually, making an outline, particularly for longer papers, is a good idea, although something a little less formal than you were probably taught is usually just as effective.

But a backward outline is something quite different. You make a backward outline *after* you have written the paper, or at least after the first draft. You use it to check the unity of the paper. In Chapter 9, you will learn that you can also use it to check organization, but we'll worry about that when we get there.

To make a backward outline, you examine each paragraph to see what its topic sentence is. This also serves as a check on your paragraphs to see if they are well unified. As you locate the topic sentences of the paragraphs, write them down in order on a numbered list. This numbered list of topic sentences is a backward outline.

But what about paragraphs that don't have topic sentences? If they should have topic sentences, then you revise them so that they do. But remember that introductory paragraphs, closing paragraphs, and transitional paragraphs usually don't have topic sentences. For them, you write the word "introductory," "closing," or "transitional" next to the appropriate number in your outline.

When you have finished the outline, read it carefully to see if there are any paragraphs that do not support the thesis. If there are any, either revise or remove them.

 EXERCISE 7B-2 _____

Now, return to the essay in Exercise 7B-1 (pp. 168–169) and make a backward outline in the space below. To do this, first write the thesis in the space provided. Then, write the topic sentence of each paragraph in the appropriate space below the thesis.

Thesis: _____

_____

Paragraph 1. _____

_____

Paragraph 2. _____

_____

Paragraph 3. _____

_____

Paragraph 4. _____

_____

Paragraph 5. _____

_____

Paragraph 6. _____

_____

Paragraph 7. _____

_____

Paragraph 8. _____

_____

Examine this outline carefully. Do any paragraphs fail to support the thesis? Cross out the topic sentence above for any paragraph that does not support the thesis.

NOTE: A discussion of the answers to this exercise can be found on page 172.

EXERCISE 7B-3

Remember the thesis you came up with back in Part A in which you told your instructor one thing about the kind of person you are? (See pages 164–165). Now you are going to put that thesis to work. On a separate piece of paper, write the essay to your instructor that you wrote that thesis for.

Do not worry about the length of the essay. Many problems crop up in essays simply because people are trying to stretch them to reach a certain length like "five hundred words" or "ten typewritten pages." To make them long enough, some people write papers that are wordy or that contain sections that wander away from the thesis. Of course at times your writing does have to be a certain length, but for now, that is one thing you won't have to worry about. Just write an essay that has several paragraphs and that satisfies the assignment. Instead of worrying about the length, worry about the thesis and unity.

EXERCISE 7B-4

Return to the essay you wrote in Exercise 7B-3 and make a backward outline. Use this outline to check the thesis and unity of the essay. Make any revisions that you feel are necessary.

After you are satisfied with the thesis and unity, revise the paper as required by the following questions and procedures:

1. Does the essay do what the assignment asked you to do?
2. Are the language and content appropriate for the audience?
3. Could the essay be strengthened by the inclusion of more concrete details?
4. Carefully proofread the essay once looking for errors with subject-verb agreement.
5. Proofread the paper a second time looking only for fragments.
6. Finally, correct any errors you can find in spelling, punctuation, or other grammar.

DISCUSSION OF INDUCTIVE EXERCISES

EXERCISE 7B-1

Based on the *last* paragraph, the thesis is something like "Police officers must be made to enforce the laws against drunk driving." Based on the *first* paragraph, the thesis is something like "This state needs to pass a tough law against drunk driving." This is a dramatic example of how a paper's thesis can subtly change as the paper progresses. The situation resembles the children's party game in which the players sit in a circle and someone whispers a secret to the person on his or her right. Each player then whispers the secret to the next person in order. By the time the secret has traveled all the way around the circle, it has changed significantly. The thesis in this paper changes the same way—a little at a time until it is quite different at the end of the paper from what it was at the beginning.

Papers with this problem always leave the reader a little puzzled. "What is the point, anyway? Does this person think we need new laws? Or does he or she think the problem is not the laws, but the way they are enforced? What we need is not new laws, but better enforcement of existing laws. What's the point?"

To correct this problem, the final sentence should read something like the following: "This state badly needs a tougher law against drunk driving."

There are a couple of techniques for preventing this problem in your writing.

First, while you are writing, you need to ensure that you are always aware of your thesis. Some writers even go so far as to write it on a three-by-five card and thumbtack it to the wall in front of them. As they write, they glance up at it at the end of each paragraph. You may not need to go that far, but you should make sure you are conscious of your thesis the entire time you are writing.

Second, when you are revising, the first thing you should check is the thesis. Does the paper have a single, clear, and effective thesis? Sometimes it helps to read the first and last paragraphs to check specifically on the problem we discovered in this essay.

EXERCISE 7B-2

Thesis: It is time this state enacted a really tough law to punish drunk drivers.

1. Introduction.
2. The number of persons killed by drunk drivers in this state has increased dramatically in the past twenty years.
3. Speeding on our highways is also increasing.
4. The major reason that drunk driving is increasing is that the penalties allowed by law are too lenient.
5. Also, the current law makes it very difficult to take a drunk driver's license away.
6. Unfortunately, too many officers are soft-hearted.
7. They too often don't charge middle-class offenders because they don't want to embarrass them or ruin their careers.
8. Closing.

If you asked yourself whether each of these paragraphs belongs in this essay, you should have discovered that the following paragraphs do not belong:

[3] This is an essay about drunk driving. Speeding is an entirely different subject and needs to come out of this essay.

[6] and [7] These two paragraphs are about drunk driving, but they still don't support the thesis. The thesis is that a tougher law should be passed. The fact that police officers are too lenient will not be affected by tougher laws. These paragraphs do discuss the *subject*, but because they don't support the *point* about that subject, they do not support the thesis, and they too should be removed.

8

Punctuating Independent Clauses

Part A   Avoiding Run-On Sentences
          and Comma Splices
Part B   Commas with Coordinating Conjunctions
Part C   Semicolons with Independent Clauses
Part D   Semicolons with Conjunctive Adverbs

In this chapter, you will learn how to punctuate sentences that have more than one independent clause. You will make much use of what you learned in Chapter 6 about independent clauses. If you are rusty on recognizing independent clauses, you might want to review that chapter before starting on this one.

Part A · Avoiding Run-On Sentences and Comma Splices

In this part, you will learn how to avoid or correct two common and very serious errors involving punctuating sentences with two independent clauses: run-on sentences and comma splices.

EXERCISE 8A-1 ─────────────────────────

The following pairs illustrate one principle about punctuating independent clauses. Study them closely and see if you can figure out why the second item in each pair is incorrect. If you are having trouble, try putting brackets around the independent clauses.

1. Correct: Alice read the paper. Kevin did the dishes.
    Incorrect: Alice read the paper Kevin did the dishes.

2. Correct: Ruth works extremely hard. She is a nurse.
    Incorrect: Ruth works extremely hard she is a nurse.

3. Correct: Getting an A in biology is very difficult. Ms. Weber is a very hard grader.
    Incorrect: Getting an A in biology is very difficult Ms. Weber is a very hard grader.

4. Correct: I was shaking all over. Two cars had collided right in front of me.
    Incorrect: I was shaking all over two cars had collided right in front of me.

5. Correct: Kathy is trying to watch her weight. She eats a lot of salads.
    Incorrect: Kathy is trying to watch her weight she eats a lot of salads.

NOTE: A discussion of the answers to this exercise can be found on page 178.

EXERCISE 8A-2

Correct any errors in the following sentences. All errors will involve run-on sentences. To correct them, just insert a period and make the first letter of the next word a capital. Of course, there are other ways to correct run-ons, but for now just make them into two sentences. If the sentence is correct, do not make any change.

Example:

a. Today is my mother's birthday. She is forty-eight.

1. Wayne dropped the fork it was very hot.

2. They do not speak to me. I don't know why not.

3. My car is broken. It needs a new water pump.

4. Sheila took a shower and changed her clothes.

5. Alexis is looking for a new job she is not making enough money at her present one.

6. The test was extremely hard it took me two full hours.

7. Al dived into the pool and swam twenty laps without stopping.

8. I gave Chuck a ride to school. He never said thanks.

9. My hometown is very small it only has one traffic light.

10. Timothy has lots of money he is a lawyer.

EXERCISE 8A-3

This exercise combines what you have just learned about run-on sentences with what you learned in Chapter 6 about fragments. Read each item carefully and correct any errors. Errors will involve run-on sentences and fragments; some items may be correct. When you join a fragment to an independent clause in this exercise, don't worry about the commas; you will learn about them in Chapter 10.

1. When I received my high school diploma. My mother and father cried.
2. David has gone fishing he will be back by six.
3. The teacher who gave me an F. Is no longer teaching at this college.
4. Since I do not speak French. I had to read the subtitles at the movie.
5. Annette loves to read Mark Twain. Because she grew up in Missouri.
6. He fixed a blue-cheese dressing she made the spaghetti.
7. The plumber fixed the furnace. He charged us seventy-five dollars.
8. Hold my books I will unlock the door.
9. The car that caused the accident. Was not even scratched.
10. Bernie was very disappointed he had hoped to get the job.

 EXERCISE 8A-4

The following pairs illustrate another principle about punctuating independent clauses. Study them closely and see if you can figure out why the second item in each pair is incorrect. If you are having trouble, try putting brackets around the independent clauses.

1. Correct: I'm not playing baseball today. It is too hot.
   Incorrect: I'm not playing baseball today, it is too hot.

2. Correct: Mr. Lloyd is giving me tennis lessons. He used to play professionally.
   Incorrect: Mr. Lloyd is giving me tennis lessons, he used to play professionally.

3. Correct: That map is out of date. It doesn't even show the beltway.
   Incorrect: That map is out of date, it doesn't even show the beltway.

4. Correct: I would never go out with Mark. He uses run-on sentences.
   Incorrect: I would never go out with Mark, he uses run-on sentences.

5. Correct: The flight to New York was very rough. We flew through two thunderstorms.
   Incorrect: The flight to New York was very rough, we flew through two thunderstorms.

NOTE: A discussion of the answers to this exercise can be found on page 179.

 EXERCISE 8A-5

Correct any errors in the following sentences. All errors will involve comma splices. To correct them, just change the comma to a period and make the first letter of the next word a capital. Again, there are other ways to correct comma splices, but for now just change them into two sentences. If the sentence is correct, do not make any change.

Examples:

a. Bob drives very carefully now; ^H/he was in a terrible accident last year.

b. When I was in the army, I had a mustache.

1. My mother has a very strong accent, she grew up in Italy.
2. This coffee is too strong. Did you make it?
3. When it started to rain, we ran into the gymnasium.
4. My job doesn't pay very well, I work at Gino's.
5. A three-story building burned down last night, no one was hurt.
6. When we went to the beach, the ocean was very rough.
7. If you see Gena, tell her to call home.
8. Fran's job is very dangerous, she drives an ambulance.
9. Michelle was late to the party. Her car had a flat tire.
10. I can't call Doug, his phone has been disconnected.

EXERCISE 8A-6

The following items contain errors involving fragments, comma splices, and run-on sentences. Read each item carefully and correct any errors. Some sentences may be correct.

1. Because I did not have any money. I had to go to the bank and cash a check.
2. At her dinner party, Ann served baklava, a Greek dessert.
3. My next-door neighbors have never invited us into their house, I think they are a little weird.
4. Rhonda loaned me twenty dollars she knows that I will pay her back.
5. John Hubbard was born in Cheyenne, the capital of Wyoming.
6. Charlene has turned into a snob, she has not spoken to me since she was elected homecoming queen.
7. The teacher gave Rob a C on his essay. Rob was furious.
8. After Margaret did the dishes, she called Gary, he is taking her to Tucson next week.
9. Our front lawn is a disgrace the grass is a foot high.
10. Donna is very lucky, she has a job as a physical therapist.

EXERCISE 8A-7

This exercise reviews everything you have learned in this section.

The following items contain errors involving fragments, run-on sentences, and comma splices. Read each item carefully and correct any errors. Some items may not have errors.

1. My mother has a very demanding job she is a reporter for the *Washington Post*. She has worked there for the past seventeen years. Except for five years while she had her children.

2. I gave my name to the woman who interviewed me and took a seat in the lounge. About five minutes later, my name was called.

3. Kevin liked to play rugby, a British form of football. He learned it while he was in the air force and stationed in England.

4. When you come to Hawaii. Give me a call. We can go out for some lobster together.

5. My daughter can't go to basketball practice today she has a fever. She should be better by Monday.

6. I ordered crab cakes, one of the specialties of the state of Maryland. Jeanette ordered clams.

7. Fix yourself a cup of coffee. I'll be there in a minute I'm on the phone. It is long distance.

8. I was upset with the jokes Ned was telling. Child abuse is no joking matter it is tragic.

9. The bridge having been washed out. There was no way to rescue the sheep. Jose could not swim across the river, the current was too strong.

10. This summer I visited Harpers Ferry, the site of John Brown's raid before the Civil War. The man who took us on the tour. He was an English teacher from the University of West Virginia.

11. Until I read the directions. I could not assemble the bike. After I read them. I still was confused.

12. A woman who lived in a convent in California for fifteen years. Just came in second in the Boston Marathon. She finished three minutes ahead of the next woman.

13. Dr. Martinez was furious with Gus this morning. He was late for class again his car wouldn't start.

14. Because I have to have something to wear to the dance tonight. I am going to buy one of these dresses, which do you like the best?

15. Lenny never delivered the TV set, my father is really mad. He told me to get the money back from Lenny.

16. My sister is going with me to the ocean she is only nine years old. We will stay for a week.

17. The woman wearing the bulky black sweater with elbow patches. She

gave the best speech in my public-speaking class. I have no idea what her name is.

18. Since Drew quit his job at the garage, he has not been able to pay his mortgage. I have loaned him forty dollars for groceries.

19. Hecht's is my favorite place to buy sweaters, they always have a large selection. Last week all their sweaters were on sale.

20. Deborah went to bed at eight o'clock she was exhausted. She didn't get up until eight-thirty this morning.

EXERCISE 8A-8

The following paragraph contains fragments, run-on sentences, and comma splices. Read the paragraph carefully and correct any errors.

Aerobics is an easy way to get some good exercise. To start with, aerobics classes are not expensive, I paid twenty dollars for ten classes. Even more important, aerobics classes are fun. The steps are fairly easy to learn, the music makes the whole experience very pleasant. Because it is all so pleasant, I don't mind going. I gave up jogging two years ago it was just too much work, aerobics is something I look forward to. I don't think that I'll ever give it up. After just two months of exercising. I've lost fifteen pounds. Also, I feel better than I ever have. Finally, I know that it is reducing my chances of having a heart attack. Aerobics is more than just exercise it is a lot of fun.

DISCUSSION OF INDUCTIVE EXERCISES

EXERCISE 8A-1

In these examples, the incorrect versions consisted of two independent clauses that were run together without punctuation. The correct versions each consisted of two sentences. Each sentence began with a capital letter and ended with a period.

You should never write two independent clauses that are run together without any punctuation. If you do, the result is known as a run-on sentence, and it is a serious error. The following diagram represents this situation.

_____ (independent clause)   (independent clause)   run-on

EXERCISE 8A-4

In Exercise 8A-4, the incorrect versions each had two independent clauses joined by just a comma. The correct versions each consisted of two sentences. Each sentence began with a capital letter and ended with a period.

You should never join two independent clauses with just a comma. If you do, the resulting sentence is called a comma splice and is a serious grammar error. The following diagram represents this situation.

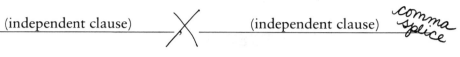

_____ (independent clause) _____ ✕ _____ (independent clause) _____ *comma splice*

Part B · Commas with Coordinating Conjunctions

EXERCISE 8B-1 ————————————————————

In Part A of this chapter, if you wanted to correct a run-on sentence or a comma splice, the only option you had was to change it into two sentences. This exercise introduces a second option for punctuating two independent clauses. Study the following examples and figure out what this second option is.

If you have trouble, try putting brackets around the independent clauses. Then look closely at the punctuation and the words used to join the independent clauses.

1. **a.** Correct: Charlie washed the clothes, and Chris cooked dinner.
   b. Incorrect: Charlie washed the clothes and Chris cooked dinner.
   c. Incorrect: Charlie washed the clothes, Chris cooked dinner.

2. **a.** Correct: The bus stopped, but no one got off.
   b. Incorrect: The bus stopped but no one got off.
   c. Incorrect: The bus stopped, no one got off.

3. **a.** Correct: You can bring a towel, or you can check one out.
   b. Incorrect: You can bring a towel or you can check one out.
   c. Incorrect: You can bring a towel, you can check one out.

4. **a.** Correct: Vince studied very hard, yet he only got a D on the midterm exam.
   b. Incorrect: Vince studied very hard yet he only got a D on the midterm exam.
   c. Incorrect: Vince studied very hard, he only got a D on the midterm exam.

5. **a.** Correct: I was getting worried, for my daughter had never stayed out this late.
   b. Incorrect: I was getting worried for my daughter had never stayed out this late.
   c. Incorrect: I was getting worried, my daughter had never stayed out this late.

6. **a.** Correct: The neighbors complained, so we turned off the stereo.
   b. Incorrect: The neighbors complained so we turned off the stereo.
   c. Incorrect: The neighbors complained, we turned off the stereo.

7. **a.** Correct: My father didn't finish the eighth grade, nor did my mother have much education.

b. Incorrect: My father didn't finish the eighth grade nor did my mother have much education.

c. Incorrect: My father didn't finish the eighth grade, did my mother have much education.

NOTE: A discussion of the answers to this exercise can be found on page 185.

EXERCISE 8B-2

Correct any errors in the following sentences. All errors will involve using commas and coordinating conjunctions to join independent clauses. In some of these sentences, you will need to add one of the seven coordinating conjunctions. Each sentence may contain no errors, one error, or more than one error.

1. Diane Walton gave one hundred dollars to the scholarship fund and her husband gave fifty.

2. Homer drove to Salem but he was too late to see the doctor.

3. Jim walked into the kitchen, he fixed himself a drink.

4. A nurse ran toward the accident, but she was too late to help.

5. Monica had to go to the library for her research paper was due on Monday.

6. I work as hard as I can, yet I never seem to have enough money.

7. Leroy dropped his books, Yvonne helped him pick them up.

8. Nancy doesn't know how to drive so she takes the bus to school.

9. We will buy some lettuce or we can pick it from Wendy's garden.

10. Inflation is going up, but unemployment is going down.

EXERCISE 8B-3

Some people have trouble deciding which of the seven coordinating conjunctions to use in a particular sentence. If you have this trouble, go back to Exercise 8B-1 and study the meaning of each coordinating conjunction in those sentences. When you know what they mean, fill in each of the blanks in the following sentences with one of them. There are other words that would make sense in these sentences, but for this exercise, use only the seven coordinating conjunctions: "and," "but," "or," "for," "so," "yet," and "nor."

1. The children were upstairs asleep, _____ my husband was in the kitchen doing the dishes.

2. I trained for more than a year, _____ I didn't make the team.

3. You must get up by seven o'clock tomorrow, _____ you will be late for class.

4. Sook Moon did not understand Chris, _____ he spoke much too fast.

5. Rachel tries very hard, _____ she is never going to be a good singer.

6. The ring cost $450, _____ the stone in it was a large ruby.

7. The bus stopped at the corner, _____ my friend didn't get off.

8. The daffodils are blooming, _____ the robins have returned.

9. It is supposed to snow heavily today, _____ the trip has been postponed.

10. Joanne took out a loan, _____ she had spent all her savings.

 ## EXERCISE 8B-4 _____

The following pairs will show you a potential problem when using coordinating conjunctions. Study these pairs closely and see if you can figure out why the second item in each pair is incorrect.

If you have trouble, try putting brackets around the independent clauses. Make sure everything you bracket is really an independent clause. Then see if you can figure out what the principle is.

1. **a.** Correct: Tamara took the milk out of the refrigerator and poured herself a glass.
    b. Incorrect: Tamara took the milk out of the refrigerator, and poured herself a glass.

2. **a.** Correct: The skater fell on the ice and slid into a little girl.
    b. Incorrect: The skater fell on the ice, and slid into a little girl.

3. **a.** Correct: We will mail your present to you or bring it by when we come to visit.
    b. Incorrect: We will mail your present to you, or bring it by when we come to visit.

4. **a.** Correct: You may turn in your paper on the last day of class or mail it to me by May 16.
    b. Incorrect: You may turn in your paper on the last day of class, or mail it to me by May 16.

5. **a.** Correct: Carol bought Ken a necktie and gave it to him on Saturday.
    b. Incorrect: Carol bought Ken a necktie, and gave it to him on Saturday.

NOTE: A discussion of the answers to this exercise can be found on page 185.

 ## EXERCISE 8B-5 _____

Correct any errors in the following sentences. All errors will involve using commas and coordinating conjunctions. Each sentence may contain no errors, one error, or more than one error.

1. George got contact lenses and grew a beard.

2. I can write my paper on Friday or I can stay home on Sunday and do it.

3. Stan likes seafood but he hates lobster.

4. Theresa will fix dinner for all of us, or we can go out to Milano's.

5. The flu always makes me feel exhausted, and gives me a headache.

6. We will put our furniture in storage, and sell the house.

7. Linda is not going to the bar with us for she is only sixteen.

8. An airplane flew low over the stadium, and dropped leaflets on the crowd.

9. We opened the door and yelled for Champ but he did not come.

10. I did not order a pizza but the man from Domino's insisted that I had.

EXERCISE 8B-6

Correct any errors in the following sentences. All errors will involve using commas and coordinating conjunctions to join independent clauses. Each sentence may contain no errors, one error, or more than one error.

1. Nancy jumped into her noisy old Ford station wagon, and drove off for California.

2. Vic was late for class, Donald didn't show up at all.

3. My check for this semester's tuition bounced for I had forgotten to deposit my paycheck.

4. Cheryl wants to have the party here at school, but Dot wants to rent a ballroom downtown.

5. I don't think we can get Gus to change his mind, but Jean wants to try.

6. George must have fallen asleep at the wheel, or hit an icy spot in the road.

7. Sally got her paper in on time and Jerry was late as usual.

8. I refuse to go to Washington, it is too expensive.

9. The horse has got to stop sleeping in the house or I am leaving.

10. We will hold the dance in the basement, and hope that not too many people show up.

11. Phillip's is a great seafood restaurant and they serve good roast beef there too.

12. My teacher and his office mate were having an argument so I left.

13. The line at the movie was very long so I decided to go home, and read a book.

14. Dawn wanted to go skydiving, but I thought it was too expensive.

15. I will vacuum the rugs, you get started on the dishes.

16. Her dress was very wrinkled and it didn't fit her very well.

17. He's easy to get along with, and doesn't take things too seriously.

18. Thelma came to school early, and went straight to the dean's office.

19. Joanne arrived in Tampa and walked into the airport but her husband was not there to greet her.

20. My mother and the woman who lives next door took a trip to Hawaii and had a wonderful time.

 ## EXERCISE 8B-7

Correct any errors in the following paragraph. All errors will involve using commas and coordinating conjunctions.

Sometimes I think teachers don't understand what it is like to be a student. Just last Wednesday, my English teacher assigned twenty-five pages of reading, and asked us to write an essay by Friday. I would have gotten it all done but my math teacher also gave us a long assignment. She asked us to do ten problems by Friday and each one of them took me thirty minutes. My psychology teacher had scheduled a quiz for the same Friday, and refused to reschedule it when we told her how things were piling up. I don't mind doing homework, but sometimes the assignments are impossible to get done. I wish some of my teachers would talk to each other, and coordinate the homework.

 ## EXERCISE 8B-8

This is a new kind of exercise, one you have not seen before in this book. Each item consists of two or more parts. In the space following each item, write one grammatical sentence that combines the given parts. For most of these items, there is more than one correct way to combine the given parts. Where appropriate, you should join them with a comma and a coordinating conjunction since that is what you have been working on in this section.

Examples:

a. 1. Maurice opened the windows.
   2. The room didn't get any cooler.

Maurice opened the windows, but the room didn't get any cooler.

b. 1. Dave climbed into the old pickup.
   2. Started the engine.

Dave climbed into the old pickup and started the engine.

1. a. Jo put a lot of ice in the cooler.
   b. Janet filled the picnic basket.

2. a. Barry opened his chemistry book to Chapter 1.
   b. Started reading about elements.

3. a. I can't go grocery shopping until Friday.
   b. I am flat broke.

4. a. I had hoped to get a B on my paper.
   b. To bring my semester's average up to a C.

5. a. Dan looked like a real cowboy.
   b. Rode a horse like a dude.

6. a. It looked like rain.
   b. We postponed the softball game.

7. a. I took a lot of notes and attended the review session.
   b. I got a C on the final exam.

8. a. Kimberly ran up to her room.
   b. Burst into tears.

9. a. Either you say you're sorry.
   b. I will punch you in the face.

10. **a.** It is too late for the early movie.
 b. I am awfully tired anyway.
 c. Let's stay home and sit by the fire.

DISCUSSION OF INDUCTIVE EXERCISES

EXERCISE 8B-1

Exercise 8B-1 illustrates that whenever you have two independent clauses joined by "and," "but," "or," "for," "so," "yet," or "nor," you must also have a comma *in front of* the joining word. The following diagram illustrates this rule:

		and		
		but		
__(independent clause)__	,	or	__(independent clause)__	
		for		
		so		
		yet		
		nor		

The seven words listed above are called coordinating conjunctions; they are the only words that can be used in this way. You should memorize this list.

Notice also that, when one of the coordinating conjunctions is used to join two *independent clauses,* a comma must be placed *in front* of the conjunction, and there is no punctuation following the conjunction.

EXERCISE 8B-4

These sentences illustrate that when a coodinating conjunction is used to join anything that is *not* two independent clauses, it is wrong to place a comma in front of the conjunction.

Part C · Semicolons with Independent Clauses

In Part B you learned to join two independent clauses with a comma and a coordinating conjunction. In this section you will learn another option for joining two independent clauses.

 ## EXERCISE 8C-1 _____

The following examples illustrate how to use a semicolon to avoid or correct comma splices or run-ons. Study the examples and make sure you understand how to use this option. It may make things clearer if you put brackets around the independent clauses.

1. **a.** Correct: My mother is very depressed; she thinks her children don't like her.
   b. Incorrect: My mother is very depressed, she thinks her children don't like her.
   c. Incorrect: My mother is very depressed she thinks her children don't like her.

2. **a.** Correct: This dress is too expensive; perhaps it will go on sale soon.
   b. Incorrect: This dress is too expensive, perhaps it will go on sale soon.
   c. Incorrect: This dress is too expensive perhaps it will go on sale soon.

3. **a.** Correct: The weather does not look promising for this weekend; the forecast calls for six inches of snow.
   b. Incorrect: The weather does not look promising for this weekend, the forecast calls for six inches of snow.
   c. Incorrect: The weather does not look promising for this weekend the forecast calls for six inches of snow.

NOTE: A discussion of the answers to this exercise can be found on pages 190–191.

EXERCISE 8C-2

Correct any errors in the following sentences. The errors will all involve comma splices or run-on sentences. Use semicolons to correct these errors.

1. My car is in the repair shop, the brakes are being relined.

2. I loved the movie last night it was about my hometown.

3. We have to go soon it is getting late.

4. Please hand me a pot holder, they are in the top left-hand drawer.

5. This book is extremely old, it was written in the eighteenth century.

6. My calculus class was cancelled this morning the teacher is sick.

7. Jack is not going to the dance, he has to work at the sub shop.

8. Arnie had never seen a sheep before, he grew up in the city.

9. I can't open the wine I don't have a corkscrew.

10. This has been a terrible day I lost my purse on the bus.

EXERCISE 8C-3

The following examples illustrate a potential problem in the use of semicolons. Study these examples carefully and try to figure out why the incorrect versions are incorrect.

If you have trouble, try putting brackets around the independent clauses. Then see if you can figure out what the principle is.

1. **a.** Correct: Charlie washed the clothes; Chris cooked the dinner.
   b. Incorrect: While Charlie washed the clothes; Chris cooked the dinner.

2. **a.** Correct: Madge took charge of things at the accident; she used to be a nurse.

     b. Incorrect: Madge took charge of things at the accident; because she used to be a nurse.

3. **a.** Correct: I'm sure that man is the new mayor; I saw his picture in this morning's paper.

     b. Incorrect: I'm sure that man is the new mayor; because I saw his picture in this morning's paper.

4. **a.** Correct: Dennis is growing the usual vegetables in his garden, like lettuce, tomatoes, and squash.

     b. Incorrect: Dennis is growing the usual vegetables in his garden; like lettuce, tomatoes, and squash.

5. **a.** Correct: I love fancy sports cars, for example, Corvettes and Porsches.

     b. Incorrect: I love fancy sports cars; for example, Corvettes and Porsches.

NOTE: A discussion of the answers to this exercise can be found on page 191.

EXERCISE 8C-4

Correct any errors in the following sentences. The errors will all involve punctuating independent clauses. In cases where you remove the semicolon, don't worry about whether to insert a comma or not. You will learn that comma rule in Chapter 10.

1.   I really liked eating at Sabatino's; since I love Italian food.

2.   My garden is not a success this year; because the rabbits have been eating everything.

3.   My aunt has a number of health problems, like high blood pressure and shortness of breath.

4.   Until the price of houses comes down, I am going to stay in this apartment.

5.   We went to visit my uncle; who has been sick for a month.

6.   Cheryl likes to do the unusual; like skydiving and scuba diving.

7.   The botany course was not easy, for we had to memorize the Latin names of a lot of plants.

8.   Nan has not been home in four years she is from New Mexico.

9.   It looks like Lou may get the job; only one other candidate is still being considered.

10. There is lots to eat in the refrigerator; like hard-boiled eggs, salad, cheese, and pickles.

EXERCISE 8C-5

Correct any errors in the following sentences. The errors will all involve punctuating independent clauses.

1. There is only one thing that really makes me mad; a man who doesn't respect women.

2. My options are very limited, I have to do something that costs less than three dollars.

3. We are not going to Larry's party; he didn't invite us.

4. I am allergic to many foods; such as tomatoes and cucumbers.

5. Ramon loaned me fifty dollars he knows I will pay him back.

6. Give me a call when you arrive in Chicago.

7. A test that requires a lot of writing; is the hardest kind.

8. I handed your note to the woman who answered the door.

9. Don't try to call Dawn tonight her phone is broken.

10. We can't go to the movie; it started a half hour ago.

11. Paul did not look at the map; because he thought he knew the way.

12. I go to the movies for entertainment I don't want to be depressed.

13. The salad had a lot of unusual things in it; for example, broccoli, alfalfa sprouts, and chick-peas.

14. I gave five dollars to the man who was collecting for the March of Dimes he seemed pleased.

15. Juanita can take care of that cut because she used to be a nurse.

16. My mother was raised in Atlanta; she still has her southern accent.

17. My baby had all the childhood diseases, like mumps and chicken pox.

18. George loves to go to the circus; because he has always wanted to be a clown.

19. I got a note from the library; it said I have an overdue book.

20. I don't have any problem with semicolons I just don't use them.

 EXERCISE 8C-6

Correct any errors in the following paragraph. Use semicolons to make corrections wherever they are appropriate.

Ms. Feldman is extremely interesting. Even though she is almost seventy years old; she often acts like she is about twenty. She loves to dress in young-looking clothes; such as, blue jeans and sweat-shirts. She always listens to rock music. Ms. Feldman is also very active, she plays tennis often and jogs every evening. She beat me easily the last time I played tennis with her. Ms. Feldman even goes out on dates her husband died over twenty years ago. I hope I have as much fun as she does when I'm seventy years old.

 EXERCISE 8C-7 _____

Each of the following items consists of two parts. In the space below each one, rewrite the two parts combined into one grammatical sentence. Use semicolons where they are appropriate.

Examples:

   a. 1. I am learning word processing at work.
      2. My boss thinks it will make me more productive.

I am learning word processing at work; my boss thinks it will make me more productive.

   b. 1. Katrina opened the letter slowly.
      2. Because she feared its contents.

Katrina opened the letter slowly because she feared its contents.

1. a. My mother has never smoked.
   b. She thinks it is sinful.

2. a. I cannot go to the concert tonight.
   b. I must study for my psych test.

3. a. Steve will not be swimming for the team this year.
   b. He broke his leg riding his bike.

4. a. I didn't like the interview of Mario Cuomo on the news last night.
   b. Because Roger Mudd was too sarcastic.

5. a. Lorna has many talents.
   b. Like playing the piano and writing poetry.

6. a. I have to get a job this summer.
   b. All of my savings are gone.

7. **a.** It was the best bird walk we had ever taken.
   b. We saw forty-five different kinds of birds.

8. **a.** Manuel reported the score of the game.
   b. To the man who answered the phone.

9. **a.** We need lots of things for our house.
   b. For example, a coffeepot, a lawn mower, and a vacuum cleaner.

10. **a.** Bernie is feeling terrible.
    b. He is coming down with a cold.

DISCUSSION OF INDUCTIVE EXERCISES

EXERCISE 8C-1

These examples show that it is sometimes correct to use a semicolon to join two independent clauses. Also, as you learned in Part A of this chapter, it is always wrong to join two independent clauses with a comma or to run them together with no punctuation.

In the English language, it is possible to get by without ever using a semicolon. There are plenty of people who have good jobs, own color televisions, take vacations in the Caribbean, have well-adjusted children, and who have never used a semicolon in their lives. Anytime a semicolon is appropriate, they just use a period and start a new sentence. Nevertheless, their writing would be improved if they learned to use semicolons because sometimes a semicolon is more effective than a period.

The following series of examples will clarify when a semicolon is appropriate, if you should choose to use one.

a. I work for a very insecure man. Cherry tomatoes are delicious in salads. Traffic is getting worse every year. Helen always gives a big Christmas party. All wars are hard on people.

Paragraph a demonstrates that, if the sentences are not somewhat linked to one another, the paragraph won't make sense. In fact, it is probably wrong to refer to something like paragraph a as a paragraph.

b. My mother is now living in Virginia. I see her often. She is sixty years old. She has an interesting occupation. She does Japanese flower arranging.

Every sentence in this paragraph has something to do with the sentence that comes before it and the one following it. If the sentences were not linked in this way, the paragraph would not make sense.

Sometimes, however, a particular pair of sentences will be more closely related than normal sentences in a paragraph. Consider, for example, the last two sentences in paragraph b:

c. She has an interesting occupation.
d. She does Japanese flower arranging.

These two sentences are even more closely related than the others in this paragraph. To indicate this closer relationship, a semicolon could be used to join them:

e. She has an interesting occupation; she does Japanese flower arranging.

A period would be completely correct here, but a semicolon indicates more exactly the close relationship between the two sentences. In cases like this, a semicolon is more sophisticated and more informative than a period.

Of course, it is always acceptable to use a period instead of a semicolon. Also, there are many cases where either punctuation mark is effective. The sentences in the following exercises, however, are good examples of the kinds of sentences that call for a semicolon.

EXERCISE 8C-3

You should have figured out from this exercise that you may not use a semicolon unless it is joining two independent clauses.
Again, a diagram:

_____(independent clause)_____ ; _____(independent clause)_____

Part D · Semicolons with Conjunctive Adverbs

Up to this point in this chapter, you have learned three options for joining independent clauses:

Option 1: You may join the independent clauses with a period.

_____(independent clause)_____ . _____(independent clause)_____

Option 2: You may join the independent clauses with a comma and a coordinating conjunction.

	and	
_____(independent clause)_____ ,	but or for so yet nor	_____(independent clause)_____

Option 3: You may join the independent clauses with a semicolon.

_____(independent clause)_____ ; _____(independent clause)_____

EXERCISE 8D-1 _____

The following examples illustrate another principle involved in punctuating independent clauses. Study these examples carefully and try to figure out why numbers 2 and 4 are incorrect.

   1. Correct: Mark loves commas, but he hates apostrophes.
   2. Incorrect: Mark loves commas, however he hates apostrophes.

   3. Correct: I did well on the final exam, but I am still getting a C in the course.
   4. Incorrect: I did well on the final exam, however I am still getting a C in the course.

NOTE: A discussion of the answers to this exercise can be found on page 197.

 EXERCISE 8D-2 _____

Study the following sentences and try to figure out an additional punctuation rule when there is a "however" in the second independent clause.

   1. a. Correct: Mark loves commas; however, he hates apostrophes.
      b. Incorrect: Mark loves commas; however he hates apostrophes.

   2. a. Correct: I did well on the final exam; however, I am still getting a C in the course.
      b. Incorrect: I did well on the final exam; however I am still getting a C in the course.

   3. a. Correct: We arrived at the station five minutes late. However, the train had not arrived.
      b. Incorrect: We arrived at the station five minutes late. However the train had not arrived.

   4. a. Correct: The price was very reasonable. However, we still could not afford the payments.
      b. Incorrect: The price was very reasonable. However we still could not afford the payments.

NOTE: A discussion of the answers to this exercise can be found on page 197.

 EXERCISE 8D-3 _____

Correct any errors in the following sentences. All errors will involve punctuating independent clauses. Each sentence may contain no errors, one error, or more than one error.

   1. Kathy looks like my sister, however, she doesn't act like her.

   2. Jim tried out for the play; however he did not get the part.

   3. My boss gives me a lot of work to do; however, he pays me well.

   4. The movie was very violent; but, I enjoyed it.

   5. Traffic was awful this morning, however; Dot was not late for work.

   6. His typing has improved; however, his spelling has gotten worse.

   7. Melanie hurt her hand; but she will play in tonight's game anyway.

8. Fred runs every morning, however, he has not lost any weight.

9. Annie opened a used clothes shop; however, she has not made any money.

10. My suitcase was lost by the airline however they paid me two hundred dollars in compensation.

In Exercises 8D-1 and 8D-2, you learned how to punctuate a sentence containing two independent clauses when the word "however" appeared in the second clause. The word "however" is a conjunctive adverb, and it is not the only one. The words in the following list are also conjunctive adverbs. Actually, the ones with two or more words are called "transitional expressions" in most books, but they are punctuated just like conjunctive adverbs, so we will just call them all conjunctive adverbs.

also	in fact
as a result	instead
consequently	meanwhile
finally	nevertheless
for example	of course
furthermore	still
however	then
in addition	therefore
indeed	thus

 EXERCISE 8D-4

Fill in the blanks in the following sentences with a word from the list of conjunctive adverbs. Be sure the word you choose for each blank really fits there. Sometimes more than one word will fit; in these cases, choose the one you think works best.

1. Dana is taking five courses this semester; _____ , she is working twenty hours per week.

2. Max is hard to get along with; _____ , he frequently is moody.

3. Stacy had intended to open a savings account; _____ , she bought a new Mustang.

4. Sylvia sprained her ankle badly; _____ , she has had to stop jogging for a few weeks.

5. I like Allison; _____ , I don't think that she would make a good chairperson.

6. I want to finish my homework; _____ , I will play cards.

7. We all went to the ocean last summer; _____ , we want to do something different this year.

8. Sid is a very good poet; _____ , he has published several poems in magazines.

9. They dried their hair and put on makeup; _____ , they were ready to go.

10. Howard took four aspirin; _____ , he went to bed.

EXERCISE 8D-5

The following examples illustrate another principle involved in punctuating independent clauses. Notice that, in these examples, both the a and the b versions are correct. Study these examples carefully and try to figure out what this principle is.

1. a. Ms. Rudick has many hobbies, for example, hunting, fishing, and clogging.
    b. Ms. Rudick has many hobbies; for example, she goes clogging every Friday night.

2. a. At first I was angry, then, sad.
    b. At first I was angry; then, I was sad.

3. a. I bought a lot of bread, in fact, four loaves.
    b. I bought a lot of bread; in fact, I bought more than we need.

NOTE: A discussion of the answers to this exercise can be found on page 197.

EXERCISE 8D-6

Now you know how to use conjunctive adverbs and how to punctuate them. Proofread the following sentences carefully and correct any errors. All errors will involve punctuating independent clauses. Each sentence may contain no errors, one error, or more than one error.

1. My bill was overdue, therefore, I carried it down to the office in person.

2. I had already seen the movie; however, I didn't mind seeing it again.

3. My hometown was sleepy and quiet, for example; we had only one stoplight.

4. Rita forgot her umbrella, as a result, she got completely soaked.

5. My brother likes very unusual sports; for example, rugby, squash, and water polo.

6. The food is really much better at the Stone Inn; also they have plenty of parking.

7. We hoped that Margie would win the tournament; yet, we knew she didn't have much of a chance.

8. The new apartment had two bathrooms, as a result; we could all sleep fifteen minutes later in the mornings.

9. Kwok had two flat tires yesterday, in addition, he did not have a spare.

10.   Gerry put away the groceries; meanwhile, Nancy made a salad.

11.   I want to go to New York this summer; but, I don't have the money.

12.   We ordered a spinach salad, instead the waiter brought us spinach pie.

13.   The war had started. Therefore most young men had to change their career plans.

14.   The parking lot was full consequently we parked across the street.

15.   Most mushrooms are harmless, still some can make you sick.

16.   For dessert Jessica ordered a chocolate mousse; instead they brought her a chocolate moose.

17.   We were irritated that Lennette was so clumsy; so, we yelled at her.

18.   We walked from Fifty-third Street to Eightieth Street; finally, we arrived at the museum.

19.   My garden is doing very well this summer, as a result I have more tomatoes than I need.

20.   This is the last of these sentences, therefore; I hope you understand them.

 EXERCISE 8D-7

Proofread the following paragraph and correct any errors. All errors will involve punctuating independent clauses.

Being a single parent is not easy, in fact it is very hard. The biggest problem is a lack of time. There is never enough time to do everything that needs to be done; for example I haven't waxed my kitchen floor in two years. Another problem is that I don't give my daughter enough attention. Just getting all the work done leaves me exhausted, as a result; I hardly ever get to just sit and talk with her. Another person who sometimes gets neglected is me. I never seem to have a chance to do anything I like to do; such as, reading a book. Sometimes I feel a little depressed; however, I always snap out of it after a few days.

 EXERCISE 8D-8

Each of the following items contains two parts. In the space below each one, rewrite the two parts combined into one grammatical sentence. Try to use a conjunctive adverb to join them. Make sure you punctuate them correctly.

Examples:

a. 1. Nguyen does not have a car.
   2. She takes a bus to work.

Nguyen does not have a car; therefore, she takes a bus to work.

b. 1. I invited Buz to dinner.
   2. I do not think that he is coming.

I invited Buz to dinner; however, I do not think he is coming.

1. a. I have a cold.
   b. I am not going to the party.

2. a. I studied my statistics assignment for four hours.
   b. I don't understand it at all.

3. a. Barb is a great dancer.
   b. She won a contest when she was in Los Angeles last summer.

4. a. I like most seafood.
   b. I hate lobster.

5. a. My car is burning too much oil.
   b. It is running very rough.

6. a. My grades are going to be much better this semester.
   b. I am getting all A's.

7. a. We should get the children to bed.
   b. We can wrap their gifts.

8. a. They worked for five hours on the chemistry homework.
   b. They gave up.

9. a. Donna is a registered nurse.
   b. She makes more money than I do.

10. a. Paula is mad at her boyfriend.
    b. She will get over it.

DISCUSSION OF INDUCTIVE EXERCISES

EXERCISE 8D-1

  1. Correct: Mark loves commas, but he hates apostrophes.
  2. Incorrect: Mark loves commas, however he hates apostrophes.

Sentence 1 is joined using option 1. It consists of two independent clauses ("Mark loves commas" and "he hates apostrophes") joined by a comma and a coordinating conjunction ("but").

     Sentence 2 is identical to sentence 1, except the word "however" has been substituted for the word "but." This one change, however, has made the sentence incorrect, because "however" is not a coordinating conjunction. Since option 1 requires that the two independent clauses be joined by a coordinating conjunction, option 1 no longer applies. To correct sentence 2, we need to use option 2 or 3 as you can see in the following examples:

    Mark loves commas; however he hates apostrophes.
    Mark loves commas. However he hates apostrophes.

As you will learn shortly, these sentences are not yet completely correct. The punctuation between the words "commas" and "however" is correct in both sentences, however. Either a period or a semicolon is acceptable in this situation, although the semicolon is probably the more frequent choice of good writers.

     Sentences 3 and 4 illustrate the same principle.

EXERCISE 8D-2

You can see from these examples that the word "however" must be followed by a comma.

EXERCISE 8D-5

The pairs of sentences demonstrate that these conjunctive adverbs are not always used in sentences with two independent clauses. You have to check. If the words following the conjunctive adverb are not an independent clause, then you may *not* put a semicolon in front of the conjunctive adverb.

REVIEW

EXERCISE 8-REVIEW-1

Correct any errors in the following items. All errors will involve punctuating independent clauses. Each item may contain no errors, one error, or more than one error.

1. I wanted Jesse to come with us, he knows his way around Ocean City.

2. I am getting a blister on my thumb, however, I do not want to quit playing.

3. She thought she had all the ingredients for a Bavarian chocolate cake; but she had forgotten about the eggs.

4. My stapler is broken it just chews up the paper.

5. I read the morning paper, and my wife reads the evening one.

6. The owner of the building pushed the door open; and stormed into my office.

7. He drank fourteen cans of beer; consequently we had to carry him home.

8. Jesus is trying to run two miles every morning, and to lose ten pounds in the next three months.

9. I hurried to the post office but it was closed when I got there.

10. I have never been to Las Vegas and I have no intention of going now.

11. The picnic has been called off; so let's all get together at my house.

12. My father made a phone call, and then drove away without saying a word.

13. This weekend I am working on my term paper; it is due next Tuesday.

14. I hoped to get a part in the play; yet, I knew my chances were not very good.

15. Marcia really liked Ben's looks, he reminded her of an old friend.

16. I wanted chocolate chip but I got mocha chocolate.

17. Sometime I like country music sometimes I hate it.

18. He ran as hard as he could yet he only came in third.

19. The cake is delicious, nevertheless, I cannot eat another bite.

20. Joanne lost fourteen pounds on her diet, I only lost six.

EXERCISE 8-REVIEW-2

Correct any errors in the following items. All the errors will involve punctuating independent clauses. Each item may contain no errors, one error, or more than one error.

1. Jeff works at University Hospital, he is a radiologist.

2. My cousin opened her own restaurant and now she is making lots of money.

3. Dolly is always volunteering to do community work; like working as a candy striper at the hospital.

4. Houng wants to buy a new stereo system, however, he knows that he can't afford it.

5. When Leroy bet one hundred dollars on a very sad-looking horse, he won.

6. Jeannine went to work for a huge firm, and hated every minute that she worked there.

7. I will not be going to school tomorrow; because it is my birthday.

8. Sue is always willing to help out her friends, for example; last week she drove me to work for three straight days.

9. The national problem with drug abuse is not a laughing matter it is tragic.

10. You had better pay me the fifty dollars that you owe me or I will have to take you to court.

11. My sister has one solution for problems; she cries.

12. Howard asked Mary Hunter to go to the dance; however he also asked Sylvia.

13. The ice on that pond is too thin for skating, we should wait until it is at least three inches thick.

14. The garbage truck backed down the street, and ran into my Volkswagen.

15. Stacy helped herself to more potatoes; because they are her favorite food.

16. I listened to every word she said; still, I had no idea what she wanted.

17. We laughed hard for at least five minutes it was one funny joke.

18. Dana will not talk to the boss and he won't write her a letter.

19. This morning the roads were treacherous; there was a thin layer of ice on them.

20. I am afraid of most reptiles; for instance, snakes, lizards, and alligators.

EXERCISE 8-REVIEW-3 _____

Each of the following items consists of two or more parts. Some of the parts are not complete sentences. In the space below each item, rewrite the parts combined into one grammatical sentence.

Example:

   a. Kim fell down.
   b. She hurt her ankle.
   c. She kept right on dancing.

Kim fell down and hurt her ankle, but she kept right on dancing.

1. **a.** The grass needs to be mowed.
   b. I am too tired.

2. **a.** Kevin was watching television.
   b. Doing his homework.

3. **a.** I finally found a parking place.
   b. I was too late to meet the plane.

4. **a.** My brother cleaned up the mess the baby had made.
   b. And cooked dinner.

5. **a.** I like to play bridge.
   b. In fact, I am pretty good at it.

6. **a.** The reporter took out his camera.
   b. He tried to take a picture of Margarita.
   c. She turned away from him.

7. **a.** I am not going to the movie.
   b. I cannot afford it this week.

8. **a.** I should have helped my daughter with her project.
   b. I went shopping.

9. **a.** They charged me forty-six dollars for a new battery.
   b. And fourteen dollars for labor.

10. **a.** I am taking anatomy this summer.
    b. It is really hard.

11. **a.** Denise is always getting mad at people.
    b. She always gets her way.

12. **a.** Gert read the paper.
    b. She did not see the article about me.

13. **a.** I enjoy many contemporary writers.
    b. Such as Saul Bellow, James Michener, and Norman Mailer.

14. **a.** My sister wants to be an accountant.
    b. Or a computer programmer.

15. **a.** We wanted to go to the ocean.
    b. I had a lot of homework.
    c. Rosa had to do her income taxes.

16. **a.** My car pool is breaking up.
    b. Several of us are changing jobs.

17. **a.** I remember buying gas for fifty-five cents a gallon.
    b. Seeing a movie for two dollars.

18. **a.** I do not smoke myself.
    b. Both of my children do smoke.

19. **a.** I asked for a raise.
    b. I got fired.

20. **a.** My roof sprang a leak.
    b. It will have to be repaired.
    c. I do not have the money to pay for it.

EXERCISE 8-REVIEW-4 _____

The errors in the following essay involve fragments, punctuating independent clauses, and subject-verb agreement. Read the essay carefully and correct any errors.

I have been having great trouble deciding what I want to do for a career. My basic problem is that my goals for a career is so different that no one profession can satisfy them all.

First, I hope to do something worthwhile with my life, I would like to feel that I am contributing something to the human race. I know that I can't solve all the world's problems but I would like to feel that I am making some contribution. When I gets ready to retire, I certainly do not want to feel that my work has made the world a worse place.

Second, I suppose it could be called egotism, but I want people to look up to me for my career. To admire my accomplishments. I do not want to be embarrassed about my job. When someone asks what I do for a living. I want them to be impressed when they hear my answer. Also, I want my parents to be proud of me, and to feel they did a good job of bringing me up. In short, I need a career that gives me a sense of accomplishment.

Finally, I want to make enough money to live comfortably; to provide my family with the things that will make them comfortable. I do not need to be a millionaire, however, I do want to be making at least $30,000 a year by the time I am thirty.

Unfortunately, I cannot find one career that satisfies all three goals. I would like the good feeling that I would get from being a social worker but the salaries are too low. I made fairly good money selling vacuum cleaners; but I knew the machines were extremely shoddy I always felt ashamed when I sold someone a piece of junk. Being a mortician would pay fairly well but I would be embarrassed to admit what I did for a living.

Maybe there are not one job that can satisfy all three of my goals but I intend to keep looking.

EXERCISE 8-REVIEW-5_____

Think of an organization you presently belong to, that you belonged to in the past, or that you might belong to in the future. This organization could be a company you work for, a social group, a neighborhood organization, an athletic team, a religious group, or any other group. The organization is looking for a place to hold a meeting, and they have asked you to investigate your school as a possible site. Look around campus and find a suitable location for the kind of meeting this group would have. Observe the concrete details necessary to support your proposal. Assume the college is willing to let your group use the site for a reasonable fee.

    You are going to write a letter *to the person or people within your group who would make the decision* and *convince them* to hold the meeting at your school. But before you write this letter, answer the following questions:

  1. Who will be the audience for this essay?_____

      _____

  2. What is the purpose of this essay? What are you trying to accomplish?_____

      _____

    Now use one of the methods you learned in Chapter 7 to develop a thesis for this piece of writing.

Thesis: _____

_____

_____

    Now you are going to check the thesis to ensure that it will be effective:

  1. Is the thesis a complete sentence?

      ☐ yes ☐ no revised thesis _____

      _____

  2. Does the thesis include a subject and a point about that subject?

      ☐ yes ☐ no revised thesis _____

      _____

  3. Is the thesis a statement rather than a question?

      ☐ yes ☐ no revised thesis _____

      _____

  4. Does the thesis make a point that needs to be proved rather than merely state a fact?

      ☐ yes ☐ no revised thesis _____

      _____

  5. Is the thesis appropriately focused (not too broad or vague)?

☐ yes ☐ no   revised thesis _____

_____

6. Will this thesis really satisfy the assignment?

☐ yes ☐ no   revised thesis _____

_____

7. Is this thesis really something I can write a good paper about? (Am I interested in it? Do I know enough about it?)

☐ yes ☐ no   revised thesis _____

_____

8. Is the thesis narrow enough for the paper I am going to write?

☐ yes ☐ no   revised thesis _____

_____

When you are satisfied with the thesis, write this letter. Again, don't worry about the length of the letter, although it will probably take several paragraphs to make the letter convincing.

EXERCISE 8-REVIEW-6

Now return to the essay you wrote in Exercise 8-Review-5 and make a backward outline. Use this outline to check the thesis and unity of the essay. Make any revisions you feel are necessary.

After you are satisfied with the thesis and unity, revise the paper in accordance with the following questions and instructions:

1. Does the essay do what the assignment asked you to do?
2. Are the language and content appropriate for the audience?
3. Could the essay be strengthened by the inclusion of more concrete details?
4. Proofread the paper once carefully looking only for errors in punctuating independent clauses.
5. Proofread the paper a second time looking only for fragments.
6. Proofread the paper a third time looking for errors in subject-verb agreement.
7. Finally, correct any errors you can find in spelling, punctuation, or other grammar.

9

Organizing Longer Pieces of Writing

Part A   Making a List
Part B   Revising for Organization

Part A · Making a List

In Chapter 7, you learned how to come up with a thesis and how to ensure that the essay is well unified to support that thesis. In this chapter, you will learn how to organize an essay so that it is most effective.

Imagine that the governmental body that makes academic policy at your campus (at many schools this body is called the Faculty Senate, although it might have a different name at your school) is reconsidering the whole question of grading. It is reviewing all the possibilities, including doing away with grades altogether. Students have been invited to write to the Senate expressing their views on the matter.

You have decided to write to the Senate and argue that grades should be abolished. So, in this case, you know your thesis right from the start. Your mind is just brimming with ideas about why grades should be abolished. The problem is that those ideas are completely disorganized. You need to get them down in writing and to organize them into an effective argument.

This is a fairly typical situation, one you are likely to experience many times when you have to write. Somewhere in your educational career, you were probably taught a technique for organizing your ideas: outlining. The problem with outlining is that most people don't ever use it again after they get free from their English teacher. With its Roman numerals and capital letters, its insistence that there not be a 1 unless there is a 2, and its complicated indentations of eight spaces, it seems much too formal, too time consuming, and too complicated. Of course, this is not the case for everyone.

A number of writers use formal outlining with great success. If you are one of these, please don't stop. Outlining is one effective way to get your ideas organized.

However, there is also a large group of writers that finds formal outlining too cumbersome. The problem is that this group has rejected outlining without finding anything to replace it. For most of them, once they know what they are going to write about, the next step is to start writing. They organize their papers in whatever order the ideas emerge in their minds. Sometimes this works. Sometimes the ideas do stream into their minds in a logical and effective order. But most of the time their papers end up organized in a way that is illogical and ineffective.

What we are suggesting in this chapter is a compromise. We recognize that many people are not going to make formal outlines for most of their writing. But that doesn't mean they have to go to the other extreme and write with no organizational plan at all. We suggest a much more informal and flexible system for getting organized, which we call "list making."

The first illustration of this technique involves a fairly lengthy piece of writing, and the list making is, therefore, fairly extensive. Our second example will show how the same method can be used effectively for a much shorter and simpler piece of writing.

Now, back to the paper you want to write to the Faculty Senate about grades. Using the list-making technique, the first step is to brainstorm on a sheet of paper. Remember that you were introduced to brainstorming in Chapter 7, where you used it to come up with a thesis. Here you are using the same technique to organize your ideas for the body of the essay.

If you have arrived at a thesis at this stage, as you have in the example we are working on, it is a good idea to start by writing that thesis at the top of the page. Then just write down every idea that pops into your head about the thesis. Don't worry. Don't censor. Don't edit. Just let the ideas flow. If some don't fit, that's okay. If some are repetitive, that's okay. If some are misspelled, that's okay. If some are contradictory, that's okay too. All you want to do, at this stage, is to get a lot of ideas down on paper.

When you run out of ideas, don't stop. Sometimes, the best ideas are the ones you think of only with hard work, only after you've gotten the more obvious ones out of the way. Sometimes taking a break when you run out of ideas is a good idea. When you come back fresh, you may come up with new ideas.

On the next page is an example of what your list making on the subject of grades might look like.

Thesis: Grades should be abolished at this school.

grades encourage cheating

our grading system came from the Germans'

teachers could write out evaluations

grades lead to dishonesty

some people do better on tests than others

some teachers grade harder than others

grades discourage asking
questions when you are
confused

placement tests are
often unfair

grades encourage
cramming

grades encourage the
giving of "safe" answers
instead of risky ones

grades inhibit creativity

teachers sometimes have
favorites

grades emphasize
memorizing facts
instead of thinking

a grade is any letter
or number assigned
to a student's perfor-
mance _and_ reported
to others

a single letter cannot
fairly represent an
entire semester's work

students could put
together a portfolio
of their best work

some people don't do
well on tests

employers and grad
schools could develop
evaluations

When the list is as complete as you can get it, you are ready to start "pruning." This is the stage at which you get rid of the bad ideas. You go through the list and cross out ideas for any of the following reasons:

1. The ideas are off the subject.
2. The ideas don't support the thesis.
3. The ideas are wrong or not provable.
4. The ideas are duplicates of others on the list.
5. The ideas are not appropriate for your audience or purpose.

The brainstorming list on grading has been "pruned" below. The reason for each "pruning" is given in parentheses.

Thesis: Grades should be abolished at this school.

grades encourage cheating

~~our grading system~~
~~came from the Germans~~
(doesn't support thesis)

teachers could write out
evaluations

~~grades lead to dishonesty~~
(duplicate)

some people do better
on tests than others

some teachers grade
harder than others

grades discourage asking
questions when you are
confused

a grade is any letter
or number assigned
to a student's perfor-
mance _and_ reported
to others

~~placement tests are
often unfair~~
(off the subject)
grades encourage
cramming

a single letter cannot
fairly represent an
entire semester's work

grades encourage the
giving of "safe" answers
instead of risky ones

students could put
together a portfolio
of their best work

grades inhibit creativity

~~some people don't do
well on tests~~
(duplicate)

teachers sometimes have
favorites

employers and grad
schools could develop
evaluations

grades emphasize
memorizing facts
instead of thinking

Of course, the key to this technique is flexibility. At any time, anything can be changed. After brainstorming, you might decide to revise the
thesis, or you may want to add items to the list.

Once your list is "pruned," you are ready to do some organizing.
Look through the list and identify ideas that belong together. An easy way
to group them is by placing the same letter in front of all the ideas that fit in
the same group. From your list on grading, for example, you might have
identified the following as belonging together by placing an A in front of
them:

Thesis: Grades should be abolished at this school.

grades encourage cheating

teachers could write out evaluations

some people do better on tests than others

A grades discourage asking questions when you are confused

placement tests are often unfair

A grades encourage cramming

A grades encourage the giving of "safe" answers instead of risky ones

A grades inhibit creativity

teachers sometimes have favorites

A grades emphasize memorizing facts instead of thinking

our grading system came from the Germans'

grades lead to dishonesty

some teachers grade harder than others

a grade is any letter or number assigned to a student's performance and reported to others

a single letter cannot fairly represent an entire semester's work

students could put together a portfolio of their best work

some people don't do well on tests

employers and grad schools could develop evaluations

Then you ask yourself what main idea all of these items add up to. Sometimes this main idea is actually one of the ideas in the group; at other times, you have to come up with the main idea at this stage. In this example, you decide that the main idea of the items in group A is the following:

Grades get in the way of real learning.

EXERCISE 9A-1 _____

We have typed the brainstorming list on grading below. (Of course, you would never need to type your lists; we only did it to make ours easier for you to work with.)

Thesis: Grades should be abolished at this school.

B   grades encourage cheating   ~~our grading system came from the Germans~~'

teachers could write out evaluations   ~~grades lead to dishonesty~~

some people do better on tests than others   B   some teachers grade harder than others

A   grades discourage asking questions when you are confused   a grade is any letter or number assigned to a student's performance *and* reported to others

~~placement tests are often unfair~~

a single letter cannot fairly represent an entire semester's work

A   grades encourage cramming

A   grades encourage the giving of "safe" answers instead of risky ones   students could put together a portfolio of their best work

A   grades inhibit creativity   ~~some people don't do well on tests~~

teachers sometimes have favorites

employers and grad schools could develop evaluations

A   grades emphasize memorizing facts instead of thinking

We have placed an A in front of each item that belongs in the group about "grades get in the way of real learning." Go through the list and place each of the other items in a group by writing a letter in front of it. We've helped you get started by placing a few B's. Find other items that belong in this B group. Then continue to identify groups until all of the items are accounted for. It is possible to have a group with only one item in it. (See how flexible this system is!)

NOTE: A discussion of the answers to this exercise can be found on page 215.

EXERCISE 9A-2 _____

Using the organization of the brainstorming list on the preceding page, decide on the main idea for each group. Remember that the main idea may be one of the items already in the group, or it may be a statement you derive from looking over the items in the group.

A.   *Grades get in the way of real learning.*

B. _____

_____

C. _____

_____

D. _____

_____

NOTE: A discussion of the answers to this exercise can be found on page 216.

EXERCISE 9A-3 _____

After you have determined what the main ideas of your paper will be, and before you are ready to start writing, you need to decide the most effective order to present the main ideas in.

Look over the four main ideas we came up with on the preceding page and decide what order you would present them in if you were actually writing the paper. What order will be most effective for your purpose with this audience?

1. _____

_____

2. _____

_____

3. _____

_____

4. _____

_____

NOTE: A discussion of the answers to this exercise can be found on page 216.

Before you do any of this organizing completely on your own, let's consider a much simpler example.

Suppose you need to send a memo to everyone in your office telling them about a meeting. Even though the process will be much simpler than the last one, because what you need to say is much less complicated, you still will benefit from list making.

First, you make a list of what you want to say in the memo:

time
date
who should come
subject of meeting
place
what to bring

Then, since this is a very short piece of writing, skip the stage of making groups. Instead, treat each item as if it were a separate group and number them in the most effective order:

⑤ time
④ date
② who should come
① subject of meeting
③ place
⑥ what to bring

Finally, using this list, you write the memo:

TO: Sales Office
FROM: Marion Wetzel
SUBJECT: Staff Meeting

I am calling a meeting to discuss a proposed revision of the policy for hiring new salespeople. If you have any interest in this issue, please come to this meeting.

We will meet in the third floor conference room on Thursday, October 23, from 3:00 to 5:00. Please bring your copy of the current hiring policy.

cc: E. B. Jimenez

Using list making in this way takes only a few minutes and ensures that what you write is well organized.

This list making is intended to be very flexible. You will probably want to adapt it to your own approach to writing, but something like what we've been working on will help greatly in improving the organization of your writing.

EXERCISE 9A-4

In this exercise you will organize a short piece of writing something like the preceding example.

Think of something you have bought that turned out to be defective. If you can't think of an actual case, just imagine one. You are going to write a brief letter asking that your money be returned because the merchandise was defective.

Don't actually write the letter; instead, answer the following questions:

1. Who will be the audience for this letter?_____

    _____

2. What is the purpose of this letter? What are you trying to

    accomplish?_____

    _____

3. What will be the thesis?_____

_____

4. Make a list of the main ideas you would include in this letter:

5. Go back to your list and eliminate any ideas that don't support the thesis. Then, number the ideas in the most effective order.

6. Finally, on a separate piece of paper, write the letter.

EXERCISE 9A-5

Revise your letter using the following checklist.

1. Does the letter have a clear thesis?
2. Does everything in the letter support that thesis?
3. Does the letter do what the assignment asked you to do?
4. Are the language and content appropriate for the audience?
5. Could the letter be strengthened by the inclusion of more concrete details?
6. Proofread the letter once carefully looking only for errors in punctuating independent clauses.
7. Proofread the letter a second time looking only for fragments.
8. Proofread the letter a third time looking for errors in subject-verb agreement.
9. Finally, correct any other errors you find.

EXERCISE 9A-6

For this assignment, you will do a slightly longer piece of writing, one that more closely resembles what you are asked to do in college courses.

Select one of the following topics and write a short essay to your English instructor about it. In this essay, you will attempt to convince your professor to agree with your position.

The possible topics are as follows:

1. In addition to the income it provides, why is work important to human beings?
2. Is there any way to defend sex and/or violence on TV?
3. Is it justifiable to require students to take certain courses?
4. Should college credit be given for developmental courses?
5. Are the laws requiring the wearing of seat belts in cars or helmets by motorcyclists a good idea?

Before you begin writing the paper, of course, you will need to do some planning. To accomplish this, answer the following questions:

1. Who will be the audience for this essay?_____
   _____
   _____

2. What is the purpose of this essay? What are you trying to accomplish?_____
   _____
   _____

3. What will be the thesis?_____
   _____
   _____

4. Now, brainstorm—make a list of ideas for this essay (if you need more room, use a separate sheet of paper):

5. Go back to your list and eliminate any ideas that don't work. Then, form your ideas into groups by placing letters in front of them.

6. In the spaces below, list the main ideas of each group. We've given you room enough for ten main ideas, but you probably won't need that many. Just use the spaces you need. Then, in the spaces in front of the letters, number them in the most effective order.

_____   A   _____
             _____

_____   B   _____
             _____

_____   C   _____
             _____

_____   D   _____
             _____

_____   E   _____
             _____

_____   F   _____
             _____

_____ G _____

_____

_____ H _____

_____

_____ I _____

_____

_____ J _____

_____

7. Finally, on separate paper, write the essay. You will revise it in Part B of this chapter.

DISCUSSION OF INDUCTIVE EXERCISES

EXERCISE 9A-1

There is some room for argument about some of these, but the following is one way you might have organized the items from the brainstorming list.

Thesis: Grades should be abolished at this school.

B grades encourage cheating

~~our grading system came from the Germans'~~

C teachers could write out evaluations

~~grades lead to dishonesty~~

B some people do better on tests than others

B some teachers grade harder than others

A grades discourage asking questions when you are confused

D a grade is any letter or number assigned to a student's performance *and* reported to others

~~placement tests are often unfair~~

A grades encourage cramming

B a single letter cannot fairly represent an entire semester's work

A grades encourage the giving of "safe" answers instead of risky ones

C students could put together a portfolio of their best work

A grades inhibit creativity

~~some people don't do well on tests~~

B teachers sometimes have favorites

C employers and grad schools could develop evaluations

A grades emphasize memorizing facts instead of thinking

EXERCISE 9A-2

Your main ideas are undoubtedly worded differently from ours, and they could be in another order, but they should look something like the following:

A. Grades get in the way of real learning.
B. The grading system is unfair.
C. There are reasonable alternatives to grades.
D. A definition of the term "grade."

EXERCISE 9A-3

The four main ideas should have been organized as follows:

1. A definition of the term "grade."

    (If you are going to define a key term, as this paper does, it makes sense to do it early in the paper—before you start using the term.)

2. The grading system is unfair.

3. Grades get in the way of real learning.

    (Numbers 2 and 3 could just as easily be reversed. There doesn't seem to be a clear preference for one before the other.)

4. There are reasonable alternatives to grades.

    (This clearly should come last. It doesn't make sense to talk about the alternatives until you have shown that there is something wrong with the current system. Once you have done that [in 2 and 3], then it makes sense to discuss alternate methods.)

Part B · Revising for Organization

Back in Chapter 7, you learned a technique, backward outlining, to check the unity of your writing. In this section you will learn how to use backward outlining to check the organization of your ideas.

EXERCISE 9B-1 _____

Use the backward outlining technique that you learned in Chapter 7 to make an outline of the following essay. To do this, you will need to follow the following steps:

1. Identify the thesis of the essay.
2. Identify the topic sentence of each paragraph.
3. Remember that introductory, closing, and transitional paragraphs usually don't have topic sentences. You just identify them as introductory, closing, or transitional.

To make this easier, we have provided spaces at the end of the essay for the outline. Read the essay and fill in the outline in the spaces provided. The letters in front of each paragraph are there for ease of identification.

[A] Of course, divorce is no fun; in fact, it's downright painful for everyone involved. My own divorce a year and a half ago was no exception. My two daughters, my husband, and I experienced a lot of pain while it was going on. At times, I thought I would never be happy again. However, some good things came out of my divorce. To be more specific, I learned a lot about myself that I never would have realized while I was "happily married."

[B] Until I had my financial situation under control, I had no interest in dating other men. But once my job and education were arranged, I started to think about dating. My problem was that I didn't have much confidence. During my marriage, I had gotten the idea that I was not very attractive because my husband often teased me about being skinny. At this time, along came Joe, my dentist's partner. He had been divorced for two years, and he was very good to me. Joe helped me realize that I really was an attractive woman, and he also fixed my kids' teeth for free.

[C] I didn't marry until I was twenty-six, but lots of kids today are getting married at seventeen or eighteen. By the time they are twenty-one, most of them have been through a divorce. I think that marrying too early is one of the major reasons so many marriages break up.

[D] When I first got divorced, I was quite worried that, if I was able to get a job and also to start dating again, I would have no time left for my children. I thought that it was essential for me always to be available in case they needed me. What I discovered after I got a job and started seeing Joe was that I had actually been spending too much time with them. Because I had felt lonely, I had focused all my attention on them. Also, because I had felt quite depressed, I was often quite cross with them. Now that I'm a lot busier, I still spend as much time with them as they need, and, because I'm feeling better about myself, I am able to respond much better to them. Even though I'm busier, I'm a better mother than ever.

[E] When my husband moved out, I found I had to support myself and my two girls on the $400 dollars he sent us each month. Since our apartment cost $265 per month, there was no way we were going to make it. It was clear that I was going to have to get a job. After a week of looking, I found a job in my dentist's office. I was sure that after a few days my dentist would realize what a terrible mistake he had made and tell me I was fired. But that didn't happen. After two months of working and my first pay raise, I began to see that I was really a fairly good receptionist. More importantly, I learned that I could support myself.

[F] After I had worked for about six months, I realized that I needed more education. I could do my job with just a high school degree, but I knew a college education would give me a lot more confidence and would help me find a better career. All it took was one phone call, and I was enrolled in my first college course. A few weeks later, I was spending every Monday and Wednesday evening in a psychology class. I found the course fascinating, and I ended up getting a B. I learned a lot of psychology, but more important to me, I learned that I was capable of doing college-level work.

[G] I used to think I was an unattractive woman who couldn't do anything but stay home and take care of the kids, and I didn't even do that very well. Now, I'm a dental receptionist, a student at Essex, a more successful mother, and a woman who has confidence in her ability to be attractive to men. I've come a long way, baby!

In the spaces below, make a backward outline of the essay you have just read. In other words, write the thesis in the first space and the topic sentence of each paragraph on the appropriate lines below.

Thesis

_____

_____

_____

Topic Sentences

[A] _____

_____

[B] _____

_____

[C] _____

_____

[D] _____

_____

[E] _____

_____

[F] _____

_____

[G] _____

_____

NOTE: A discussion of the answers to this exercise can be found on page 223.

EXERCISE 9B-2

Return to the backward outline you made in Exercise 9B-1 and decide which paragraphs you would eliminate because they don't belong in the essay. Enter the letters of any paragraphs you would like to eliminate in the following brackets: [   ]   [   ]   [   ]

Then, rearrange the remaining items in a more logical order in the spaces provided below. Place the *original* letter designations in the brackets. (There may be more spaces than you need.)

    Thesis: From my divorce, I learned a lot about myself that I never would have realized while I was "happily married."

    1. [   ] _____

_____

    2. [   ] _____

_____

3. [   ] _____
        _____

4. [   ] _____
        _____

5. [   ] _____
        _____

6. [   ] _____
        _____

7. [   ] _____
        _____

8. [   ] _____
        _____

NOTE: A discussion of the answers to this exercise can be found on pages 223–224.

EXERCISE 9B-3

The following letter is one student's response to the assignment in Chapter 8 to write a letter to an organization and recommend that they hold a meeting on your campus.

Read the letter and make a backward outline in the space following.

Dear Neal,

[A] I strongly recommend that starting in August our Dungeons and Dragons club hold its monthly meetings in Room 201 of the Student Union at Washington College.

[B] We can use this room for a very reasonable fee. Even though most of the members of the club are not students, the fact that I am a student at Washington College makes it possible for us to hold our meetings in the Student Union for a mere $4.00 per meeting. This fee covers the cost of cleaning up the room after we leave.

[C] The college is conveniently located for most of our members; it is just three blocks west of McKinley Avenue on Calvert Street. The Student Union is a large brick building right in the middle of the campus. It is easy to find because it is visible from Calvert Street as one approaches the campus.

[D] The room I recommend is a large, pleasant meeting room on the second floor; it will be perfect for our group. The room is big enough to seat seventy-five people at tables for four. Since fifty is the biggest turnout we have ever had, that should be plenty of room. Most important, the Student Union is air-conditioned. The room is extremely pleasant with a bright green rug and large windows that look out on the green campus. The ceiling lights can be adjusted to whatever brightness suits our needs.

[E] The easy availability of food will be a major addition to our meetings. Just downstairs from Room 201 is a snack bar that serves the usual junk food but also has a health food section. Everyone should be able to find something to suit his or her taste.

[F] I also recommend that we hold the business meeting at the end of our meetings instead of at the beginning as we have been doing. Since a number of the members arrive late, they miss most of the business meeting. If we hold the business meeting at the end of the evening, everyone will be there for it.

[G] Parking will be no problem if we meet at Washington College. There is a large lot right behind the Student Union in which we can park for only a quarter a night. This lot always has spaces; I've never seen it full. Also, it is well lit at night and is watched over by a security guard, so there is no safety problem.

[H] Our meeting in July convinced me that something has to be done about the location for our meetings, or we are going to start losing members. Although I arrived at the downtown Y ten minutes before eight, I reached the meeting fifteen minutes late because it took me twenty minutes to find a parking place. When I got inside, I remembered why the June meeting had been so terrible—there is no air-conditioning at the Y, and the room we meet in is too crowded for our group. The crowning blow occurred when I returned to my car and found that someone had stolen my tape deck.

[I] I strongly urge that, beginning in August, we hold our meetings in the Student Union at Washington College. Please think my proposal over, and I will call you on Friday to see if you agree.

In the spaces below, make a backward outline of the essay you have just read. In other words, write the thesis in the first space and the topic sentence of each paragraph on the appropriate lines below.

Thesis

_____

_____

_____

Topic Sentences

[A] _____

_____

[B] _____

_____

[C] _____

_____

[D] _____

_____

[E] _____

_____

[F] _____

_____

[G]　———————————————————————
　　　———————————————————————

[H]　———————————————————————
　　　———————————————————————

[I]　———————————————————————
　　　———————————————————————

NOTE: A discussion of the answers to this exercise can be found on page 224.

EXERCISE 9B-4 _____

Return to the backward outline you mde in Exercise 9B-3 and decide which paragraphs you would eliminate because they do not belong in this letter.

　　　Enter the letters of any items you would like to eliminate in the following brackets:　　[　]　　[　]　　[　]

　　　Next, rearrange the remaining items in a more logical order in the spaces provided below. Place the *original* letter designations in the brackets. (There may be more spaces than you need.)

Thesis:　I strongly recommend that starting in August our Dungeons and Dragons club hold its monthly meetings in Room 201 of the Student Union at Washington College.

1. [　]　———————————————————
　　　———————————————————

2. [　]　———————————————————
　　　———————————————————

3. [　]　———————————————————
　　　———————————————————

4. [　]　———————————————————
　　　———————————————————

5. [　]　———————————————————
　　　———————————————————

6. [　]　———————————————————
　　　———————————————————

7. [　]　———————————————————
　　　———————————————————

8. [　]　———————————————————
　　　———————————————————

9. [　]　———————————————————
　　　———————————————————

NOTE: A discussion of the answers to this exercise can be found on pages 224–226.

EXERCISE 9B-5 _____

In this exercise, you will revise the essay you wrote in Exercise 9A-6. In the space below, make a backward outline of your essay.

Thesis

_____

_____

_____

Topic Sentences

[A] _____

_____

[B] _____

_____

[C] _____

_____

[D] _____

_____

[E] _____

_____

[F] _____

_____

[G] _____

_____

[H] _____

_____

[I] _____

_____

[J] _____

_____

[K] _____

_____

[L] _____

_____

Using your backward outline and the following checklist, revise your essay.

1. Does the essay have a clear thesis?
2. Does everything in the essay support that thesis?
3. Is the essay organized logically?
4. Does the essay do what the assignment asked you to do?
5. Are the language and content appropriate for the audience?
6. Could the essay be strengthened by the inclusion of more concrete details?
7. Proofread the essay once carefully looking only for errors in punctuating independent clauses.
8. Proofread the essay a second time looking only for fragments.
9. Proofread the essay a third time looking for errors in subject-verb agreement.
10. Finally, correct any other errors you find.

DISCUSSION OF INDUCTIVE EXERCISES

EXERCISE 9B-1

The backward outline of the essay in this exercise should look something like this:

> **Thesis:** From my divorce, I learned a lot about myself that I never would have realized while I was "happily married."

[A] Introduction.
[B] Joe helped me realize that I really was an attractive woman.
[C] I feel that people today are getting married much too early.
[D] Even though I'm busier, I'm a better mother than ever.
[E] I learned that I could support myself.
[F] I learned that I was capable of doing college-level work.
[G] Closing.

EXERCISE 9B-2

Paragraphs eliminated:
[C] I feel that people today are getting married much too early.

The first decision you needed to make was to eliminate any items that didn't support the thesis. In this case, only one paragraph didn't really support the thesis: paragraph [C]. This paragraph was about divorce, but it did not say anything about the thesis. It may be true that early marriages are a cause of divorce, but that has nothing to do with what this woman learned from her divorce; in fact, she didn't marry until she was twenty-six.

The most logical order for organizing these items is as follows:

1. [A] Introduction.
2. [E] I learned that I could support myself.
3. [F] I learned that I was capable of doing college-level work.
4. [B] Joe helped me realize that I really was an attractive woman.
5. [D] Even though I'm busier, I'm a better mother than ever.
6. [G] Closing.

The number of ways to organize essays is probably infinite. To arrive at the most effective organization, you need to use your common sense to arrange the paper in an order that will make sense to the reader.

Did the original order of this essay make sense? Could you figure out why the writer presented the ideas in the order she did? Perhaps she intended to organize them in order of importance, starting with what she considered most important and continuing to the least important. That is a perfectly logical way to organize an argument, but if that was her intention in this case, she did not make it clear to the reader. Nothing in the essay indicates that the writer considers learning that a man found her attractive more important than learning that she was capable of supporting herself. If the writer chooses to organize her essay in order of the importance of the ideas, then she will have to make the relative importance of the ideas much clearer. If there is any logic to the organization of this essay as it is currently written, it is not clear to the reader, and that is a problem.

If the writer does not make clear which ideas are the most important, however, she does make something else very clear. She shows us exactly the order in which the events occurred. It is quite clear that the first problem she tackled was her financial one: She got a job. It is also clear that she didn't start dating until she had a job and had started back to school. Further, she didn't realize that she could be a better mother until she had a job, was attending classes, and was dating. Therefore, a way of organizing these ideas that seems much more logical than the original order is to organize them according to the order in which they actually occurred. This kind of organization is known as chronological or time order.

The point here is not that you should always organize your writing in chronological order, but rather that, if you will make a backward outline of your writing and then ask yourself whether the organization will seem logical to the reader, you will produce much more effective papers.

EXERCISE 9B-3

The backward outline for this piece of writing should look like this:

Thesis: I strongly recommend that starting in August our Dungeons and Dragons club hold its monthly meetings in Room 201 of the Student Union at Washington College.

[A] Introduction.
[B] We can use this room for a very reasonable fee.
[C] The college is conveniently located for most of our members.
[D] The room I am recommending is a large, pleasant meeting room on the second floor; it will be perfect for our group.
[E] The easy availability of food will be a major addition to our meetings.
[F] I also recommend that we hold the business meeting at the end of our meetings instead of at the beginning as we have been doing.
[G] Parking will be no problem.
[H] Our meeting in July convinced me that something has to be done about the location for our meetings, or we are going to start losing members.
[I] Closing.

EXERCISE 9B-4

Paragraphs eliminated:

[F] I also recommend that we hold the business meeting at the end of our meetings instead of at the beginning as we have been doing.

The thesis is that the meetings should be held in the Student Union. Paragraph [F] is about the organization of the meeting, not the location, and therefore does not support the thesis.

Revised organization:

1. [A] Introduction.
2. [H] Our meeting in July convinced me that something has to be done about the location for our meetings, or we are going to start losing members.
3. [C] The college is conveniently located for most of our members.
4. [G] Parking will be no problem.
5. [D] The room I am recommending is a large, pleasant meeting room on the second floor; it will be perfect for our group.
6. [E] The easy availability of food will be a major addition to our meetings.
7. [B] We can use this room for a very reasonable fee.
8. [I] Closing.

The biggest change was to make paragraph [H], the paragraph describing what went wrong at the July meeting, into the second paragraph. Paragraph [H] is really a description of the problem; it tells what is wrong with the old meeting place. It makes sense to tell what is wrong with the way things have been done in the past before you propose a change. Stuck near the end of the essay as it was in the original version, this paragraph seemed like an afterthought without any real purpose. Now it is clearly there to explain why the group needs to change its meeting place.

Paragraphs [C], [G], and [D] are the heart of the argument. They explain how the new location will solve the problems raised in paragraph [H]; there is plenty of parking, the room is air-conditioned, the room is large enough, and the parking is secure. We have organized these three paragraphs in this order because it is roughly chronological. First, people are going to have to find the place, then they will have to park, and finally they will come into the room.

Paragraphs [E] and [B] provide additional reasons for locating the meeting at the college, other than the ones raised by problems with the old location. [E], the paragraph on the snack bar, was placed first because it seemed a little more connected to the previous paragraph that was describing the room itself; [E] tells about another physical advantage to the proposed location. [B] points out an administrative advantage, the low fee, and, therefore, was saved until last.

Of course, there are other logical ways to organize this essay. The purpose of this chapter is not to tell you a correct format for organizing an essay, but to teach you a technique that will allow you to check the organization of your writing and to revise it when that is appropriate.

To illustrate that there can be more than one effective way to organize a piece of writing, we have organized this letter in a slightly different way below. This organization is interesting because it doesn't start with the introductory paragraph; it opens with a more interesting paragraph, the one describing the meeting in July, and doesn't actually present the thesis until the second paragraph. See what you think.

Dear Neal,

[H] Our meeting in July convinced me that something has to be done about the location for our meetings, or we are going to start losing members. Although I arrived at the downtown Y ten minutes before eight, I reached the meeting fifteen minutes late because it took me twenty minutes to find a parking place. When I got inside, I remembered why the June meeting had been so terrible—there is no air-conditioning at the Y, and the room we meet in is too crowded for our group. The crowning blow was when I returned to my car and found that someone had stolen my tape deck.

[A] I strongly recommend that starting in August our Dungeons and Dragons club hold its monthly meetings in Room 201 of the Student Union at Washington College.

[C] The college is conveniently located for most of our members; it is just three blocks west of McKinley Avenue on Calvert Street. The Student Union is a large brick building right in the middle of the campus. It is easy to find because it is visible from Calvert Street as it passes the campus.

[G] Parking will be no problem. There is a large lot right behind the Student Union which only costs a quarter a night to park in. This lot always has spaces; I've never seen it full. Also, it is well lit at night and is watched over by a security guard, so there is no safety problem.

[D] The room I am recommending is a large, pleasant meeting room on the second floor; it will be perfect for our group. The room is big enough to seat seventy-five people at tables for four. Since fifty is the biggest turnout we have ever had, that should be plenty of room. Most important, the Student Union is air-conditioned. The room is extremely pleasant with a bright green rug and large windows which look out on the green campus. The ceiling lights can be adjusted to whatever brightness suits our needs.

[E] The easy availability of food will be a major addition to our meetings. Just downstairs from Room 201 is a snack bar that serves the usual junk food but also has a health food section. Everyone should be able to find something to suit his or her taste.

[B] We can use this room for a very reasonable fee. Even though most of the members of the club are not students, the fact that I am a student at Washington College makes it possible for us to hold our meetings in the Student Union for a mere $4.00 per meeting. This fee covers the cost of cleaning up the room after we leave.

[I] I strongly urge that, beginning in August, we hold our meetings in the Student Union at Washington College. I will be calling you on Friday to see if you agree.

Again, the point of all this is not to teach you any particular organizational format. In fact, in this exercise, we have shown you two different organizations, each of which would be quite effective. The point is to show you a technique, backward outlining, which you can use to check and perhaps improve the organization of your writing.

10

Punctuating Introductory Elements

Part A   Commas with Introductory Phrases
Part B   Commas with Introductory Clauses

In this chapter, you will learn an additional set of punctuation rules. We will focus on punctuating phrases and clauses at the beginning of the sentence, although we will also consider several related situations.

Part A · Commas with Introductory Phrases

In this part, the primary skill you will learn is to punctuate a sentence with an introductory phrase. You will also learn to distinguish these from phrases that are not introductory.

 EXERCISE 10A-1

The following examples illustrate the basic principle involved in punctuating introductory phrases. In this exercise, *all* the examples are correct. Study them carefully and try to figure out what the principle is.

If you have trouble, try putting brackets around the independent clauses. Then see if you can figure out what the principle is.

1. Running after the bus, I sprained my ankle.
2. Hoping to get an A in biology, I stayed up all night studying.
3. To open the car door, I had to use a coat hanger.
4. To run in the Boston Marathon, you have to be very good.
5. In the month of June, she started her new job.
6. In the bottom of the closet, Mac found his sunglasses.

NOTE: A discussion of the answers to this exercise can be found on page 233.

EXERCISE 10A-2

Correct any errors in the following items. All errors will involve punctuating introductory elements. Some items may contain fragments that need to be corrected. Each item may contain no errors, one error, or more than one error. If the item contains no errors, just leave it alone.

Examples:

 a. With a pink scarf around her head, my daughter looked like a hippy.
 b. Letting my dog out early in the morning, I run the risk of waking my neighbors.
 c. To finish her paper by today, Connie had to stay up all night.

 1. Picking up the change from the table. Dottie noticed a foreign coin.

 2. To arrive in New York by ten-thirty, you have to take the eight o'clock train.

 3. To get the top off the peanut butter Mike had to use a screwdriver.

 4. In the top dresser drawer Kelly discovered an address book.

 5. Lifting the chair onto the platform, Lou strained his back.

 6. Driving all the way to Houston. Bonnie put five hundred miles on her car.

 7. Watching the television, Marty fell asleep. She had been up all night.

 8. From the bottom of the stairs Sue saw that I was not ready.

 9. Closing the door Fred said good night.

 10. To find a present, Victor went to eight stores.

EXERCISE 10A-3

The following examples illustrate another principle involved in punctuating introductory phrases. Study these examples carefully and try to figure out what this principle is.

  If you have trouble, try putting brackets around the independent clauses. Then see if you can figure out what the principle is.

 1. **a.** Correct: Running after the bus, I sprained my ankle.
   b. Incorrect: Running after the bus I sprained my ankle.
   c. Correct: Running after the bus is dangerous.
   d. Incorrect: Running after the bus, is dangerous.

 2. **a.** Correct: Asking a question, Ginny made a fool of herself.
   b. Incorrect: Asking a question Ginny made a fool of herself.
   c. Correct: Asking a question can be embarrassing.
   d. Incorrect: Asking a question, can be embarrassing.

 3. **a.** Correct: Finding a ten-dollar bill, Marc shouted.
   b. Incorrect: Finding a ten-dollar bill Marc shouted.
   c. Correct: Finding a ten-dollar bill was lucky.
   d. Incorrect: Finding a ten-dollar bill, was lucky.

NOTE: A discussion of the answers to this exercise can be found on page 233.

EXERCISE 10A-4

Correct any errors in the following. All errors will involve punctuating introductory elements. Some items may contain fragments that need to be corrected. Each sentence may contain no errors, one error, or more than one error. If an item contains no errors, just leave it alone.

1. Looking for a job. Can be very frustrating.

2. Hanging his coat behind the door Ken sat down at his desk.

3. Giving me an angry look. Carrie stomped out of the room.

4. Watching a baseball game, is very relaxing on a summer afternoon.

5. Having already eaten dinner. Judy only ordered a cup of coffee.

6. Watching his oatmeal, Tim buttered the toast.

7. Picking up the wet towel I yelled at Emily.

8. Cursing under his breath the cowboy rode after the escaped calf.

9. Getting angry usually does not solve anything.

10. Taking a menu, Denny ordered a whiskey sour.

EXERCISE 10A-5

The following examples illustrate another principle involved in punctuating introductory phrases. Study these examples carefully and try to figure out what this principle is.

If you have trouble, try putting brackets around the independent clauses. Then see if you can figure out what the principle is.

1. a. Correct: To catch the train, Dave had to run.
   b. Incorrect: To catch the train Dave had to run.
   c. Correct: To jump onto a moving train is dangerous.
   d. Incorrect: To jump onto a moving train, is dangerous.

2. a. Correct: To check your coat, you must pay a dollar.
   b. Incorrect: To check your coat you must pay a dollar.
   c. Correct: To pay that much is stupid.
   d. Incorrect: To pay that much, is stupid.

3. a. Correct: To see the heron, we had to use a telescope.
   b. Incorrect: To see the heron we had to use a telescope.
   c. Correct: To see a great blue heron is very exciting.
   d. Incorrect: To see a great blue heron, is very exciting.

NOTE: A discussion of the answers to this exercise can be found on pages 233–234.

EXERCISE 10A-6

Correct any errors in the following items. All errors will involve punctuating introductory elements. Some items may contain fragments that need to be corrected. Each item may contain no errors, one error, or more than one error. If an item contains no errors, just leave it alone.

1. To remember her name, I always thought about Ginger Rogers.

2. To forget her name, was very embarrassing.

3. Running up to the boss Lew asked for a day off.

4. To count all the beans in that jar. Was an unreasonable assignment.

5. To carry my tray out of the cafeteria, I had to balance my notebook on my head.

6. To run into Jeff at the conference, was quite a coincidence.

7. To be accepted into that club, Maria had to write a long letter.

8. Giving more than twenty-five dollars to the Heart Fund. Entitles you to a Heart Fund tee shirt.

9. To make me laugh Gwen told a long joke.

10. To get to heaven you must be able to punctuate introductory elements.

EXERCISE 10A-7

The following examples illustrate another principle involved in punctuating introductory phrases. Study these examples carefully and try to figure out what this principle is.

1. a. Correct: In the month of June, Jill started her new job.
   b. Incorrect: In the month of June Jill started her new job.
   c. Correct: In June, Jill started her new job.
   d. Correct: In June Jill started her new job.

2. a. Correct: At seven o'clock in the morning, the phone rang.
   b. Incorrect: At seven o'clock in the morning the phone rang.
   c. Correct: At seven o'clock, the phone rang.
   d. Correct: At seven o'clock the phone rang.

3. a. Correct: With a coat hanger, Nelly opened her trunk.
   b. Incorrect: With a coat hanger Nelly opened her trunk.
   c. Correct: With a hanger, Nelly opened her trunk.
   d. Correct: With a hanger Nelly opened her trunk.

NOTE: A discussion of the answers to this exercise can be found on page 234.

EXERCISE 10A-8

Correct any errors in the following sentences. All errors will involve punctuating introductory elements. Each sentence may contain no errors, one error, or more than one error. If an item contains no errors, just leave it alone.

1. To my surprise no one answered the phone.

2. Licking his fur Snowball cleaned up after dinner.

3. Kicking a football, is a good way to get rid of frustrations.

4. In spring a young man's fancy turns to love.

5. By mistake I opened the wrong locker.

6. To drive home Helen needed her glasses.

7. Feeling tired I lay down for a nap.

8. To my little sister every day is a holiday.

9. In China people eat a lot more rice than potatoes.

10. To leave we had to answer a lot of questions.

 EXERCISE 10A-9

This exercise reviews everything you have learned about punctuating introductory phrases. Correct any errors in the following sentences. All errors will involve punctuating introductory phrases. Some items may contain fragments that need to be corrected. Each sentence may contain no errors, one error, or more than one error. If an item contains no errors, just leave it alone.

1. In the middle of her recital she got a cramp in her hand.

2. To join the Jaycees he had to pay a lot of money.

3. Organizing a Girl Scout troop was more demanding than she thought.

4. Looking carefully in the ditch, she spotted the wounded quail.

5. Opening the envelope, Barb became very excited.

6. Checking the dictionary is the only way to be sure about spelling.

7. In spite of my doubts about his discretion. He did not tell Marcie about the rumors.

8. To get a camping spot on the Fourth of July. Is almost impossible in Yosemite.

9. To get commas in the right places you have to understand everything about sentences.

10. To be accepted by the Naval Academy was quite an honor.

11. Giving me a knowing look. She answered the phone.

12. Looking down I didn't see Joanie. She was just getting home from her trip.

13. Objecting to Vivian's comments. Brian stormed out of the room.

14. To my way of thinking we should invite the entire class to the party.

15. Letting the potatoes boil for half an hour. You can mix the ingredients for the topping.

16. Listening to Mahler always makes me depressed.

17. Arguing with her about religion, is just a waste of time.

18. In the middle of the play, Gordon stood up and shouted to his friends.

19. To go to temple every week, was more than he could do.

20. After bargaining for half an hour. Sue got the man to sell her the camera for twenty dollars.

EXERCISE 10A-10 _____

Each of the following items consists of two or more parts. Some of the parts are not complete sentences. In the space below each one, rewrite the parts combined into one grammatical sentence.

1.   a. To replace your oil filter.
     b. Should take only about thirty minutes.

2.   a. Glancing out the window.
     b. Charles saw someone stealing his bike.

3.   a. In the middle of the night.
     b. A terrible explosion shook the building.

4.   a. To escape the long arm of the IRS.
     b. Is not possible.

5.   a. To buy a new house.
     b. Will use up all our savings.

6.   a. Fixing my cycle on the side of the Interstate.
     b. I was taking a big chance.

7.   a. Without saying a word to any of us.
     b. Mr. Greif passed out a test and left the room.

8.   a. In the cities and in the towns.
     b. Of this great country.
     c. People are asking, "Where's the beef?"

9.   a. Losing a game of tennis.
     b. Is not the same as losing a scholarship to college.

10. **a.** Seizing the police officer by the neck.
    b. Was not the best way to get out of the ticket.

 EXERCISE 10A-11 _____

Correct any errors in the following paragraph. All errors will involve punctuating introductory elements. There may be some fragments.

Watching television, always makes me feel degenerate. To put it mildly television is not very challenging to the mind. As a matter of fact making out the grocery list is more challenging. To sit in front of the TV for an entire Saturday afternoon. Makes me feel like I've just wasted a day. I always know there are other things I should be doing. Cleaning my room would be more productive than watching TV. Instead, I just sit and stare. To turn off the "boob tube," is sometimes the hardest thing in the world. So, I just sit there and feel guilty.

DISCUSSION OF INDUCTIVE EXERCISES

EXERCISE 10A-1

This exercise demonstrates that when any kind of a phrase occurs in front of the independent clause in a sentence, that phrase must be followed by a comma. This general rule can be illustrated by the following diagram:

___(any phrase)___ , _____(independent clause)_____

EXERCISE 10A-3

This exercise shows that if a phrase beginning with an "ing" verbal appears at the beginning of a sentence, it is only followed by a comma when the rest of the sentence is an independent clause. If the rest of the sentence is not an independent clause, then it is wrong to insert a comma.
    Perhaps a diagram will help:

___("ing" phrase)___ , _____(independent clause)_____

___("ing" phrase)___ _____(anything other than an independent clause)_____

EXERCISE 10A-5

The principle in these sentences is much like the one you learned in Exercise 10A-3, only this time it involves a phrase beginning with "to" + verb. If a phrase starting with "to" + verb appears at the beginning of the sentence, it should be followed by a comma only if the rest of the sentence is an independent clause. If the rest of the sentence is not an independent clause, then it is wrong to put in a comma.

Another diagram:

| _____(any phrase)_____ , _____(independent clause)_____ |

| _____(any phrase)_____ _____(anything other than an independent clause)_____ |

EXERCISE 10A-7

This exercise shows that the comma is optional following short prepositional phrases (three words or less) at the beginning of the sentence.

Part B · Commas with Introductory Clauses

In Part A you learned that a *phrase* that precedes an independent clause must be followed by a comma. In this part, the primary skill you will learn is to punctuate a sentence with an introductory *clause*. You will also learn to distinguish these from clauses that are not introductory and to punctuate dependent clauses when they occur at the end of the sentence.

A dependent clause is a group of words that contains a subject and a verb but does *not* express a complete thought. They generally begin with one of the "sentence busters" that you learned in Chapter 6.

EXERCISE 10B-1 _____

The following examples illustrate one principle involved in punctuating dependent clauses. Study these examples carefully and try to figure out what this principle is.

1. Correct: Max was angry until he heard my explanation.
2. Correct: Max was angry, until he heard my explanation.

3. Correct: Mark laughed a lot even though he was afraid.
4. Correct: Mark laughed a lot, even though he was afraid.

5. Correct: You had better arrive by seven o'clock unless you have a reserved seat.
6. Correct: You had better arrive by seven o'clock, unless you have a reserved seat.

If you are having trouble figuring this one out, look closely at the punctuation in the sentences.

NOTE: A discussion of the answers to this exercise can be found on pages 237–238.

EXERCISE 10B-2 _____

Correct any errors in the following items. All errors will involve punctuating introductory elements. Some items may contain fragments. Each sentence may contain no errors, one error, or more than one error.

1. My plate cracked when I dropped it.

2. Debbie worked on her term paper, until she fell asleep last night.

3. Marty jogs for an hour every morning. Before he eats breakfast.

4. Mr. Devos was willing to loan Ed five hundred dollars. Because he has known Ed for years.

5. Jim was willing to go to the circus if we would promise to leave by nine o'clock.

6. My neighbors have been extremely careful about locking their doors. Since they were robbed last month.

7. Mr. Jackman has a foul mouth, even though he goes to church every Sunday.

8. Neal is always trying to meet my sister. Although he knows she is engaged to Peter.

9. Sonja opened a comic book store after she won ten thousand dollars in the lottery.

10. Pat sat out in the back yard. Until her skin turned bright red.

 EXERCISE 10B-3

The following examples illustrate another principle involved in punctuating dependent clauses. Study these examples carefully and try to figure out what this principle is.

1. a. Correct: I had a headache when I woke up.
   b. Correct: I had a headache, when I woke up.
   c. Correct: When I woke up, I had a headache.
   d. Incorrect: When I woke up I had a headache.

2. a. Correct: Mark laughed a lot because he was nervous.
   b. Correct: Mark laughed a lot, because he was nervous.
   c. Correct: Because he was nervous, Mark laughed a lot.
   d. Incorrect: Because he was nervous Mark laughed a lot.

3. a. Correct: You had better arrive by seven if you want to get a seat.
   b. Correct: You had better arrive by seven, if you want to get a seat.
   c. Correct: If you want to get a seat, you had better arrive by seven.
   d. Incorrect: If you want to get a seat you had better arrive by seven.

If you are having trouble figuring this one out, try putting brackets around the independent clauses. Then see if you can figure out what the principle is.

NOTE: A discussion of the answers to this exercise can be found on page 238.

EXERCISE 10B-4 _____

Correct any errors in the following. All errors will involve punctuating introductory elements. Some items may contain fragments. Each item may contain no errors, one error, or more than one error.

1. When I arrived at the party Tom was already there.

2. Unless the Orioles play a lot better after the All-Star break. They will
   be lucky to finish in fourth place.

3. To learn computer programming Ms. Makowski took a course at a
   community college.

4. Since no one knows the answer, I will ask Professor Maccentelli.

5. After the creek flooded we were not able to use the bridge.

6. Because my sister was not invited to the meeting. I am not going either.

7. If the weather looks good this weekend, let's go camping.

8. Being a member of the Audubon Society Paula goes on lots of bird-
   watching trips.

9. If you get this letter before you leave give me a call.

10. Until Donna gets a job. She should not think about buying a house.

EXERCISE 10B-5 _____

The following examples illustrate another principle involved in punctuating
dependent clauses. Study these examples carefully and try to figure out what
this principle is.

1. Correct: Whenever you return from the office, I will have dinner
                ready.
2. Incorrect: Whenever you return from the office I will have dinner
                ready.

3. Correct: Whenever you return from the office will be okay with me.
4. Incorrect: Whenever you return from the office, will be okay with
                me.

5. Correct: Whatever you wear, I'm wearing jeans.
6. Incorrect: Whatever you wear I'm wearing jeans.

7. Correct: Whatever you wear will be fine.
8. Incorrect: Whatever you wear, will be fine.

If you are having trouble figuring this one out, try putting brackets
around the independent clauses. Then see if you can figure out what the
principle is.

NOTE: A discussion of the answers to this exercise can be found on page 238.

EXERCISE 10B-6 _____

Correct any errors in the following. All errors will involve punctuating introductory elements. Some items may contain fragments. Each sentence may
contain no errors, one error, or more than one error.

1. When you begin work at the agency, is up to you.
2. Even though he apologized, I never want to see him again.
3. Whoever stole my bike will be sorry when he tries to ride it.
4. Sliding down the stairs I injured my leg.
5. As long as that television is blaring. I cannot do my homework.
6. When she gets off the plane, is when I will stop worrying.
7. Whoever guesses the correct number of beans. Is the winner.
8. If you don't want to go tell him you are too busy.
9. How you raise the money is up to you.
10. If a man bites a dog that is news.

DISCUSSION OF INDUCTIVE EXERCISES

EXERCISE 10B-1

These examples illustrate that, when a dependent clause comes after an independent clause, a comma at the end of the independent clause is optional.

| _____(independent clause)_____ | _____(dependent clause)_____ |

or

| _____(independent clause)_____ , | _____(dependent clause)_____ |

Actually, the situation in these cases is a little more subtle than these diagrams indicate. While there is no *general* rule about the comma in front of a dependent clause at the end of the sentence, in specific cases, experienced writers often have a preference. In fact, experienced writers generally prefer that the comma be left out in most cases. In the following, for example, most writers would omit the comma.

1. We always have good weather when we are at the beach.
2. Joseph had a cup of coffee while he waited for Helene to finish dressing.
3. Mr. Liu was hurrying because he was late to work.
4. I will pick you up if your car won't start.
5. Things have been a lot quieter around my house since my children moved out.

Most experienced writers would use a comma in the following sentences:

6. I telephoned Ramon, even though I was fairly certain that he was out of town.

7. Sandy will graduate this year, unless she fails statistics.
8. I did not run in the marathon, although I had trained for it.
9. I am going fishing tomorrow, whether it rains or not.
10. Denise had been selected for a promotion, though she didn't know it at the time.

Even in this second group of sentences, some experienced writers would omit some of the commas.

The difference between the two groups of sentences is not very obvious. Most people, however, feel that there is a bigger "pause" at the point where the comma is inserted in the second group than there is at the corresponding point in the first. Others would say that in the second group, they "lower their voice" a little for the dependent clause at the end.

The best advice we can give you on these sentences is that, unless you feel there is a big "pause" or that you "lower your voice" significantly for the dependent clause, leave the comma out. There is no hard-and-fast rule, but, unless you feel it is really necessary, you are better off omitting the comma.

Now that we have raised the issue of putting in commas when you pause, we should discuss it in more detail. Many inexperienced writers put too many commas in their writing. When asked why they put a particular comma in, they often reply, "I thought I needed a comma because I paused there." As we have seen in the above exercise, pauses sometimes do require commas. Furthermore, historically, commas were invented to represent pauses.

But there are several reasons why putting in a comma wherever you pause is a risky practice. First, a number of other punctuation marks were also invented to represent pauses; periods, semicolons, colons, and dashes all also represent pauses. So, putting in a comma whenever you pause may mean you are using a comma when you should be using some other mark of punctuation. Secondly, your pauses may be different from other people's; you may pause more or less often than the average person and, as a result, put in too many or too few commas.

The "pause theory," however, is not completely worthless. It is a very good way to locate places where you *may* need a comma. Then ask yourself whether there is any *rule* that requires a comma at that point. If so, put one in; if not, leave the comma out.

EXERCISE 10B-3

These sentences show that, when the dependent clause comes before the independent clause, it must be followed by a comma.
        Another diagram:

_____(dependent clause)_____ , _____(independent clause)_____

EXERCISE 10B-5

These sentences show that you have to be careful about setting off dependent clauses at the beginning of the sentence. You must make sure that the part of the sentence following the dependent clause is really an independent clause. If it is not, then you must *not* put a comma after the dependent clause.

R E V I E W

EXERCISE 10-REVIEW-1 _____

The following items contain errors in punctuating introductory elements. Some of them may contain fragments. Proofread these closely and correct any errors. Each item may contain no errors, one error, or more than one error.

1. In the early morning hours there was a loud explosion.
2. If you haven't even read his book. Why are you criticizing it?
3. If it snows we'll have to stay home because I don't have snow tires.
4. To sneak into my house without waking the dog, is impossible.
5. Confirming my suspicions Joy showed up at the party with Art.
6. Balancing my checkbook is a job I hate.
7. To close my refrigerator door I have to use two hands.
8. To go sailing, is my idea of a great weekend.
9. As I walked into the room a giant panda was sitting on the couch.
10. Of the two of them I would rather get in a fight with George.
11. Whenever you finish your work, will be the time for us to have a beer.
12. To avoid paying taxes on the gift, she paid for it in cash.
13. The phone's ringing, gave me an excuse to cut short the conversation.
14. To visit the National Gallery, we had to take a bus.
15. Running after her dog. She showed her determination.
16. Whenever you finish work, I'll be waiting for you.
17. To err, is human.
18. When you are promoted, will depend on how hard you work.
19. To jump out of an airplane wearing a parachute. You have to be crazy.
20. Unless you have some objection we will spend our first night in Denver.

EXERCISE 10-REVIEW-2 _____

The following contain errors involving punctuating introductory elements. Read each item carefully and correct any errors. Some items may contain fragments. Each item may contain no errors, one error, or more than one error.

1. As soon as I saw the car I knew I had to have it.
2. In the middle of my party, the fire alarm went off.
3. Fixing the garbage disposal, took about four hours.

4. When he is angry, he becomes very silent.

5. Why he didn't return the package, is a mystery to me.

6. If you want to save some money. You should start saving coupons.

7. If it rains I'll pick you up.

8. As the car slowly drove over the crest of the hill. Three deer stepped out of the woods.

9. After school is out kids flock to our neighborhood pool.

10. Before church on Sundays. We would usually have a big breakfast.

11. Shaking his head my father picked up the broken plate.

12. Running five miles a day is nothing to her.

13. In the second place I have already seen the movie.

14. While I was taking a bath. The phone rang three times.

15. To call long distance on Mother's Day, was nearly impossible.

16. Running for a seat on the city council, took all of Brian's money.

17. Being an hour late for the party, didn't bother Mark at all.

18. In the middle of the lake we saw a rocky island.

19. When Helene makes up her mind no one can change it.

20. As I suspected, the furnace had gone out.

EXERCISE 10-REVIEW-3

Each of the following items consists of two or more parts. Some of the parts may not be sentences. In the space below each item, rewrite the parts combined into *one* grammatical sentence.

Example:

    a. When Betsy fell down.
    b. She hurt her knee.

When Betsy fell down, she hurt her knee.

1.   **a.** Even if he doesn't remember what happened last night.
     b. I still feel terrible about it.

2.   **a.** To get his name before the committee.
     b. He wrote them a twenty-page letter.

3. a. Whenever you finish your homework.
    b. Is when we'll have dinner.

4. a. To get this car running again.
    b. Will cost over a hundred dollars.

5. a. When I first came to college.
    b. I wanted to become an accountant.
    c. Because that's what my father is.

6. a. If you wear that hat.
    b. Everyone will make fun of you.

7. a. After the interest rates have come back down to a reasonable level.
    b. I will consider buying a house.

8. a. When I think about what she has been through in her life.
    b. I wonder how she has remained so sane.

9. a. Running after the bus.
    b. He sprained his ankle.

10. a. Leaning against the railing.
    b. We talked about the argument we had had.

11. a. Singing at the top of my lungs.
    b. Is very therapeutic for me.

12. a. Whatever the two of you decide.
    b. Will be okay with the rest of us.

13.   **a.** Because I got too much sun yesterday.
      b. I am not going to the beach this afternoon.

14.   **a.** To become so upset over a little thing like that.
      b. Shows just how immature he is.

15.   **a.** Just to finish the race.
      b. Was quite an accomplishment.

16.   **a.** In the middle of his lecture.
      b. An alarm went off.

17.   **a.** If Helen is late this time.
      b. I think we should just leave her.

18.   **a.** To be given a chance to compete.
      b. Was all that she asked.

19.   **a.** If you can get that stain out.
      b. You should wear that dress on Saturday.

20.   **a.** When I have time to relax and think.
      b. I get very depressed about my situation.

EXERCISE 10-REVIEW-4 ⎯⎯⎯⎯⎯⎯⎯⎯⎯⎯⎯⎯

The following letter contains errors in punctuating introductory clauses and contains several fragments. Proofread it carefully and correct any errors.

Dear Ms. Heidel:

For the past three-and-one-half years I have been living in apartment 101 of your complex. During that time I have never been late with my rent, never bounced a check, never lost my key, never allowed my dog to bother anyone else, and never asked you to do anything for me. In other words, I have been an ideal tenant.

However, that must now change. I must ask you to do something about the new family that has moved into apartment 102. To live next to people like the Bryants, is more than anyone should have to endure. Since they moved in I have not a single moment's peace.

From early in the morning till late at night. That teenage son of theirs, plays rock music so loudly that I can hear it in every corner of my apartment. If I ask him to turn it down he does so. However, in fifteen minutes he turns it right back up. His parents are no help since they seem to enjoy the music as much as he does.

Furthermore, the outside appearance of the building has degenerated considerably since the Bryants moved in. To get past all of their "big wheels," is like crossing an obstacle course. In addition, they have piled up junk on their balcony, and they let bags of garbage sit for days in the hall outside their front door.

Climaxing the past two months of this behavior the Bryants had a party this past weekend. More than thirty cars arrived taking up every parking place and spilling over onto the lawn. Since all the guests didn't fit into the apartment, they spread onto the stairs and into the lobby. At two in the morning they were still going strong. When I asked them to quiet down. They responded with choruses of "For He's a Jolly Good Fellow." Today, a week later, the stairs are still littered with beer cans and bottles.

I respectfully request that you do something about these people by the end of the week. If you do not take action I intend to break my lease.

 EXERCISE 10-REVIEW-5 ⎯⎯⎯⎯⎯⎯⎯⎯⎯⎯⎯⎯⎯⎯⎯⎯⎯⎯

This exercise reviews what you learned in this chapter as well as what you learned in Chapter 8 about punctuating independent clauses.

    Proofread the following essay carefully and correct any errors. All errors will involve punctuating independent clauses or introductory elements.

    I think love is overrated. Most people would probably say that love is an essential ingredient for a successful marriage but I don't agree. Of course, it is nice when there is love in a marriage, but it is not essential.

    Since the beginning of civilization poets, artists, and philosophers have tried to define love, recently psychiatrists and psychologists have added their definitions. The meaning I intend for the word is much simpler and more understandable than what these great thinkers have come up with. When I talk about love I simply mean a heightened emotional state in which the subject feels an intense attraction for another person. This state can often cause the subject to think about the other person much of the time, and to want to be with the other person as much as possible. In extreme cases, it can conceal faults that the other person has, it can make him or her appear perfect.

With this definition in mind, it should be clear why I feel love is not essential to marriage. Most people have been in such a heightened emotional state at one time or another in their lives, however, such a state usually lasts only a relatively short time. The feeling of love is very pleasant; but it is also very distracting. Few of us could sustain this drain on our time and energy for more than a few months. Nevertheless, when people claim that the love has gone out of their marriage, they are revealing their expectation that this emotional high will last for a lifetime. Of course, it can't but that is no reason to give up on the marriage. People must recognize that the kind of emotion we usually think of as love is not something that can endure forever. After a certain period of time it is bound to be replaced by a less intense, and less exciting emotion, which I will refer to as deep affection. Expecting love to last for the lifetime of a marriage, may be one of the chief causes of our high divorce rate.

Besides the fact that it won't last there is another reason why love is not a necessary ingredient for a good marriage. Most of us who have fallen in love know that very often the person whom we fall in love with is exactly the wrong person for us to marry. This is not always true but many of us seem to be fatally attracted to just the kind of person with whom marriage would be disastrous. There is nothing wrong with falling in love in this way, but we should be very cautious about marrying a man or woman who will make us miserable.

To fall in love, often means that we are incapable of seeing any imperfections in the other person. Of course, he or she is not perfect, so when we do begin to see his or her flaws, we may feel betrayed. We may even decide to break off the relationship because the other person has let us down. He or she hasn't really let us down we have just experienced another of the dangers of a relationship based too strongly on love.

If love isn't essential to a good marriage what is? I suggest the phenomenon I referred to earlier as deep affection. Building a marriage on deep affection is a much safer approach than building it on love. Deep affection includes a large amount of respect and considerable attraction as well. However it doesn't make us blind. It still allows us to recognize that the other person is a human being with a normal collection of faults. It doesn't make us feel that we must be with the other person all the time, but it does mean that we enjoy the time that we do spend together. Deep affection only develops when two people have spent enough time together to have experienced both joy and sadness. Luckily, it often develops just as the emotional excitement known as love is beginning to mellow.

If people will just recognize the value of what I have called deep affection, and the dangers of love, we will be on the road back to healthier, and more mature relationships.

 ## EXERCISE 10-REVIEW-6

For this essay, as in many college assignments, we will merely give you a general area to write about. You will be responsible for developing a specific subject and then a thesis. Imagine that this assignment was given to you by one of your present instructors; he or she will be the audience.

For the general area you are to write about, select one of the following:

1. Why we punish criminals.
2. How to be happy about your career.
3. Whether ambition is a good or a bad quality.
4. Whether revenge is a good or a bad motive.
5. Whether selfishness is good or bad.
6. The problems with health care in America.
7. The problems with education in America.

Just as you did on the last essay, before you do any writing, you will need to do some planning. To help you with this, answer the following questions:

1. Who will be the audience for this essay?_____

_____

_____

2. What is the purpose of this essay? What are you trying to accomplish?_____

_____

_____

3. What will be the thesis?_____

_____

_____

4. Now, brainstorm—make a list of ideas for this memo (if you need more room, use a separate sheet of paper):

5. Go back to your list and eliminate any ideas that don't work. Then, form your ideas into groups by placing letters in front of them.

6. In the spaces below, list the main ideas of each group. We've given you room enough for ten main ideas, but you probably won't need that many. Just use the spaces you need. Then, in the spaces in front of the letters, number them in the most effective order.

_____   A   _____

_____

_____   B   _____

_____

_____   C   _____

_____

_____   D   _____

_____

_____   E   _____

_____

_____   F   _____

_____

_____   G   _____

_____

_____   H   _____

_____

_____   I   _____

_____

_____   J   _____

_____

7. Finally, on separate paper, write this essay using the plan you have just made. You will revise it in the next exercise.

 EXERCISE 10-REVIEW-7

Make a backward outline of the essay you wrote for the previous exercise. Then use this backward outline and the following checklist to revise your essay.

1. Does the essay have a clear thesis?
2. Does everything in the essay support that thesis?
3. Is the essay organized logically?
4. Does the essay do what the assignment asked you to do?
5. Are the language and content appropriate for the audience?
6. Could the essay be strengthened by the inclusion of more concrete details?
7. Proofread the essay once carefully looking only for errors involving fragments, punctuating independent clauses, or introductory elements.
8. Proofread the essay a second time looking for errors in subject-verb agreement.
9. Finally, correct any other errors you find.

11

Developing Ideas

Part A   Assertions and Evidence
Part B   Asking What Needs to Be Proved

Part A · Assertions and Evidence

Imagine yourself sitting in your English classroom waiting for the teacher to arrive. You're about fifteen minutes early, so you have plenty of time to observe everyone as they arrive for class. You remember that, for your psychology class, you have to write a paper in which you observe men and women and draw conclusions about the differences in their behavior. You decide to watch for the differences in your classmates.

As you sit watching everyone come into the room, you jot down notes about their behavior. The following notes were actually made, in a very unscientific way, watching men and women at a college on the East Coast arrive for an English class on an April morning:

The first man makes a lot of noise as he arrives—laughs loudly and slams his books down on his desk.

The next two men rearrange some of the desks so they can sit together in the back of the room.

These first three men are all wearing blue jeans and running shoes.

Two women arrive and sit quietly in the front row.

The women smile at the men, who say something to each other and laugh loudly.

The women are wearing makeup; one takes out a mirror and adjusts her hair.

A group of men and women arrive simultaneously. The men call out noisily to the two men in the back row and move some more desks so they can sit together.

One man walks over and looks out the window.

A woman in the front row takes out her notebook and a pen, places them on her desk, and smiles.

Another woman is combing her hair and then puts on lipstick.

More men and women arrive.

Of the nine women now in the room, three have on shorts and blouses, two have on jeans, three have on skirts, and one has on some kind of jumpsuit.

Of the men, eleven have on jeans, and two have on corduroy shorts.

Two women on the left side of the room are combing their hair.

A man knocks his books off the desk with a loud crash. The woman sitting next to him picks them up.

Women are more helpful than men.

Men are less imaginative than women about their clothes; they are more conformist.

The professor, a male, arrives, but there are still five minutes until class begins.

Two women in the front row smile at the professor.

A woman walks up to the front desk, waits a second, smiling, and, when the professor has arranged his books, asks him something in a quiet voice. He answers; she smiles, nods, and returns to her seat.

Women smile much more often than men.

Two more women arrive and sit quietly in the front row.

A man in the back of the room says in a loud voice, "Professor Pierce, are our papers due today?" The professor says that they are. Groans from the back of the room.

Four or five women and one man get their papers out and place them on their desks.

Women are more likely than men to behave like "good" students.

Men are noisier than women.

There are three rows of desks in the room. Of the eleven women, eight are sitting in the front row, two in the middle row, and one in the back right-hand corner. Of the thirteen men, ten are sitting in the back row, two are sitting in the middle row, and one is still standing and staring out the window.

Women tend to sit near the front of the room; men, toward the back.

Women care more about their appearance than men do.

The professor asks the students to pass their papers to the left. Three of the men don't have their papers done. The men in the back row pass theirs to the right. The woman in the back row collects them and carries them up to the professor.

The professor asks, "What is the one thing every one of your papers should have?" Three women raise their hands, and a man in the back row says, "A thesis."

Professor Pierce says, "Right. I hope you all checked your papers to make sure they have a single clear thesis."

Women are more anxious to please other people than men are.

 # EXERCISE 11A-1

The notes about men and women have been reorganized into two groups below. Study these two groups and figure out what the difference between them is. What determines whether an item is placed in group 1 or group 2?

Group 1

1. Women are more helpful than men.
2. Men are less imaginative than women about their clothes; they are more conformist.
3. Women smile much more often than men.
4. Women tend to sit near the front of the room; men, toward the back.
5. Women are more likely than men to behave like "good" students.
6. Women care more about their appearance than men do.
7. Men are noisier than women.
8. Women are more anxious to please other people than men are.

Group 2

1. The first man makes a lot of noise as he arrives—laughs loudly and slams his books down on his desk.
2. The next two men rearrange some of the desks so they can sit together in the back of the room.
3. These first three men are all wearing blue jeans and running shoes.
4. Two women arrive and sit quietly in the front row.
5. The women smile at the men, who say something to each other and laugh loudly.
6. The women are wearing makeup; one takes out a mirror and adjusts her hair.
7. A group of men and women arrive simultaneously. The men call out noisily to the two men in the back row and move some more desks so they can sit together.
8. One man walks over and looks out the window.
9. A woman in the front row takes out her notebook and a pen and places them on her desk and smiles.
10. Another woman is combing her hair and then puts on lipstick.
11. More men and women arrive.
12. Of the nine women now in the room, three have on shorts and blouses, two have on jeans, three have on skirts, and one has on some kind of jumpsuit.
13. Of the men, eleven have on jeans, and two have on corduroy shorts.
14. A man knocks his books off the desk with a loud crash. The woman sitting next to him picks them up.
15. Two women on the left side of the room are combing their hair.
16. The professor, a male, arrives, but there are still five minutes until class begins.
17. Two women in the front row smile at the professor.
18. A woman walks up to the front desk, waits a second, smiling, and, when the professor has arranged his books, asks him something in a quiet voice. He answers; she smiles, nods, and returns to her seat.
19. Two more women arrive and sit quietly in the front row.
20. A man in the back of the room says in a loud voice, "Professor Pierce, are our papers due today?" The professor says that they are. Groans from the back of the room.
21. Four or five women and one man get their papers out and place them on their desks.
22. There are three rows of chairs in the room. Of the eleven women, eight are sitting in the front row, two in the middle row, and one in the back

right-hand corner. Of the thirteen men, ten are sitting in the back row, two are sitting in the middle row, and one is still standing and staring out the window.

23. The professor asks everyone to pass their papers to the left. Three of the men don't have their papers done. The men in the back row pass theirs to the right. The woman in the back row collects them and carries them up to the professor.

24. The professor asks, "What is the one thing every one of your papers should have?" Three women raise their hands, and a man in the back row says, "A thesis."

25. Professor Pierce says, "Right. I hope you all checked your papers to make sure they have a single clear thesis."

What is the difference between the items in group 1 and those in group 2?

_____

_____

_____

_____

NOTE: A discussion of this exercise can be found on pages 259–260.

 EXERCISE 11A-2 _____

Notice that the list given at the beginning of this chapter looks a lot like the brainstorming lists you made in earlier chapters. Often, a brainstorming list includes both facts and assertions based on those facts. In earlier chapters, when we picked the main ideas out of the brainstorming lists, we were really picking out (or thinking up) the assertions that could be made from the evidence.

To organize this list of ideas, first decide on a thesis based on the evidence in the list:

_____

_____

_____

NOTE: Check your thesis against ours, which can be found on page 260.

 EXERCISE 11A-3 _____

Now organize the ideas in the list that begins on page 248.

1. First eliminate any ideas that won't work in this paper.
2. Then group the ideas into logical clusters by putting letters in front of each idea on the list.
3. In the spaces below, list the main ideas of each group. We've given you room enough for eight main ideas, but you probably won't need that many. Just use the spaces you need. Then, in the spaces in front of the letters, number them in the most effective order.

Thesis: Women are more anxious to please other people than men are.

	A	_____
		_____
	B	_____
		_____
	C	_____
		_____
	D	_____
		_____
	E	_____
		_____
	F	_____
		_____
	G	_____
		_____
	H	_____
		_____

NOTE: A discussion of the answers to this exercise can be found on pages 260–261.

 EXERCISE 11A-4

The outline below takes the evidence left after we have eliminated the items that don't work and arranges it under the appropriate main idea.

This is a step you probably would never do in writing a paper because it is too time consuming. We've done it here because it makes the differences between assertions and evidence very clear.

Thesis: Women are more anxious to please other people than men are.

1.   Women are more likely than men to behave like "good" students.

The next two men rearrange some of the desks so they can sit together in the back of the room. (could go under 2)

A woman walks up to the front desk, waits a second, smiling, and, when the professor has arranged his books, asks him something in a quiet voice. He answers; she smiles, nods, and returns to her seat. (could go under 3)

A man in the back of the room says in a loud voice, "Professor Pierce, are our papers due today?" The professor says that they are. Groans from the back of the room. (could go under 3)

Four or five women and one man get their papers out and place them on their desks.

The professor asks everyone to pass their papers to the left. Three of the men don't have their papers done. The men in the back row pass theirs to the right. The woman in the back row collects them and carries them up to the professor.

2. Women tend to sit near the front of the room; men, toward the back.

   There are three rows of chairs in the room. Of the eleven women, eight are sitting in the front row, two in the middle row, and one in the back right-hand corner. Of the thirteen men, ten are stitting in the back row, two are sitting in the middle row, and one is still standing and staring out the window.

3. Men are noisier than women.

   The first man makes a lot of noise as he arrives—laughs loudly and slams his books down on his desk.

   Two women arrive and sit quietly in the front row. (could go under 2)

   A group of men and women arrive simultaneously. The men call out noisily to the two men in the back row and move some more desks so they can sit together. (could go under 2)

   Two more women arrive and sit quietly in the front row. (could go under 2)

   The professor asks, "What is the one thing every one of your papers should have?" Three women raise their hands, and a man in the back row says, "A thesis."

4. Women care more about their appearance than men do.

   The women are wearing makeup; one takes out a mirror and adjusts her hair.

   Another woman is combing her hair and then puts on lipstick.

   Two women on the left side of the room are combing their hair.

5. Women smile much more often than men.

   The women smile at the men, who say something to each other and laugh loudly. (could go under 3)

   A woman in the front row takes out her notebook and a pen and places them on her desk and smiles.

   Two women in the front row smile at the professor.

6. Women are more helpful than men.

   A man knocks his books off the desk with a loud crash. The woman sitting next to him picks them up. (could go under 3)

   Review this outline and see if there are any points you would eliminate from your paper. If there are, identify which points you would eliminate and why in the space below.

NUMBER   REASON FOR ELIMINATING

_____   _____

           _____

_____   _____

           _____

_____   _____

           _____

NOTE: A discussion of the answers to this exercise can be found on page 261.

EXERCISE 11A-5

Read each of the following paragraphs and underline any assertions. In the space provided, list briefly the points that support the assertion. If there is no evidence to support the assertion, just leave the space blank. Then, check the appropriate box to indicate whether the assertion is adequately supported or not.

The first one is done for you.

1. <u>Chincoteague Island is a great place for a family vacation.</u> The beach there is one of the prettiest on the East Coast, and it's not too crowded. Besides the beach, there are miles of bike trails that are beautiful and, most important, level. The birds at Chincoteague are among the most impressive anywhere. In one afternoon, I saw great blue herons, little green herons, glossy ibis, and three kinds of egrets. Finally, the motel where we stay has a swimming pool, a tennis court, and a weight-lifting room.

Evidence:

a. _beach is pretty_

b. _beach is not crowded_

c. _bike trails_

d. _bird watching_

e. _motel has pool, tennis, weight-lifting_

f. _____

g. _____

h. _____

☑ adequate support   ☐ inadequate support

2. First, I overslept this morning and, therefore, didn't have time to take a shower. Then, the toast got stuck in the toaster and burned up. To make matters worse, it was the last piece of bread in the house. I decided to drink my coffee as I drove to work. But when I tried to start my car, the battery was dead. After a half hour, my neighbor managed to get it started with a jump from his battery. I arrived at work an hour late and quite frazzled. It was a terrible morning.

Evidence:

a. _____

b. _____

c. _____

d. _____

e. _____

f. _____

g. _____

h. _____

☐ adequate support   ☐ inadequate support

3. Something has to be done about terrorism. Madmen cannot be allowed to get away with the things they have been doing. Terrorists must learn that there is a price to be paid for violating the laws of natural decency. It's time we stopped letting these thugs push us around. It's time America took a stand.

Evidence:

a. _____

b. _____

c. _____

d. _____

e. _____

f. _____

g. _____

h. _____

☐ adequate support   ☐ inadequate support

4. The local news on channel 4 is a joke. Even the newscasters don't seem to take it seriously. They hardly ever cover any real news; the show is almost all sensationalism. And the reporters are incompetent. They don't even understand the stories they are covering. They always ask the people they are interviewing dumb questions. The show is so bad that I only watch it for laughs.

Evidence:

a. _____

b. _____

c. _____

d. _____

e. _____

f. _____

g. _____

h. _____

☐ adequate support   ☐ inadequate support

5. American society is getting older. The percentage of Americans over seventy has doubled since 1960. There are twice as many people between the ages of fifty and seventy as there were in 1960. Even the number between thirty and fifty is increasing, up by 20 percent in the same period. The only groups that have a smaller percentage now than in 1960 are those below thirty. The twenty-to-thirty age group is down by 16 percent, and the under-twenties are down 28 percent.

Evidence:

a. _____

b. _____

c. _____

d. _____

e. _____

f. _____

g. _____

h. _____

☐ adequate support   ☐ inadequate support

6. This town is in better shape than it's been in for the last twenty-five years. Mayor Washington reports that the average income is at its highest level ever. He further points out that unemployment is at 6½ percent, the lowest since 1967. Chief of Police Daniels has repeatedly pointed out that the crime rate is lower than at any time since 1962. The president of the Chamber of Commerce has announced that this year will be the best business year the town has experienced in twenty years; sixteen new businesses have opened, and only two have gone out of business in the past twelve months. Even the president of the PTA has good news; our children's scores on the College Boards have gone up for three years in a row, after fifteen years of decline. Everywhere you look this town is really improving.

Evidence:

a. _____

b. _____

c. _____

d. _____

e. _____

f. _____

g. _____

h. _____

☐ adequate support   ☐ inadequate support

7.   Living in the city has many advantages for me. All my ordinary needs
     can be satisfied within two blocks of my apartment building. There is
     a supermarket across the street and a dry cleaners just down the block.
     A large movie house with four different theaters is located two blocks
     away, and my doctor's office is right in my building. Getting around
     in the city is easy and inexpensive. One block from my house, I can
     catch a bus that takes me right to Memorial Hospital where I work.
     By walking another block, I can catch another bus that takes me all
     the way downtown for shopping, dinner, or the theater. I don't even
     own a car. But most important, I love meeting lots of interesting peo-
     ple. The other night I couldn't sleep, so I went across the street to a
     café and found myself in a great conversation for two hours.

Evidence:

a. _____

b. _____

c. _____

d. _____

e. _____

f. _____

g. _____

h. _____

☐ adequate support   ☐ inadequate support

NOTE: A discussion of the answers to this exercise can be found on pages 261–263.

EXERCISE 11A-6

For this essay, think about a job you now hold, one you have held in the
past, or one you could hold in the future. You know that you will be eligible
for a promotion in about six months. You are anxious to convince your
boss that you are a valuable employee who deserves a promotion. You
decide that one way to increase your chances of getting promoted is to come
up with a suggestion that will demonstrate how valuable your ideas are to
the business.

  Write a memo to your boss in which you recommend a change; this
could be a change in procedures, a change in personnel, a change in equipment, or any other change that you would like to propose.

  Sometimes students think that a memo is necessarily very short. This
is sometimes true, but often memos are several pages long. Your memo

should be long enough to effectively argue your point, probably about the same length as the essays you have written in this course.

Before you do any writing, you will need to do some planning. To help you with this, answer the following questions:

1. Who will be the audience for this memo?_____

   _____

   _____

2. What is the purpose of this memo? What are you trying to accomplish?_____

   _____

   _____

3. What will be the thesis?_____

   _____

   _____

4. Now, brainstorm—make a list of ideas for this memo (if you need more room, use a separate sheet of paper):

5. Go back to your list and eliminate any ideas that don't work. Then, form your ideas into groups by placing letters in front of them.

6. In the spaces below, list the main idea of each group. We've given you room enough for ten main ideas, but you probably won't need that many. Just use the spaces you need. Then, in the spaces in front of the letters, number them in the most effective order.

_____ . ____A____ _____

   _____

_____ ____B____ _____

   _____

_____ ____C____ _____

   _____

_____ ____D____ _____

   _____

_____ ____E____ _____

   _____

_____ ____F____ _____

   _____

	G	_____
____		_____
	H	_____
____		_____
	I	_____
____		_____
	J	_____
____		_____
		_____

7. Now check the assertions in your paper (this will probably be all of your main ideas, but perhaps also some of your supporting ideas) to see if you have adequate evidence to support each one.
8. Finally, on separate paper, write this memo. You will revise it in the next exercise.

EXERCISE 11A-7 _____

Make a backward outline of the essay you wrote for the previous exercise. Then use this backward outline and the following checklist to revise your memo.

1. Does the memo have a clear thesis?
2. Does everything in the memo support that thesis?
3. Is the memo organized logically?
4. Does the memo do what the assignment asked you to do?
5. Are the language and content appropriate for the audience?
6. Could the memo be strengthened by the inclusion of more concrete details?
7. Do you make any unsupported assertions?
8. Next, carefully proofread the memo, looking only for errors involving fragments or punctuating independent clauses and introductory elements.
9. Proofread the essay a second time looking for errors in subject-verb agreement.
10. Finally, correct any other errors you find.

DISCUSSION OF INDUCTIVE EXERCISES

EXERCISE 11A-1

All the items in group 2 are actual observations. They are, in some sense, "facts." There is not much room for argument about these. If you put them in your psychology paper, the reader would probably not disagree with you or ask, "What evidence do you have for that?"

The items in group 1, on the other hand, are not facts. They are your opinions based on your observations, but they are extremely arguable. If you put one of them into your paper, the chances are quite good that the reader would ask, "What evidence do you have for that?" or something not so polite, like "Says who?"

The distinction between these two kinds of ideas is very important. The first group are known as "assertions." Those in the second group are "evidence." The reason this distinction is so important is that a convincing piece of writing must be a combination of both types.

If I write "Smoking in public places must be outlawed," all I have done is express my opinion. If I add to it, "The Congress must make it illegal for people to smoke in places where nonsmokers will be affected," I have only repeated my assertion. I still have not given my reader one reason why he or she should agree with me. I am unlikely to have convinced anyone. Assertions do a good job of expressing your opinion, but by themselves, they are not very convincing.

On the other hand, if I write a paper full of facts but with no general assertions about what those facts add up to, then my writing will be equally unconvincing. The assertions are what make sense out of the facts. They are the conclusions you reach after you think about your facts.

Thus, it is important that you know the difference between assertions and evidence, so that you can make sure your writing is a combination of both. In fact, a well-constructed argument usually consists of an assertion followed by evidence to back it up, then another assertion followed by more evidence. This sequence continues until the main point or thesis is proved.

EXERCISE 11A-2

Our thesis is the last statement in group 1:

Thesis: Women are more anxious to please other people than men are.

You may have worded your version of the thesis a little differently, but it should have been something like ours.

EXERCISE 11A-3

1. We eliminated the following items because they did not support the thesis:

    a. One man walks over and looks out the window.
    b. These first three men are all wearing blue jeans and running shoes.
    c. More men and women arrive.
    d. Of the nine women now in the room, three have on shorts and blouses, two have on jeans, three have on skirts, and one has on some kind of jumpsuit.
    e. Of the men, eleven have on jeans, and two have on corduroy shorts.
    f. Professor Pierce says, "Right. I hope you all checked your papers to make sure they have a single clear thesis."

2. Our list of main ideas looked like this:

Thesis: Women are more anxious to please other people than men are.

3. A   Men are noisier than women.
4. B   Women care more about their appearance than men do.
5. C   Women smile much more often than men.
6. D   Women are more helpful than men.
2. E   Women tend to sit near the front of the room; men, toward the back.
1. F   Women are more likely than men to behave like "good" students.

In this case, the order does not seem to make much difference. We thought that F was probably our major and most convincing point, so we put it first. E and A are closely related to F, so we put them next. They both talk about traits that are similar to the one about women being more likely to play the "good student" role. B, C, and D are then arranged in order of descending importance.

Narrowing the main ideas out of all this material down to these six is fairly crucial. In this case, however, the order in which the six arguments are presented is less crucial. We arranged them in what seemed to us to be a descending order from the most important to the least.

Notice, however, that the six main ideas all came from group 1 in Exercise 11A-1. The main ideas are almost always assertions. Evidence is almost never a main idea.

EXERCISE 11A-4

The only one of the six points that we would eliminate is number 6. Number 6 asserts that women are more helpful than men. There is only one fact to support it. The only evidence is that *one* woman picked up *one* man's books for him. This is certainly not *convincing* evidence. No one is going to be won over by one example. Therefore, this point is not convincing. Before deciding to remove it from the paper, however, two questions must be answered:

1.   Could we come up with some more evidence to support it?

    Often it is possible to find more evidence to support an assertion like this. The evidence might come from thinking a little harder about the point. Or, we might strengthen the point by shifting some evidence from elsewhere in the argument. We could also do some more research.

2.   Will eliminating it seriously weaken the overall argument?

    Before you eliminate an unsupported argument from your paper, you need to make sure that it is not essential to your thesis. If it is essential, then eliminating it may result in the entire paper being unconvincing.

We found that number 6 is not essential to the argument and that it was not feasible to find more evidence to support it, so we decided to eliminate it.

But what about point number 2? Like number 6, it only has one piece of evidence to support it. However, deciding whether a particular assertion has enough support is not just a matter of counting the number of supporting points. In the case of number 2, the one supporting point is an analysis of the seating pattern of the eleven women and thirteen men. This analysis is a very convincing way of showing that the assertion is true. It would have a good chance of convincing those who are unconvinced. Therefore, point number 2 is not eliminated.

This, then, is the major point of this section: Your writing will be severely weakened if it includes assertions that are not supported with adequate evidence.

EXERCISE 11A-5

2.   The main assertion in this paragraph is, "It was a terrible morning." The evidence to support this assertion is quite solid and convincing:

a. I overslept   d. no more bread
b. no shower   e. battery dead
c. toast burned   f. hour late for work

☑ adequate support   ☐ inadequate support

3. The main assertion in this paragraph is, "Something has to be done about terrorism." There is no convincing support for this assertion. Instead of evidence, the paragraph includes a series of broad assertions that are no more convincing than the first one.

   ☐ adequate support   ☑ inadequate support

4. The main assertion in this paragraph is, "The local news on channel 4 is a joke." There are a number of statements following this assertion that might look like evidence:

   a. newscasters don't take it seriously
   b. don't cover any hard news
   c. show is sensationalistic
   d. don't even understand the stories they are covering
   e. always ask the people they are interviewing dumb questions
   f. I only watch it for laughs

If you look more closely at each of these statements, however, you will see that each of them is a mere assertion also. There is, in reality, not one piece of hard evidence to support any of these assertions.

      Look, for example, at the first statement: the newscasters don't even take it seriously. This isn't evidence; it is merely an opinion. The writer doesn't provide any examples to back it up. Each of the statements is like that—just the writer's opinions rather than real evidence.

   ☐ adequate support   ☑ inadequate support

5. The main assertion in this paragraph is, "American society is getting older." The evidence that supports this assertion is in the form of data or statistics. For certain kinds of arguments, this is the most convincing kind of evidence.

   a. the percentage over seventy has doubled since 1960
   b. twice as many between the ages of fifty and seventy as there were
   c. number between thirty and fifty is up by 20 percent
   d. twenty-to-thirty age group is down by 16 percent
   e. under twenties are 28 percent smaller

   ☑ adequate support   ☐ inadequate support

6. The main assertion in this paragraph is, "This town is in better shape than it's been in for the last twenty-five years." The evidence to support this assertion includes some data, but is primarily "expert opinion"—statements from the mayor, the police chief, and the presidents of the Chamber of Commerce and of the PTA. This kind of expert opinion is often good support for your assertions, as it is here.

   a. Mayor Washington reports that the average income is at its highest level ever.
   b. Unemployment is at 6½ percent, the lowest since 1967.
   c. Chief of Police Daniels has repeatedly pointed out that the crime rate is lower than at any time since 1962.
   d. The president of the Chamber of Commerce has announced that

this year will be the best business year the town has experienced in twenty years.

    e. Sixteen new businesses have opened, and only two have gone out of business in the past twelve months.

    f. The president of the PTA has good news: our children's scores on the College Boards have gone up for three years in a row.

☑ adequate support   ☐ inadequate support

  7. The main assertion in this paragraph is, "Living in the city has many advantages for me." There are several statements that seem to support this assertion:

    a. All my ordinary needs can be satisfied within two blocks of my apartment building.

    b. Getting around in the city is easy and inexpensive.

    c. Most important, I love meeting lots of interesting people.

Each of these three statements, however, is also an assertion. The difference between this paragraph and number 4 is that each of these assertions does have some evidence to support it:

    a. All my ordinary needs can be satisfied within two blocks of my apartment building.

        (1) a supermarket across the street
        (2) a dry cleaners just down the block
        (3) large movie house with four different theaters is located two blocks away
        (4) doctor's office right in my building

    b. Getting around in the city is easy and inexpensive.

        (1) one block from my house, I can catch a bus that takes me right to Memorial Hospital where I work
        (2) another bus that takes me all the way downtown for shopping, dinner, or the theater
        (3) I don't even own a car

    c. Most important, I love meeting lots of interesting people.

        (1) the other night I went across the street to a café and found myself in a great conversation for two hours

☑ adequate support   ☐ inadequate support

The last paragraph illustrates very clearly the most important principle in this section: it is perfectly all right to make assertions, but when you do, you must provide some kind of evidence to back them up. The evidence can be facts, observations, statistics, expert opinion, or reasons, but you must support every assertion with some kind of evidence.

Part B · Asking What Needs to Be Proved

The purpose of this section is to teach you to ask one question: What needs to be proved? This is a question that will help you improve your writing both when you are planning and when you are revising.

EXERCISE 11B-1 _____

In the memo you wrote for the last section, you might have come up with a thesis something like this:

Thesis: This store should buy a new cash register.

While you were planning this memo, you could have asked yourself, "To convince my boss that the store should purchase a new cash register, what points need to be established?"

In the spaces below, list what you think would need to be proved in this case. To get you started, we have entered the first one for you.

1. *There is a problem with the current cash register.*

2. _____

3. _____

4. _____

5. _____

6. _____

7. _____

8. _____

Select one of the following theses and make a list in the space below of the points you would need to make in order to prove it:

1. Tuition at this school should be lowered.
2. An office needs one more worker.
3. You should buy a new car.

1. _____

2. _____

3. _____

4. _____

5. _____

6. _____

_____

7. _____

_____

8. _____

_____

When revising a paper, this question can also come in handy. As you reread a piece of writing, you can ask yourself, "What did I need to prove in order to prove my thesis?" Then, you can examine the paper to see if it did, in fact, prove those points.

NOTE: A discussion of this exercise can be found on page 266.

EXERCISE 11B-2 _____

Return to the memo you wrote for Exercise 11A-6 and ask yourself what points you needed to make in order to prove your thesis. List the points you needed to establish in the spaces below.

Thesis: _____

_____

_____

Points that needed to be established:

1. _____

_____

2. _____

_____

3. _____

_____

4. _____

_____

5. _____

_____

6. _____

_____

7. _____

_____

8. _____

_____

DISCUSSION OF INDUCTIVE EXERCISE

EXERCISE 11B-1

You may have thought of some things we didn't, but you should have included at least the following:

1. There is a problem with the current cash register.
2. A new cash register will solve the problem.
3. There is not a better solution to the problem. (For example, why not get the old one fixed?)
4. This solution won't create worse problems. (For example, if it costs too much, it might eat up all our profit.)

Some other ideas you might have listed include the following:

5. This is an appropriate time to buy a new register. (For example, they have just gone on sale.)
6. Management won't be opposed to this proposal.

12

Coherence

Part A   Transitions
Part B   Consistent Point of View
Part C   Consistent Tense

Coherence, literally, means "sticking together." When applied to writing, it refers to how well the writing "sticks together," how well it "flows" from one idea to the next. Writing that is coherent is easy to read; each idea flows logically into the next one. The reader doesn't have trouble following the argument, doesn't have to back up and reread a passage to figure out what it means.

One of the best ways to make sure your writing is coherent is to organize it effectively as you learned in Chapter 9. There are, however, several other techniques that can also be used to improve coherence, and you will learn about them in this chapter.

Part A · Transitions

EXERCISE 12A-1

Take a look at the following two paragraphs and decide which one is more effective.

Paragraph 1

I have several good reasons for not going to work today. I was stung several times in the foot by bees while walking in my yard last night. I cannot get my shoe on. My son is staying home from school.

He has a bad cold. The computer is being repaired at work. I won't be able to get much done anyhow.

Paragraph 2

I have several good reasons for not going to work today. First, I was stung several times in the foot by bees while walking in my yard last night. As a result, I cannot get my shoe on. Also, my son is staying home from school because he has a bad cold. Finally, the computer is being repaired at work, so I won't be able to get much done anyhow.

After you have decided which one is more effective, figure out why. What is the difference between them?

NOTE: A discussion of the answers to this exercise can be found on pages 270–271.

EXERCISE 12A-2 _____

As a user of the English language, you are undoubtedly already familiar with many transitional expressions. This exercise will give you some sense of the ones you know. In the spaces below each of the following sentences, write as many transitional expressions as you can think of *that would work gracefully* in the blank space.

We have provided a blank line for every transitional expression we could think of. However, don't feel you have to think of exactly as many as we did. Just fill in as many as you can.

1. I am not going out tonight. My car is not running well; _____ , the forecast is for snow.

    _____   _____

    _____   _____

    _____   _____

2. She wore a clove of garlic around her neck; _____ , she was never attacked by a werewolf.

    _____   _____

    _____   _____

    _____   _____

    _____   _____

3. I studied very hard for my astrology test; _____ , I failed it.

    _____   _____

4. I am allergic to many things; _____ , I break out in a rash whenever I am around aardvarks.

    _____   _____

    _____   _____

5. Emily made lemonade; _____ , she took the cat for a swim.

_____   _____

_____   _____

_____   _____

NOTE: The answers to this exercise can be found on pages 271–272.

EXERCISE 12A-3

In the following sentences, write the transitional expression that is most effective on the blank lines. Also insert the appropriate punctuation.

1. I wanted to go home _____ I waited for Susan.

2. My daughter learned a lot at the aquarium _____ she learned that sharks will not eat stingrays.

3. Lonnie washed her car _____ she mowed the lawn.

4. Julio put an ad in the paper _____ he put notices up on the bulletin boards at work.

5. Tanya got an A on every quiz _____ she wrote a wonderful research paper _____ she only got a B in the course.

6. Mr. Lee's mother is quite sick _____ he is flying to Korea.

7. We painted every room and sanded all the floors. Next, we added a deck in the back. _____ we put the house up for sale.

8. Greg was putting up the tent _____ Bruce was starting a fire for dinner.

9. The tornado did damage to our roof _____ it destroyed the garage. _____ the damage could have been a lot worse.

10. I made lots of mistakes while driving to Pennsylvania _____ I missed the exit for the Pennsylvania Turnpike.

EXERCISE 12A-4

Revise the following paragraph to improve its transitions. In some places, this will mean adding a transitional expression; in other places, you may need to change or delete one that is already there.

A word of caution. Too many transitional expressions can make your writing seem cluttered and cumbersome. Don't insert a transitional expression unless it really makes the writing clearer. In the following passage, only a few are needed. Don't overdo it.

The trouble with American foreign policy is that it sees the world as if it were a Hollywood Western. This means that we act as if all the people in the world fit into two groups—good guys and bad guys. The world is not like that. Most people are a combination of good and bad and mainly want to be left alone with a reasonable chance for a decent life. Our cowboy mentality means that too often we see violence as the only solution to problems. When some of our citizens are taken hostage, there are always many voices crying out for a military raid to rescue them. Like those heroes of the Hollywood Western, we think courage requires that we speak very little. If we sat down with those "bad" guys and talked over our differences, we might look "weak." Perhaps American foreign policy would be improved if our leaders would watch a few musicals.

DISCUSSION OF INDUCTIVE EXERCISES

EXERCISE 12A-1

We hope that you agree that paragraph 2 is much more effective than paragraph 1. Paragraph 2 is much easier to read; it flows more smoothly; it is easier to follow.

To understand why this is so, think about a modern interstate highway. It is composed of a series of large white rectangles of concrete laid end to end for hundreds of miles. Where these concrete rectangles are joined, there is a seam of an inch or so that is filled with black tar. As you drive over an interstate highway that is in good shape, your tires make a reassuring "whump, whump, whump" noise rolling at fifty-five miles per hour over the seams.

On an interstate that is not in such good shape, however, the noise may not be so reassuring. Freezing and thawing may have caused the concrete rectangles to shift so that their seams are no longer small cracks filled with tar. They may have shifted so that there is a large crack or so that one concrete block is much higher than the other. Perhaps a diagram will help:

On this kind of highway, when your tires hit the seam, the sound is a resounding bang that vibrates all the way up the steering wheel. In particularly severe cases, the impact may even knock your front wheels out of alignment.

Whoever is responsible for maintaining the roads needs to get out there and fix the highway. What is needed is some more tar at the point where the two concrete blocks are out of alignment. This tar would provide a smooth transition from one block to the other so that your car would not be jolted. The repaired highway would then look like this:

Of course, this lesson in highway engineering is going to end up having something to do with writing. The connection is this. Sentences are a lot like those big blocks of concrete that make up the interstate. When they are in good shape, when the writing is coherent, they flow along smoothly with no jarring as the reader moves from one sentence to another. But occasionally large gaps develop between them. The reader is jarred as he or she makes the transition from one sentence to the next. To fix this problem, the writer must provide a smoother transition from one sentence to the next. Instead of pouring hot tar in the gap, writers use a word or phrase to make the transition smooth. These words and phrases are, logically enough, called transitional expressions. Inserting them in a piece of writing that has transitional problems is a good way to provide coherence. Of course putting them in where they are not needed can also cause problems, just as putting extra tar on a seam that doesn't need it can cause an unnecessary bump.

EXERCISE 12A-2

Listed below each of the sentences are as many transitional expressions as we could think of.

1. I am not going out tonight. My car is not running well; _____ , the forecast is for snow.

in addition	also
moreover	furthermore
what is more	besides

2. She wore a clove of garlic around her neck; _____ , she was never attacked by a werewolf.

as a result	therefore
consequently	for this reason
thus	hence
because of this	

3. I studied very hard for my astrology test; _____ , I failed it.

nevertheless	still

4. I am allergic to many things; _____ , I break out in a rash whenever I am around aardvarks.

for example	for instance

5. Emily made lemonade; _____ , she took the cat for a swim.

later	then
next	after a while
afterward	finally

In the space below, we have listed all the transitional expressions from the sentences above, as well as other common ones. They are grouped according to their function.

Addition:

also	furthermore	next
and	in addition	similarly
besides	moreover	what is more
first (second, etc.)		

Cause and effect:

accordingly	for this reason	then
and so	hence	therefore
as a result	so	thus
consequently		

Contrast:

although	in contrast	on the contrary
but	instead	still
even though	nevertheless	though
however	on the other hand	yet

Example:

for example	for instance

Summary:

all in all	finally	in short
and so	in brief	on the whole
after all	in closing	to conclude
at last	in conclusion	to summarize

Time:

afterward	formerly	next
after a while	in the future	previously
at last	in the meantime	simultaneously
at the same time	in the past	soon
currently	immediately	suddenly
earlier	later	then
eventually	meanwhile	until now

Part B · Consistent Point of View

EXERCISE 12B-1 _____

The following are three versions of the same paragraph. Which do you like best? Which is the least effective?

Version 1

Students coming to register should arrive on campus by ten o'clock. They should bring their SAT scores, a number two pencil, and their driver's license to room 212 of the Administration Building, where they will be told what to do next. The entire process will take about three hours.

Version 2

Students coming to register should arrive on campus by ten o'clock. You should bring your SAT scores, a number two pencil, and your driver's license. They should go to room 212 of the Administration Building, where you will be told what to do next. The entire process will take about three hours.

Version 3

When you come to register, you should arrive on campus by ten o'clock. You should bring your SAT scores, a number two pencil, and your driver's license to room 212 of the Administration Building, where you will be told what to do next. The entire process will take about three hours.

NOTE: A discussion of the answers to this exercise can be found on pages 274–275.

EXERCISE 12B-2 —————————————————————

Revise the following paragraphs for shifts in point of view.

Paragraph 1

James Michener is a very popular writer today, but that doesn't necessarily mean he is a great writer. He usually writes novels that have lots of characters and that are spread over several centuries. Once you start one of his novels, you will have a hard time putting it down. He writes another best seller about every two years. Nevertheless, his real stature as a novelist will only be clear in the future when his novels have had a chance to pass the test of time.

Paragraph 2

You will find using a word processor to be much easier than you think. You merely type your paper using the keyboard of the computer exactly like a typewriter. Then, the writer uses various combinations of keys to make changes in his or her paper. He or she can move words around, erase words, and insert words with just the flick of a key. The writer who has used a word processor will never go back to an old-fashioned typewriter.

Paragraph 3

People who win large prizes in lotteries often find that all that money only makes them miserable. They have to put up with a lot of people trying to get their hands on a chunk of the money. They may even find that their friends expect them to share the prize money. All these pressures take a lot of the fun out of winning. You discover that you can no longer trust anyone. You have to be on your guard constantly to make sure you aren't taken advantage of. You no longer can relax and enjoy life.

EXERCISE 12B-3 _____

The following paragraph is written from the point of view of "you." Revise it using the point of view of "they." The first sentence has been done for you.

           people   *their* *they*

If ~~you~~ want to be careful about ~~your~~ health, ~~you~~ should consider taking vitamins. Your body requires certain amounts of vitamins in order to remain healthy. You may think that eating healthily should provide all the vitamins you need, and it should, but it may not. Even if you eat a fairly well-balanced diet, you may, by chance, be missing one or more crucial vitamins. If you regularly eat a lot of junk food, your body may be missing even more essential vitamins. To be on the safe side, you need only to take a good multivitamin, one that will supply all the essentials.

DISCUSSION OF INDUCTIVE EXERCISE

EXERCISE 12B-1

It should have been fairly easy to decide which of these three paragraphs was least effective: version 2 is quite confusing. First, it talks about what *students* should do. Then, in the middle, it shifts and talks about what *you* should bring. Then it shifts back to *they* and says *they* should go to room 212. And when *they* get to room 212, *you* will be told what to do. This shifting back and forth between "they" and "you" is quite confusing and makes version 2 the least effective.

    Deciding which you prefer between versions 1 and 3 is not so easy. They are both perfectly correct, and which one would be more effective depends somewhat on the purpose the writer has in mind. If part of the purpose is to make potential students feel more relaxed and more welcome, then version 3 would be more effective; it talks directly to potential students and sounds friendlier. On the other hand (notice that transitional expression?), if part of the purpose of the letter was to make sure that students realize this is "serious business" and that they had better show up on time and with the proper information, then version 1 would be more effective. Its use of "they" all the way through makes it sound more stern and authoritarian.

    And there are other options that could be used for a letter like this. The writer might have decided to describe how the average student accomplishes registration. The letter would have started, "When the student comes to register, he or she usually tries to arrive on campus by ten o'clock." If the writer was a fellow student, then he or she could have written, "When I come to register, I usually arrive on campus by ten o'clock" or "When we come to register, we should arrive on campus by ten o'clock." All of these are perfectly correct, but each one conveys a slightly different tone. Perhaps a chart will make the choices clearer:

If the writer	he or she would say	If the writer	he or she would say
talks as a student	I come to register	talks as one of the students	we come to register
talks directly to the student	you come to register	talks directly to the students	you come to register
talks about the student	he or she comes to register	talks about the students	they come to register

From this chart, you can see that there are at least six different ways the letter to incoming students could have been written. Each would have been correct, but each would have added a slightly different tone to the letter. We've already seen that using "you" makes writing sound more personal, while "they" makes it seem more authoritarian. Each of the other choices would change the tone slightly.

These different choices are known as different "points of view." The best point of view for a particular piece of writing depends on the purpose of the writing and the effect the writer wants to create.

There is only one choice that is always incorrect: choosing to mix several different points of view. Shifting point of view in the middle of a piece of writing is almost always wrong. That is why version 2 in this exercise was so confusing. It didn't have a consistent point of view.

Once you start using a particular point of view, make sure you don't accidentally slip into a different one. The most common mistake in consistent point of view is to begin with one of the other choices and then accidentally to slip into the use of "you." Therefore, when you are revising your writing, any time that you see the word "you," check it closely to make sure you have not made a shift in point of view.

Part C · Consistent Tense

EXERCISE 12C-1 _____

Back in Chapter 4, you learned from the following sentences that the present tense is used to describe events that are happening "right now," as the person is speaking. Each of the following sentences is true "right now."

1. The Red River is nearly at flood stage.
2. My watch is about five minutes fast.
3. My husband has the car.
4. Rose is in the swimming pool.
5. Lynn has a great idea.

In the next five sentences, these sentences have been revised slightly. When are these sentences occurring? When are they true?

6. The Red River was nearly at flood stage.
7. My watch was about five minutes fast.
8. My husband had the car.

9.   Rose was in the swimming pool.
10. Lynn had a great idea.

NOTE: A discussion of this exercise can be found on page 280.

EXERCISE 12C-2

In Chapter 4, you also encountered the following sentences. These are written in the present tense, just like the first five in Exercise 12C-1, but the present tense here indicates something a little different from what it indicated in the last exercise. Here it indicates that statements are true *always,* in the present and in the past and in the future. *Moby-Dick* is not a novel about whaling only right now; it was in the past, and it will be in the future. The same is true for each of these.

1.   *Moby-Dick* is a novel about whaling.
2.   Rome is the capital of Italy.
3.   Mr. Curran takes the 7:28 train to work.
4.   The Congo River flows into the Atlantic Ocean.
5.   The Chinese alphabet consists of thousands of characters.

Notice that each of these statements could also be written in the past tense. With these changes, when is each of these sentences true?

6.   *Moby-Dick* was a novel about whaling.
7.   Rome was the capital of Italy.
8.   Mr. Curran took the 7:28 train to work.
9.   The Congo River flowed into the Atlantic Ocean.
10. The Chinese alphabet consisted of thousands of characters.

NOTE: A discussion of this exercise can be found on page 280.

EXERCISE 12C-3

Now that we have reviewed the use of present and past tense, we will work on a problem that sometimes occurs in the use of these tenses.
     Read the following and decide which is most effective and which is least.

Version 1

     Robert Frost's poetry has a very simple and straightforward outer surface, but underneath, it is quite complicated. He writes about farms, trees, brooks, ponds, walls, and paths, but all the time he is discussing something much more serious. For example, when he writes about himself and his neighbor going out to repair the wall between their lands, he raises profound questions about relationships between people. His neighbor insists that "good fences" are necessary if people are to get along, but Frost wonders why. He even suggests that there may be mysterious natural forces that want to tear down the walls between people. Beneath the simple surface of Frost's poetry, there is powerful thinking about the human experience.

Version 2

Robert Frost's poetry had a very simple and straightforward outer surface, but underneath, it was quite complicated. He wrote about farms, trees, brooks, ponds, walls, and paths, but all the time he was discussing something much more serious. For example, when he wrote about himself and his neighbor going out to repair the wall between their lands, he raised profound questions about relationships between people. His neighbor insisted that "good fences" were necessary if people were to get along, but Frost wondered why. He even suggested that there might be mysterious natural forces that wanted to tear down the walls between people. Beneath the simple surface of Frost's poetry, there was powerful thinking about the human experience.

Version 3

Robert Frost's poetry had a very simple and straightforward outer surface, but underneath, it was quite complicated. He writes about farms, trees, brooks, ponds, walls, and paths, but all the time he is discussing something much more serious. For example, when he wrote about himself and his neighbor going out to repair the wall between their lands, he raises profound questions about relationships between people. His neighbor insists that "good fences" are necessary if people are to get along, but Frost wondered why. He even suggested that there might be mysterious natural forces that wanted to tear down the walls between people. Beneath the simple surface of Frost's poetry, there is powerful thinking about the human experience.

NOTE: A discussion of the answers to this exercise can be found on pages 280–281.

EXERCISE 12C-4

Correct any errors in the following. All errors will involve inconsistent use of verb tense. Each sentence may contain no errors, one error, or more than one error.

1. When I first saw the ring he had bought me, I am amazed.

2. Since London was located on a major river, it was a center of trading in the Middle Ages.

3. My car was in the garage, so I ride to work with Donna.

4. Gloria was an actress and plays mostly flaky roles.

5. If Charles sees someone kissing, he makes a big fuss.

6. Every Sunday last year, I get up at six and delivered newspapers to three hundred houses.

7. The judge sentences me to one month in jail, and he smiled while he was giving the sentence.

8. This book is written by George Orwell; he also was the author of *1984*.

9.   While I lived in Hawaii, I learned to snorkel.

10.   When you worked for Mr. Hall, does he ever give you a bonus?

EXERCISE 12C-5

Proofread the following paragraph carefully and correct any errors. All errors will involve inconsistent verb tense.

Looking for a prom dress with my daughter was quite an experience. She announced that the girls in her school had decided they would not wear "real" prom dresses. Then she tries to explain what they would wear, but I couldn't understand it. We went to a huge mall with four major department stores. After five hours, I had held up forty-one dresses and asked, "Would you like something like this?" And the answer is consistently "No." So we try a fancy ladies' dress shop, but nothing there will do. After a break for dinner, we drive to the last department store in town, but nothing there will do. Finally, we stopped at one last dress shop, and there she finds the dress she wanted. It was a white strapless dress with a lot of gauzy material around the bottom. I could not see how it was any different from a traditional prom dress, but I am so relieved to have found a dress that I do not say a word.

EXERCISE 12C-6

In the preceding exercises, you learned that tenses must be consistent. If you start out in past tense, you may not switch to the present tense for no reason. In the following perfectly correct sentences, however, you will find that the verb tenses are not consistent. Study these sentences carefully and see if you can figure out why these shifts in verb tense are acceptable.

1.   I was born in Kansas City, but now I live in Omaha.
2.   Laurie gave me a ring, but now she wants it back.
3.   When I first met her, my wife was still in school; now she is an accountant.
4.   Today I love tomatoes, but I hated them when I was a child.
5.   I studied for five hours, but I do not remember a thing I read.

NOTE: A discussion of the answers to this exercise can be found on page 281.

EXERCISE 12C-7

Now you know all you need to know about tense shifts. Proofread the following sentences and correct any errors. All errors will involve unnecessary tense shifts. Each sentence may contain no errors, one error, or more than one error.

1. When I saw Tony, he is waiting for a bus and talking to a beautiful woman.

2. As a boy, I loved to play baseball, but now I am just a loyal fan.

3. Joe and Barb live in the city, but they are looking for a house in the suburbs.

4. Susan Toler drove to California and gets herself a part in a movie.

5. We watch Cathy open her gifts and laughed when we saw what she got from you.

6. Ben hands me a quarter and took my newspaper off my desk.

7. Kevin had hoped to get a job this summer, but he is going to summer school instead.

8. I opened the letter anxiously, but it is only a bill.

9. Ms. Myers stops and looks at something on the floor; then, she went into the kitchen and started whistling.

10. I hoped to be finished with this homework by now, but I am only on number nine.

11. My neighbor bought a new lawn mower, and he mows his grass every Saturday morning at seven-thirty.

12. Ed opens the refrigerator and looks inside but he did not find anything to drink.

13. When I lived in New York, I paid a lot of rent, and I can not keep a car because there is nowhere to park it.

14. Now I go to a lot of movies, but I used to think they were boring.

15. We buy our tickets and walk into the lobby; then, my brother remembered that he had forgotten to turn off the coffee pot.

16. Mr. Vasquez used to hire a lot of high school students, and he pays them fairly well.

17. Debbie tells a long, funny story while she was waiting for the dentist.

18. Shakespeare uses British history to create great drama, and he borrowed some history from the Romans as well.

19. I lived next door to the Hadleys until they moved to Texas.

20. Lew jumps out of his chair when Ms. Branagan came into the room.

 EXERCISE 12C-8

Correct any errors in the following paragraph. All errors will involve tense shifts.

I used to believe that it was wrong to lie. When my house burned down last year, I told the truth on the claim I filed with my insurance company. However, they seem to assume that everyone lies when they file a claim. They tell me that my house was not worth the eighty-five thousand a realtor told me it was worth, so they offer me sixty thousand. They say about half the possessions I reported as destroyed were not even covered, and they reduce the value of everything else by about 50 percent for depreciation. When I finally go to a lawyer, he told me that most people make such dishonest claims that insurance companies have to reduce the value of claims in order to stay in business. Now that I know this, I am a lot wiser, and I intend to lie like crazy if I ever have to file another claim.

DISCUSSION OF INDUCTIVE EXERCISES

EXERCISE 12C-1

By changing the form of the verb slightly, we have changed each sentence so that it makes a statement that was true in the *past*. In this form, sentence 1 indicates only that the river was near flood stage at some time in the past; we don't know whether it is still near flooding or not. The sentence only indicates that, in the past, the river *was* near flooding. The same is true for each of the other sentences.

EXERCISE 12C-2

As in sentences 6 through 10 in Exercise 12C-1, each of these sentences, written in the past tense, makes a statement that was true in the past; in this form, they don't indicate whether these statements are still true in the present.

The following rules summarize what we know from these two exercises about the present and past tenses.

The present tense has two uses:

- to express events that are going on right now, in the present;
- to express events that are true always, continually, or repeatedly, in the past, present, and future.

The past tense has only one use:

- to express events that were true in the past.

EXERCISE 12C-3

You may have had some trouble deciding which of these is the most effective, but you should have seen fairly quickly that version 3 is the least effective. Version 3 confuses the reader because it can't decide whether to talk about Frost in the present tense or the past tense. First it says Frost's poetry *had* a simple surface but *was* complicated underneath. In the next sentence, it says that Frost *writes* about rural subjects, but by the third sentence, it has switched back to the past tense, as it discusses when he *wrote* about repairing a wall. This switching back and forth between present and past tenses makes the passage very confusing.

Version 1 is written in the present tense, and version 2 in the past. These are both perfectly correct, and, in this case, they are just about equally effective. Occasionally, when you have a choice, one will sound better than the other, but if not, you can use either one.

The only thing you can't do is to switch back and forth. Just like with point of view in the last section, it is important that you keep your tenses consistent. Don't switch back and forth for no reason.

EXERCISE 12C-6

Each of these sentences shifts between present and past tense, but these shifts are for a reason. Each time there is a tense shift, it indicates that one part of the sentence happened in the past and another part is in the present. In the first sentence, "I was born in Kansas City" in the *past,* so I am using the past tense "was born." But in the second half of the sentence, I am no longer talking about the past. Right now, in the *present,* "I live in Omaha." Since the sentence shifts from the past to the present, the verb tense shifts from past to present.

Each of the shifts in these sentences is for a reason; each indicates that one part of the sentence is occurring in the past and one part in the present. This is the only time it is acceptable to shift tenses.

13

Noun Use

Part A   Singular and Plural
          of Regular Nouns
Part B   Singular and Plural
          of Irregular Nouns
Part C   Capitalization

Part A · Singular and Plural of Regular Nouns

In this section you will learn how to form the plurals of regular nouns.

 EXERCISE 13A-1 —————————————————————

The following sentences illustrate the basic rule for forming plural nouns in English.

1.   One <u>boy</u> was playing in the street.
2.   Two <u>boys</u> were playing in the street.
3.   A <u>book</u> fell off my desk in the middle of the night.
4.   Several <u>books</u> fell off my desk in the middle of the night.
5.   There is only one <u>typewriter</u> remaining in stock.
6.   There are only two <u>typewriters</u> remaining in stock.

Study these sentences and figure out the basic rule for forming plural nouns.

NOTE: A discussion of the answers to this exercise can be found on page 284.

EXERCISE 13A-2 _____

The following sentences contain errors involving plural nouns. Proofread these sentences and correct any errors. Each sentence may contain no errors, one error, or more than one error.

1. Many bird landed in my front yard at dusk.

2. I saw a rainbows as I was driving to Larry's house.

3. Several of the desk in this room are broken.

4. Greg bought a bag of apple for all of us.

5. John doesn't believe in ghost.

6. The wave are quite big this afternoon.

7. Shirley sets three alarm clock every night.

8. Lou Anne bought some disk for her computer.

9. Her proposal contained a number of hidden cost.

10. There are many risk in following Mary's suggestion.

 EXERCISE 13A-3 _____

The following sentences illustrate a variation on the basic rule for forming plural nouns.

1. One <u>class</u> was cancelled this morning.
2. All <u>classes</u> were cancelled this morning.
3. Last night a <u>fox</u> ran out of our garage.
4. Last night two <u>foxes</u> ran out of our garage.
5. I gave Jocelyn a large <u>dish</u> for a wedding present.
6. I gave Jocelyn a set of <u>dishes</u> for a wedding present.
7. I sliced a <u>tomato</u> for the salad.
8. I sliced some <u>tomatoes</u> for the salad.
9. I had one <u>hero</u> when I was growing up.
10. I had two <u>heroes</u> when I was growing up.

Study these sentences and figure out the basic rule for this variation.

NOTE: A discussion of this exercise can be found on pages 284–285.

 EXERCISE 13A-4 _____

Proofread the following sentences and correct any errors. All errors will involve the formation of plural nouns. Each sentence may have no errors, one error, or more than one error.

1. There were three brush on Maria's dresser.

2. He works for a company that builds patio.

3. Debby and Marc need a lot of box because they are moving.

4. These three book belong to the city library.

5. Mr. Martin has two boss in this company.

6. Would you bring me the box of match?

7. Empty those ash into the garbage can in the garage.

8. We planted a row of bush in front of our house.

9. Steve gave three reason why he could not quit his job.

10. Stacey gets herself into more fix than anyone else I know.

EXERCISE 13A-5

Proofread the following paragraph and correct any errors. All errors will involve plural nouns.

Classes in college are a lot different from classes in high school. In high school the desk were arranged in neat little rows and always seemed too small. In college, the desk are big enough so that I don't hit my knees, and they are often arranged in a circle. High school teacher often gave test, sometimes without any warning. In college, we have only two or three test a semester, and they are always announced well in advance. In high school, we always had to raise our hand and wait to be called on. Here in college, class are more like conversations; if we have something to say, we just wait for a pause in the discussion and then say it. The basic difference between high school class and college class is that, in college class, it is assumed that the student are adults.

DISCUSSION OF INDUCTIVE EXERCISES

EXERCISE 13A-1

The basic rule for forming plural nouns is as follows:

To make a regular noun plural, add an "s."

EXERCISE 13A-3

These sentences show that it is sometimes necessary to add an "es" ending instead of just an "s" to make words plural. This is generally true when a word ends in the following: "ch," "sh," "ss," "x," and "z."

In addition, most words that end in "o" form their plurals by adding an "es"; however, the following form their plurals by adding just an "s." You should probably memorize these:

one lasso	two lassos
one patio	two patios

one piano	two pianos		
one photo	two photos		
one radio	two radios		
one solo	two solos		
one soprano	two sopranos		

With these changes, the rule for forming plural nouns looks like this:

To make a regular noun plural, add an "s" or "es."

Part B · Singular and Plural of Irregular Nouns

In Part A, you learned to form plurals of regular nouns. The rule you learned was as follows:

To make a regular noun plural, add an "s" or "es."

In this section, you will learn some rules for making irregular nouns plural.

 EXERCISE 13B-1 ———————————————————

The following examples illustrate one way irregular nouns form their plurals:

half	halves	self	selves
hoof	hooves	shelf	shelves
knife	knives	thief	thieves
leaf	leaves	wife	wives
life	lives	wolf	wolves

Study these examples and write this exception to the regular rule for forming plurals in the space below.

_____

_____

_____

_____

_____

NOTE: A discussion of the answer to this exercise can be found on page 288.

 EXERCISE 13B-2 ———————————————————

Use the rule for forming plural nouns as you proofread the following sentences and correct any errors. All errors will involve plural nouns. Each sentence may contain no errors, one error, or more than one error.

1. The students in my writing class are very proud of themselves.

2. It required two knife to cut the watermelon into two halfs.

3. The leaf had fallen off the trees by October thirty-first last year.

4.   There were several boxs on the shelfs in the basement.

5.   Angie made two list, one of the husbands and one of the wifes.

6.   My cat, Cooper, really does have nine life.

7.   Linda repairs roofs during the summer.

8.   Scott's beliefs won't allow him to serve in the army.

9.   The knifes are in the top left drawer.

10. Do your new pants have cuff?

EXERCISE 13B-3

The following examples illustrate another addition to the rule for forming plural nouns:

one beauty	two beauties	one pony	two ponies
one cry	two cries	this sky	these skies
one enemy	two enemies	one spy	two spies
one fly	two flies	one study	two studies
one French fry	two French fries	one try	two tries
one jury	two juries	one worry	two worries
one lily	two lilies		

In the space below, write the addition to the rule that is illustrated by the preceding examples.

_____

_____

_____

_____

_____

        The following group illustrates an addition to the preceding addition:

one attorney	two attorneys	one Monday	two Mondays
one boy	two boys	one monkey	two monkeys
one bay	two bays	one ray	two rays
one day	two days	one Sunday	two Sundays
one jay	two jays	one Tuesday	two Tuesdays
one key	two keys	one way	two ways

How are all the words on this list different from the ones on the list before? Once you figure this out, write the addition to the preceding addition in the space below.

_____

_____

_____

_____

_____

NOTE: A discussion of the answer to this exercise can be found on pages 288–289.

EXERCISE 13B-4

Proofread the following sentences using the rule for forming plural nouns and correct any errors. Each sentence may contain no errors, one error, or more than one error.

1. After the children rode the ponys, they had hamburgers and French frys at McDonald's.
2. On Mondaies, I usually pick up the two key in the manager's office.
3. More and more jury are refusing to hand down the death penalty.
4. The monkies and the wolfs usually attract the biggest crowds at the zoo.
5. The skys are beautiful in Alaska.
6. The morning sun brought out the beauty of the lilys.
7. Wilma's studies keep her very busy.
8. There are three boxs of knifes in the truck.
9. When I was in high school, I had no worry and no enemy.
10. Everyone is entitled to his or her own believes.

EXERCISE 13B-5

The following examples illustrate yet another group of irregular noun plurals:

one deer	two deer
one fish	two fish (or fishes)
one moose	two moose
one sheep	two sheep

In the space below, write the addition illustrated by the preceding examples.

_____

_____

_____

_____

NOTE: A discussion of the answer to this exercise can be found on page 289.

EXERCISE 13B-6

Proofread the following sentences and correct any errors. All errors will involve noun plurals. Each sentence may contain no errors, one error, or more than one error.

1. Three man were hunting deers in the woods behind my house.
2. The last apartment Gene rented had mouses.
3. Her studies included the migration patterns of goose and fishs.
4. The women in this picture are the wife of the astronauts.

5. Two sheeps were grazing in Vera's front yard.

6. Zack had beautiful tooths.

7. Roxanne's husband never ate the meat of mooses on Tuesdayes.

8. There were lilys on the table when I arrived at Jackie's house.

9. Mooses have been known to eat mices when they were very hungry.

10. What would a James Bond movie be without spys?

DISCUSSION OF INDUCTIVE EXERCISES

EXERCISE 13B-1

From the examples, this exception to the rule for forming plural nouns appears to be the following:

Regular Rule: To make a regular noun plural, add an "s" or "es."

First Exception: To make a noun that ends in "f" or "fe" plural, change the "f" or "fe" to a "v" and add "es."

There are, however, several exceptions to this latest addition:

one belief	two beliefs
one chief	two chiefs
one cuff	two cuffs
one roof	two roofs
one safe	two safes

It is probably best to memorize these. If you are ever in doubt, a dictionary lists the plural forms of all nouns that do not follow the regular rule, that is, all nouns that do not add an "s" or "es" to form their plurals. The following, for example, are portions of the entries for "thief" and "chief" in the *American Heritage Dictionary*:

• **thief** (thēf) n. pl. thieves (thevz) 1. A person who steals property. . . .

• **chief** (chēf) n. Abbr. C., ch., Ch. 1. One who is highest in rank. . . .

Notice that the plural for "thief" is listed as "thieves," but the plural for "chief" is not listed. This is because "thieves" is irregular; to form it you must change the "f" to a "v" and then add an "es." However, the plural of "chief" is "chiefs." This is a regular noun; it forms its plural merely by adding an "s"; therefore, the dictionary doesn't list the plural form.

EXERCISE 13B-3

The words on both lists on page 286 all end in a "y." The ones at the top of the page end in a consonant and a "y"; the ones at the bottom end in a vowel and a "y." With these two additions, the rule for forming plurals now looks like the following:

Regular Rule: To make a regular noun plural, add an "s" or "es."

First Exception: To make a noun that ends in "f" or "fe" plural, change the "f" or "fe" to a "v" and add "es."

| Second Exception: | To make a noun that ends in a consonant and a "y" plural, change the "y" to "i" and add "es." |
| Third Exception: | To make a noun that ends in a vowel and a "y" plural, just add an "s." |

EXERCISE 13B-5

These examples show that the plurals of some irregular nouns are the same as their singular forms.

The following examples illustrate the most irregular group of all:

one child	two children	one mouse	two mice
one foot	two feet	one tooth	two teeth
one goose	two geese	one woman	two women
one man	two men		

These words are very irregular. You probably already know most of them, and you may want to just memorize the others. If you are ever in doubt, check a dictionary. Dictionaries list the plural forms of all irregular nouns.

Now you know all the ways nouns form their plurals. The rule with all its exceptions is listed below.

Regular Rule:	To make a regular noun plural, add an "s" or "es."
First Exception:	To make a noun that ends in "f" or "fe" plural, change the "f" or "fe" to a "v" and add "es."
Second Exception:	To make a noun that ends in a consonant and a "y" plural, change the "y" to "i" and add "es."
Third Exception:	To make a noun that ends in a vowel and a "y" plural, just add an "s."
Fourth Exception:	Some very irregular nouns do not change their form from singular to plural.
Fifth Exception:	Other highly irregular nouns form their plurals in completely unpredictable ways.

Part C · Capitalization

 EXERCISE 13C-1 _____

The following sentences illustrate the basic rule for capitalization.

1. Lance Branagan attended Essex Community College for three years.
2. I once lived in Kabul, Afghanistan, for a year.
3. *The Scarlet Letter* is still one of the greatest novels ever written in America.
4. Nancy and Debra are driving us all crazy with their grammatical blunders.
5. *Connections* is very exciting reading; I wonder how it will end.
6. The General Electric Corporation built a washing machine for me.
7. Laredo, Texas, is an awfully hot town.
8. My son is going to Franklin High School.
9. Elvis Presley shocked our parents.
10. The Empire State Building is no longer the tallest building in the world.

The first word of every sentence above is capitalized, but so are a lot of other words. Can you figure out one thing all these other words have in common?

If you are having trouble, look at the capitalized words in numbers 1 (Lance Branagan), 4 (Harry, Debra), and 9 (Elvis Presley). What do these words have in common? What are they? Is there some sense in which all the other capitalized words are the same thing as these?

NOTE: A discussion of the answers to this exercise can be found on page 294.

EXERCISE 13C-2

The following sets of sentences illustrate some of the problems in applying this capitalization rule. Study them carefully and try to figure out why the incorrect ones are incorrect.

1.	Correct:	I attended Marshall High School for four years.
2.	Incorrect:	I attended High School for four years.
3.	Correct:	I attended high school for four years.
4.	Correct:	West Virginia University will be closed all of next week.
5.	Incorrect:	The University will be closed all of next week.
6.	Correct:	The university will be closed all of next week.
7.	Correct:	I still owe Doctor Fong three hundred dollars.
8.	Incorrect:	I still owe my Doctor three hundred dollars.
9.	Correct:	I still owe my doctor three hundred dollars.
10.	Correct:	I am going to visit Aunt Gail next Sunday.
11.	Incorrect:	I am going to visit my Aunt next Sunday.
12.	Correct:	I am going to visit my aunt next Sunday.
13.	Correct:	My mother lives in the western part of New York.
14.	Incorrect:	My mother lives in the western part of this State.
15.	Correct:	My mother lives in the western part of this state.
16.	Correct:	The Colorado River is not very deep at this time of year.
17.	Incorrect:	The River is not very deep at this time of year.
18.	Correct:	The river is not very deep at this time of year.

NOTE: A discussion of the answers to this exercise can be found on pages 294–295.

EXERCISE 13C-3

Proofread the following sentences and correct any errors. All errors will involve capitalization. Each sentence may contain no errors, one error, or more than one error.

1. My Doctor told me I needed a rest.

2. My mother often had to come in and talk with my High School Principal.

3. I plan to go to Miami Dade Community College next year.

4. I spent the summer with Aunt Dolores.

5. I am thinking about buying my Professor a one-way ticket to Siberia.

6. This State does not spend nearly enough of its budget on my salary.

7. The Lake has gotten a little polluted in recent years.

8. My family Doctor is going to testify before a committee of Senators and Delegates about how much I deserve a pay raise.

9. Kenwood high school gave me a great preparation for College.

10. The Building where my Uncle works is right next to the Trump Tower.

 ## EXERCISE 13C-4 _____

Now you know that *names* of particular persons, places, or things must be capitalized and words that are *not* names may not be capitalized. There are several other problem areas in the capitalization rules, however. This exercise will teach you one of these. Study the following examples carefully and try to figure out what addition to the capitalization rule they illustrate.

1. I have an appointment with my astrological advisor next <u>December</u>.

2. I have an appointment with my astrological advisor next <u>fall</u>.

3. Wilma is moving to Tashkent in <u>December</u>.

4. Wilma is moving to Tashkent in the <u>summer</u>.

5. On <u>Wednesday</u> my car was hit by a bus.

6. Last <u>winter</u> my car was hit by a bus.

7. Every <u>Monday</u> I have to drag myself out of bed.

8. Every <u>spring</u> I have to drag myself out of bed.

NOTE: A discussion of the answers to this exercise can be found on page 295.

 ## EXERCISE 13C-5 _____

Proofread the following sentences and correct any errors. All errors will involve capitalization. Each sentence may contain no errors, one error, or more than one error.

1. In Spring a young man's fancy turns to thoughts of love.

2. I bought this toaster on wednesday, and it broke on thursday.

3. Our reunion was held on a lovely summer Sunday afternoon.

4. My Doctor takes a vacation every August.

5. Vera will graduate from High School next Spring.

6. The new Library will be completed in the fall.

7. On Wednesdays, we eat lunch in the Park behind our Building.

8. My uncle goes to Jamaica every Winter.

9. Linda Hubbe will begin work on Monday.

10. David hopes to finish his computer project this Summer or, at the latest, by september.

EXERCISE 13C-6

Study the following examples and try to determine an additional rule concerning capitalization.

1. My mother grew up in the <u>South</u>.
2. A well-designed house should have most of its windows facing <u>south</u>.
3. The greatest population growth during the 1980s was in the <u>West</u>.
4. This river flows <u>west</u> for about two hundred miles.
5. Major financial institutions in the <u>East</u> control most banking decisions for the country.
6. Moslems always face <u>east</u> when they pray.

NOTE: A discussion of the answers to this exercise can be found on page 295.

EXERCISE 13C-7

Proofread the following sentences and correct any errors. All errors will involve capitalization. Each sentence may contain no errors, one error, or more than one error.

1. There has been a lot of flooding in the west this Spring.
2. Marlene and Bruce were driving north on the New Jersey Turnpike when their brakes went out.
3. Our professor is spending his vacation in the south.
4. We will try to sell this house next Summer.
5. The sun is very bright if you are driving West late in the afternoon.
6. Donald was born in the south, but he doesn't have any accent.
7. My Aunt's store is located three blocks North of the post office.
8. Will you return these books to the Library for me on sunday?
9. This College does not attract many students from the East.
10. I grew up just a few miles North of the Mexican border.

EXERCISE 13C-8

Study the following words and try to determine one more rule for capitalization.

1. Lloyd is studying <u>mathematics</u> this summer.
2. Lloyd is taking <u>Math 110</u> this summer.
3. My favorite subject is <u>history</u>.
4. My best course this semester is <u>History of Russia</u>.
5. Richelle has Professor Crawford for <u>Introduction to Modern Poetry</u>.
6. Richelle has Professor Crawford for her <u>poetry</u> class.

NOTE: A discussion of the answers to this exercise can be found on page 295.

EXERCISE 13C-9

The following are lists of subjects of study. While subjects are usually not capitalized, there are a few exceptions. Study the following lists and figure out why the exceptions are capitalized.

mathematics	English
history	French
nursing	Spanish
computer programming	Chinese

NOTE: A discussion of the answers to this exercise can be found on page 295.

EXERCISE 13C-10

Proofread the following sentences and correct any errors. All errors will involve capitalization. Each sentence may contain no errors, one error, or more than one error.

1. In my Anatomy class, we all are nervous about the midterm exam.
2. When my mother studied Swahili, she did not learn to read it.
3. There are usually three exams in chemistry 201.
4. Is psych 101 offered in the Spring?
5. Wanetta is worried about her grades in calculus and english.
6. The Professor in my accounting class always tells too many jokes.
7. I studied Typing in High School, but I have forgotten everything I learned.
8. Mike is on the waiting list for American History I.
9. I would love to take a course about the Literature of the South.
10. My botany class was cancelled on monday.

EXERCISE 13C-11

Study this list of words that are *not* capitalized. What general groups do these words represent?

daisy	poodle
iris	boxer
poppy	terrier
nasturtium	collie
chrysanthemum	beagle

NOTE: A discussion of the answers to this exercise can be found on page 296.

EXERCISE 13C-12

The following examples illustrate one last rule about capitalization. Study these examples and try to determine what this last rule is.

1. My brother is majoring in <u>American history</u>.
2. Dick's <u>German shepherd</u> is really very friendly.
3. My uncle raises a special flower called the <u>Americana rose</u>.
4. A <u>Norwegian elkhound</u> makes a very good pet.
5. An <u>Indian doctor</u> operated on my father.

NOTE: A discussion of the answers to this exercise can be found on page 296.

EXERCISE 13C-13

This exercise summarizes everything you have learned about capitalization. Proofread the following paragraph carefully and correct any errors.

I have an Uncle who seems to have figured out the secret to being happy. About twenty years ago, he was a Doctor making lots of money and working seventy hours a week. One day, he announced he was quitting his practice and living for himself from then on. When he was in College, he worked his way through school by renovating houses, mostly for his friends. Now that he has quit medicine, he has gone back to what he always enjoyed most—renovation. He only works about four days a week and takes a vacation for two months every Winter. Last year he flew to Florida and rented a sailboat. He and his Irish Setter just sailed East into the Ocean for a month and then sailed back for a month. Then he was ready to go back to his work with a fresh outlook. The combination of doing a job he loves and not working too hard seems to guarantee that he is always happy.

DISCUSSION OF INDUCTIVE EXERCISES

EXERCISE 13C-1

"Lance Branagan," "Harry," "Debra," and "Elvis Presley" are all names of people. The other capitalized words in the sentences are also names. They are not necessarily names of people but each of them is the name of a *particular* person, place, or thing. You may have learned that the name of a particular person, place, or thing is called a proper noun. The term is not really that important, but you must remember the principle: we capitalize the *names* of *particular* persons, places, or things.

EXERCISE 13C-2

The incorrect versions are incorrect because words are capitalized which are not the *names* of *particular* persons, places, or things.

In number 2, "High School" is not the *name* of a *particular* high school. The name was "Marshall High School," and when you use that name (as in number 1) you do capitalize all three words. However, since "high school" is just a general term and is not the *name* of any particular thing, it should not be capitalized. "University" in number 5 is much the same.

Apparently, my doctor's name is "Doctor Fong," and so it is capitalized in number 7. Titles, like "Doctor," are capitalized when they are used as a part of the name. However, when I refer to him as "my Doctor" in number 8, I am not using his name; "Doctor" is not the *name* of a *particular* person. Therefore, it is incorrect to capitalize it.

"Aunt Gail" (in number 10) is the *name* of a *particular* person, so it is capitalized; however, when she is referred to as "my Aunt" in number 11, I am no longer using her *name*, so "Aunt" should not be capitalized.

"New York" is the *name* of a *particular* place, so (in number 13) it is correctly capitalized. When the same place is referred to as "this State" (in number 14), you are no longer using its *name*, so it is incorrect to use a capital.

"Colorado River" (in number 16) is the *name* of a *particular* thing (or place?), so it is correctly capitalized. The "river" is not the *name* of any particular thing, so it is not capitalized.

The principle remains the same: the *names* of *particular* persons, places, or things are capitalized; words that are *not* names of particular persons, places, or things are *not* capitalized.

EXERCISE 13C-4

These sentences show that days of the week and months of the year are capitalized, but the seasons are not. This may seem completely illogical to you, but there is a reason. Most of the days of the week and months are named for Greek, Roman, or Norse gods or goddesses; the seasons were not named for anyone. For example, "January" is derived from the name of the Greek god Janus; "Wednesday" comes from the name of the Norse god Woden. Words that are derived from proper nouns are also considered proper nouns, so we capitalize them.

Whether you remember the explanation or not, remember that days of the week and months are capitalized; seasons are not.

EXERCISE 13C-6

These sentences show that words indicating directions are capitalized when they represent a geographic area (the South) and are not capitalized when they indicate a direction (we drove north).

EXERCISE 13C-8

These examples show that *names of courses* are capitalized, but *subjects of study* are not.

EXERCISE 13C-9

While academic subjects are generally not capitalized, if the subject is derived from the name of a country (like England or Spain), then it is capitalized.

EXERCISE 13C- 11

These lists indicate that names of plants or breeds of dogs are not capitalized.

EXERCISE 13C-12

These examples show that, when a word is derived from (that is, when it "comes" from) a word that is always capitalized, the derived word is also capitalized. Since "America" is the name of a particular place, it is capitalized. Since the word "American" is derived from "America," it too is capitalized.

Further, when a word that needs to be capitalized is combined with one that doesn't, only the first is capitalized. For example, in the phrase "American history," "American" is capitalized because it is derived from "America," but "history" is not capitalized because it is not the name of a particular person, place, or thing, nor is it derived from a word that is.

R E V I E W

 ## EXERCISE 13-REVIEW-1 _____

Proofread the following sentences carefully and correct any errors. All errors will involve noun plurals or capitalization. Each sentence may contain no errors, one error, or more than one error.

1. Carmella is a member of two churchs.
2. A polygamist is usually thought of as a man with two or more wife, but why couldn't a woman be a polygamist too?
3. The new High School was completed five years ago.
4. Nancy's father's warehouse was filled with school desk.
5. We have two safe at my work.
6. When Mr. Stokes was in High School, every student took Latin.
7. Check these list to see if Sandy left anything off.
8. The crys of the children woke our pet armadillo.
9. I will stay with Uncle Lou while I am in San Francisco.
10. Robin's tomato are almost ripe.
11. I would rather baby-sit monkies than her children.
12. My Doctor does not believe in vitamins.
13. Vic took a lot of photo at Mary's wedding.
14. Vince raises sheeps on his farm.
15. We bought a German Shepherd last Fall.
16. I promised to trim some bushs for Lina this weekend.

17. Eddie Murray's home run was foul by two feets.

18. If you live in the south, you have to have air conditioning.

19. All my class were cancelled today.

20. To get rid of all the mouses, I brought in some cats; now how do I get rid of the cats?

EXERCISE 13-REVIEW-2

Proofread the following sentences carefully and correct any errors. All errors will involve noun plurals or capitalization. Each sentence may contain no errors, one error, or more than one error.

1. There were three box under the basement steps.

2. I hope they catch those thief before they rob anyone else.

3. Benjamin's Aunt lives in Hawaii.

4. We saw two foxs when we were camping.

5. Marlene works for a company that puts rooves on houses.

6. Roberta goes to a College in New York City.

7. At camp the kids are not allowed to have radioes.

8. Angela's daughter is always talking about riding ponys.

9. Greg and Mona plan to get married next Summer.

10. We threw several tomato at the politicians.

11. The attornies in this case are sure they can win.

12. To get to Barry's farm, you have to drive south for about six miles.

13. Don't take risk unless you have to.

14. Three moose were crossing the highway and stopping traffic.

15. I hope to study Nursing, if I am accepted into the program.

16. There are no left-handed desk in this room.

17. I need work done on several of my tooth.

18. Terrie gave her daughter a beagle for her birthday.

19. The only heros in this mess were the firemen who put the fire out.

20. I brought two knifes for us.

EXERCISE 13-REVIEW-3

Proofread the following essay and correct any errors. All errors will involve noun plurals or capitalization.

When we were childrens, our parents told us we should never lie. At some point, most of us realized that this wasn't so. There are times when it seems to be necessary or at least advisable to tell a lie. In our society, lying seems to have become necessary for survival. When we were young, we believed all lie were wrong; when we found out that that was not so, we seem to have decided that all lies are all right. In other words, many of us reject our youthful morality, but we haven't found any more mature morality to replace it.

Most peoples I know lie without hesitation when people ask them to do thing they don't want to do. My Aunt always makes up things she has to do when we invite her to come to a party. All my friends lie when their parents want them to spend some time together. "Oh, Mom, We'd love to come for a visit this Summer, but Joe can't take any vacation because he wants to be promoted. Maybe we could come next Winter." Most of the kids in my Psychology class lie about their absences because they don't want the Professor to lower their grades. Even at work, people use this kind of lie to avoid the unpleasant. We tell our bosses or our coworkers that we couldn't possibly take on that project because we have an important meeting at just the same time. We often excuse this kind of lying by saying we are doing it to avoid hurting someone else's feelings. The truth is we are doing it to save ourselfs a lot of hassles and to make sure no one gets mad at us.

From the time we were little kid, Doctors have been telling us, "This won't hurt." And it always hurts like crazy. Doctors often lie when they have bad news for patients. They say they don't want to tell the truth to the patient with terminal cancer because it will only depress him. They say they don't want to tell the man who thinks he's sick that it's all in his head, because it's more effective to give him a placebo (a sugar pill that has no medicine in it). The patient thinks he's getting medicine and so feels better, and the doctor doesn't have to tell him his illness is imaginary. But are these lies really for the good of the patient? Don't they often save the Doctor a lot of hassles? More importantly, don't they undermine our trust in doctors? If we know they think it's okay to lie to us, how can we ever trust them?

Sometimes we say it's okay to lie if the person we are lying to is corrupt or dishonest. This kind of lying is often defended when it is directed at big organizations like insurance firms, corporations we want to hire us, or government agencys like the IRS. It may be true that very few people ever tell the truth to these big organizations because they are seen as too powerful and they are suspected of making huge profits by exploiting us, but once most people make the decision to lie to these kinds of agencies, there are no limits to their dishonesty. They assume that they have to lie to protect themselves from these companys without ever thinking that they might be lying just to save some money or to gain some other benefit. If this attitude becomes widespread, the society then becomes completely dishonest, and no one trusts anyone.

I don't know what the answer is to all this. It is true that sometimes lying seems necessary in order to cope with the world. It is also true that the truth sometimes hurts people's feelings. And it's certainly true that sometimes lying to a sick person seems merciful. But I can't get over the feeling that lots of us have just abandoned honesty completely without thinking about when it might still be wrong to tell a lie.

C H A P T E R

14

Future Tense and Perfect Tenses

Part A   Future Tense
Part B   Perfect Tenses
Part C   Irregular Verbs

In Chapter 12 you learned about the present tense and past tense. The present tense is used:

- to express events that are going on right now, in the present;
- to express events that are true always, continually, or repeatedly, in the past, present, and future.

The past tense has only one use:

- to express events that were true in the past.

In this chapter you will learn about other tenses.

Part A · Future Tense

EXERCISE 14A-1 _____

In the following, the only difference between the a versions and the b versions is a change in the verb. Study these sentences and figure out how the meaning of the b versions is different from that of the a versions.

1. a. Juanita opens the store at nine o'clock.
    b. Juanita will open the store at nine o'clock.

2. a. Nan rides her motorcycle to school.
    b. Nan will ride her motorcycle to school.

3. **a.** The waitresses put a flower on every table.
   b. The waitresses will put a flower on every table.

4. **a.** Genetics is making agriculture more productive.
   b. Genetics will make agriculture more productive.

5. **a.** The moon is full tonight.
   b. The moon will be full tonight.

NOTE: A discussion of the answers to this exercise can be found on page 302.

EXERCISE 14A-2 _____

The following paragraph is written in the past tense. In the space provided, rewrite it in the future tense. The first sentence has been done for you.

Even though I retired last May, the summer was very busy. My car was paid for, and my mortgage was paid off, so my expenses were minimal. I was working part-time for a landscaping company, which meant lots of sun, fresh air, and exercise. In my spare time, I took a computer-programming course at the local college. It was wonderful to take a course just out of intellectual curiosity. I also planted a good-sized vegetable garden in my back yard. Besides all that, I saw every movie that looked interesting.

Even though I will retire next May, the summer will be very busy.

_____

_____

_____

_____

_____

_____

_____

_____

_____

_____

_____

_____

_____

_____

_____

_____

_____

_____

_____

_____

_____

DISCUSSION OF INDUCTIVE EXERCISE

EXERCISE 14A-1

In each of these pairs, the a version states that something is true in the present, at the time that the sentence is being spoken. The b version states that something will be true in the future.

To indicate that a sentence is making a statement about the future, we use the helping verb "will" in front of the main verb.

Part B · Perfect Tenses

EXERCISE 14B-1 _____

Each of the following sentences is written with several different forms of the verb. For each sentence, select the form that sounds best and write it on the line at the end of the sentences.

1. a. Today, Fran lives in a teepee.
    b. Today, Fran has lived in a teepee.
    c. Today, Fran lived in a teepee.

2. a. These days, Emily makes cookies for a living.
    b. These days, Emily has made cookies for a living.
    c. These days, Emily made cookies for a living.

3. a. At this moment, Vinnie waits for a bus.
    b. At this moment, Vinnie has waited for a bus.
    c. At this moment, Vinnie waited for a bus.

1. a, b, or c: _____ verb: _____

2. a, b, or c: _____ verb: _____

3. a, b, or c: _____ verb: _____

Now do the same thing for these three sentences:

4. a. As of today, Fran lives in a teepee for three years.
    b. As of today, Fran has lived in a teepee for three years.
    c. As of today, Fran lived in a teepee for three years.

5. a. So far Emily makes eight hundred chocolate chip cookies.
    b. So far Emily has made eight hundred chocolate chip cookies.
    c. So far Emily made eight hundred chocolate chip cookies.

6. a. As of now, Vinnie waits for forty-five minutes.
    b. As of now, Vinnie has waited for forty-five minutes.
    c. As of now, Vinnie waited for forty-five minutes.

4. a, b, or c: _____ verb: _____

5.   a, b, or c: _____   verb: _____

6.   a, b, or c: _____   verb: _____

If you did these correctly, you should have come up with the regular present tense form of the verbs for sentences 1, 2, and 3; for sentences 4, 5, and 6, you should have chosen the version with the word "has" in front of the verb.

Now for the hard part. When do you use a verb with the word "has" in front of it? What is it about sentences 4, 5, and 6 that makes them sound better with the "has" form of the verb? If you have trouble, try asking yourself when the action of each of these verbs takes place. In number 1, for example, when does Fran live in a teepee? In number 4, when does Fran live in a teepee?

NOTE: A discussion of the answers to this exercise can be found on pages 306–309.

EXERCISE 14B-2

The following sentences are all correct, and all use the present perfect tense. What else can you learn about how to form the present perfect from these sentences?

1.   a. Marcy has slept for eleven hours.
     b. The children have slept for eleven hours.

2.   a. A student has objected to Dr. Laubheim's grading policy.
     b. Some students have objected to Dr. Laubheim's grading policy.

3.   a. Mr. Raudebaugh has walked fifteen miles.
     b. Mr. and Ms. Raudebaugh have walked fifteen miles.

4.   a. A bluebird has built a nest on Nancy's back porch.
     b. Two bluebirds have built a nest on Nancy's back porch.

NOTE: A discussion of the answers to this exercise can be found on page 309.

EXERCISE 14B-3

Correct any errors in the following sentences. All errors will involve the use of present perfect tense.

1.   As of this summer, the Liu family lived in Sacramento for fifty years, so they are having a celebration.

2.   My brother have been a student for six years, but this year he is going to graduate.

3.   The population of the United States have grown at a slower rate during the past ten years than at any time since the Census Bureau started keeping records.

4.   This turkey cooked for three hours; shall I take it out?

5.   Each of these people have filed a grievance.

6. My knee bothers me for the past six months.

7. Jackie did not solve the problem, but she is still working on it.

8. Rita lives in Rosedale for eight years, but she says she has to move this year.

9. Both of my parents has opened IRAs at First National Bank.

10. Has you met my roommate?

 EXERCISE 14B-4 _____

In each of the following pairs of sentences, decide which one sounds better.

1. a. While Kate washed the dishes, I read the newspaper.
    b. While Kate washed the dishes, I had read the newspaper.

2. a. When Kate called, I read the newspaper already.
    b. When Kate called, I had read the newspaper already.

3. a. Last summer, my parents lived in Little Rock.
    b. Last summer, my parents had lived in Little Rock.

4. a. Last summer, my parents lived in Little Rock for ten years.
    b. Last summer, my parents had lived in Little Rock for ten years.

5. a. Last night, I worked for two hours.
    b. Last night, I had worked for two hours.

6. a. By nine o'clock, I worked for two hours.
    b. By nine o'clock, I had worked for two hours.

NOTE: A discussion of this exercise can be found on pages 309–312.

 EXERCISE 14B-5 _____

Correct any errors in the following sentences. All errors will involve the use of verb tense.

1. When the bank finally opened, I waited for forty-five minutes.

2. This restaurant serves family meals in this neighborhood for twenty years.

3. By the time the fireworks started, the children have fallen asleep.

4. In 1985, my parents had been married for fifty years.

5. When I finished the book, I had not understood the ending.

6. Last Saturday, we worked on this project for six weeks.

7. By noon, they had sorted sixteen zip codes.

8. When I bought my computer, they lowered the price the day before.

9. The fire department is fighting this fire for three hours.

10. When the phone rang, I had jumped out of my seat.

EXERCISE 14B-6

In each of the following pairs of sentences, decide which one is correct.

1. a. When I finish this page, I will take a break.
   b. When I finish this page, I will have taken a break.

2. a. When I finish this page, I will write ten pages.
   b. When I finish this page, I will have written ten pages.

3. a. On March 20, Susan will be fifty years old.
   b. On March 20, Susan will have been fifty years old.

4. a. On March 20, Susan will live for fifty years.
   b. On March 20, Susan will have lived for fifty years.

NOTE: A discussion of the answers to this exercise can be found on pages 312–314.

 EXERCISE 14B-7

Correct any errors in the following sentences. All errors will involve the use of verb tense.

1. By the time I get my next paycheck, I will spend it.

2. I have worked fifty-two hours by the end of this week.

3. I taught myself to operate the ditto machine by the time Mr. Williams decided to teach me.

4. I ate dinner, so I am baby-sitting for my sister's sons while everyone else goes to dinner.

5. If they had had any money, they would not have asked to borrow it from us.

6. In 1990, I will live in Boise for twenty-five years.

7. When my alarm clock went off, I was already awake for a half hour.

8. After three hours of searching, Margie have not found a coat.

9. Believe it or not, I have had two years of guitar lessons.

10. In fifteen more minutes, I will wait three hours for the ferry.

11. By the time an ambulance gets here, she will bleed to death.

12. Pete had practiced a lot, so his playing has improved dramatically.

13. In 1990, this school will be established for one hundred years.

14. By noon, he has loaded only thirty boxes, so I told him he would have to work a lot faster, or he would be fired.

15. I don't want to go to the new Woody Allen movie because I already saw it.

16. If you will have been ready by seven o'clock, I can give you a ride to work.

17. When the fire truck arrives, the fire was burning for an hour.

18. When Lee opened the box, he had looked very worried.

19. In the year 2000, my son will live for twenty years.

20. The party has ended, and everyone but Greg went home.

DISCUSSION OF INDUCTIVE EXERCISES

EXERCISE 14B-1

The correct sentences are the following:

1. a. Today, Fran lives in a teepee.
2. a. These days, Emily makes cookies for a living.
3. a. At this moment, Vinnie waits for a bus.
4. b. As of today, Fran has lived in a teepee for three years.
5. b. So far Emily has made eight hundred chocolate chip cookies.
6. b. As of now, Vinnie has waited for forty-five minutes.

To see why these are correct, take a look at sentences 1 and 4. Sentence 1 takes place right now, in the present. It states that Fran is living in that teepee at the moment that the sentence is being written. How about in the past? We don't know about the past, at least not from sentence 1. It only says she is living in that teepee right now.

Sentence 4, on the other hand, says something different. It states that Fran lives in a teepee right now, but also that she has been living there for the past three years.

A couple of diagrams may make this distinction clearer:

PAST   PRESENT   FUTURE

Fran in a | *lives teepee*

Sentence 1

PAST   PRESENT   FUTURE

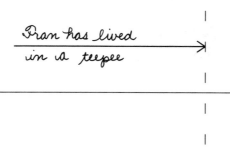

Sentence 4

You already know that the verb in sentence 1 is in present tense. The verb in sentence 4 is said to be in present perfect tense. The present perfect tense is formed by placing "has" in front of the main verb. The form of this main verb can sometimes cause trouble, but for now we'll ignore that possibility and just focus on getting the correct helping verb. We'll work on the form of the main verb in Part C of this chapter.

The other four sentences in this exercise are similar to 1 and 4. Sentence 2 states that, at the present time, Emily makes cookies for a living:

PAST   PRESENT   FUTURE

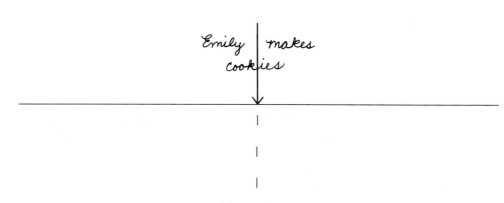

Sentence 2

Sentence 5 states that, in the past and up to the present moment, Emily has been turning out those cookies:

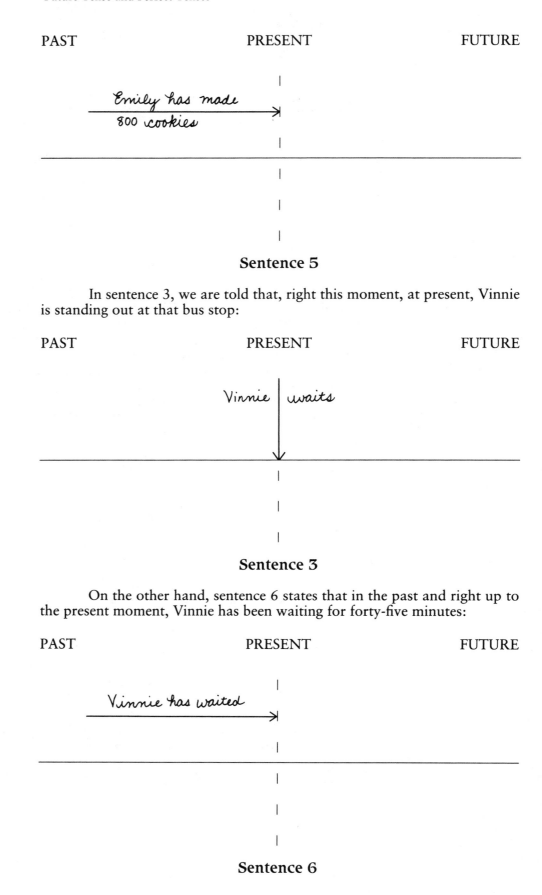

PAST   PRESENT   FUTURE

Emily has made 800 cookies

Sentence 5

In sentence 3, we are told that, right this moment, at present, Vinnie is standing out at that bus stop:

PAST   PRESENT   FUTURE

Vinnie | waits

Sentence 3

On the other hand, sentence 6 states that in the past and right up to the present moment, Vinnie has been waiting for forty-five minutes:

PAST   PRESENT   FUTURE

Vinnie has waited

Sentence 6

To summarize, the present perfect tense is used to describe an action that began in the past and continued up to and including the present moment. The present perfect tense is formed by placing a "has" in front of the main verb.

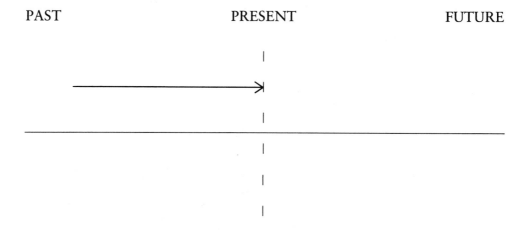

PAST   PRESENT   FUTURE

Present Perfect Tense

EXERCISE 14B-2

These sentences show that the helping verb "has" follows the subject-verb agreement rules that you learned in Chapter 4. When the subject is singular, the verb is "has"; when the subject is plural, the verb is "have."

EXERCISE 14B-4

The following are the correct versions of these sentences:

1. **a.** While Kate washed the dishes, I read the newspaper.
2. **b.** When Kate called, I had read the newspaper already.
3. **a.** Last summer, my parents lived in Little Rock.
4. **b.** Last summer, my parents had lived in Little Rock for ten years.
5. **a.** Last night, I worked for two hours.
6. **b.** By nine o'clock, I had worked for two hours.

To see why these are correct, let's take a close look at numbers 1 and 2. Sentence 2 refers to two events: when Kate called and my reading the paper. Both events occurred in the past. As the following diagram shows, however, they did not occur at the same time. The reading of the paper took place *before* Kate's calling:

PAST   PRESENT   FUTURE

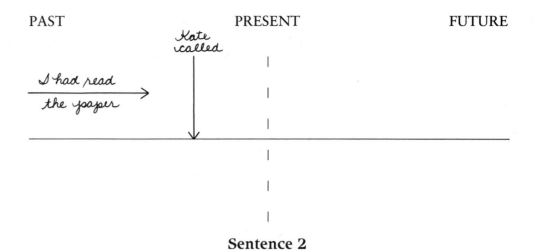

Sentence 2

Sentence 1 also refers to two events. The first is Kate's washing the dishes, and the other is my reading the paper. Both are going on in the past; in this sentence, however, they are going on at the same time; neither occurred before the other:

PAST   PRESENT   FUTURE

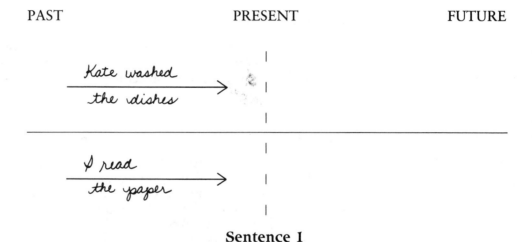

Sentence 1

These two examples reveal that when a sentence reports two events that both occurred in the past, if one occurred before the other, the one that occurred earlier is reported using a verb with the word "had" in front of it. This form of the verb is known as past perfect tense. If it involves a verb, the later event is reported in the regular past tense.

Let's see how this works with sentences 3 and 4. Sentence 3 reports two events, "last summer" and my parents' living in Little Rock. Both occurred at the same time in the past. Therefore, the verb is "lived," the past tense, rather than "had lived," the past perfect.

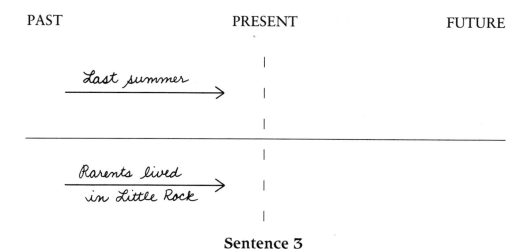

Sentence 3

In sentence 4, there are also two events, "last summer" and my parents living in Little Rock. However, this time they are not going on at the same time. Last summer, of course, took place last summer. In this sentence, however, my parents' living in Little Rock went on for the ten years prior to last summer. Therefore, "had lived," the past perfect form of the verb, is used.

PAST   PRESENT   FUTURE

Last
summer

Parents had lived
in Little Rock

Sentence 4

In sentence 5, the two events are "last night" and my working for two hours. They occurred at the same time, so the past tense, "worked," is used.

PAST   PRESENT   FUTURE

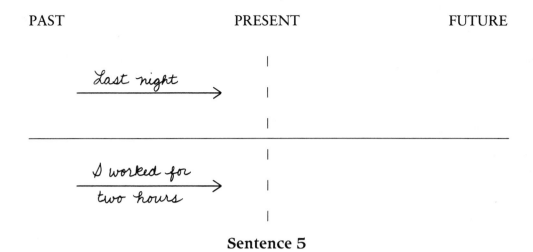

Sentence 5

In sentence 6, the two events are "nine o'clock" and my working for two hours. While "nine o'clock" occurred at exactly nine o'clock, my working for two hours went on from seven until nine. Since one event occurred before the other, the earlier one is reported in the past perfect tense, "had worked."

PAST   PRESENT   FUTURE

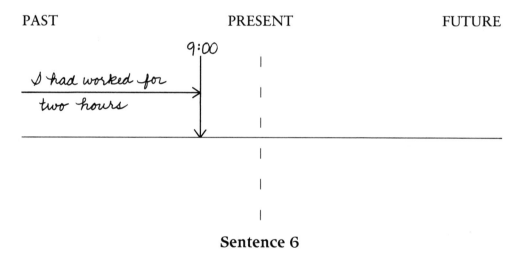

Sentence 6

In summary, when two events occur in the past but not at the same time, the past perfect tense is used to report the one that occurred earlier. The past perfect is formed by placing the verb "had" in front of the main verb.

EXERCISE 14B-6

The correct answers to this exercise are the following:

1. **a.** When I finish this page, I will take a break.
2. **b.** When I finish this page, I will have written ten pages.
3. **a.** On March 20, Susan will be fifty years old.
4. **b.** On March 20, Susan will have lived for fifty years.

These sentences, like the ones in the previous exercises, involve two events. This time, however, both events are taking place in the future. In sentence

1, for example, the two events are finishing this page and taking a break. These two events will take place at exactly the same time, so the regular future tense is used for both of them.

PAST   PRESENT   FUTURE

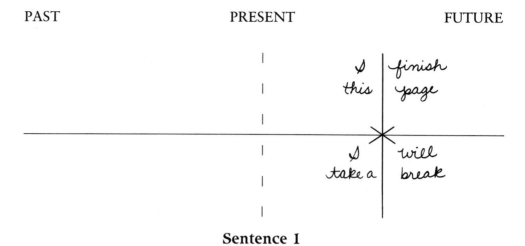

Sentence 1

In sentence 2, on the other hand, the two events do not take place at the same time. The writing of the ten pages will have occurred in the future, but *before* "I finish this page." To describe this situation—two events in the future but one earlier than the other—we need another "perfect" tense. We need a future perfect tense, and that's exactly what we have in sentence 2b. The future perfect tense uses "have" between the "will"and the main verb. In this case, the verb is "will have written."

PAST   PRESENT   FUTURE

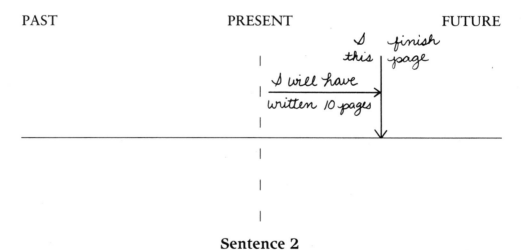

Sentence 2

In sentence 3, the two events occur at the same time, so the future tense, "will be," is used.

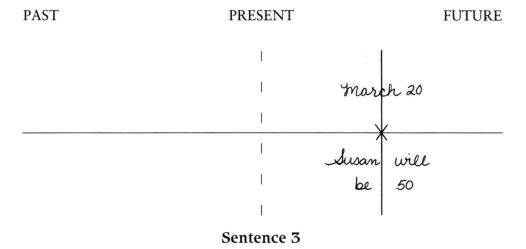

Sentence 3

In sentence 4, the two events are both in the future, but one occurs before the other, so it is expressed in future perfect tense: "will have lived."

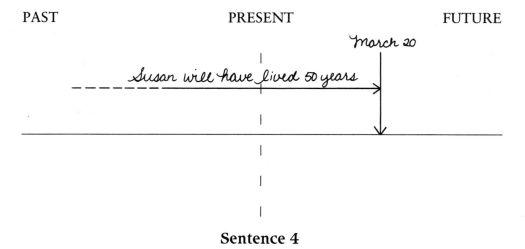

Sentence 4

In summary, the future perfect tense is used when two events both occur in the future but not at the same time. Future perfect is used for the one that will occur earlier. It is formed by placing the word "have" in between the "will" and the main verb.

Part C · Irregular Verbs

You now know how to use the six major tenses in the English language. In Chapter 4, you also learned that not all verbs follow the regular rules for their singular and plural forms. The verbs "be," "have," and "do" were quite irregular. In this section, you will learn how to handle the many irregular verbs in the past and perfect tenses.

EXERCISE 14C-1 ⸻

In the present tense you learned that the very common verb "be" is also one of the most difficult to use because it is so irregular. The past tense versions of this verb are also highly irregular, as you will see in this exercise.

The following pairs of sentences illustrate the use of the past tense of the verb "be." Study them closely and try to figure out the rule for forming the past tense with "be."

1. I was late for the meeting.
2. You were late for the meeting.
3. Pam was late for the meeting.
4. Pam and Benita were late for the meeting.

5. I was very noisy during dinner last night.
6. You were very noisy during dinner last night.
7. A child at the next table was very noisy during dinner last night.
8. Two children at the next table were very noisy during dinner last night.

9. I was a very sick person.
10. You were a very sick person.
11. My father was a very sick man.
12. My parents were very sick people.

13. I was extremely violent.
14. You were extremely violent.
15. The movie was extremely violent.
16. The movies were extremely violent.

Figure out a rule that will account for these examples and write it in the space below.

_____

_____

_____

_____

_____

NOTE: A discussion of this exercise can be found on pages 325–326.

EXERCISE 14C-2 ⸻

In the following sentences, fill in either *was* or *were* as appropriate.

1. Liza Minnelli _____ my favorite singer.

2. The Gilberts _____ in an accident.

3. Edith or her parents _____ going to return these books.

4. The cover of these notebooks _____ very pretty.

5. There _____ two dogs in our garbage.

6. I _____ sick of your complaining.

7. Dan and Diane _____ planning a surprise party for you.

8. The children or their mother _____ bringing a snack.

9.   I _____ interested in learning to program in COBOL.

10.   There _____ a hole in the garbage bag.

EXERCISE 14C-3 _____

Besides the verb "be," a number of other verbs have irregular past tense forms. The following sentences demonstrate some of the more common of these.

1.   Today I do my homework.
2.   Yesterday I did my homework.

3.   Today he goes to Boston.
4.   Yesterday he went to Boston.

5.   Today I have a cold.
6.   Yesterday I had a cold.

7.   Today I eat my dinner.
8.   Yesterday I ate my dinner.

9.   Today she comes for a visit.
10.   Yesterday she came for a visit.

These sentences, using just a handful of the irregular verbs, show how differently some of them form their past tenses. There are basically two ways you can avoid errors with these irregular verbs:

1.   You can learn the irregular forms. In fact, you probably already know many of them.
2.   You can look the ones you don't know up in a dictionary.

EXERCISE 14C-4 _____

Listed below are the present tense forms of the most common irregular verbs. Write the correct past tense form next to each one that you know. If you don't know, just leave the line blank. Don't guess. In the following exercises, you will get a chance to look up the ones you don't know.

are	_were_	wear	_wore_
is	_was_	win	_won_
go	_went_	steal	_stole_
see	_saw_	drive	_drove_
fall	_fell_		
grow	_grew_	write	_wrote_
blow	_blew_	eat	_ate_
fly	_flew_	get	_got_
throw	~~through~~ _ew_	bite	_bit_
know	_knew_	meet	_met_
		forget	_forgot_
		sit	_sat_

freeze	froze	feel	felt
choose	chose	spend	spent
rise	rose	keep	kept
teach	taught	lose	lost
fight	faught	sleep	slept
seek	sought	dwell	dwelt
think	thought	bend	bent
catch	caught	build	built
buy	bought	send	sent
bring	brought	leave	left
do	did	break	broke
stand	stood	awake	awoke
find	found	wake	woke or waked
tell	told	take	took
sell	sold		
hide	hid	shrink	shrank
hear	heard	stink	stank
say	said	drink	drank
have	had	ring	rang
hold	held	sing	sang
read	read	sink	sank
lead	lead		
slide	slid		
hit	hit	begin	began
quit	quit	run	ran
cut	cut	swim	swam
let	let	come	came
hurt	hurt	become	became
set	set	give	gave
put	put		
cost	cost		

The entry for a verb in most dictionaries starts out something like this:

- **walk** (wôk) v. walked, walking, walks. -intr. 1. To move over a surface by taking steps with the feet. . . .

The first item in the dictionary definition is always the word itself, usually printed in boldface type and divided into syllables. The next item, usually inside parentheses, is the phonetic spelling to indicate pronunciation. The third item is an abbreviation to indicate the part of speech; verbs are indicated by the abbreviations "v," "vb," "vi" (verb intransitive), or "vt" (verb transitive). The next item is the one we are interested in: the different forms of the verb. In the above example, the forms are "walked, walking, walks." The first form listed is always the past tense, so we know that for the verb "walk," the correct past tense is "walked."

Here is the entry for "walk" from another dictionary.

- **walk** (wôk) v [fr ME walken, fr OE wealcan] 1. to move along on foot at a moderate pace. . . .

This dictionary organizes its entries differently in two ways. First, inside brackets [ ] it indicates the history of the word, how it was spelled in Middle English and Old English. Second, it does not show the different forms of the verb. Before you decide that this dictionary is defective, remember that the verb "walk" is regular and that regular verbs all form their past tense in the same way, by adding an "ed" ending. Since this is so predictable, many dictionaries don't bother to list the forms for regular verbs.

Here is the same dictionary's listing for an irregular verb.

- **drive** (drīv) v drove, driven, driving [ME driven, fr. OE drifan; akin to OHG triban] 1. to impart a forward motion to by physical force. . . .

Since "drive" is an irregular verb, all dictionaries will list the various forms, starting with the past tense. In this case, the correct past tense form is "drove."

So, for irregular verbs, you have two choices. You can learn the past tense form, or you can look it up in a dictionary.

Looking up the correct past tense forms can be very time consuming, so some people just decide to learn them all. If you decide to do this, putting them on flash cards is probably the easiest method. Just write the present tense form on the front and the past tense on the back. Then look at the present tense forms and see if you can remember the past tense. Working on them for about fifteen minutes a day will produce dramatic results (or your money back).

EXERCISE 14C-5

In the following sentences the present tense of each verb is given in parentheses. Write the appropriate *past tense* form of each verb on the line provided. If you know the past tense form, you may just write it in. If you don't know it, look it up in a dictionary. In addition to writing it on the line in this exercise, also return to exercise 14C-4 and enter the correct form on the appropriate line there.

1.   My uncle _____ (go) to Florida for the winter.

2.   Yesterday, Karl _____ (wear) a necktie for the first time in three years.

3.   Last year we _____ (grow) enough tomatoes to supply the entire office.

4. It was so cold in Minnesota that my feet nearly _____ (freeze).

5. I _____ (think) long and hard before I accepted this job.

6. When I was in the navy, I only _____ (write) my girlfriend one time. She wasn't my girlfriend when I got home.

7. Doreen _____ (feel) terrible about her mistake, but she couldn't bring my pet cockroach back to life.

8. Do you know what Helen _____ (do) to her hair?

9. In 1963 I just _____ (hit) the road for a few years.

10. In his last paper, Mark _____ (break) the world record for number of fragments.

11. The rodeo _____ (begin) at two o'clock.

12. My dog _____ (hear) me turn on the bath water, and he took off running.

13. I guess Helen bought that hat before she _____ (see) what it looked like on her.

14. My brother _____ (drive) to Texas to try to find a job. All he found was cactus.

15. I _____ (know) the answer when I raised my hand, but the moment she called on me, I _____ (forget) it.

16. Some days I wonder why I _____ (choose) this course.

17. Rosetta _____ (bring) a wonderful dessert, but my dog _____ (eat) it when she left it in the kitchen.

18. I _____ (spend) my tuition money on a new Betamax.

19. Kris _____ (quit) smoking about once a month last year.

20. Brad _____ (take) a quick look at your car before he _____ (come) over. He says it has mononucleosis.

 EXERCISE 14C-6_____

The following sentences are written in the present tense. Change them to the past tense by crossing out each verb and writing the past tense form above it.

1. My favorite vegetable is chocolate ice cream.

2. The Red Sox win the opening game.

3. A hot southern wind blows into my window on many summer nights.

4. Lisa rises at six every morning and leaves for work at seven.

5. Jerry and Angela fight a lot when they drink too much.

6. Ms. Bohmer buys her cars at garage sales.

7. This suit costs only fifty dollars.

8. Allen finds studying to be too much trouble, so he sleeps with his book under his pillow.

9. Pat sings for a living, but she does not make much of a living.

10. I give at the office.

EXERCISE 14C-7

Correct any errors in the following. All errors will involve irregular past tense forms. Each sentence may contain no errors, one error, or more than one error.

1. David stoled my idea for a Halloween costume.

2. Ellis and Joy was in love until she meeted me.

3. When I went to the Burger King, I chose to eat a salad.

4. Irregular verb forms made me so mad that I bited my English teacher.

5. Cheryl throwed the cat so hard that he flied out the window.

6. Because you bended the cover of that book, you will have to buy it.

7. Gary keeped Denise in suspense until she finally toll him to get lost.

8. Mr. Quarles read my paper to the entire class, and I become very embarrassed.

9. My mother sayed I should talk to my father when he come home.

10. Yesterday, my head hurted a lot, but I runned in the marathon anyway.

EXERCISE 14C-8

Correct any errors in the following paragraph. All errors involve past tense.

As I was growing up, my parents was a little strict with me, but now I am a better person for it. When I was in the second grade, they help me to learn responsibility by getting me a job at my father's company. I empty the waste baskets for 148 offices every afternoon after school. This was a very convenient job because the company was located just thirty blocks from my school, so I just walk over when I get out of class at quarter past three. I also learned how to be punctual because my father punish me mildly if I didn't arrive at my job by 3:30. Once when I was late, he maked me spend the night alone in the building. I was never late again after that. I keeped my office job through high school, but as I growed up, my father wisely recognize that I was ready for more responsibility. Therefore, in my fourteenth year, he choosed a second job for me. I becomed responsible for painting the center lines on highways during the evenings when traffic was very light. I especially learned alertness during this job. I use to listen carefully and to hustle out of the way when I hear cars coming. Once I was a little slow getting out of the way, and I ended up in the hospital for six weeks. I learn a lot about staying alert from that experience. As I said, my parents was a little strict with me, but it maked me a stronger person. Everyone here at the institution says I am very responsible, punctual, and alert. If I am ever released, I will go far because of these qualities.

 EXERCISE 14C-9

Now that you know how to form irregular verbs in the past tense, let's take a look at how to form the main verb with perfect tenses.

The following sentences illustrate how the main verb is formed with *regular* verbs in the perfect tenses.

1. a. Alfred has lived in California all his life.
   b. Alfred and Kelly have lived in California all their lives.
   c. Alfred had lived in California all his life.

2. a. Molly has kissed every boy in her class.
   b. Molly and Karen have kissed every boy in their class.
   c. Molly had kissed every boy in her class.

3. a. He has frowned all day.
   b. They have frowned all day.
   c. She had frowned all last week.

Can you figure out the rule for forming the main verb with perfect tenses? Look closely at the endings of the main verbs. Are there any differences among the endings of the various main verbs in these sentences?

NOTE: A discussion of the answers to this exercise can be found on page 326.

 EXERCISE 14C-10

In Exercise 14C-3, you learned that there are two ways to make sure you use the past tense of irregular verbs correctly:

1. You can learn the irregular forms. In fact, you probably already know many of them.
2. You can look up the ones you don't know in the dictionary.

When you look up these irregular verbs in the dictionary, you find entries that start out like the following:

- **drive** (drīv) v drove, driven, driving. . . .

- **eat** (ēt) v ate, eaten, eating. . . .

- **grow** (grō) v grew, grown, growing. . . .

- **read** (rēd) v read, reading. . . .

- **tell** (tĕl) v told, telling. . . .

The following examples show how to use these dictionary entries to get the right form of the main verb when it is used with the perfect tenses. Look closely at them and try to figure out how to get the correct form of the verb from the dictionary entry.

1.   Irregular verbs <u>have driven</u> me looney.
2.   Phil <u>has eaten</u> in this restaurant and says it is wonderful.
3.   By the time we got to the movie, Tarzan <u>had grown</u> into a young man.
4.   I <u>had read</u> the homework, but I didn't understand her question.
5.   Chandra <u>has told</u> that story a million times; I wish she would shut up.

Do you see how the dictionary entry can be used to get the correct form for perfect tenses? Look especially closely at the last two definitions and sentences. They are a little different from the first three.

NOTE: A discussion of the answers to this exercise can be found on page 326.

EXERCISE 14C-11 ⎯⎯⎯⎯⎯⎯⎯⎯⎯⎯⎯⎯⎯⎯⎯⎯

To insure that you know how to use a dictionary to look up past participles, look up each of the following. Even if you know what the correct form is, look it up to make sure you know how to use the dictionary.

1.   Bruce has _____ (see) a number of unicorns.
2.   Martha had _____ (forget) our date, or so she says.
3.   My brother and I have _____ (fight) for years.
4.   The party had _____ (begin) when we arrived.
5.   Ms. Isaac had _____ (have) a cold for two weeks.

Adding the past participle in number 5 results in a sentence that may seem unusual to you, but it is perfectly correct. The first "had" is there as a helping verb. The second "had" is a main verb; it means "to possess," as in the sentence "I had an idea." We very often use such expressions as "has had," "have had," and "had had." They are perfectly correct.

EXERCISE 14C-12 ⎯⎯⎯⎯⎯⎯⎯⎯⎯⎯⎯⎯⎯⎯⎯⎯

Now let's complete the list of irregular verbs that you worked on in Exercise 14C-4. Below we have listed the present and past tense forms for all the verbs in that exercise. If you know the past participle, enter it on the line. If you don't know it, for now just leave it blank. As you do the following exercises, you will be filling in the ones you don't know.

PRESENT TENSE	PAST TENSE	PAST PARTICIPLE	PRESENT TENSE	PAST TENSE	PAST PARTICIPLE
are	were	_____	wear	wore	_____
is	was	_____	win	won	_____
go	went	_____	steal	stole	_____

PRESENT TENSE	PAST TENSE	PAST PARTICIPLE	PRESENT TENSE	PAST TENSE	PAST PARTICIPLE
see	saw	_____	drive	drove	_____
fall	fell	_____	write	wrote	_____
grow	grew	_____	eat	ate	_____
blow	blew	_____	get	got	_____
fly	flew	_____	bite	bit	_____
throw	threw	_____	meet	met	_____
know	knew	_____	forget	forgot	_____
			sit	sat	_____
freeze	froze	_____	feel	felt	_____
choose	chose	_____	spend	spent	_____
rise	rose	_____	keep	kept	_____
teach	taught	_____	lose	lost	_____
fight	fought	_____	sleep	slept	_____
seek	sought	_____	dwell	dwelt	_____
think	thought	_____	bend	bent	_____
catch	caught	_____	build	built	_____
buy	bought	_____	send	sent	_____
bring	brought	_____	leave	left	_____
do	did	_____	break	broke	_____
stand	stood	_____	awake	awoke	_____
find	found	_____	wake	woke	_____
tell	told	_____	take	took	_____
sell	sold	_____			
hide	hid	_____	shrink	shrank	_____
hear	heard	_____	stink	stank	_____
say	said	_____	drink	drank	_____
have	had	_____	ring	rang	_____
hold	held	_____	sing	sang	_____
read	read	_____	sink	sank	_____
lead	led	_____			
slide	slid	_____			
hit	hit	_____	begin	began	_____
quit	quit	_____	run	ran	_____
cut	cut	_____	swim	swam	_____

PRESENT TENSE	PAST TENSE	PAST PARTICIPLE	PRESENT TENSE	PAST TENSE	PAST PARTICIPLE
let	let	_____	come	came	_____
hurt	hurt	_____	become	became	_____
set	set	_____	give	gave	_____
put	put	_____			
cost	cost	_____			

EXERCISE 14C-13

On the blank line in the following sentences, write the correct form of the verb indicated in parentheses. If you know the form, just write it on the line. If you don't know it, look it up in a dictionary, enter it on the line, and return to Exercise 14C-12 and fill it in there too.

1. The young gremlin had _____ (steal) the golden apple.

2. My luck has _____ (take) a turn for the worse.

3. I think Stephen has _____ (drink) enough for tonight. He has fallen asleep in the closet.

4. Mr. Lindauer has _____ (grow) tomatoes every summer.

5. I wish I had _____ (know) that you were driving to Boston.

6. I have _____ (have) Leslie's umbrella since last Saturday.

7. My sister had _____ (tell) my mother about the accident before I got home.

8. Nancy wishes she had _____ (quit) doing the twist before she dislocated her hip.

9. Leroy has _____ (do) all the chemistry problems for you.

10. Their vacation had _____ (cost) them a thousand dollars by the end of the first week.

EXERCISE 14C-14

Now you know everything you need to know about forming main verbs with perfect tenses. This exercise will review what you have learned.

Correct any errors in the following sentences. All errors will involve main verb forms with perfect tenses. Each sentence may contain no errors, one error, or more than one error. If you have to look any of these up, return to Exercise 14C-12 and enter the correct form on the appropriate line there also.

1. My mother has leaved for Tucson without her suitcase.

2. Mr. Alzamora has been sick for a week.

3. Roosevelt had brung a llama to his senior prom.

4. Kent has slud safely into third base, but the other team has protested.

5. My cat has hurt her paw.

6. Bob said that he had gave at the office.

7. My parents have sang in the Handel Choir for ten years.

8. Jim has broke Debbie's heart.

9. The school had bended the rules for her, and she knew it.

10. Have you ate yet?

11. Joseph has not wore the new tie I gave him.

12. Perhaps I should not have chose a purple tie with pink roses on it.

13. Prices have went so high that I have to quit school.

14. I think they have hit an all time high.

15. My father has ran his business the same way for thirty years.

16. I hate Linda Sadler, and I have feeled that way for a long time.

17. I had wrote a letter, but she has not wrote back.

18. These irregular verbs have drove me crazy.

19. In addition, they have threw me for a loop.

20. I will probably have trouble with these until hell has freezed over.

EXERCISE 14C-15

Read the following paragraphs carefully and correct any errors.

Looking for a job has been harder than I ever imagined. First, I have to write my résumé. Since I has worked at a number of different jobs, this was very complicated. After I had wrote my résumé, I had to write a cover letter to each employer. Then I bought a new suit to wear to the interviews. As of today, I has went for interviews at six companies, and I am waiting to hear from them. Whenever I have got depressed, my husband have told me not to worry, and so far that has worked.

I have waited for three days, and I have not heard anything yet. I worry a lot about the jobs, but I know I have did everything I can. If all of these companies have chose someone else, then I will just have to start over.

DISCUSSION OF INDUCTIVE EXERCISES

EXERCISE 14C-1

The rule for forming the past tense of the verb "be" is as follows:

1. If the subject is singular, including the pronoun "I," use the verb "was."
2. If the subject is plural or is the pronoun "you," use the verb "were."

The verb "be" is the *only* verb that has different forms for singular and plural subjects in the past tense. Other than the verb "be," you only need to worry about subject-verb agreement in the present tense.

EXERCISE 14C-9

These sentences show that with any form of the helping verb "has," the main verb ends with an "ed." At least, this is the rule for *regular* verbs. In the next exercise you will learn how to form the main verb for irregular verbs.

EXERCISE 14C-10

Here again are the first three dictionary entries from page 321. The form that is used with "has," "have," or "had" is underlined:

- **drive** (drīv) v drove, <u>driven</u>, driving. . . .

- **eat** (ēt) v ate, <u>eaten</u>, eating. . . .

- **grow** (grō) v grew, <u>grown</u>, growing. . . .

In each of the examples, the main verb that is used with the perfect tense is the form listed immediately after the past tense. This form of the verb is called the past participle. The last entry, the "ing" form, is called the present participle, but we are not concerned with it right now.

The basic form of each of these dictionary entries is as follows:

[present tense] [pronunciation] [part of speech] [past tense form] [past participle] [present participle]

Now let's take a look at the other two dictionary entries:

- **read** (rēd) v <u>read</u>, reading. . . .

- **tell** (tĕl) v <u>told</u>, telling. . . .

Notice that for these entries only one form is listed after the part of speech and before the present participle. This means that the past tense is identical with the past participle. Therefore, you should select the form immediately after the part of speech both for past tense and for the perfect tense.

Take a look at the following, for example:

1. I <u>had read</u> the homework, but I didn't understand her question.
2. Last night I <u>read</u> the homework too quickly.
3. Chandra <u>has told</u> that story a million times; I wish she would shut up.
4. She <u>told</u> it to me at lunch last week.

In 1 and 2, you can see that the verb "read" is used for both the past perfect and the past tense. In 3 and 4, you can see that the verb "told" is used for both the present perfect and the past tense.

R E V I E W

EXERCISE 14-REVIEW-1

Proofread the following sentences carefully and correct any errors. All errors will involve verb use, including tense shifts, which you learned in Chapter 12. Each sentence may contain no errors, one error, or more than one error.

1. Mr. Sabiston waste a lot of money on his yard last summer.
2. Your car do not have enough room for me and my pet hippo.
3. When I had heard the crack of the rifle shot, I jumped.
4. Last night Karen tell her boyfriend she does not love him.
5. Julie had drove her car right through a fence before I arrived.
6. When Ms. Garcia saw Ben, he is standing in the road and screaming.
7. In January, Raymond will be working here for one year.
8. This be the best party I have ever gone to.
9. Behind the bookshelves were a valuable old coin.
10. It hurt when I was not selected to defend our school from icebergs.
11. I have never sang this song before, but I will give it a try.
12. When the game was over we realized that it was so late that we missed the last bus home.
13. Francis give me a ride to work on Saturdays.
14. Barry do a lot of odd jobs, but he never has any money.
15. Betsy or her parents are taking pictures at the party.
16. The impact of the accident throwed me through the windshield.
17. Have you went to the new pizza restaurant on Harford Road?
18. By the time Raphael was sixteen, he studied Chinese for three years.
19. The seam of these trousers are not straight.
20. When Mr. Gross come to work, he found me sleeping in the storeroom.

EXERCISE 14-REVIEW-2

Proofread the following sentences carefully and correct any errors. All errors will involve verb use, including tense shifts, which you learned in Chapter 12. Each sentence may contain no errors, one error, or more than one error.

1. Until seven o'clock, a beer cost only fifty cents at the Rusty Scupper.
2. My sister have a cold, but she went to school anyway.
3. A collection of antique dolls were on sale at the auction.
4. Before she moved to Baltimore, Melia has lived in many cities.

5.   Rich has broke several of the college records for swimming.

6.   Paul stands up and yelled for his dog.

7.   Carol Freidman ask a lot of questions before she buys anything.

8.   Since I waited for thirty minutes, I left without Rebecca.

9.   The players or the coach is going to be embarrassed.

10.   Last week, my father help me fix the carburetor on my car.

11.   George's back has gave him trouble for years.

12.   Rose Torres hands me a note and ran back into the kitchen.

13.   The index list every important word in the book.

14.   We does a lot of warm-up exercises before we start practice.

15.   Chuck was waiting for two hours when Carla finally showed up.

16.   When her car started skidding, Joyce kept her head.

17.   We have ate dinner, but we could use a cup of coffee.

18.   I was on the committee for three years, so they asked me to be the chair.

19.   We has packed our suitcases.

20.   There is two reasons why I cannot go to the party.

 ## EXERCISE 14-REVIEW-3 _____

Proofread the following essay and correct any errors. All errors will involve verb use, including tense shifts, which you learned in Chapter 12.

It seems obvious that work is something human beings are not fond of. We all knows how hard some people will try to avoid work. We all knows how great it feel when work is unexpectedly called off because of a power failure or a big snowstorm. From all the evidence, it seemed clear that we do not like to work.

However, it also appears to be true that, at least in some ways, human beings like to work. In fact, in some circumstances we will fight to be allowed to work. Think about the person who had been laid off. Do he or she think of being laid off as a blessing? Of course not. How many people are ready to retire when the company says they should? Even if their retirement benefits and social security are as much as their salary, many people would do anything to keep working.

Now you may be thinking, "Not me, baby. Try offering me retirement at full pay and see how fast I accept." But how long would you be happy? All of us would welcome a week or a month or even a year without working. But how many people would be willing never to work again? Not too many, I'll bet.

What is it about work that makes us want it, even though, on a day-to-day basis, we would do anything to get out of it? I think there is several answers to this question. Of course, there is the money. But there is several other factors as well.

Work is one important way that we give meaning to our lives. Work, at least if we are lucky, allows us to feel that we are making some contribution to society. It is at work that we gain a sense of success. Being able to do something useful in the workplace makes us feel needed.

Also, work provides a social outlet. Our bosses might not approve, but a lot of the reason we come to work is to interact with other people. There is a lot of satisfaction to be gained from day-to-day contact with our fellow workers. We laugh and cry at work. We has fights, and we make up. In some ways the workplace replaced the extended family as our social arena.

Finally, we goes to work because we would feel strange if we didn't. Going to work is what adults do in this society. This used to be true mainly for men, but lately it became somewhat true for women too. If we stay home on weekdays and sit out in a lawn chair, the mailman will think we have came down with some disease or that we have went off our rocker. This feeling that it is necessary to go to work is understandable, since five mornings a week we have been getting up, getting dressed, and going off somewhere ever since kindergarten. It just feels wrong to stay home.

So, no matter how much we complain about work and no matter how good if feels to take a day off, there is still some powerful forces in our personalities that make us want to work.

C H A P T E R

15

Pronoun Reference and Agreement

Part A   Identifying Pronouns
Part B   Identifying Antecedents
Part C   Clear Reference
Part D   Pronoun Agreement

Part A · Identifying Pronouns

In this chapter you will learn about a group of words called pronouns. When you finish with this part, you will be able to identify pronouns in sentences. The following parts will teach you how to avoid some common errors with pronouns.

EXERCISE 15A-1 _____

Study the underlined words in the following sentences carefully. These words are all pronouns. Try to get a sense of what these words have in common. How are they all alike?

1. I can give you a ride to school.
2. He told me about the accident.
3. We are keeping them from dinner.
4. They loaned her the money, and she paid it back the next day.
5. Carol left him a message about the game.

NOTE: A discussion of the answers to this exercise can be found on page 336.

EXERCISE 15A-2 _____

In the following sentences, underline all pronouns. Each sentence may contain no pronouns, one pronoun, or more than one pronoun.

330

1. We gave them the phone number for the security office.

2. Do you want me to tell Mr. Hillman about the mistake?

3. I brought a swimming suit, but I left it in the car.

4. If they will give us a ride, we can still get to the movie on time.

5. He was still angry at her when I saw him the next day.

6. She told me about the mistake, but I soon forgot about it.

7. Marcy invited them to the party, but they were already going to the ocean.

8. Teddy gave the purse to Molly and then forgot to tell Ann.

9. If you see Jennie, tell her about Brian and me.

10. While Mr. Beck was chasing us, he tripped and fell.

EXERCISE 15A-3

Study the underlined pronouns in the following sentences carefully. How are these similar to the ones in Exercise 15A-1? How are they different?

1. My car is in the garage.
2. Pete would like to borrow your jumper cables.
3. Our chances of winning are very slim.
4. Barbara lent one hundred dollars to her brother.
5. Did the children bring their lunches?

NOTE: A discussion of the answers to this exercise can be found on pages 336–337.

EXERCISE 15A-4

In the following sentences, underline all pronouns. Each sentence may contain no pronouns, one pronoun, or more than one pronoun.

1. I can't find my wallet.

2. Craig did not eat his dinner.

3. Marty and Dottie are renting their house.

4. Have you had your iron today?

5. Hank gave Donna a beautiful ring for Valentine's Day.

6. My dog is having its rabies shots today.

7. I love your new sweater.

8. Their answer did not seem right to me.

9. Cathy lowered her head and walked right past me.

10. The movie was not as good as its reputation.

EXERCISE 15A-5

Study the underlined words in the following sentences carefully. These words are all pronouns. Try to get a sense of what these words have in common. How are they all alike?

1. <u>Everybody</u> needs <u>somebody</u>.
2. Did <u>anybody</u> pack the mustard?
3. There was <u>nothing</u> in the mailbox.
4. <u>Something</u> tells me that <u>everything</u> is going to work out for the best.
5. <u>No one</u> told me that <u>anything</u> had been decided.

These pronouns all belong to a group known as *indefinite* pronouns. Can you think of any more pronouns that would fit in this group? List any that you can think of in the space below.

NOTE: A discussion of the answers to this exercise can be found on page 337.

 EXERCISE 15A-6

In the following sentences, underline all pronouns. Each sentence may contain no pronouns, one pronoun, or more than one pronoun.

1. Everyone knew that Tony was innocent.
2. I hope someone rememered to bring a corkscrew.
3. He lost nothing in the flood, but she was not so lucky.
4. James didn't say anything to make her so angry.
5. Nothing can be done to help a chocolate addict.
6. Did anyone help you with the flat tire?
7. Evelyn gave somebody a ride to last week's game.
8. I squeezed everything into one suitcase.
9. Nobody could sleep with three cats in the bed.
10. Arnold gave something to everyone in the office.

 EXERCISE 15A-7

Study the underlined words in the following sentences carefully. These words are also all indefinite pronouns, but they are different from the ones in Exercises 15A-5 and 15A-6. Try to get a sense of what these words have in common. How are they all alike?

1. <u>Each</u> of the children gave a speech.
2. <u>Some</u> of the apples were rotten, but <u>many</u> of them were fine.
3. <u>One</u> of the cars went out of control and wrecked <u>most</u> of the fence.
4. <u>Either</u> of the answers is correct.
5. <u>None</u> of us missed <u>all</u> of the questions, but <u>most</u> of us missed a <u>few</u> of them.

NOTE: A discussion of the answers to this exercise can be found on page 337.

EXERCISE 15A-8

In the following sentences, underline all pronouns. Each sentence may contain no pronouns, one pronoun, or more than one pronoun. These sentences contain personal pronouns as well as both kinds of indefinite pronouns. Underline them all.

1. Both of Emerson's feet were broken in the accident.

2. Neither of the people we hired can start work until September.

3. Belinda didn't like any of the tee shirts, but she bought several of them nevertheless.

4. Most of the students failed the final exam.

5. Everyone should eat some of the gazpacho.

6. Much of Shawn's paper was merely a summary of the plot.

7. Either of the ties will look fine with that shirt.

8. Each of her dives was perfect.

9. Any of the hikers can ride in the baggage truck if he or she develops blisters.

10. None of the teachers got all of the questions right.

EXERCISE 15A-9

Study the underlined words in the following sentences carefully. These words all belong to another group of pronouns. Try to get a sense of what these words have in common. What obvious similarity do you notice about their spelling?

1. My mother, who lives in Virginia, is coming to visit.
2. Whomever Richard dates is fine, just so he leaves me alone.
3. The clock, which had not worked for years, suddenly struck twelve.
4. I knew a man who slept in a cowboy hat and spurs.
5. I am certain you will be happy with whichever house you buy.
6. The woman whom I used to work for is now the president of the company.
7. Alice is one person whose values have never changed.
8. Whatever you buy in Palm Springs will be very expensive.
9. Whomever you invite must be able to do the tango.
10. What is your chemistry professor's name?

NOTE: A discussion of the answers to this exercise can be found on pages 337–338.

EXERCISE 15A-10

In the following sentences, underline all pronouns. Each sentence may contain no pronouns, one pronoun, or more than one pronoun. Some of the pronouns may be from the earlier groups.

1. The Mustang that we bought is bright green.

2. Some of the children did not know who I was.

3. What did you buy at the yard sale?

4. Do you remember the man who went skinny-dipping?

5. Whomever the club elects will be a good president.

6. I will go along with whatever you decide to do, as long as it doesn't involve grammar.

7. The family whose house burned down had no insurance.

8. The wheel on Carrie's bike was damaged.

9. Some of the strawberries that the children had picked were not ripe.

10. The song that she sang was one of my favorites.

EXERCISE 15A-11 _____

Study the underlined words in the following sentences carefully. These words are all pronouns. Try to get a sense of what these words have in common. How are they all alike?

1. <u>This</u> is a delicious pie.
2. <u>These</u> are the best seats in the theater.
3. Did you see <u>that</u>?
4. <u>Those</u> are the biggest tomatoes I have ever seen.

NOTE: A discussion of the answers to this exercise can be found on page 338.

EXERCISE 15A-12 _____

In the following sentences, underline all pronouns. Each sentence may contain no pronouns, one pronoun, or more than one pronoun. All the types of pronouns you have studied thus far may be included.

1. That is the ugliest hat I have ever seen.

2. The Safeway's apples were not as beautiful as those.

3. Then Jerry walked into the drugstore and bought a newspaper.

4. This is a test of the emergency broadcasting system.

5. Did you tell her that, or did she just make it up?

6. Everyone should have one of those.

7. There aren't enough of these for everyone.

8. Most of the Girl Scouts won't believe this, but it is true.

9. May I have a look at that?

10. Those are impressive credentials.

EXERCISE 15A-13 _____

This exercise will introduce you to the one kind of pronoun remaining. Study the underlined words in the following sentences carefully. These words are all pronouns. Try to get a sense of what these words have in common. How are they all alike?

1. I have been taking care of <u>myself</u> since I was fourteen.
2. Every morning Warren makes <u>himself</u> a cup of coffee and a bowl of oatmeal.
3. My parents are getting too old to take care of <u>themselves</u>.
4. You make <u>yourself</u> right at home.
5. We surprised <u>ourselves</u> by getting to Denver in six hours.

NOTE: A discussion of the answers to this exercise can be found on page 338.

EXERCISE 15A-14

In the following sentences, underline all pronouns. All of the kinds of pronouns you have studied may be included. Each sentence may contain no pronouns, one pronoun, or more than one pronoun.

1. My dog had better behave himself, or we will have to put him in a kennel.
2. Robin cleaned the entire downstairs by herself, but she had a little help with the upstairs.
3. I helped myself to a beer and joined the party on the patio.
4. Some of us really like to throw ourselves into a project.
5. Ed allowed himself only thirty minutes to drive downtown.
6. All the seats were taken by the time Joan arrived.
7. Stephanie is trying to teach herself how to play tennis.
8. Most of the shoes that were on sale were very large sizes.
9. My cat was grooming itself in the middle of the living room window as Sarah drove up.
10. I don't trust myself alone in a room with a bowl of potato chips.

EXERCISE 15A-15

Now you know all the pronouns in the English language. This exercise will review your knowledge of pronouns.

In the following sentences, underline all pronouns. Each sentence may contain no pronouns, one pronoun, or more than one pronoun.

1. We should buy some of their strawberries because they are on sale.
2. Carl was helping himself to the desserts.
3. Everybody brought something to the party.
4. Ruth gave us good advice.
5. These are Debbie's shoes.
6. Tim and Gail said they would be here by nine o'clock.
7. The movie that we saw was about the town that we had grown up in.

8. Most of the children don't believe in Santa Claus, but many of them pretend that they do.

9. Linda gave herself a hard time because she didn't get the job.

10. Half of the children had colds, but that didn't slow them down.

11. Jeff drove all the way to Kansas City and delivered the ring to Liz in person.

12. Chris gave herself a party when she turned twenty-one.

13. Anything you donate will be greatly appreciated.

14. Rosemary's bed was covered with stuffed animals, so we couldn't sit on it.

15. Don's daughters were very proud of themselves because they won a prize for one of the cows they had raised.

16. Police officers expect to be treated with a little respect.

17. A few of the problems on the midterm were harder than I expected, but most of them were easy.

18. My math book is extremely funny.

19. Elaine told us about what she had done during the summer.

20. Whoever gets all of these right really understands pronouns.

DISCUSSION OF INDUCTIVE EXERCISES

EXERCISE 15A-1

These words are known as personal pronouns. You don't have to remember this term, nor do you need to memorize the following list, but you do need to be able to recognize these as pronouns whenever you see them. Here is a complete list of personal pronouns.

I	me
you	him
he	her
she	us
it	them
we	they

EXERCISE 15A-3

These pronouns are merely variations on the ones you learned in the first exercise. The only difference is that these are possessive; that is, they indicate that someone or something is "owning" something else. In sentence 1, for example, I am owning the car; it is *my* car. In sentence 2, you own the jumper cables; they are *your* jumper cables.

All the possessive pronouns in English are listed below:

my	mine	its	
your	yours	our	ours

his   their   theirs
her   hers

EXERCISE 15A-5

Here is a list of all the pronouns that are similar to the ones in this exercise. How many were you able to list? Study this list and see if you can come up with an easier way to remember them than memorizing the entire list.

everyone	no one
everybody	nobody
everything	nothing
someone	anyone
somebody	anybody
something	anything

These words are easier to remember if you realize that they are made up of all the combinations of the following.

every
no   and   one
some   body
any   thing

All of these words are indefinite pronouns. As with personal pronouns, you don't need to remember this term, nor do you need to memorize the list. You must, however, be able to recognize these words as pronouns when you see them. There are other words that are also indefinite pronouns. We will take a look at them in Exercise 15A-7.

EXERCISE 15A-7

What this group of indefinite pronouns has in common is that they all refer to a quantity—how much or how many—of something. The following is a complete list of indefinite pronouns:

all	more
another	most
any	much
both	neither
each	none
either	one (or any other number)
few	several
half (or any other fraction)	some
many	

EXERCISE 15A-9

The most obvious similarity in these pronouns is that they all begin with the letters "wh." For this reason, the easiest way to think of them is as "wh" words. Other books refer to them as relative pronouns and interrogative pronouns, but there is no real reason to learn either of these terms.

The following is a complete list of these "wh" words. Look closely at the first word on the list.

that	who
what	whoever
whatever	whom

which   whomever

whichever   whose

The first word, "that," of course, doesn't begin with a "wh." Since it is the only exception, however, it is fairly easy to remember, so we will continue to refer to this group as the "wh" words.

EXERCISE 15A-11

These four, "this," "that," "these," and "those," are known as demonstrative pronouns. Again, you do not need to remember the term, but you should know that these are pronouns when you see them.

These pronouns all begin with the letters "th." Notice that "that" is also on this list. Can you see a difference in how it is used here and how it was used in Exercise 15A-9?

EXERCISE 15A-13

These are merely pronouns that you learned earlier with the ending "self" added to them. They are called reflexive pronouns, but once again, there is no reason to learn the term. If you have learned the earlier pronouns, you should have no trouble recognizing these.

Part B · Identifying Antecedents

EXERCISE 15B-1 _____

In the following sentences, certain words have been underlined, and then arrows have been drawn from these words to other words in the sentence.

1. Malcolm told Jan that she was supposed to bring salad to the party.
2. When Kris kissed Jim, he burst into tears.
3. Louise buys her makeup from a catalog.
4. Skip bought his car in 1983, and it is still running fine.
5. When Felix saw Fran, he gave her the letter, and she read it.

    The following questions refer to the above sentences.

1. What are the underlined words?
2. What is the relationship of the underlined words to the words their arrows point to?

NOTE: A discussion of the answers to this exercise can be found on page 339.

EXERCISE 15B-2 _____

In the following sentences, underline each pronoun and draw an arrow from it to its antecedent. Each sentence may contain no pronouns, one pronoun, or more than one pronoun.

1. Maria ran until she thought her lungs would burst.
2. Greg saw the man who was passing out leaflets.
3. One of the children had lost her mitten, and Jimmie found it.

4. Saul Bellow and Norman Mailer attended the ceremony even though they don't get along.

5. Kathy checked the instructions, but they didn't say anything about malfunctions.

6. The car that was broken down was parked on the shoulder of the road.

7. The groceries are still in the car because they are too heavy for one person to carry.

8. When he is feeling good, Jason is a marvelous dancer.

9. If the phone rings, let Cindy answer it.

10. Mario gave Judy his keys, but she can't remember what she did with them.

DISCUSSION OF INDUCTIVE EXERCISE

EXERCISE 15B-1

1. The underlined words are all pronouns.
2. The words their arrows point to are the nouns that these pronouns are taking the place of or standing for. Pronouns are said to "refer" to these nouns. The nouns that the pronouns refer to are their "antecedents." The antecedent for a pronoun is almost always a noun, although occasionally it is another pronoun.

Part C · Pronoun Reference

EXERCISE 15C-1 _____

There is something wrong with all of the following sentences. Study them and see if you can figure out why these sentences are not effective.

1. Beverly sent Helen a message before she went on vacation.
2. Mr. Ng says he sent his landlord a check, but he has no record of it.
3. The officers have ignored the wishes of the members because they are extremely unreasonable.
4. My brother thanked my father when he arrived at the airport.
5. Ms. Caldwell opened the present from Ms. White while she was sitting in our living room.

NOTE: A discussion of the answers to this exercise can be found on page 341.

EXERCISE 15C-2 _____

These sentences illustrate another kind of problem with pronoun reference. In Exercise 15C-1, there were two or more possible antecedents for the pronoun, so the sentences were ambiguous. What is the problem in these?

1. The road was very slick, and visibility was limited because of the fog. As Peter returned home, he was driving too fast. This is what caused the accident.
2. Jill yelled across the library that she was quitting her job. This upset her sister.
3. Fred's daughter broke an antique pitcher that his grandmother had given him. Orange juice spilled all over the kitchen floor. This is really going to upset Fred when he gets home.
4. California is famous for its modern life-style. They eat a lot of yogurt there.
5. Gail owns two tennis rackets although she has never learned how to play it.

NOTE: A discussion of the answers to this exercise can be found on pages 341–342.

 EXERCISE 15C-3——————————————

The following sentences have problems caused by vague pronoun reference. Read each sentence carefully and correct any problems either by inserting words where needed or by rewriting the entire sentence.

1. My mother never graduated from college and works as a volunteer at Good Samaritan Hospital; this is what is so depressing to her.
2. Gert gave the message to Donna before she left for the day.
3. Pedro owned bowling shoes although he didn't do it very often.
4. In movies, they often expect us to believe the most improbable events.
5. If you see Laura and her sister, will you make sure she knows that the party has been postponed?
6. My sister is now a well-known mathematician, which she got a D in when she was in high school.
7. I read in the paper that hospital costs are going up, and this started an argument between my brother and me.
8. The book was lying on the table, and it was soaking wet.
9. I bought a leather purse because it lasts longer than vinyl.
10. Rick asked Herb about his pet anaconda.
11. When he was crying, I became very upset. This was why no one answered the phone when you called.
12. I used to want to be an accountant, but I got a C in it, so I changed my mind.
13. Each cashier is assigned a bagger for her work period, but they have been unable to keep up with the increased flow of customers.
14. I didn't realize that Ben had not read your letter before he called you. This is what caused all the trouble.

15. Kate explained to Marie that she had not done the correct assignment.

16. In the *New York Times,* they say that there is too much vocationalism in higher education.

17. The parents told their boys they would have to spend some time cleaning their room.

18. She graduated and joined the navy, which surprised me greatly.

19. The year George taught a course with Dennis, he did most of the work.

20. I took your pants to be cleaned; it's on my way to school.

DISCUSSION OF INDUCTIVE EXERCISES

EXERCISE 15C-1

In each of these sentences the meaning is unclear because of a pronoun. In number 1, it is not clear whether Beverly or Helen went on a vacation. This ambiguity results from the pronoun "she." The way "she" is used here, it is impossible to tell whether its antecedent is Beverly or Helen. This problem is known as vague pronoun reference. It is not clear which noun the pronoun is referring to.

The other sentences have similar problems. In number 2, one can't tell whether it is Mr. Ng or the landlord who has no record of the check. In number 3, the pronoun "they" is the problem. Which "they" is unreasonable? The officers, the wishes, or the members? It is impossible to know. In number 4, did the father or the brother arrive at the airport? And in number 5, was it Ms. Caldwell or Ms. White who was sitting in our living room?

This kind of vague reference can make your writing extremely ineffective and should always be avoided.

EXERCISE 15C-2

In Exercise 15C-1, the pronoun reference was unclear because there were two possible antecedents. In this exercise, the pronoun reference is unclear because there is no real antecedent.

There is, for example, no antecedent for the pronoun "this" in the last sentence of number 1. Remember that an antecedent is a noun, or occasionally a pronoun. "This" seems to refer to some vague idea—perhaps that the road was slick or that visibility was limited or that Peter was speeding or some combination of all of these. But there is no noun or pronoun that "this" is clearly referring to.

Similarly, in number 2, there is no clear antecedent for "this." Is it the fact that Jill is quitting or the fact that she was yelling in the library? And in number 3, there is the same problem. What does the "this" refer to?

The situation in the last two sentences is a little different. In number 4, there is no antecedent for "they." It seems like California is the antecedent, but that can't be because the pronoun would have to be "it." The antecedent for "they" is really something like "people who live in California." But that phrase, or more specifically the noun "people," doesn't actually appear, so there really is no antecedent. The situation in number 5 is similar. One thinks that the noun "tennis" is the antecedent for the pronoun "it," but, on closer examination, there is no *noun* "tennis." The word tennis, in this sentence, is an adjective describing "racket." So, there is no noun to serve as antecedent for "it."

Part D · Pronoun Agreement

The rules you will learn in this section are quite similar to the rules you learned in Chapter 4 for subject-verb agreement. You might want to review those rules before starting this section.

EXERCISE 15D-1 _____

The following sentences all have serious problems. Examine the sentences closely and figure out what the problems are.

1. My lawn is so brown that I watered them all night.
2. The two dogs opened its eyes when I walked up.
3. The telephone broke when I dropped him.
4. The panda was taking their nap when I got to the zoo.
5. My father emptied their pipe out the window.

What words in these sentences cause them to sound so strange? What is wrong with these words?

NOTE: A discussion of the answers to this exercise can be found on pages 346–347.

EXERCISE 15D-2 _____

The sentences in Exercise 15D-1 were so strange that it is unlikely anyone would ever write them, but they illustrated the principle of pronoun agreement very clearly. In this exercise, the problems are not nearly as obvious. Nevertheless, each of the following sentences has an error involving pronoun agreement. Study these sentences until you understand what the error is in each one.

1. The taxpayer must sign their return before mailing it.
2. The teacher who cares about their students will be available for conferences.
3. The representative who doesn't accept contributions from lobbyists will soon lose their seat in Congress.
4. The consumer who doesn't compare prices will spend their money foolishly.
5. The traveler who doesn't make reservations in advance may end up sleeping in their car.

NOTE: A discussion of the answers to this exercise can be found on pages 347–348.

EXERCISE 15D-3 _____

Correct any errors in the following sentences. All errors will involve pronoun agreement. Each sentence may contain no errors, one error, or more than one error.

1. The voter should make sure their registration is up to date each year.

2. When a person tells one lie, sooner or later they will need to tell another.

3. A student should take their writing courses early because good writing will help them in most of their other courses.

4. You must have confidence in what your spouse is doing when they are not with you.

5. When a telephone rings, not very many people can avoid answering them.

6. The police officer should make sure their uniform is always spotless.

7. Nurses often feel compassion for their patients.

8. A cat often sharpens their claws on the furniture.

9. When a gardener purchases a lot of bulbs, they expect that most of them will actually come up the following spring.

10. A newspaper reporter should have their questions written down before they start to interview someone.

 EXERCISE 15D-4 _____

The following sentences illustrate a slight complication to the basic rule for pronoun agreement. Study these examples until you understand this complication.

1. a. Lynn and Marie lent Mr. Washington their lawn mower.
    b. The Hansons and the Johnsons lent Mr. Washington their lawn mowers.
    c. Lynn and the Hansons lent Mr. Washington their lawn mowers.
    d. The Hansons and Lynn lent Mr. Washington their lawn mowers.
    e. Lynn or Marie lent Mr. Washington her lawn mower.
    f. The Hansons or the Johnsons lent Mr. Washington their lawn mower.
    g. Lynn or the Hansons lent Mr. Washington their lawn mower.
    h. The Hansons or Lynn lent Mr. Washington her lawn mower.

2. a. My daughter and her friend left their books in my car.
    b. My daughters and their friends left their books in my car.
    c. My daughter and her friends left their books in my car.
    d. My daughters and their friend left their books in my car.
    e. My daughter or her friend left her books in my car.
    f. My daughters or their friends left their books in my car.
    g. My daughter or her friends left their books in my car.
    h. My daughters or their friend left her books in my car.

NOTE: A discussion of the principles illustrated by these sentences can be found on pages 348–349.

EXERCISE 15D-5———————————————

Correct any errors in the following sentences. The errors will involve all the types of pronoun agreement you have learned thus far. Each sentence may contain no errors, one error, or more than one error.

1. A cardinal or a blue jay can be easily identified by the crest on top of their heads.

2. Joyce or Fran will lend you her umbrella.

3. Ken and Kevin were flexing his muscles.

4. The teacher or the students will have to compromise his principles.

5. Either the cabinet officers or the president will place their initials on the document.

6. If you buy avocados or tomatoes, make sure it is ripe.

7. The bishops and cardinals make their flight reservations with Pan Am.

8. Massachusetts or Michigan cast their electoral votes for George McGovern.

9. Billy Joe or his parents will lend you their binoculars.

10. My cat and my dog had spilled its water.

———————————————

Sometimes the antecedent for a pronoun is not a noun, but another pronoun. Frequently these pronouns are the indefinite pronouns you first met in Part A of this chapter. However, sometimes it can be a little difficult to figure out whether a particular indefinite pronoun is singular or plural. In this exercise you will learn how to figure this out.

The first group of indefinite pronouns we will look at are *always singular:*

anybody	everyone	nothing
anyone	everything	one
anything	neither	somebody
each	nobody	someone
either	no one	something
everybody		

Notice that this group includes all the combinations of the following:

$$
\left.\begin{array}{l} \text{any} \\ \text{every} \\ \text{no} \\ \text{some} \end{array}\right\} \text{ and } \left\{\begin{array}{l} \text{body} \\ \text{one} \\ \text{thing} \end{array}\right.
$$

The words that cause people the most trouble in this group are *either,* *everyone,* and *everybody.* Remember that these three, as well as all the others listed above, are *always singular.*

The next group of indefinite pronouns is *always plural:*

both   many   two (or any number other than one)

This group does not cause much trouble.

EXERCISE 15D-6

Using what you have learned above, draw an arrow from the underlined pronouns to their antecedents in each of the following sentences.

1.   Both of my sisters broke off their engagements.

2.   Each of my sisters broke off her engagement.

3.   Many of my friends wrote their representatives about the new taxes.

4.   One of my friends wrote her representatives about the new taxes.

5.   Two of the men can make their speeches tonight.

6.   Either of the men can make his speech tonight.

NOTE: A discussion of the principles illustrated by these sentences can be found on pages 349–350.

EXERCISE 15D-7

Correct any errors in the following sentences. The errors will involve all the types of pronoun agreement you have learned thus far. Each sentence may contain no errors, one error, or more than one error.

1.   Everybody should bring their lunches on the bus; we will supply soft drinks.

2.   Each of the contestants performed their act in three minutes.

3.   Both of the horses tossed its head to the music.

4.   Someone should donate his or her guitar to the band.

5.   Has anyone seen an orange cat lurking around their house in the past three days?

6.   The student who works hard in her course will raise their average considerably.

7.   Half of the children saved their money.

8.   Everyone who forgets their receipt will have to go home and get them.

9.   Either of my sons can bring you his jumper cables.

10.   The doctor who lowers their fees is a rarity.

EXERCISE 15D-8

There is a third group of indefinite pronouns that is a little more complicated because the pronouns in this group can be either singular or plural. The group includes the following:

any	most	none
all	much	some
half (or any other fraction)		

Study the following sentences and figure out how to decide when these pronouns are singular and when they are plural.

1. Some of the wine had lost its flavor.
2. Some of the books had lost their covers.
3. Half of the cake had disappeared from its plate.
4. Half of the flowers had dropped their petals.
5. Most of the milk smells like it is sour.
6. Most of the tomatoes look like they are rotten.

NOTE: A discussion of the principles illustrated by these sentences can be found on page 350.

EXERCISE 15D-9 _____

Correct any errors in the following sentences. The errors will involve all the types of pronoun agreement you have learned thus far. Each sentence may contain no errors, one error, or more than one error.

1. Some of the champagne had lost their fizz.

2. Most of the noise was so loud that they made my ears ache.

3. Each of the cats had its tail bandaged.

4. A woman who wants to work in this agency should have their career goals clearly decided.

5. None of those accountants knew their own state's tax laws.

6. Many of the birds in this refuge have already laid their eggs.

7. Each of the boys closed their eyes and pretended to be asleep.

8. Everybody should have their part memorized by Friday.

9. Each of the dogs gave their special bark as the mailman worked his way up the street.

10. Some of the boys lost their cool when the bus skidded.

DISCUSSION OF INDUCTIVE EXERCISES

EXERCISE 15D-1

The problems with these ludicrous sentences all involve pronouns and their antecedents. In the list below, we have isolated the pronouns and their antecedents so that the difficulty is more obvious:

1. lawn...................them
2. dogs...................its
3. panda ....their
4. telephone ....him
5. father.................their

The trouble in each of these is that a pronoun has been used that conflicts with its antecedent. In number 1, for example, the "lawn" is not a "them"; it is an "it." Notice that the sentence sounds fine when "it" is substituted for "them":

   1. My lawn is so brown that I watered it all night.

Similarly, in each of the others, replacing the erroneous pronoun with an appropriate one results in a sentence that sounds fine:

   2. The two dogs opened their eyes when I walked up.
   3. The panda was taking its nap when I got to the zoo.
   4. The telephone broke when I dropped it.
   5. My father emptied his pipe out the window.

      Does this remind you of the relationship between subjects and verbs that you worked on in Chapter 4? Remember that when you had a singular subject, you had to have a singular verb to go with it. And, remember that this relationship between the subject and verb was called subject-verb *agreement*.

      The similar relationship between pronouns and their antecedents is also called agreement—pronoun agreement. The rule is as follows:

> Pronouns must agree with their antecedents. Singular pronouns must have singular antecedents, and plural pronouns must have plural antecedents. Similarly, male pronouns must have male antecedents, female must have female, and neuter must have neuter.

EXERCISE 15D-2

The problem in these sentences is exactly the same as the problem with the sentences in Exercise 15D-1: pronoun agreement. The list below shows the problem pronouns and their antecedents:

   1. taxpayer .... their
   2. teacher .... their
   3. representative .... their
   4. consumer .... their
   5. traveler .... their

In each of these sentences, the pronoun "their," which is plural, refers back to a singular antecedent. Therefore, the sentences are incorrect because they violate the rule for pronoun agreement.

      To see how to correct these problems, let's look closely at sentence 1:

   1. The taxpayer must sign their return before mailing it.

The most obvious way to correct this is to make the pronoun agree, to change the plural "their" to a singular pronoun like "his."

   6. The taxpayer must sign his return before mailing it.

      There is, however, one problem with this solution. Although it is grammatically correct, many people find it offensive because of its use of the masculine pronoun "his." Using a masculine pronoun ignores the fact that roughly half of the taxpayers are women. A solution to this problem is the following:

   7. The taxpayer must sign his or her return before mailing it.

This solution, however, also presents a problem. Those who are less concerned about sexual politics find the use of "his or her" to be somewhat awkward. This awkwardness becomes more apparent in an extended passage:

8. Once the taxpayer has checked his or her arithmetic, he or she should make sure he or she has signed the return. Then he or she should insert it in the envelope, fill in his or her return address, and mail it to his or her regional office of the IRS.

It would appear that one has to choose between two solutions, neither of which is completely satisfactory. In many cases, however, there is a way around this problem. Instead of changing the pronoun, one can change the antecedent:

9. Taxpayers must sign their returns before mailing them.

By changing the antecedent from the singular "the taxpayer" to the plural "taxpayers," the entire problem is avoided. When it is possible, this is undoubtedly the best solution.

You can see from the following revisions of the other four sentences in this exercise that this solution often works very well:

10. Teachers who care about their students will be available for conferences.
11. Representatives who don't accept contributions from lobbyists will soon lose their seats in Congress.
12. Consumers who don't compare prices will spend their money foolishly.
13. Travelers who don't make reservations in advance may end up sleeping in their cars.

These sentences have eliminated the pronoun agreement problems and have avoided offending anyone. When it is possible, making the antecedent plural is the best solution. When this is not possible, one must decide which is the lesser evil—offending people by using the masculine pronoun or sounding slightly awkward by using the expressions "his or her" and "he or she."

EXERCISE 15D-4

In these sets of eight sentences, the first four use the conjunction "and" and the second four use the conjunction "or." Let's look at the first four first.

The following shortened versions make it easier for you to see the pronouns and their antecedents.

1. a. Lynn and Marie .... their lawn mower
   b. The Hansons and the Johnsons .... their lawn mowers
   c. Lynn and the Hansons................. their lawn mowers
   d. The Hansons and Lynn .... their lawn mowers

2. a. My daughter and her friend .... their books
   b. My daughters and their friends .... their books
   c. My daughter and her friends .... their books
   d. My daughters and their friend .... their books

From these examples it should be clear that when the antecedent is a combination of two nouns and those nouns are joined by "and," the antecedent is always considered plural. In these cases, that means that the pronoun will be the plural "their."

Now let's look at the second four sentences in each set, the ones in which the two nouns in the antecedent are joined by "or":

1. e. Lynn or Marie lent Mr. Washington her lawn mower.
   f. The Hansons or the Johnsons lent Mr. Washington their lawn mower.
   g. Lynn or the Hansons lent Mr. Washington their lawn mower.
   h. The Hansons or Lynn lent Mr. Washington her lawn mower.

2. e. My daughter or her friend left her books in my car.
   f. My daughters or their friends left their books in my car.
   g. My daughter or her friends left their books in my car.
   h. My daughters or their friend left her books in my car.

The situation here is a little more complicated. In 1e, the two nouns in the antecedent are both singular. If Lynn or Marie lent someone her lawn mower, how many people lent a lawn mower? One, of course. We don't know whether it was Lynn or Marie, but we do know it was only one of them. Therefore, the antecedent is singular and the correct pronoun is "her." Sentence 2e works the same way.

In 1f, the two nouns in the antecedent are both plural. We don't know whether it was the Hansons or the Johnsons who did the lending, but in either case it was more than one person. If it was the Hansons, it was more than one person; if it was the Johnsons, it was more than one. Either way, the antecedent is plural, so the correct pronoun is "their." Sentence 2f works the same way.

The g and h sentences are the most complicated of all. In each of these, the antecedent is composed of two nouns joined by "or." In each case, however, one of the nouns is singular and the other is plural. This makes it impossible to figure out logically whether the antecedent is singular or plural. In sentence 1g, for example, if it was Lynn who did the lending, then it should be *her* lawn mower. But if it turns out that the Hansons did the lending, then it should be *their* lawn mower. Since we don't know who did the lending, we can't figure out logically whether the antecedent is singular or plural.

Where logic fails, however, grammar provides an answer. Somewhat arbitrarily, the grammatical rule states that when a singular and a plural antecedent are joined by "or," the pronoun must agree with the antecedent that it is closer to. Thus, in sentence 1g, the pronoun is closer to the plural "Hansons," so we use the plural "their." In sentence 1h, on the other hand, the pronoun is closer to the singular "Lynn," so we use the singular "her." Sentences 2g and 2h work the same way.

The rules for pronoun agreement with antecedents joined by "and" or "or" are summarized below:

1. If the antecedent is two nouns joined by "and," use a plural pronoun.
2. If the antecedent is two singular nouns joined by "or," use a singular pronoun.
3. If the antecedent is two plural nouns joined by "or," use a plural pronoun.
4. If the antecedent is one singular and one plural noun joined by "or," use a pronoun that agrees with the nearer of the two nouns.

EXERCISE 15D-6

What these sentences show is that when an indefinite pronoun is followed by a prepositional phrase, it is the pronoun and not the noun in the prepositional phrase that is the antecedent.

To demonstrate this, let's look at the first two sentences:

1. Both of my sisters broke off <u>their</u> engagements.
2. Each of my sisters broke off <u>her</u> engagement.

In sentence 1, you might think the antecedent is either "both" or "sisters." They are both plural, and the plural pronoun "their" agrees with either of them. In sentence 2, however, the antecedent must be "each." "Each" is singular, and the singular pronoun "her" agrees with it. If the noun in the prepositional phrase, "sisters," were the antecedent, the pronoun would have to be the plural "their." The correct conclusion from this is the following:

> In a sentence with an indefinite pronoun followed by a prepositional phrase, the antecedent is always the pronoun preceding the prepositional phrase and is never the noun at the end of the prepositional phrase.

Thus, in sentences 3 and 4, the antecedent is not "friends." In sentence 3, it is "many," so the plural pronoun "their" agrees with it. In sentence 4, the antecedent is "one," so the singular pronoun "her" agrees with it.

In sentence 5, the antecedent is "two," and the plural pronoun "their" refers back to it. In sentence 6, the antecedent is "either," and the singular pronoun "his" refers back to it.

EXERCISE 15D-8

From sentences 1 and 2, it is clear that "some" can be either singular or plural. To see how this works, let's look in some detail at these sentences.

1. Some of the wine had lost its flavor.

We know that the pronoun "its" has to agree with its antecedent "some." We also learned, in this exercise, that "some" can be either singular or plural. To figure out which it is, we have to look at the noun in the following prepositional phrase, "wine." Since "wine" is singular, "some" is singular, and since "some" is singular, the pronoun "its" must be singular to agree with it.

2. Some of the books had lost their covers.

In sentence 2, "some" is plural because the noun in the following prepositional phrase, "books," is plural. Because "some" is plural, the pronoun that refers to it, "their," must be plural.

The other four sentences work in a similar way.

R E V I E W

 ## EXERCISE 15-REVIEW-1 _____

The following sentences contain errors involving pronoun reference or agreement. Read each sentence carefully and correct any errors. To correct some of the errors, it may be necessary to completely rewrite the sentence.

1. Actually visiting Jerusalem was something of a disappointment for Debbie. She had dreamed about the trip since she was a child. This is what was so disappointing to her.

2. While Ken shook George's hand, he never looked at him.

3. My best friend is a psychologist, which I also studied for several years in college.

4. Each of the kittens had been licking their paws.

5. Either Karen or her daughter had left her purse in my car.

6. An engineer should never leave home without their slide rule.

7. Either of those police officers could get down off their horse and help that lady.

8. Susan was valedictorian of her class and gave a speech at her graduation. This was the result of a lot of hard work.

9. Helen's brothers never came to see her parents while they were on welfare.

10. Sandie and Chris watch birds on weekends, which is a very pleasant hobby.

11. Cathy or her parents will have to eat her words.

12. Why don't you ask Joan and Catherine to lend you her notes?

13. Each of the children brought their lunch with them on the field trip.

14. After Juanita paid the salesclerk, she whistled.

15. Jane Pauley asked the President's wife a question before she even had time to sit down.

16. In New York City, they are much friendlier than you would expect.

17. He checked the correct answers, but they didn't show very clearly because he didn't press down hard enough.

18. Each of the ducks was so damaged by the oil that they could not fly.

19. Both the players and the coach will get to tell his side of the story to the commissioner.

20. Would everyone please bring an extra towel with them on Monday.

 EXERCISE 15-REVIEW-2

The following sentences contain errors involving pronoun reference or agreement. Read each sentence carefully and correct any errors. To correct some of the errors, it may be necessary to completely rewrite the sentence.

1. The sky was beginning to get darker, and I had missed the last bus to Washington. This was making me very worried.

2.   Kathy smiled at Audrey, but she looked very solemn when I saw her.

3.   My friend Joe gave me a squash racquet even though I had never played it in my life.

4.   Each of the waiters checked their table assignments before leaving for the kitchen.

5.   Donna and her parents showed me their new condominium.

6.   Someone left their umbrella at my apartment.

7.   Either Victor or Stanley will lend you his car.

8.   I got my résumé typed on a word processor, and after three interviews, I was hired as a data processor for the Social Security Administration. I really appreciated Maxine's help with this.

9.   Ralph gave Marc the letter from Gloria; he turned and walked away without saying a word.

10.   Each of the candidates must do their own work.

11.   When Kirby or Ned raises their hand, I know the class is in for a big laugh.

12.   Each of the guests brought a plant with them.

13.   Either the players or the coach will have to be more reasonable about his demands.

14.   Most of the children could not even write his or her own name.

15.   I bought these shoes at Ward's during their spring sale. This is why they are so cheap.

16.   A member of a jury must make up their own mind about the guilt or innocence of the accused.

17.   Bob passed the sugar to Max, and he never even said a word.

18.   By early April the dogwoods had flowered, and by the middle of May, they had fallen to the ground.

19.   A person going to a job interview should make sure they understand what the job they are applying for consists of.

20.   George's boss had offered him a raise before he left on vacation.

 EXERCISE 15-REVIEW-3 _____

The following essay contains errors involving pronoun reference or agreement. Read the essay carefully and correct any errors. To correct some of the errors, it may be necessary to rewrite the sentence completely.

     The best professor I've had since I came to college didn't care about students. Most of my teachers have at least made some efforts to seem to be concerned about his or her students. They have tried to learn all of our names, they have given us their home phone numbers and assured us it was all right to call, and they have responded sympathetically when we have come to them with problems. Dr. Lupton didn't do any of those things; in fact, she really didn't seem to care about students at all. What she did care about was biology.

When my friend Joan came in late to Dr. Lupton's class with a bandage around her head, she didn't even seem to notice. She was too caught up in the ecological balance of the tidewater marsh even to notice Joan. Come to think of it, I don't think Dr. Lupton ever even took attendance. This bothered me a lot at the time because Joan was my best friend.

Dr. Lupton was very careful about keeping her office hours and her appointments. However, one afternoon when she didn't have office hours, I stopped in without an appointment. I needed some help with a water quality project she had assigned. I was quite surprised that she made no effort to make me feel welcome. What I did feel was that she was more interested in the project she was working on than she was in me. Each of the teachers I had had before Dr. Lupton had made me feel that they were glad to have me come and ask them questions at any time. I was furious at Dr. Lupton for her lack of concern. The next day in class, when she asked that everyone please confine their visits to her office hours, I was mortified. I decided that she was just one teacher I couldn't respect.

However, as the semester progressed, a funny thing happened. I got used to Dr. Lupton's attitude toward students. When I stopped worrying about how she felt about us, I began to see that the biology we were studying was fascinating. Maybe her enthusiasm for her subject was what made me begin to take it seriously. I realized that a teacher who cares more about their subject than their students can still be a good teacher. By the end of the semester, I had discovered that I wanted to become a biologist myself, but I never did become friends with Dr. Lupton.

16

Commas with Series, Places, and Dates

Part A   Items in a Series
Part B   Commas with Places
Part C   Commas with Dates

Part A · Items in a Series

In Chapter 8 you learned to use commas with coordinating conjunctions to join independent clauses. In Chapter 10 you learned to use commas to set off introductory elements. In this chapter you will learn three additional comma rules.

EXERCISE 16A-1 _____

The following sentences illustrate the first of these three rules. These sentences are all correct. Study these sentences and try to figure out what this rule is.

1.   **a.** I keep underwear, socks, and handkerchiefs in my top drawer.
     b. I keep underwear, socks and handkerchiefs in my top drawer.

2.   **a.** Bob, Jim, and Terry are going with us to the hog wrestling contest.
     b. Bob, Jim and Terry are going with us to the hog wrestling contest.

3.   **a.** There are primaries this week in Maine, New Hampshire, Vermont, and Connecticut.
     b. There are primaries this week in Maine, New Hampshire, Vermont and Connecticut.

4.   **a.** Nelson looked in the kitchen, in the basement, and in the backyard without finding his daughter.

     b. Nelson looked in the kitchen, in the basement and in the backyard without finding his daughter.

  5. **a.** We will cancel the picnic if it rains, if it snows, or if Jennie Manning tries to come to it.

     b. We will cancel the picnic if it rains, if it snows or if Jennie Manning tries to come to it.

  6. **a.** Cucumbers and asparagus make me break out in a rash.

NOTE: A discussion of this exercise can be found on pages 355–356.

EXERCISE 16A-2 _____

The following sentences contain errors involving items in a series. Proofread the sentences and correct any errors. Each sentence may contain no errors, one error, or more than one error.

  1. If you are going to the Safeway, would you get milk Cheerios and sugar?

  2. Debbie, Linda, and Theresa, are going to California for the summer.

  3. Mike served, sandwiches, potato salad, coleslaw, and iced tea for lunch.

  4. Leslie put mothballs in her suitcases in her closet and in her footlocker.

  5. I expected Randy and Howard to help me with the deliveries.

  6. Airlines, trains, and buses, were delayed by this weekend's snowstorm.

  7. The salad contained spinach lettuce cabbage cucumbers and tomatoes.

  8. I found sand in my pockets in my purse and in my ears when I got back from the beach.

  9. Tom's car chokes, coughs, and sputters when it first starts, but it always runs fine once it is warmed up.

 10. The high jump the discus throw and the pole vault are my favorite events in the Olympics.

DISCUSSION OF INDUCTIVE EXERCISE

EXERCISE 16A-1

These sentences illustrate the rule for commas with items in a series. The basic principle is that you separate items in a series with commas. The b versions of each sentence, however, show that the comma before the final "and" is optional. But because leaving this comma out can sometimes make a sentence unclear, we recommend that it *not* be omitted.

    A series can be three or more items. Number 3 has four items. Notice that, when there are only two items, as in number 6, the words are not considered a series and you do not use commas.

The items in the series can be words, phrases, or clauses. The first three examples are words in series. Number 4 has phrases in a series, and number 5 has clauses in a series.

Notice also that you do not put a comma following the final item in the series.

Part B · Commas with Places

EXERCISE 16B-1

The following sentences illustrate a second rule for commas. Study these sentences carefully and try to determine what this rule is.

1. I was born in Denver, Colorado, in 1963.
2. Pasadena, California, is the home of the Rose Bowl.
3. A hurricane hit Biloxi, Mississippi, last fall.
4. We sent the package to you at 1737 Bolton Street, Detroit, Michigan 52556.
5. My brother has lived at 812 Lesley Road, Bozeman, Montana 85638, for the past ten years.

NOTE: A discussion of this exercise can be found on page 357.

EXERCISE 16B-2

Proofread the following sentences and correct any errors. The errors will involve the rule for commas with places. Each sentence may contain no errors, one error, or more than one error.

1. I took a bus to Tulsa Oklahoma and never went back to Ardmore again.
2. Lake Havasu Arizona is now the home of the London Bridge.
3. Becky addressed the letter to Ms. Doris Eisenhart 11009 South Shore Road Rockville Maryland 21255.
4. President Johnson lived at 8844 Royce Boulevard Abilene Texas 44859 for six weeks when he was a boy.
5. We are flying to Chicago, Illinois for a conference next week.
6. The zoo in San Diego California is famous around the world.
7. Our company headquarters is at 1500 Concord Pike Boston Massachusetts 01046.
8. This plane stops in Dallas Texas before it arrives in Los Angeles.
9. Send your check to Million Dollar Drawing The Market Building 623 York Road Cincinnati Ohio 33405.
10. The train station in Boise, Idaho is very large and modern.

DISCUSSION OF INDUCTIVE EXERCISE

EXERCISE 16B-1

What these sentences show is the following:

1. When using city and state, place a comma before and after the state (except when it is the final word in a sentence, in which case a period replaces the comma).
2. When writing out an address, place a comma after each item that would be on a separate line if you were writing the address on an envelope. In addition, place a comma between the city and state but not between the state and the zip code.

Part C · Commas with Dates

EXERCISE 16C-1 _____

The following sentences illustrate the third of these rules for comma use. Study these sentences carefully and try to determine what this third rule is.

1. George was hired on March 17, 1984, and was fired the next day.
2. Monday, September 21, 1941, was the beginning of a new era.
3. This contract expires in January 1992 unless it is renewed.
4. This contract expires in January, 1992, unless it is renewed.
5. My parents were married on 6 April 1970 at five o'clock in the afternoon.
6. My parents were married on 6 April, 1970, at five o'clock in the afternoon.

NOTE: A discussion of this exercise can be found on page 358.

EXERCISE 16C-2 _____

The following sentences contain errors involving the comma rules you have studied in this chapter. Proofread these sentences and correct any errors. Each sentence may contain no errors, one error, or more than one error.

1. My accident occurred on Friday June 27, 1984 at ten o'clock in the evening.
2. The Allied Company has asked for a delivery date in November, 1986.
3. My first daughter was born in Colorado Springs Colorado on Wednesday October 11 1966.
4. Lenny, Marc, and Bill, were all hired on August 30 1983.
5. January 25 1988 is the deadline for applying for these benefits.
6. Clifford Still began work on this painting in May, 1981 and completed it in August of that year.
7. I lived in Kansas City Missouri until October 2 1984.
8. Do you know what happened on December 7 1941?

9. The meeting I missed was scheduled for Thursday April 16 1986 instead of Thursday April 23.

10. As of May 20 1987 I will never make another comma error.

DISCUSSION OF INDUCTIVE EXERCISE

EXERCISE 16C-1

The sentences demonstrate that the correct way to punctuate dates is as follows:

. . . month day, year, . . .
or
. . . day of week, month day, year, . . .

If only the month and year are used, the options are as follows:

. . . month year . . .
or
. . . month, year, . . .

If the day of the month is given before the month, the options are as follows:

. . . day month year . . .
or
. . . day month, year, . . .

R E V I E W

 ## EXERCISE 16-REVIEW-1

Proofread the following sentences carefully and correct any errors. All errors will involve commas with series, places, or dates. Each sentence may contain no errors, one error, or more than one error.

1. On the morning of March 28 1983 I got out of bed got dressed ate breakfast and walked out of my apartment only to find that my car had been stolen.

2. On September 29 1992 we will have been married for ten years.

3. In Colorado Springs Colorado there is a wonderful hotel called the Broadmore.

4. I applied for a scholarship for a student loan and for a work-study position, but I didn't get any of them.

5. I ordered her present from a store in Dallas Texas.

6.   For lunch I ate only a salad a piece of toast and a cup of tea.

7.   This weekend, I need to do my laundry to balance my checkbook and to wash my car before I can go to a movie.

8.   I remember that I mailed the check on Friday October 13 1985.

9.   If we don't receive a response from her by May 4 1986 we can sell the house without her permission.

10. My boss owns a house in Toledo, Ohio and another one in St. Louis Missouri.

11. My only options seem to be dropping a course quitting my job or not sleeping for the next three months.

12. I told Mike and Kathy that Atlanta Georgia was a place they might consider moving to.

13. By Monday March 15 1987 I will either be promoted or quit my job.

14. On Sundays we often see a movie go to a concert or have friends over.

15. When I lived in Minot North Dakota, I really didn't mind the cold.

16. Biting my fingernails, cracking my knuckles, and smoking, are all bad habits that I've had to break.

17. I got out of the navy on February 23 1979.

18. We spent the first night of our trip in Blacksburg Virginia and the second night in Akron Ohio.

19. The warranty on my car expires on August 27, 1987.

20. If you go to the grocery store, would you pick up a gallon of milk, and a head of lettuce?

EXERCISE 16-REVIEW-2 —————————————————

Proofread the following sentences carefully and correct any errors. All errors will involve commas with series, places, or dates. Each sentence may contain no errors, one error, or more than one error.

1.   When I took my car in last week, it needed a tune-up a new fuel pump and a lubrication.

2.   My father was born in Hortense Georgia and lived there until he was fifteen.

3.   On April 30, 1987 I will be twenty-one years old.

4.   Smoking can give you cancer can set your house on fire and can give you bad breath.

5.   The address on the envelope was Ms. Penelope Quaithwright 18359 South Park Plaza Santa Fe New Mexico 77890.

6. I started working for General Motors in February, 1978 and have never missed a day of work.

7. This year I am growing tomatoes lettuce corn squash and cucumbers.

8. I was living in Pocatella, Idaho in 1976.

9. I was born on September 21 1941 at two in the morning.

10. Without a moment's hesitation, Helen ripped off her jacket pulled off her shoes and dove into the lake to rescue her grandson.

11. On our vacation we spent a week in Orlando, Florida and a week in Mobile, Alabama.

12. Do you remember where you were in June, 1977 or in January of the following year?

13. Marcy Goldberg, Kevin Bona, and Marc Frank, were all hired at the same time I was.

14. A fire in a stable in Chicago Illinois spread to half the city.

15. My student loan will not be paid off until December 18 1991.

16. I have looked in my closet, in my dresser, and under my bed, and have not been able to find my earring.

17. You should mail your application to Mr. Timothy Adams 871 Beacon Avenue Providence Rhode Island 02906.

18. I can use my GI Bill benefits anytime until December 31 1989.

19. The terrible floods in Mississippi, and in Louisiana have caused a lot of anguish.

20. Memphis Tennessee is one of the fastest-growing cities in the East.

EXERCISE 16-REVIEW-3 ⸻⸻⸻⸻⸻⸻⸻⸻⸻⸻⸻

Proofread the following essay and correct any errors. All errors will involve commas with series, places, or dates.

Growing up in Reading Pennsylvania in the fifties, I always thought that people who lived in places that were far away and exotic would be very different from the people I knew. My three years in the army taught me that this is not so. Of course, there are differences, but people from very different cultures can also have a lot in common.

On Thursday May 16 1955 at ten o'clock at night in Reading General Hospital, I was born. For the next seventeen years, I grew up in a middle-class northern community. All the people I knew lived in this same cultural environment. We all thought that people from big cities people from other sections of the country and people from foreign countries must be very different from us. In fact, when my mother, who is a Lutheran, married a Catholic, her family objected strongly. Only after they got to know my father, did they really accept him.

In August, 1972 I enlisted in the army. I was ordered to report to Fort Benning Georgia for basic training. During these eight weeks of training, I became good friends with three of the guys in my squad. They were from Georgia New York and Puerto Rico. I could barely understand the New Yorker because he spoke so fast. But that was easy compared to the Southerner and the Puerto Rican; it took me three weeks to understand them because of their accents. However, once we could understand each other, we found that we had a lot in common. All three of us were happy to be out of high school and away from our parents. In addition, we all missed our girlfriends and were sure they would wait for us while we were in the army. Also, we all hated being on KP.

After eight weeks of marching shooting and physical training, I received orders for my first permanent assignment: Korea. Wayne Larry and Juan were all going to Germany. However, before we left Fort Benning, all four of us had received "Dear John" letters from our girlfriends.

When I arrived in Korea, my first impressions were that the Koreans had a strange language, strange food, and strange clothes. After a few months of living in Seoul Korea, however, I found out that my impression that they were very different from me was not completely accurate. I met a family named the Kims and found out that we, in fact, had a lot in common. From the Kims, I learned to appreciate Korean food music and hospitality. I also learned about cultural issues in Korea. Mr. Kim had been raised as a Christian, and Ms. Kim was a devout Buddhist. Her family had objected strongly to their marriage, but now they really liked Mr. Kim. It seemed just like my family back in Reading.

On June 7 1975 I returned to the States and was discharged from the army. I was extremely happy to be back with my friends in Reading Pennsylvania, but I also had learned a lot about people who seemed different from me.

17

The Apostrophe

Part A   Recognizing Possessive Situations
Part B   Forming Possessives
Part C   Using Contractions
Part D   Contractions versus Possessives

Part A · Recognizing Possessive Situations

There are three major reasons why people sometimes make mistakes with apostrophes. They fail to recognize when a word is possessive, or they don't know where to place the apostrophe, or they confuse the two major uses of apostrophes. In this chapter you will learn how to avoid each of these problems.

EXERCISE 17A-1 ⎯⎯⎯⎯⎯⎯⎯⎯⎯⎯⎯⎯⎯

In the following sentences, the possessive words have been underlined. Study these words and figure out what it means to say that a word is possessive.

1. <u>Bobby's</u> car was stolen.
2. I borrowed <u>Ms. Burkart's</u> dictionary while I wrote my paper.
3. The <u>teacher's</u> coat was covered with chalk dust.
4. The <u>doctor's</u> new office is located on the third floor of this building.
5. <u>Bernie's</u> yellow notebook was covered with graffiti.

NOTE: A discussion of the answers to this exercise can be found on page 366.

EXERCISE 17A-2 ⎯⎯⎯⎯⎯⎯⎯⎯⎯⎯⎯⎯

In the following sentences, underline every word that is possessive. The apostrophes have all been omitted because they would make the exercise too easy. You do not have to put in the apostrophes, just underline the words that are possessive. Each sentence may contain no possessive words, one possessive word, or more than one possessive word.

1. Have you seen Annettas hat?

2. The students pen was green with a black cap.

3. In the grass John saw a snake.

4. I was not impressed by Marks new suit.

5. When I saw the twins, Ms. Holmen was taking them for a walk.

EXERCISE 17A-3

The sentences in Exercise 17A-1 illustrate the most basic way a word can be possessive. The term "possessive," however, can also be applied to words in several other situations. The underlined words in the following sentences are all possessive. Take a good look at them and try to figure out why they are possessive.

1. Judith's hair is thick and curly.
2. I accidentally spilled coffee on Karl's leg.
3. Mr. Ireland's collarbone was fractured in the accident.
4. Do you know what color Margaret's eyes are?
5. The doctor examined George's back and found nothing wrong.

NOTE: A discussion of the answers to this exercise can be found on page 366.

EXERCISE 17A-4

The underlined words in the following sentences are also possessive. Study them and try to determine what additional situation is considered possessive in English.

1. The car's tires need to be rotated.
2. This table's surface is very sticky.
3. The house's front porch was in very bad shape.
4. That book's cover is badly stained.
5. This computer's memory is nearly full.

NOTE: A discussion of the answers to this exercise can be found on page 366.

EXERCISE 17A-5

In the following sentences, the underlined words are all possessive. Study these words and try to figure out yet another situation which is possessive.

1. Gina's sister is not coming home for the spring break.
2. After the dance, I met Robin's mother for the first time.
3. Ms. Slowinski's son is in my calculus class.
4. Did you see Barb's daughter when you were at her house?
5. The mayor of this city is Diane's aunt.

NOTE: A discussion of the answers to this exercise can be found on page 367.

EXERCISE 17A-6

Now you have learned four different ways in which a word can be possessive:

- **a.** When you are talking about something belonging to someone.
- **b.** When you are talking about a part of someone's body.
- **c.** When you are talking about a part of an inanimate object.
- **d.** When you are talking about someone's relative.

The following exercise includes examples of all these possessive situations. Read each sentence carefully and underline each word that is possessive. The apostrophes have all been omitted so that the exercise will not be too easy. You do not need to add apostrophes; just underline words that are possessive. Each sentence may contain no possessive words, one possessive word, or more than one possessive word.

1. I used Freds knife to open the wine.
2. I wrote the phone number on the palm of Lindas hand.
3. Have you seen my cars new seats?
4. Because you know Mr. Raab, Carville wants you to ask him to speak to the freshman class.
5. The woman in this film is Bills niece.
6. I sent Chris luggage when he graduated from college.
7. Steves trousers were ripped in the back.
8. Hollys hair has never looked as nice as it did the first time I met her.
9. This lamps switch is broken.
10. Cynthias parents are away this weekend.

EXERCISE 17A-7

There are even more situations in which words are considered possessive. The underlined words in the following sentences are possessive. Study these examples carefully and try to figure out what it is about these words that makes them possessive.

1. <u>Michael's</u> honesty is well known among his friends.
2. I was shocked to learn about <u>Sophia's</u> reputation.
3. <u>Eugene's</u> sense of humor has won him many friends.
4. <u>Al's</u> moods are beginning to get on my nerves.
5. Vicky was pleased by the <u>boss's</u> enthusiasm for the proposal she wrote.

NOTE: A discussion of the answers to this exercise can be found on page 367.

EXERCISE 17A-8

The underlined words in the following sentences are all possessive. Study each example and try to determine yet another situation in which words are considered possessive.

1. Annamarie's answer shocked the professor.
2. I read Phil's paper, and it was not too bad.
3. Did you get a look at Debbie's design for the new poster?
4. The class really liked Mr. Bladgett's suggestion.
5. Jerry's contribution was much less than we expected from him.

NOTE: A discussion of the answers to this exercise can be found on page 367.

EXERCISE 17A-9

The underlined words in the following sentences are all possessive. These examples are probably the hardest kind of possessive situation to recognize. Study them carefully and try to figure out what this last possessive situation is.

1. Last year's prices were a lot less than we are paying now.
2. I look forward to next fall's fashions.
3. Tomorrow's homework will not be collected, but I am going to do it anyway.
4. Ten minutes' delay and the house would have been a total loss.
5. I would not put up with an hour's wait to get into the concert.

NOTE: A discussion of the answers to this exercise can be found on page 367.

EXERCISE 17A-10

Now you have learned how many different situations are considered possessive in the English language. In each case, the ingredient seems to be that something "belongs," in some sense, to something or someone else. It is this sense of "belonging" to someone or something that is meant by the term "possessive."

The following exercise includes examples of all the different types of possessive situations you have learned. Underline all possessive words in the following sentences. All apostrophes have been omitted so that the exercise will not be too easy. You do not need to insert apostrophes; just underline the words that are possessive. Each sentence may contain no possessive words, one possessive word, or more than one possessive word.

1. My psych books cover was stained when I bought it.

2. It will be to Felixs advantage if he takes English this summer.

3. The childrens rooms are usually messy.

4. This years clothing styles do not look good on me.

5. I was worried about Kays cough.

6. In the bananas James found a tarantula.

7. George had done time in the Mens Detention Center.

8. A cab drivers life is often in danger.

9. The mens club voted to allow women as members.

10. Students in the sixties were more rebellious than todays students.

11. The tables surface was marred by the girls roller skates.

12. Jacks grades were better than he expected.

13. Marias answer was a complete surprise.

14. The shoes Peter bought were too small for him.

15 Juanitas fathers death has made her very depressed.

16. This months special at the A&P is strawberry ice cream.

17. In the mornings Susan is always very cheerful.

18. This years movies are just what teenagers like best.

19. I heard about the job from my friends uncle.

20. The volunteer armys problems are not just low pay.

DISCUSSION OF INDUCTIVE EXERCISES

EXERCISE 17A-1

These examples show that a word is possessive when something belongs to it, when it "owns" something. In the previous sentences, the car belonged to Bobby, the dictionary belonged to Ms. Burkart, the coat belonged to the teacher, the office belonged to the doctor, and the notebook belonged to Bernie.

Also notice that it is always the first word that is possessive. In number 1, it is "Bobby" that is possessive, not "car." The possessive word is always the one doing the possessing, not the one being possessed.

Further, notice that an adjective can come in between the possessive word and the word being possessed. In number 4, "new" comes between "doctor's" and "office." In number 5, "yellow" comes between "Bernie's" and "notebook."

The examples also seem to show that a possessive word ends with an apostrophe and an "s." This is not always true, however. Sometimes possessive words have other forms. You will learn about these other forms a little further on.

EXERCISE 17A-3

The sentences in Exercise 17A-3 show that references to a part of someone's body are possessive. In a sense, that hair "belongs" to Judith, and that leg with coffee burning it "belongs" to Karl.

EXERCISE 17A-4

The examples in Exercise 17A-4 show that a possessive situation exists when you are talking about a part of an inanimate object like a car or a desk. There is a sense in which those tires "belong" to that car and that surface "belongs" to that table.

A number of years ago, some writers objected to using apostrophes with inanimate objects, but that objection has almost completely disappeared today.

EXERCISE 17A-5

In each of the sentences in Exercise 17A-5, the possessive situation involves someone's relative (such as a sister, a mother, a son, a daughter, or an aunt). Like it or not, at least grammatically, your relatives "belong" to you.

EXERCISE 17A-7

In each of the possessive situations in Exercise 17A-7, the sentence is discussing some general quality that belongs to someone. In number 1, for example, "honesty" is a general quality belonging to Michael. In number 2, the reputation is a general quality belonging to Sophia. In each of these a general quality belongs to someone, and this kind of "belonging" is also considered a possessive situation.

EXERCISE 17A-8

Each of these situations involves a product that someone has produced, something someone has made. These products, in a sense, "belong" to the person who made them. The answer in number 1, for example, was made by Annamarie and, therefore, belongs to her. In number 2, the paper was produced by Phil and so belongs to him. In each case something someone has produced can be said to "belong" to him or her.

EXERCISE 17A-9

The key fact about these possessive words is that they represent periods of time. Thus, it is possible to think of something "belonging" to a particular period of time. Those prices "belonged" to last year, and the fashions "belong" to next fall.

Part B · Forming Possessives

To form a possessive, add an apostrophe or an apostrophe and the letter "s" to a word.

In Part A you learned that a word is possessive when something "belongs" to it. To form possessives, then, the first step is to determine whether the word in question possesses anything, whether it is in a possessive situation. If it is not, then you may not form a possessive with it.

 ### EXERCISE 17B-1 _____

Once you determine that a word is possessive, you must check something else before you form a possessive. Take a look at the underlined words in the following sentences. They are all possessive and they all have apostrophes. What else do they all have in common? More specifically, what part of speech are they all?

1. I lost <u>Bruce's</u> ring when I was washing the dishes at <u>Valerie's</u> house.
2. This <u>city's</u> mayor is running for reelection.
3. When I looked across the theater, <u>Jack's</u> arm was around <u>Katrina's</u> waist.

4. The <u>teacher's</u> voice was too quiet to be heard in the back of the room.
5. <u>Eric's</u> <u>car's</u> brakes need to be rebuilt.

NOTE: A discussion of the answers to this exercise can be found on page 372.

EXERCISE 17B-2 _____

The underlined words in the following sentences are all possessive. What do they have in common? Can you think of any other words that fit in this group? If so, write them on the lines following the sentences.

1. <u>Everyone's</u> paper will be returned to him or her next Monday.
2. Patrick found <u>somebody's</u> wallet in the locker room.
3. Who will win the election is <u>anybody's</u> guess.
4. <u>Something's</u> shadow lay across my floor, making it hard to find my contact lens.
5. <u>No one's</u> arguments are going to change Chris's mind.

_____

_____

_____

_____

NOTE: A discussion of the answers to this exercise can be found on page 372.

EXERCISE 17B-3 _____

Once you have determined that a word is possessive and is a noun or indefinite pronoun, you are ready to actually form the possessive. In the following sentences, the underlined words are correctly formed possessives. Study these examples carefully and try to determine what the basic procedure for forming possessives is.

1. One <u>boy's</u> hat was left in the classroom.
2. My <u>dog's</u> bed is located in the kitchen.
3. The <u>lawyer's</u> advice was to accept the offer.
4. <u>Someone's</u> car was parked in my driveway.
5. I need to replace my <u>car's</u> battery.

NOTE: A discussion of the answers to this exercise can be found on page 373.

EXERCISE 17B-4 _____

The following sentences contain errors involving the formation of possessive nouns and indefinite pronouns. Proofread these sentences and correct any errors. Each sentence may contain no errors, one error, or more than one error.

1. I found a students notebook in the back seat of my car.
2. Todays students are very hardworking.

3. In the mornings, birds often are waiting at my bird feeder.

4. I ran into Erics girlfriend in the Giant.

5. Someones dog had tipped over the garbage.

6. My husbands sister is taking care of somebodys house at the beach.

7. We sent Kris flowers for her birthday.

8. Mr. Zandts garden was ruined by the storm.

9. Last years party was a disaster, so this year we are having it at Sues house.

10. This is the story of one cats bravery.

EXERCISE 17B-5

In Exercise 17B-3, you learned the basic form for making nouns and indefinite pronouns possessive. The sentences from that exercise are repeated below as the a version of each number. The b version demonstrates a variation on the method for forming possessives. Study the following pairs of sentences closely and try to figure out why the b versions end in "s' " rather than in " 's". In particular, look at what all the words being made possessive in the b versions have in common.

1. a. One <u>boy's</u> hat was left in the classroom.
   b. Two <u>boys'</u> hats were left in the classroom.

2. a. My <u>dog's</u> bed is located in the kitchen.
   b. My two <u>dogs'</u> beds are located in the kitchen.

3. a. The <u>lawyer's</u> advice was to accept the offer.
   b. The three <u>lawyers'</u> advice was to accept the offer.

4. a. <u>Someone's</u> car was parked in my driveway.
   b. Several <u>guests'</u> cars were parked in my driveway.

5. a. I need to replace my <u>car's</u> battery.
   b. I need to replace my two <u>cars'</u> batteries.

NOTE: A discussion of the answers to this exercise can be found on page 373.

EXERCISE 17B-6

The following sentences contain errors involving possessives. Proofread these sentences and correct any errors. Each sentence may contain no errors, one error, or more than one error.

1. Two squirrels were sitting on my patio.

2. My parent's house is located in Washington, D.C., but they are moving soon.

3. My wifes' parents live in Dallas.

4. The three students questions seemed to make the teacher angry.

5. One Volkswagens horn was beeping in the wilderness.

6. Fifty elephants danced across my kitchen floor.

7. The three actors lines are very complicated in this play.

8. This stores' prices are much too high for my budget.

9. My two daughters' dates were sitting patiently in the living room.

10. These book's covers were soaking wet, but now they are fine.

EXERCISE 17B-7

The following pairs of sentences reveal one additional variation in the formation of possessives.

1. a. Two <u>boys'</u> hats were left in the classroom.
    b. Two <u>children's</u> hats were left in the classroom.

2. a. My two <u>dogs'</u> bowls are located in the kitchen.
    b. Several <u>deer's</u> footprints were visible in the mud.

3. a. The three <u>lawyers'</u> advice was to accept the offer.
    b. The three <u>clergymen's</u> advice was to accept the offer.

4. a. Several <u>guests'</u> cars were parked in my driveway.
    b. Several <u>people's</u> cars were parked in my driveway.

5. a. I need to replace my two <u>cars'</u> batteries.
    b. I need to purchase two <u>women's</u> bicycles.

Write the plural form of each of the underlined words in the spaces below. Be careful. Write just the *plural* form, not the possessive of each word. The first two are done for you.

1. a. _____*boys*_____   b. _____*children*_____
2. a. _____   b. _____
3. a. _____   b. _____
4. a. _____   b. _____
5. a. _____   b. _____

What do all the plural words in the a column have in common? What do all the ones in the b column have in common? Now can you figure out the third variation on the rules for forming possessives?

NOTE: A discussion of the answers to this exercise can be found on pages 373–374.

EXERCISE 17B-8

The following sentences contain errors in possessive formation. Proofread them carefully and use the four-step process to correct any errors. Each sentence may contain no errors, one error, or more than one error.

1. The mens room is located in the basement.

2. The three childrens' were playing with an ostrich in my front yard.

3. This years styles have even influenced childrens' clothes.

4. Six Corvette's were parked in my driveway.

5. Have women's issues been addressed at this conference?

6. Our three sheeps pasture is located across the street.

7. The radio stations' in this town play only rock music.

8. Nancy saw three deer's tails as she glanced out of the tent.

9. I changed into my swimming suit in the men's locker room.

10. Three children's were trying to sell Girl Scout cookies to Audrey.

 ## EXERCISE 17B-9

This exercise reviews everything you have learned about forming possessives. Read each sentence carefully and correct any errors, using the rules given on pp. 373–374. Each sentence may contain no errors, one error, or more than one error.

1. The childrens screams could be heard all over the neighborhood.

2. Several teachers were eating lunch in the student union.

3. My cars' tires are low on air, so I am driving it to a gas station.

4. The presidents' speech to Congress was very misleading.

5. In the evening's Derrell works at Gino's.

6. Several police officers cars were vandalized.

7. Six childrens' jackets were stolen from this department over the week-end.

8. The players union did not agree to negotiate around the clock.

9. Todays economy makes it necessary that peoples budgets be rigid.

10. Can you tell me where the womens room is located?

11. These doctors' offices are too crowded.

12. The two deers antlers became locked during their battle.

13. The chairpersons' absence caused us to cancel the meeting.

14. Nelson was awakened by sixty sheeps bleating.

15. My bikes tires are easy to patch.

16. In my class, the nine womens preference was that we cancel class next week.

17. Yesterdays vote in the student senate surprised everyone.

18. No ones name was on this locker, so I put Toms books in it.

19. Walters' pants are drying in the kitchen, so he is hiding in the bathroom.

20. My daughters friend had borrowed someones bicycle for the weekend.

 ## EXERCISE 17B-10

The following paragraph contains errors in possessive formation. Read the paragraph carefully and correct any errors.

Taking my grandparents out to dinner at Randolphs Seafood Restaurant last Saturday night was a complete disaster. When we arrived at the restaurant, there were about thirty people waiting for tables. My grandparents' hate to wait, but there was nothing else we could do. After forty-five minutes, we were finally seated. My grandparent's dinners were served cold, and mine was burned. When my grandmother went to the womens room, she found a line of women waiting to get in. The restaurants air conditioning was not working, so we sweltered throughout the meal. Finally, when we left, my cars front left tire was flat. We'll never go back to Randolphs.

DISCUSSION OF INDUCTIVE EXERCISES

EXERCISE 17B-1

All of the possessive words in Exercise 17B-1 are nouns. So, nouns are one kind of word that can form its possessive by adding some combination of an apostrophe and the letter "s."

EXERCISE 17B-2

The words in this group include the following:

anybody	nobody
anyone	no one
anything	nothing
everybody	somebody
everyone	someone
everything	something

An easy way to remember these words is to think of them as all the possible combinations of the following:

any
every
no   and
some

body
one
thing

These words are all indefinite pronouns. While it is not necessary that you remember the term, it is important that you remember the words in this group.

In the English language, then, there are only two groups of words that show possession by adding some combination of an apostrophe and an "s": nouns and this group of indefinite pronouns. Therefore, the second step in forming a possessive is to ask yourself whether the possessive word is a noun or indefinite pronoun. If the answer to that question is no, then you may not form the possessive by adding an apostrophe and an "s."

EXERCISE 17B-3

Each of the possessives in this exercise was formed by adding an apostrophe and an "s" to the possessive word. The steps for forming possessives, then, are as follows:

1. Ask yourself whether the word in question is possessing anything. Is it in a possessive situation? If not, do not make it possessive.
2. Ask yourself whether the word in question is a noun or indefinite pronoun. If not, do not use an apostrophe and an "s" to make it possessive.
3. Form the possessive by adding an apostrophe and the letter "s."

EXERCISE 17B-5

What the possessive words in the b versions of these sentences have in common is that they are all plural. As a result, their possessives are formed by adding an apostrophe following the "s" that makes them plural. Thus, the rules for forming possessives are now as follows:

1. Ask yourself whether the word in question is possessing anything. Is it in a possessive situation? If not, do not make it possessive.
2. Ask yourself whether the word in question is a noun or an indefinite pronoun. If not, do not use an apostrophe and an "s" to make it possessive.
3. Ask yourself if the word is singular or plural. Write the word in its singular or plural form as appropriate. Remember that at this point you are only making the word singular or plural; do *not* make it possessive until step 4.
4. Form the possessive as follows:
   a. If the word is singular, add an apostrophe and the letter "s."
   b. If the word is plural, add just an apostrophe.

EXERCISE 17B-7

All the plural words in the a column end in the letter "s." All the plural words in the b column end in some letter other than "s." Looking at the sentences themselves, it is clear that, when the plural form ends in the letter "s," you make it possessive by adding just an apostrophe. When the plural form ends in anything other than the letter "s," you add an apostrophe and the letter "s."

Now you know all the variations in the four-step process for forming possessives. The complete process is outlined below:

1. Ask yourself whether the word in question is possessing anything. Is it in a possessive situation? If not, do not make it possessive.
2. Ask yourself whether the word in question is a noun or indefinite pronoun. If not, do not use an apostrophe and an "s" to make it possessive.
3. Ask yourself if the word is singular or plural. Write the word in its singular or plural form as appropriate. Remember that at this point you are only making the word singular or plural; do *not* make it possessive until step 4.
4. Form the possessive as follows:
   a. If the word is singular, add an apostrophe and the letter "s."
   b. If the word is plural and ends in "s," add just an apostrophe.

c. If the word is plural and ends in anything other than an "s," add an apostrophe and the letter "s."

Part C · Using Contractions

In Parts A and B of this chapter, you learned how to use apostrophes to form possessives with nouns and indefinite pronouns. In this part you will learn about a completely different use of apostrophes.

EXERCISE 17C-1 _____

The following pairs of sentences illustrate another use of apostrophes. Study these sentences and try to determine what this use is.

1. a. We will show you the way back to town.
    b. We'll show you the way back to town.

2. a. Larry could not see past his nose.
    b. Larry couldn't see past his nose.

3. a. Parker has not read the paper this morning.
    b. Parker hasn't read the paper this morning.

4. a. My brother is very happy that he is working for the state.
    b. My brother is very happy that he's working for the state.

5. a. I will send you a postcard when I arrive in Portugal.
    b. I'll send you a postcard when I arrive in Portugal.

NOTE: A discussion of the answers to this exercise can be found on page 375.

EXERCISE 17C-2 _____

The words in question from Exercise 17C-1 are listed below:

1. a. We will   b. We'll
2. a. could not   b. couldn't
3. a. has not   b. hasn't
4. a. he is   b. he's
5. a. I will   b. I'll

Take a close look at these examples and try to figure out where the apostrophe is placed in contractions. Look especially closely at numbers 2 and 3.

NOTE: A discussion of the answers to this exercise can be found on page 375.

EXERCISE 17C-3 _____

Now you know all you need to know about using contractions. This exercise reviews everything you have learned in this part. Proofread each sentence and correct any errors. All errors will involve the use of contractions. Each sentence may contain no errors, one error, or more than one error.

1. Theres no reason for you to feel embarrassed.

2. My essay is'nt finished, but Im not worried about it.

3. Larry couldn't see why we were angry.

4. My sister wo'nt let me open doors for her.

5. Has'nt the bus stopped running on this street?

6. I wonder what they're going to do when their daughter does'nt come home from college for the summer.

7. Havent you read the morning paper yet?

8. I dont like asparagus.

9. Jazz is'nt for everyone, but I love it.

10. Whats for dinner tonight?

DISCUSSION OF INDUCTIVE EXERCISES

EXERCISE 17C-1

The sentences in Exercise 17C-1 show that you may join some words and leave out a letter or two if you use an apostrophe. The words that are formed by joining two other words are called contractions. They are permissible most of the time, but are considered inappropriate for very formal writing.

EXERCISE 17C-2

From these examples you can see that, in general, the apostrophe is placed where the letter or letters have been omitted, *not* necessarily where the two words are joined. "Couldn't," for example, would be incorrect if it were written "could'nt."

There is one contraction that does not follow any rule:

will not → won't

It is probably best just to memorize this one.

Part D · Contractions versus Possessives

One of the biggest causes of errors in the use of apostrophes is confusion between contractions and possessives. In this part you'll learn to avoid this confusion.

 ### EXERCISE 17D-1 ————————————

The following pairs of sentences illustrate something new about forming possessives. The b version of each sentence is obviously incorrect; no one would ever write such sentences. But why are they incorrect? Check back to the four-step process for forming possessives in Part B (pp. 373–374) and see if you can figure out which step in that process prevents you from forming the incorrect versions of these possessives.

1.　a.　Correct:　　My wife and I have ordered <u>our</u> passports.
　　b.　Incorrect:　My wife and I have ordered <u>we's</u> passports.

2. **a.** Correct: Ms. Doyle has lost <u>her</u> keys.
   b. Incorrect: Ms. Doyle has lost <u>she's</u> keys.

3. **a.** Correct: I was angry about <u>my</u> grade in physics.
   b. Incorrect: I was angry about <u>I's</u> grade in physics.

NOTE: A discussion of this exercise can be found on page 378.

EXERCISE 17D-2 _____

As Exercise 17D-1 illustrates, the separate possessive forms for "we," "she," and "I" are "our," "her," and "my." In the chart below, these three have been filled in. Fill in as many of the others as you know.

SINGULAR		PLURAL	
REGULAR FORM	POSSESSIVE FORM	REGULAR FORM	POSSESSIVE FORM
I	<u>my (mine)</u>	we	<u>our (ours)</u>
you	_____	you	_____
he	_____	they	_____
she	<u>her (hers)</u>		
it	_____		
who	_____	who	_____

NOTE: A discussion of this exercise can be found on page 378.

EXERCISE 17D-3 _____

Although it is unlikely that you would use "we's" instead of "our" or "I's" instead of "my," the three pairs of possessive pronouns and pronoun contractions listed below are often confused:

> its/it's
> your/you're
> their/they're

The following examples illustrate the differences between the use of these possessives ("its," "your," and "their") and the use of the corresponding contractions ("it's," "you're," and "they're"). Study these examples until you know when to use the possessive form and when to use the contraction.

1. The wind was so strong that my kite lost <u>its</u> tail.
2. My car has a mind of <u>its</u> own.
3. I am afraid that <u>it's</u> too late to register for courses.
4. <u>It's</u> not too far to walk from here.
5. Have you sent in <u>your</u> money yet?
6. <u>Your</u> car is sitting in my driveway.
7. I heard <u>you're</u> going to Mexico this summer.
8. <u>You're</u> going to like the service in this writing center.
9. My parents are celebrating <u>their</u> thirtieth wedding anniversary tonight.
10. Orangutans take care of <u>their</u> young for two years.

11. I think <u>they're</u> going to have dinner at the Hyatt.
12. I love blueberries, but <u>they're</u> too expensive for my budget.

NOTE: A discussion of the answers to this exercise can be found on pages 378–379.

EXERCISE 17D-4

Now you know how to distinguish between contractions and possessives. This exercise will review everything you have learned in this part. Proofread the following sentences and correct any errors. All errors will involve the distinction between contractions and possessives. Each sentence may contain no errors, one error, or more than one error.

1. Their looking for oil in Virginia, but it's unlikely that they will find any.
2. I got my application in the mail, but Marlene hasn't gotten her's.
3. It's too late to go swimming.
4. I hear your going to New York this weekend.
5. I don't like they're attitude.
6. Tony's dog hurt it's leg, but it's better now.
7. Michael isn't going to flunk his' accounting course.
8. Jesse isn't invited to they're party, so I'm not going either.
9. They're giving tickets to illegally parked cars this afternoon.
10. I would like to transfer to the state university, but they're tuition is too high.
11. Its possible that your going to get the job.
12. I like you're new shoes.
13. I love doing grammar exercises because they're so much fun.
14. They haven't gotten their income tax refund yet, but we got our's.
15. Your going to have to take a detour when you reach the Mississippi River.
16. It's not a bad drive to Ocean City, if there isn't a lot of traffic.
17. Evelyn had two umbrellas, so I borrowed one of her's.
18. It's a shame that the election is so early.
19. Is therapy covered by you're insurance?
20. I wonder if their going to discover a cure for cancer in my lifetime.

EXERCISE 17D-5

The following paragraph contains errors involving contractions and possessives. Proofread the paragraph and correct any errors.

My car is on it's last legs. Last week it lost it's muffler, and this week it's extremely hard to start. I am afraid the battery may be almost dead. I would like to take it to Rip-Off Motors to be worked on tomorrow. Their located on Route 40, just east of town. If you could follow me out there in the morning, I could ride to work in you're car. If your going to be too busy to give me a ride, don't worry; I can ask Toby for a ride.

DISCUSSION OF INDUCTIVE EXERCISES

EXERCISE 17D-1

Obviously "our" is correct, and "we's" is incorrect. Just as clearly, "her" and "my" are correct, and "she's" and "I's" are incorrect. These are not exceptions to the four-step process for forming possessives, however. Step 2 in that process says "Ask yourself whether the word in question is a noun or indefinite pronoun." The four-step process applies *only* to nouns and indefinite pronouns. Since "we," "she," and "I" in the sentences on the preceding page are *pronouns* and not nouns or indefinite pronouns, the four-step rule does *not* apply. Pronouns (other than indefinite pronouns) *never* form their possessives by adding " 's." Instead, there is always a separate form of the pronoun to indicate possession.

EXERCISE 17D-2

SINGULAR		PLURAL	
REGULAR FORM	POSSESSIVE FORM	REGULAR FORM	POSSESSIVE FORM
I	my (mine)	we	our (ours)
you	your (yours)	you	your (yours)
he	his	they	their (theirs)
she	her (hers)		
it	its		
who	whose	who	whose

EXERCISE 17D-3

From these sentences you can conclude the following:

1. "It's" is always the possessive. "It's" is always the contraction for "it is." Anytime that you use an "it's," ask yourself whether "it is" would make sense in its place. If it would, then the "it's" is correct. If not, you need to use "its."

2. "Your" is always the possessive. "You're" is always the contraction for "you are." Anytime that you use a "you're," ask yourself whether "you are" would make sense in its place. If it would, then the "you're" is correct. If not, you need to use "your."

3. "Their" is always the possessive. "They're" is always the contraction for "they are." Anytime that you use a "they're," ask yourself whether "they are" would make sense in its place. If it would, then the "they're" is correct. If not, you need to use "their."

R E V I E W

EXERCISE 17-REVIEW-1 ⎯⎯⎯⎯⎯⎯⎯⎯⎯⎯⎯

Proofread the following sentences carefully and correct any errors. All errors will involve the use of apostrophes. Each sentence may contain no errors, one error, or more than one error.

1. Its very difficult to cope with todays inflation rate.
2. Cecil's choice is to eat at Burger King, but Kathy does'nt want to.
3. It's all right with me if your late for the party.
4. Mockingbird's have been known to attack cats.
5. My sons' teacher doesnt like him.
6. This stores' prices' are quite reasonable.
7. My neighbors' have not mowed they're grass in three weeks.
8. The childrens coats were soaking wet, but they did'nt seem to mind.
9. The mens' names were Walter and George.
10. Walters sister was married to George, who is a friend of you're father.
11. The two dogs bowls are on top of the refrigerator.
12. We were'nt late for our parents' anniversary, but we had to speed to get there.
13. I think its going to rain before we get to you're uncles store.
14. Is there a good womens' dress shop in your neighborhood?
15. They're taking too long to finish that job.
16. Why doesnt you're cat like it's kittens?
17. My sisters' are all younger than I am.
18. I saw Sharons' parents in the Giant last night.
19. When your in the army, you give up a lot of you're rights.
20. In the books' Craig studied, there was no mention of suicide.

EXERCISE 17-REVIEW-2 ⎯⎯⎯⎯⎯⎯⎯⎯⎯⎯⎯

Proofread the following sentences carefully and correct any errors. All errors will involve the use of apostrophes. Each sentence may contain no errors, one error, or more than one error.

1. In his clothes' John looked much younger.

2. My cats' eyes are giving him trouble.

3. We were'nt ready when the bell rang.

4. I hope its not going to rain.

5. Todays students are worried about the job situation.

6. Is the mens' room downstairs?

7. Rachel doesnt look like she enjoys square dancing.

8. They're test was not nearly as hard as ours.

9. I just did not understand the plays ending.

10. I could hear my two boy's voices from all the way in the kitchen.

11. Im hoping to get an A in my math class.

12. I heard you're looking for a new job.

13. My two sisters' have opened a shop in the new mall.

14. Do you make the childrens' lunches?

15. Karen is hoping that shes invited to play in the citywide tournament.

16. My job has its advantages.

17. This years TV programs are worse than ever.

18. The three deers' footprints were plainly visible in the snow.

19. You shouldnt worry so much about offending someone.

20. Have you finished you're homework yet?

EXERCISE 17-REVIEW-3 _____

Proofread the following essay and correct any errors. All errors will involve the use of apostrophes.

Just once in my life, I would like to take an extreme position. However, on every issue I can think of, I end up in the middle of the road. I have come to the conclusion that I am compulsively moderate.

Take, for example, the matter of dress. My childrens clothes are interchangeable with those of their friends. There is'nt an ounce of individuality in anything they wear. I dont like that kind of conformity, but I also dont approve of my friend who tries to shock everyone by wearing the most bizarre outfits she can contrive. She's always showing up wearing large floppy hats, long feather earrings, and transparent blouses. You can see from this that my preference is for clothes that express individuality without being too extreme. And that is the problem: I never do anything extreme.

At my job I disapprove of people who can only say "yes" to the boss. I think people should have the courage to express they're opinions even when those opinions are different from the boss's. On the other hand, there are two men at work who seem to disagree with everything our boss says. They waste everyones time by objecting to every decision. They're negative attitudes are very disruptive. So once again, I approve of a little rebelliousness, but not too much.

Nothing can ruin a visit to someones house more quickly than unruly children. Todays parents are often overly permissive. Lenient parents' who let they're children interrupt conversations and annoy the guests bother me more than almost anything. I say "almost" because there is one thing that offends me even more: tyrannical parents. I hate to see parents who have turned they're children into robots who can only say "Yes, Sir" or "Thank you, Ma'am." Spending an evening in this kind of militaristic environment can leave me depressed for three weeks. Its not that I object to discipline, but I do object to an excess of it. Once again, I end up as a moderate.

Of course, moderation is all right in it's place. My problem is that I am always moderate. I never take an extreme position. You might say that Im extremely moderate, but, at least, that means I've found something that I'm extreme about.

C H A P T E R

18

Confusing Words

Part A   Words That Are Confused Because
          They Sound Alike
Part B   Words That Are Confused Because
          They Sound Similar
Part C   A, An, and And
Part D   Words That Are Confused with Incorrect Words
Part E   Contractions and Possessive Pronouns

Part A · Words That Are Confused Because They Sound Alike

In the English language, there are a number of words that can easily be confused with other words. In this chapter you will learn how to avoid or correct mistakes that result from these confusions. In this part of the chapter you will learn about eight pairs of words that people confuse because they are pronounced exactly alike but are spelled differently and have very different meanings. Words like these are sometimes called homophones.

 EXERCISE 18A-1 _____

The following sentences include examples of homophones used correctly. Study these sentences and try to figure out the differences in meaning between these words.

The first three illustrate the word "here."

1. Alice doesn't live <u>here</u> any more.
2. Let's pitch the tent <u>here</u>.
3. <u>Here</u> is your assignment for today.

Compare the word "here" in the sentences above with the word "hear" in the following sentences:

4. Peter can't <u>hear</u> at all with his left ear.
5. I <u>hear</u> you are getting married.
6. Can people <u>hear</u> their own heartbeats?

Some people find it helpful in keeping these straight to remember that "hear," the one that means to hear something with your ear, has the word "ear" in it: "h*ear*."

Now look at another set.

7. I believe there is a terrible secret in his <u>past</u>.
8. Those who do not understand the <u>past</u> are doomed to repeat it.
9. Hawthorne believed that the <u>past</u> had a large influence on the present.

Compare "past" in the preceding sentences with its homophone, "passed," in the following sentences:

10. A bright red truck <u>passed</u> me at a high rate of speed.
11. We <u>passed</u> the Kansas state line about twenty minutes ago.
12. It's hard to believe that I actually <u>passed</u> statistics.

The next two groups illustrate the difference between "know" and "no."

13. I don't <u>know</u> anything about calculus.
14. Laura and Jane <u>know</u> how to read blueprints.
15. I <u>know</u> how busy you are, but this will only take a minute.

16. If Will asks you to serve on his committee, you should just say <u>no</u>.
17. There is <u>no</u> reason why you shouldn't accept her offer.
18. Our schedule allows <u>no</u> time for shopping.

The next two groups show the difference between "knew" and "new."

19. I <u>knew</u> Catherine when she was just two years old.
20. Jacqueline <u>knew</u> that there would be trouble if she was late.
21. We <u>knew</u> that the price would be high, but not that high.

22. Veronica is the <u>new</u> kid in our class.
23. Is that dress <u>new</u>?
24. Boppo Soda is <u>new</u> and improved.

The next five sentences illustrate a number of uses of the word "break."

25. Did Mark <u>break</u> his ankle or just sprain it?
26. We sure could use a <u>break</u> in this weather.
27. Give me a <u>break</u>.
28. Patricia's mistake turned out to be a lucky <u>break</u>.
29. Let's take a ten-minute <u>break</u>.

Compare the above uses of "break" with the uses of "brake" in the following sentences:

30. Jo Ann needs to have the <u>brakes</u> adjusted on her Volkswagen.
31. It helps to use the hand <u>brake</u> when you stop on steep hills.
32. I <u>brake</u> for unicorns.

The next two groups illustrate the difference between "patience" and "patients."

33. If you want to catch any fish, you must have <u>patience</u>.
34. You need a lot of <u>patience</u> to do these grammar exercises.
35. This hospital has enough beds for two hundred <u>patients</u>.
36. Theresa enjoys working with <u>patients</u> more than anything else about her job.

The next groups demonstrate the difference between "personal" and "personnel."

37. The <u>personnel</u> office has made another mistake with my vacation time.
38. You should send your application to the <u>personnel</u> officer.
39. Whitney is absent today because of a <u>personal</u> problem.
40. Please don't use the copier to copy <u>personal</u> papers.

The final group causes special problems because it includes three words, "to," "too," and "two" and because "to" and "too" each have two meanings.
The first three sentences illustrate one meaning for the word "to."

41. Steve usually rides his bike <u>to</u> school.
42. I sent a letter <u>to</u> the president.
43. Omar is going <u>to</u> college this summer.

The next three sentences illustrate the second use for the same word, "to."

44. I hope <u>to</u> go visit Canada this summer.
45. Tom wanted <u>to</u> go into business for himself.
46. <u>To</u> dance with Mary Ann can be very risky.

The next three sentences illustrate one use of "too."

47. Is it okay if Bob comes to the beach <u>too</u>?
48. Susan did her homework and studied for the test <u>too</u>.
49. Ed knows how to start a fire without matches, and he knows how to use commas <u>too</u>.

The next group illustrates the second meaning of "too."

50. It is <u>too</u> late to think about that now.
51. Charles is <u>too</u> young to start school this year.
52. The price for that house is <u>too</u> high.

Some people find it helpful to think of "too," the one that means "also" or "more than enough" as the one with "more than enough o's" because it has two of them.

EXERCISE 18A-2 _____

Now you know the homophones that cause people the most trouble. The following sentences contain errors involving the use of these homophones. Proofread them and correct any errors. Each sentence may contain no errors, one error, or more than one error.

1. The ship was to late too save the drowning witch.

2. The breaks on the bus were defective, and this caused the accident.

3. I don't no why my parents didn't call us when they past through town.

4. I did not here anything knew while I was in California.

5. On Mondays I have little patience for interruptions.

6. Her personal goals are very high, and I think she has a good chance of accomplishing them.

7. Bobby wants to get to no Shirley, and she would like to get to no him to.

8. Did you see the look on the face of the woman who past me?

9. Hear is the book you asked me to pick up for you.

10. I don't have the patients too wait for the bus.

Part B · Words That Are Confused Because They Sound Similar

In this part you will learn about seven pairs of words that are often confused because their pronunciations are similar. For many people, the easiest way to avoid mistakes with these is to learn the differences in pronunciation. If you pronounce them precisely, it will be clear that they are two separate words; as a result, the differences in meanings will be much easier to keep straight.

 ### EXERCISE 18B-1

The sentences in this exercise illustrate the differences in meaning of seven pairs of words with very similar pronunciations. The first two groups of sentences demonstrate the difference between "fine" and "find." As with all of the words in this part, if you will pronounce the words precisely, the difference in meaning will be easier to remember. In this case, the difference in pronunciation is the "d" sound at the end of "find."

1. Shirley was feeling <u>fine</u> the day after her operation.

2. Simon paid the <u>fine</u> because he didn't have the time or money to go to court.

3. Max cannot <u>find</u> his keys.

4. Darlene made a real <u>find</u> at a yard sale last weekend.

The following groups of sentences illustrate the difference between "mine" and "mind." As was the case with "fine" and "find," if you pronounce the final "d" sound in "mind," it will be a lot easier to keep these two words separate in your mind.

5. This book is <u>mine</u>, but you may borrow it.

6. A friend of <u>mine</u> gave me these shoes.

7.   Darlene's father worked in a <u>mine</u> for thirty years.
8.   The ship struck a <u>mine</u> that was left over from World War II.

9.   A <u>mind</u> is a terrible thing to waste.
10. You have to make up your <u>mind</u> about the vacation so we can make reservations.
11. I won't <u>mind</u> if you pick some of my tomatoes.
12. Will you <u>mind</u> the baby for a few minutes while I run to the store?

The next two groups of sentences illustrate one of the errors people make more often than any of the others in this chapter: the confusion of "then" and "than." Once again, pronouncing the two words precisely will help a lot.

13. I fixed dinner and <u>then</u> noticed that the TV was missing.
14. Way back <u>then</u>, people didn't have electric lights.
15. Did you know <u>then</u> that your car wouldn't start?

16. Donald is taller <u>than</u> Jeff.
17. This exercise is more difficult <u>than</u> I expected.
18. We started later <u>than</u> we had planned.

The next two groups show the difference between "weather" and "whether." Here the difference in pronunciation is at the beginning of the two words. The "w" sound at the beginning of "weather" is different from the "wh" sound at the beginning of "whether" in the same way that the "w" sound in "win" is different from the "wh" sound in "when."

19. The <u>weather</u> in Monterey is delightful all year.
20. We really need a break in this <u>weather</u>.

21. I don't care <u>whether</u> you are mad or not.
22. Paula wondered <u>whether</u> she really had a chance of being promoted.

The next groups of sentences demonstrate the difference between "lose" and "loose." This time the pronunciation difference is in the sound of the letter "s." In "lose" the "s" is pronounced like a "z"; in "loose" the "s" is pronounced like an "s."

23. Did the Red Sox <u>lose</u> last night?
24. If we <u>lose</u> our way, I have a map in the glove compartment.

25. This knot is too <u>loose</u> to hold the boat.
26. Turn me <u>loose</u>, you scoundrel.

The following sentences show the difference between "affect" and "effect." Here the pronunciation difference is in the vowel sound at the beginning of the words. These sentences illustrate the most common meaning of these two words; there are other meanings, but they are much less common than these.

27. His pleas did not <u>affect</u> the judge's sentence.
28. Will this quiz <u>affect</u> my grade?
29. This medicine does not <u>affect</u> my ability to drive.

30. The <u>effect</u> of his pleas was that the judge became angry.
31. The only <u>effect</u> this quiz can have on your grade is to raise it.
32. One side <u>effect</u> of this medicine is drowsiness.

The next groups of sentences illustrate the differences among four words that are sometimes confused: "were," "we're," "wear," and "where."

33. My parents <u>were</u> born in Poland.
34. We <u>were</u> sleeping when the fire broke out.
35. What <u>were</u> the results of your study?

36. For dinner, <u>we're</u> having stir-fried vegetables.
37. <u>We're</u> not getting anything done just standing around talking.
38. This year <u>we're</u> celebrating my birthday by going to New York.

39. I don't have anything to <u>wear</u> to the party.
40. Becky Ramos would like to <u>wear</u> a clown costume tonight.
41. Did you have to <u>wear</u> a necktie when you worked at the Sloan Company?

42. I don't know <u>where</u> I put my keys.
43. <u>Where</u> are you going tonight?
44. This is the place <u>where</u> we camped last year.

The next group demonstrates the differences among a threesome of confusing words: "quit," "quite," and "quiet." The pronunciations of these three are quite different, but the spellings are similar enough to give some people trouble. If you will pronounce these just the way they are spelled, you should get them right.

45. Megan <u>quit</u> her job when she didn't get a raise.
46. Lou decided to <u>quit</u> smoking.
47. The fullback on that team just won't <u>quit</u>.

48. The new restaurant is <u>quite</u> expensive.
49. Jerry said that the movie is <u>quite</u> long.
50. I don't think that light is <u>quite</u> enough for me to read by.

51. My children can't stay <u>quiet</u> for more than five minutes.
52. Suddenly, the entire room became totally <u>quiet</u>.
53. We could use a little peace and <u>quiet</u> around here.

"Dessert" and "desert" are two words a lot of people have trouble telling apart:

54. She never eats <u>dessert</u>.
55. For <u>dessert</u> we are serving carrot cake, chocolate mousse, and lemon sherbet.
56. Mr. Rodriguez brought a beautiful strawberry pie for <u>dessert</u>.

57. I spent my vacation camping in the <u>desert</u>.
58. The <u>desert</u> is beautiful in the spring.
59. To me she looks like an oasis in the <u>desert</u>.

Some people confuse the words "course" and "coarse." "Course" is by far the more common term, and it has several related uses:

60. My psychology <u>course</u> meets on Monday evenings.
61. The <u>course</u> I wanted to take was already full.
62. The ship was two hundred miles off its <u>course</u>.
63. The <u>course</u> for tomorrow's race is very hilly.

64.   Of course, you will want to sleep late tomorrow.

The other "coarse" has a much narrower range of meaning:

65.   Her husband was a very coarse fellow.
66.   He told a very coarse joke.
67.   This sandpaper is too coarse.

        Finally, "accept" and "except" cause lots of people trouble:

68.   I cannot accept the job because the salary is too low.
69.   Dottie finds it difficult to accept compliments.
70.   I did every problem except number ten.
71.   Except for Lucy, everyone agrees that we should refuse their offer.

 EXERCISE 18B-2

Proofread the following sentences and correct any errors. The errors will involve confusing words, both the ones you've learned in this part and the homophones you learned in Part A.

1.   It will be find with me if your brother comes to.

2.   The effect of her decision is that were going to get a new computer.

3.   I don't no weather Karl understands what a mess his llama makes with its continual spitting.

4.   Donna is know better at swimming then John is.

5.   I'll bet Yolanda will loose that application before she fills it out.

6.   Michael made up his mine and past the reading coarse in one semester.

7.   Do you know if this hotel has a nice restaurant were we can have a little quite talk?

8.   Accept for Monday, the weather was really find while we were at the Cape.

9.   I wish I new how to brake this news to my parents.

10.   I would rather lose the contest then be thought of as a cheater.

11.   Mark came hear, ate his dinner, and than left without eating desert.

12.   Your advice had a good effect on Joan's attitude.

13.   If I haven't passed statistics this time, I'll lose my mine.

14.   When the weather is hot, you should we're lose clothes.

15.   Were not sure if staying home wouldn't be a better idea then going to the picnic.

16.   She went to the personal office to find out about her retirement benefits.

17.   There are too reasons why this restaurant is better then Vallegio's.

18.   I didn't here from the teacher, so I guess I past the course.

19.   The affect of his insecurity is that he has very little patience.

20.   I can't quiet except his explanation for his mistake; it's not like him.

Part C · A, An, and And

Because the use of "a," "an," and "and" is a little more complicated than the use of the words you have studied thus far, we will treat them separately in this section.

EXERCISE 18C-1 _____

On the line in front of each of the words below, write either the word "a" or the word "an." For now, don't try to figure out why, just write the one that sounds better.

A

_____ apple

_____ orangutan

_____ elephant

_____ oboe

_____ armchair

_____ artist

_____ engineer

_____ effort

B

_____ banana

_____ gorilla

_____ giraffe

_____ violin

_____ desk

_____ detective

_____ lawyer

_____ mistake

When you've finished, compare your list with the following list:

A

___an___ apple

___an___ orangutan

___an___ elephant

___an___ oboe

___an___ armchair

___an___ artist

___an___ engineer

___an___ effort

B

___a___ banana

___a___ gorilla

___a___ giraffe

___a___ violin

___a___ desk

___a___ detective

___a___ lawyer

___a___ mistake

How are all the nouns in column A different from all the nouns in column B? Write the rule for choosing between "a" and "an" in the space below:

_____

_____

_____

_____

NOTE: A discussion of this exercise can be found on page 392.

 ## EXERCISE 18C-2 _____

Now you know the basic rule for choosing between "a" and "an." In this exercise you will learn a modification of that rule.

Write either "a" or "an" on the blank in front of the following two-word phrases:

A

_____ old apple

_____ angry orangutan

_____ irritated elephant

_____ imaginary violin

_____ empty armchair

B

_____ red apple

_____ large orangutan

_____ wise elephant

_____ mystical violin

_____ leather armchair

When you have finished, compare your answers with the following list:

A

___an___ old apple

___an___ angry orangutan

___an___ irritated elephant

___an___ imaginary violin

___an___ empty armchair

B

___a___ red apple

___a___ large orangutan

___a___ wise elephant

___a___ mystical violin

___a___ leather armchair

Study these examples and write the rule for choosing between "a" and "an" with the necessary modification in the space below:

_____

_____

_____

_____

_____

NOTE: A discussion of this exercise can be found on page 392.

EXERCISE 18C-3 _____

There is one further modification needed before you have the complete rule for choosing between "a" and "an." This exercise will teach you this modification.

Write either "a" or "an" on the blank line in front of each of the following:

A   B

_____ hour   _____ hotel

_____ honest man   _____ happy man

_____ honor   _____ help

_____ umbrella   _____ unicorn

_____ utter disaster   _____ uniform policy

_____ undersecretary   _____ ukulele

When you've finished, compare your list with the following list:

A   B

___an___ hour   ___a___ hotel

___an___ honest man   ___a___ happy man

___an___ honor   ___a___ help

___an___ umbrella   ___a___ unicorn

___an___ utter disaster   ___a___ uniform policy

___an___ undersecretary   ___a___ ukulele

How are all the nouns in column A different from all the nouns in column B? If you are having trouble, say these words out loud and listen to the difference between the beginning sound of each of the words. What kind of sound does each of the words in column B begin with? Now write the final version of the rule for choosing between "a" and "an" in the space below.

_____

_____

_____

_____

_____

_____

NOTE: A discussion of the answers to this exercise can be found on page 392.

EXERCISE 18C-4

The following sentences illustrate the difference between "an" and "and." These two are very much like the pairs of words with similar sounds that you studied in Part B. If you will be careful to pronounce the final "d" sound in "and," you probably will not have any trouble keeping these two straight.

1. I have <u>an</u> awful headache.
2. There is <u>an</u> orangutan in the bathtub.

3. When it comes to grammar, English teachers have <u>an</u> edge on normal people.

4. We called <u>and</u> whistled, but our dog never came.

5. Democrats <u>and</u> Republicans agreed to back the president.

6. I jumped into bed <u>and</u> went right to sleep.

NOTE: A discussion of this exercise can be found on page 393.

EXERCISE 18C-5

Now you know how to use "a," "an," and "and." Proofread the following sentences and correct any errors. The errors will involve confusing words, including those you learned in Parts A and B as well as "a," "an," and "and."

1. Rita an Florence will here from me about their gossiping.

2. Sheree doesn't no how to play an ukulele.

3. In the refrigerator, you can fine an orange or an grapefruit.

4. Were looking for an yellow sweater with blue stripes.

5. A orangutan is smaller then a gorilla.

6. We just past a couple on a bicycle built for too.

7. Carla did not quiet except my offer, but she didn't say no either.

8. Do you no an good Italian restaurant?

9. The movie was about the affects of a atomic bomb.

10. An elephant is not larger than a whale.

DISCUSSION OF INDUCTIVE EXERCISES

EXERCISE 18C-1

Based on these examples, it appears that you should use "a" when the following noun begins with a consonant and "an" when the following noun begins with a vowel.

EXERCISE 18C-2

Based on these examples, it appears that the use of "a" or "an" depends on the following *word,* regardless of whether that word is a noun or an adjective.

EXERCISE 18C-3

Compare your version with ours. While your wording may be different, the meaning should be fairly close to ours.

> Use "a" when the following word begins with a vowel *sound;* use "an" when the following word begins with a consonant *sound.*

EXERCISE 18C-4

"An" is used much like an adjective to modify a noun, as in "an orangutan" or "an edge"; "and" is used to join two words, phrases, or clauses in a sentence, as in "called and whistled" or "jumped into bed and went right to sleep."

Part D · Words That Are Confused with Incorrect Words

Some people confuse the correct version of some words with an incorrect version. In this part you will learn to avoid or correct this kind of mistake.

 ## EXERCISE 18D-1 _____

In the following sentences, the incorrect versions are incorrect because of the underlined word or phrase. These words or phrases are not correct at any time in the written English language. If you have been using the incorrect versions of any of these, this is the time to learn the correct version.

1. Correct: We paid <u>a lot</u> of money for that painting.
2. Incorrect: We paid <u>alot</u> of money for that painting.

3. Correct: Thanks <u>a lot</u> for the ride.
4. Incorrect: Thanks <u>alot</u> for the ride.

In other words, there is *no such word* in the written English language as "alot." If you write it, you are always wrong.

5. Correct: We were <u>supposed to</u> be home by midnight.
6. Incorrect: We were <u>suppose to</u> be home by midnight.

7. Correct: My parents <u>used to</u> wait up until I got home.
8. Incorrect: My parents <u>use to</u> wait up until I got home.

"Supposed to" and "used to" must have the "d" ending.

9. Correct: Randy's dinner was <u>all right</u>.
10. Incorrect: Randy's dinner was <u>alright</u>.

The word "alright" is generally considered unacceptable in written English.

11. Correct: I will <u>try to</u> be there by eight o'clock.
12. Incorrect: I will <u>try and</u> be there by eight o'clock.

13. Correct: Our company will <u>try to</u> deliver your order by March 15.
14. Incorrect: Our company will <u>try and</u> deliver your order by March 15.

In other words, you should always write "try to" rather than "try and."

15. Correct: Kevin <u>would have</u> made a good grammarian.
16. Incorrect: Kevin <u>would of</u> made a good grammarian.

17. Correct: We <u>should have</u> called when we reached the ocean.
18. Incorrect: We <u>should of</u> called when we reached the ocean.

19. Correct: Shawn <u>could have</u> offered to serve on the committee.
20. Incorrect: Shawn <u>could of</u> offered to serve on the committee.

With "would," "should," and "could," the correct word is always "have," not "of." The reason "of" sounds right to some people is that they pronounce "have" as "of." The pronunciation is not what we're worried about here, but when you write these words, you must use "have," not "of."

EXERCISE 18D-2

This exercise reviews all the confusing words you have learned so far in this chapter. Proofread each sentence and correct any errors. Each sentence may contain no errors, one error, or more than one error.

1. This medicine is not suppose to make you sleepy.

2. I fine that I like most foods once I get use to them.

3. The weather could of been alot better, but we had a good time anyhow.

4. Were worried about the affect this experience may have on her career.

5. The knew cafeteria is alright, but it could of been alot better.

6. We should of gone too a Chinese restaurant because Mary likes Chinese food much better then Italian.

7. To help you quite smoking, perhaps you should try and eat a apple whenever you feel like a cigarette.

8. Students are suppose too read an chapter of the text each week.

9. We would of been hear an hour ago, but we had a flat tire.

10. I think Joe could of past this coarse, accept for the statistics.

11. Is it alright with you if I take tomorrow off to take care of some personnel matters?

12. Troy use to live in Phoenix until he quite his job and moved back here.

13. Penny said she would try and remember too bring your binoculars tomorrow.

14. Two dollars would of been enough for a tip; the desert was terrible.

15. It is really to hot for Camilla to walk over here.

16. We didn't want to loose the game, but they we're just to good for us.

17. The whether this summer is going to brake the record for heat.

18. Do you mine if Robin and Norm try and fine her earring?

19. There are alot of mistakes in my essay, but Mr. Cimino passed it anyway.

20. It is alright if they make fun of me; I'm use to it.

Part E · Contractions and Possessive Pronouns

The use of apostrophes to form possessives and contractions is discussed at great length in Chapter 17. Here you will focus on the confusion between four pairs of words: its and it's, your and you're, their and they're, and whose and who's. You will also learn to avoid confusing "there" with "their" and "they're."

 EXERCISE 18E-1 _____

Study the following pairs of sentences and try to figure out the difference between "its" and "it's."

1. I think that bus is off <u>its</u> route.
2. My dog hurt <u>its</u> leg.
3. I think <u>it's</u> going to rain.
4. John hopes <u>it's</u> not too late to apply.

If you're having trouble figuring out the difference between these words, try to figure out what two words can be substituted for "it's." What happens if you try to substitute the same two words for "its"? Now, how can you tell when to use "its" and when to use "it's"?

NOTE: A discussion of the answers to this exercise can be found on page 396.

 EXERCISE 18E-2 _____

Study the following groups and see if you can figure out how to tell when to use each of these confusing words.

1. I found <u>your</u> wallet in the locker room.
2. If <u>you're</u> ready, we'll leave now.
3. I have forgotten <u>whose</u> car we came in.
4. I have an aunt <u>who's</u> married to an orangutan.
5. Yvette says her parents have lost <u>their</u> senses.
6. <u>They're</u> allowing her to go to the beach for a week by herself.
7. Did you park your car over <u>there</u>?

NOTE: A discussion of this exercise can be found on pages 396–397.

 EXERCISE 18E-3 _____

The following sentences contain errors involving confusion between possessives and contractions as well as the other confusing words you have studied in this chapter. Proofread each sentence and correct any errors. Each sentence may contain no errors, one error, or more than one error.

1. Its to late to put oil in your car now.
2. The Banigans have sold they're house for more then they expected.

3. Do you know your lights are on?

4. Brian told a very course joke, so Vicky told him to be quite.

5. It's possible that Jackie forgot to pick us up.

6. It's not your fault that the tire is flat.

7. I hope Marion and Brenda find they're cat soon.

8. You're new haircut is perfect.

9. This car has a mine of it's own.

10. Do you know who's aardvark this is?

11. Donald wants to use your lawn mower.

12. This road is supposed to be a shortcut to there house.

13. Whose responsible for the mess in the bathroom?

14. There are alot of reasons why your the best person for this job.

15. I waited a hour for Wanda, and than I left.

16. Terry wondered who's car that silver Toyota is.

17. I like all kinds of desert accept custard pies.

18. They're dog is so mean that it's not allowed out of it's pen.

19. Lee wants you to try and call her this weekend to tell her your plans.

20. The effect of you're decision is that I will loose my job.

DISCUSSION OF INDUCTIVE EXERCISES

EXERCISE 18E-1

"It's" is called a contraction; it is formed by contracting "it" and "is" into one word. "Its" is a possessive; it indicates that something belongs to "it." In number 1, for example, we are talking about the "route" that belongs to "that bus."

EXERCISE 18E-2

The sentences in this exercise show that the versions with apostrophes can always be rewritten as the two words that have been contracted. To make sure you have the right version, all you need to do is mentally try out the two separate words and see if they make sense. If they do, the version with the apostrophe is correct; if not, then the version with the apostrophe is wrong.

For example, consider the following sentence:

8. My club has exceeded its budget.

To see whether "it's" should be used in sentence 8, you mentally substitute "it is" for "its," producing the following:

9. My club has exceeded it is budget.

Sentence 9 does not make sense, so you know that "it's" is the wrong word, and you leave "its" in the sentence as in number 8.

Now look at one more:

10. I hope your coming to the party.

Now try out the two contracted words to see if they make sense:

11. I hope you are coming to the party.

Number 11 does make sense, so that means the version with the apostrophe is correct and the sentence should be as follows rather than as it is in number 10.

12. I hope you're coming to the party.

The distinction between "whose" and "who's" can be figured out in exactly the same way. If you can substitute "who is," then "who's" is the word you want; if not, use "whose" to show possession.

The distinctions among "they're," "their," and "there" are a little more complicated. If you can substitute "they are," then the word you want is "they're"; if not and if you want to show possession, then "their" is correct. If "they are" doesn't fit and you want to show location (as in "over there"), then "there" is the correct form.

R E V I E W

EXERCISE 18-REVIEW-1 ————————————

Proofread the following sentences carefully and correct any errors. All errors will involve confusing words. Each sentence may contain no errors, one error, or more than one error.

1. Did Horace here weather Shawn is alright or not?

2. Ms. Powers will try and visit you in California, but she will be even busier then she planned to be.

3. Patricia past her exam, and I hope Faith did to.

4. My dog always spills it's water on the kitchen floor and than walks through it, making footprints everywhere.

5. I new you're knapsack wouldn't hold all this food.

6. This loss won't affect our standing because this was not a league game.

7. Let's take a brake an have a beer before we work on the final problem.

8. You'll have to except the fact that you will be crossing a dessert.

9. We bought alot of clothes that we should of bought weeks ago.

10. Did you no that Bob and Jay use to own a cigar shop?

11. Would Adrian mine if I use his omelet pan?

12. The Dodgers we're suppose to loose this game, but there ahead.

13. I don't have any idea who's responsible for these fire drills, but I wish they would quiet holding them.

14. Ann's lecture didn't have any effect on Donna's behavior.

15. We paid a find and vowed never too speed again.

16. I think Jeff could of had a little more patients with his children.

17. Andre mailed an letter to the personal office inquiring about openings.

18. Juan thought you would of been angry if he had past you on the freeway.

19. They're is know reason to have trouble with these sentences.

20. After these exercises, your not suppose to miss alot of these.

 ## EXERCISE 18-REVIEW-2

Proofread the following sentences carefully and correct any errors. All errors will involve confusing words. Each sentence may contain no errors, one error, or more than one error.

1. I hope this coarse is not to hard.

2. Randall will fine his wallet on the secretary's desk.

3. There is a angry customer in the lobby, and he wants to speak to the manager.

4. We have wasted alot of time, so now I want to work on this project.

5. Be quite while we watch Rosalee except her award on the television.

6. Sandra did not here anything from Guy the whole time he was in Mexico.

7. Brian plays the piano much better then I expected.

8. We are going back to the A&P, an we are demanding our money back.

9. I am not suppose to eat anything that contains salt for the next six months.

10. Have you finished you're homework for English yet?

11. I think we past the turnoff for Jose's house about ten minutes ago.

12. This medicine is not having any affect on my cold.

13. I bought my daughter an uniform for Girl Scouts.

14. Marilyn use to live next door to me, but now she lives in the city.

15. Jerry and Norman have forgotten to turn in they're applications for financial aid.

16. Paul didn't no that he had to have the first assignment done by Friday.

17. Angela always has alot of lose change on the floor of her car.

18. I worked for only a hour on Saturday, but they paid me for a whole day.

19. Will you try and remember who told you about Rosalind and me?

20. I have a friend who's going to join the navy next month.

 EXERCISE 18-REVIEW-3

Proofread the following essay and correct any errors. All errors will involve confusing words.

My brother went too West Point, and he hated every minute of it. He should of known that he wouldn't like all that discipline, but he didn't really think alot about it before he went. When he was a junior, he wrote a essay on Melville's *Moby-Dick*. He was very depressed when he got it back with an F on it. Even though he past the course, I don't think he ever forgave that professor or West Point for that grade.

A few months later, he resigned an transferred too Virginia Tech. After a year there, he disappeared and, six months later, reappeared living in New York, married, and enrolled in Columbia. At Columbia he majored in English and got straight A's. I don't no weather it was New York, getting married, or Columbia, but something sure had a good affect on him.

In his last semester before graduation, he took a seminar on Herman Melville. For that course, he had too do a paper on one of Melville's novels, so he pulled out his old paper from West Point. Now, he did retype the paper and correct a few obvious typos, but basically he submitted the same paper he had turned in several years earlier at West Point. Of course, he new he wasn't suppose to do this, but he just wanted to prove how wrong those military instructors had been. After waiting about to weeks, he got the paper back, and he got an F on it at Columbia also.

Now he thinks there was some kind of conspiracy.

C H A P T E R
19
Wordiness

Part A   Wordiness
Part B   False Humility

Part A · Wordiness

 EXERCISE 19A-1 _____

In each of the following pairs, select the one that makes its point more clearly and effectively.

1. a. At the same time that he was working at the bank, he also owned a real estate type of a business.
    b. While he was working at the bank, he also owned a real estate business.

2. a. Because of the fact that Jody was expecting a baby, she quit her job.
    b. Because Jody was pregnant, she quit her job.

3. a. I had a fear of speaking in front of people. The reason for this fear was because of an experience I had in high school. This experience was when I forgot my lines in a high school play.
    b. I feared speaking in front of people because I once forgot my lines in a high school play.

4. a. In this day and age, many American citizens forget their responsibilities and duties to their government.
    b. These days, many Americans forget their responsibilities to their government.

5. **a.** The dog was large in size and made a fierce growling noise as I proceeded to walk up the sidewalk.

    b. The large dog growled fiercely as I walked up the sidewalk.

Once you have decided which version of these sentences is more effective, try to figure out why. What makes the less effective versions less effective?

NOTE: A discussion of this exercise can be found on page 402.

 EXERCISE 19A-2

In each of the following pairs of sentences, decide which version you prefer.

1. **a.** The heavy rain had caused the tent to collapse into a pile of bright orange material, yellow nylon ropes, and pools of water.

    b. The rain had caused the tent to collapse.

2. **a.** The shiny black Porsche rumbled quietly next to me at the stoplight.

    b. The car rumbled next to me at the stoplight.

3. **a.** A plate of golden spaghetti covered with a deep red sauce waited for me on the dining room table.

    b. A plate of spaghetti sat on the table.

4. **a.** The heavily creased face of the seventy-three-year-old man broke into a broad smile when I handed him his newspaper.

    b. The man smiled when I handed him his newspaper.

5. **a.** A shiny green bug was making its way up the pink cotton sleeve of her blouse.

    b. A bug was crawling up her arm.

NOTE: A discussion of this exercise can be found on page 402.

 EXERCISE 19A-3

Proofread the following sentences for wordiness. Sometimes the wordiness can be eliminated by crossing out words; in other cases, it will require that you rewrite all or part of the sentences.

1. The true fact about the sport of tennis is that who wins is mostly a matter of luck.

2. This course has too many requirements that we have to do.

3. The sticky brown syrup covered the kitchen table and dripped onto the floor.

4. Much to my amazement and dismay, no one else objected.

5. The dead corpse was lying on a table in the middle of the room.

6. A low, moaning noise rose up from beneath the floor.

7. The giraffe was watching us in a suspicious manner.

8. After we voted, Jeff wanted to reconsider the proposal again.

9. In spite of the fact that she is a careless driver, she was not the one who had responsibility for the accident.

10. In her tiny room, Ms. Drachman had collected hundreds of dusty and yellowed, paperback mystery novels.

DISCUSSION OF INDUCTIVE EXERCISES

EXERCISE 19A-1

Almost everyone would agree that the b versions of these sentences are much more effective than the a versions. In every case the b version makes the same point using fewer words. Unnecessary words that merely get in the way of the reader have been eliminated from the a versions to form the b versions.

Notice that the b sentences were shorter than the a versions in every case.

EXERCISE 19A-2

You probably agreed with most readers that the a versions in this exercise were more effective. Did you also notice that the a versions, in every case, were wordier and, therefore, longer than the b versions? Doesn't this contradict what you learned in the previous exercise?

No, it doesn't. Notice that, in Exercise 19A-1, we said that the b versions were preferable because "unnecessary words that merely get in the way of the reader" were eliminated. In the b versions of this exercise, the words that were eliminated were *not* unnecessary; they did *not* get in the way of the reader. The words that were eliminated contributed a great deal to the effectiveness of the sentences, and when they were removed, the sentences were less effective.

Look, for example, at number 1. The following words were removed:

heavy
into a pile
of bright orange material
yellow nylon ropes
pools of water

These words are what made the sentence especially effective. They were the concrete details that made the description come alive and seem like a real experience described by a real person.

If you combine what you have learned in this exercise with what you learned in the first one, then you will understand what it means to get rid of wordiness. It means to get rid of excess words that contribute nothing to the effectiveness of the sentence. But it does not mean that a shorter sentence is always more effective than a longer one. If effective words are eliminated, the result will be a less effective sentence.

Part B · False Humility

EXERCISE 19B-1 _____

Which of the following paragraphs gives you the feeling that the writer is confident and really believes in what he or she is saying? Which is more convincing?

Paragraph 1

In my opinion, it seems that this country is becoming too materialistic. I feel that we place entirely too much importance on material possessions. It's only my opinion, but it seems like whether people are considered successful or not is determined by the car they drive and the house they live in. Young people are choosing their careers, not according to what would be satisfying work, but strictly according to what will make them the most money. I feel that a little materialism is only human, but it seems to me that things in this country have gone too far.

Paragraph 2

This country is becoming too materialistic. We place entirely too much importance on material possessions. Whether people are considered successful or not is determined by the car they drive and the house they live in. Young people are choosing their careers, not according to what would be satisfying work, but strictly according to what will make them the most money. A little materialism is only human, but things in this country have gone too far.

After you have decided which paragraph is more convincing, figure out why. What makes the less convincing one less convincing?

NOTE: This exercise is discussed on page 404.

EXERCISE 19B-2 _____

Revise the following sentences to make them sound like the writer is more confident.

1. In my opinion, it is unlikely to rain tomorrow.

2. It seems to me that the White Sox are going to win the American League pennant.

3. I believe that the price of gasoline is much too high.

4. The solution to hunger, it seems to me, is for the wealthy nations to be more willing to share their food with the poorer nations.

5. I think the speed limit should be raised to sixty-five.

DISCUSSION OF INDUCTIVE EXERCISE

EXERCISE 19B-1

The writer of paragraph 2, of course, seems much more confident, and as a result, the writing is much more convincing.

The only difference between the two paragraphs is the presence of the following phrases in paragraph 1:

> in my opinion,
> it seems
> I feel
> it's only my opinion
> it seems
> I feel
> it seems to me

This kind of phrase is known as a "qualifier." To see what these qualifiers do to a piece of writing, consider the following two sentences:

1. In my opinion, unemployment is our most serious problem.
2. Unemployment is our most serious problem.

What is the difference between these two statements? You might answer that number 1 merely states the writer's opinion, and that would certainly be true. But what about number 2? Doesn't it also state the writer's opinion? Yes, it does. The difference is that in sentence 1, the writer is being very cautious and *pointing out* that it is his or her opinion. But it is perfectly clear, in both sentences, that someone's opinion is being stated.

The effect of these qualifiers, especially if they are used repeatedly as in paragraph 1, is to give the impression that the writer is being extremely cautious, that the writer is worried that the reader might get the impression that the writer is overstating his or her case. Now, there are times when such caution is appropriate. If you are a rank amateur about baseball and write the manager of your nearest major league team to give him advice, you might want to sound a little humble and throw in a few "in my opinions." If you are an undergraduate student taking your first psychology course and you have an idea about the theories of R. D. Laing, you might decide to write him a letter. In a letter to such an authority in his field, a little humility is probably in order. Most of the time, however, the more confident you sound, the more effective the writing will be. Since the kind of expressions listed above make you sound *less* sure of yourself, they should be avoided in most writing.

R E V I E W

 ## EXERCISE 19-REVIEW-1 _____

In the following sentences, assume that you would like to sound as confident as possible. These sentences include problems with false humility and with wordiness. Correct any errors. Each sentence may contain no errors, one error, or more than one error.

1. I found myself frequently at odds with my sister on a constant basis.

2. There are many words and ways to describe procrastination.

3. I would have had much less trouble had I not avoided the problem and dealt with it when it had first come to my attention.

4. This company, in my opinion, pays its employees fairly well.

5. I recognized that she had a higher level of maturity in comparison with my two brothers.

6. We heard a high wavering noise as we entered into the tunnel.

7. This course is too hard due to the fact that it requires a lot of writing.

8. Juan closed the door in a careless manner and walked to his car.

9. The value of television for educating our youth is, it seems to me, highly overrated.

10. I had the foresight to look ahead, and that saved me many headaches.

11. When I get home from work, I have to undertake the task of fixing dinner for my family.

12. The rules that existed when I was in school were rigid and inflexible.

13. It is only my opinion, but I think that the president should serve a six-year term.

14. During the same time that the professor was writing the quiz on the blackboard, two students were looking up the answers in their books and writing them on slips of paper.

15. When I bought it, this blouse was a deep purple in color, but now it is more of a lavender.

16. Even an inexperienced beginner could have avoided making the mistakes that she made.

17. Bert's total and complete disregard for other people is more than I can tolerate.

18. At eight o'clock A.M. in the morning, I expect to see you in my office.

19. Karl's mistake on the telephone combined together with his not showing up for the meeting caused us to lose the contract.

20. A giant brown turtle with mud still caked on its feet was entered into the race by my brother.

 EXERCISE 19-REVIEW-2

In the following sentences, assume that you would like to sound as confident as possible. These sentences include problems with false humility and with wordiness. Correct any errors. Each sentence may contain no errors, one error, or more than one error.

1. I need your check prior to the time that the bank closes tomorrow.

2. Because of the fact that I had forgotten my driver's license, I could not cash a check at the Safeway.

3. It seems to me that Morty should try to forget about Doreen and start going out with a woman who will treat him decently.

4. The outcome of his inquiry could have resulted in the loss of my job.

5. The first step begins with the realization that no one is perfect.

6. Maurice's talk lasted thirty-five minutes in length, which I think is too long for an in-class report.

7. This stove has the capability of keeping my house warm in temperatures down to thirty degrees below zero.

8. That is the oldest line in the book, so don't let it sway your mind.

9. I believe that total honesty should be one of our true values.

10. I will be finished paying for my car in the not-too-distant future.

11. A tall, thin man wearing a baseball cap and a green shiny jacket walked up to Mick and shoved him into a taxi.

12. It seems to me that Nicole should, in my opinion, stop taking what she does from her husband.

13. In these modern days of today, it is not even safe to visit our public places and institutions.

14. This weekend I am supposed to stay home and clean my room, which is filthy and dirty.

15. I have encountered many obstacles and problems that are making it difficult for me to continue in school.

16. He entered into the room without ever suspecting that anyone might be waiting for him.

17. In his hand was a beautiful gold ring with a large sparkling diamond.

18. In the event that you are late for work tomorrow, give me a call.

19. I have mastered the basic essentials of word processing, but I still don't feel very sure of myself.

20. My mother was of the opinion that women shouldn't work.

EXERCISE 19-REVIEW-3

Proofread the following essay and correct any errors. All errors will involve wordiness.

I don't know about other men, but, in my opinion, my drive to compete is the strongest component of my personality. It is a true fact that there isn't anything I do that isn't motivated by competition.

Of course, I compete in all the obvious ways. At work, I view every project, every report, and every meeting as an opportunity for me to prove myself. But that's not so unusual; most men I know are like that at work.

And any time that I play a sport, I play to win. At my company's annual picnic that they hold every year, I can't wait till they get out the softball equipment. I know I'm good at the game, and by the time the game is over I've proved it to everyone else. I've had to find a new partner for my Thursday-night racquetball game as a result of the fact that my friend Craig, with whom I've played for years, just wasn't taking it seriously enough. In the last year, I've beaten him nine times out of ten, and I need more competition and challenge than that.

Even when we go on vacation, I view everything as a competition. For example, last summer we went camping in Yosemite National Park. We all rented bikes, and, of course, I got one with ten speeds. Then I proceeded to challenge my wife to a race. At least she had enough sense to refuse. On our first bike ride, my daughters noticed a waterfall, and then they saw another. I announced that we were going to try to see all eight waterfalls in the park before dinner.

I'm also the kind of person who loves and adores games. I'll play almost anything—Monopoly, Clue, Hearts, even Trivial Pursuit. Luckily, when my daughters were growing up, they liked to play games too. But I knew there was something wrong about me when I found myself trying my best to beat them. Then one day, I discovered that I was cheating during a game of Clue. I found myself leaning over to see if Emily had the Professor Plum card or not.

You may think that I'm exaggerating all this, but, in my opinion, I'm not. Perhaps you'll believe how extreme my situation is when I tell you that I entered into therapy to cure my competitive tendencies. I thought I was making great progress. I seemed to be relaxing. I hadn't tried to prove how good I was at anything in weeks. At the company picnic, I just ate a lot of watermelon.

I was so proud of myself that I reported to my therapist that I thought I was cured. I heard myself saying to him, "Yes, Doctor. I'm a lot better, and I'm determined to be the least competitive person around." Then I knew I was in big trouble.

C H A P T E R
20

Awkwardness

Part A   Parallelism
Part B   Misplaced Modifiers

Part A · Parallelism

 EXERCISE 20A-1 ———————————————————

Compare the following pairs of sentences. Decide which version is more effective and why.

1.   **a.** To start my research for a term paper, I like to browse around in a number of books and making notes as I go.
    b. To start my research for a term paper, I like to browse around in a number of books and to make notes as I go.

2.   **a.** The final exam in biology will require that we know how to identify all the bones in the human body and dissecting a frog.
    b. The final exam in biology will require that we know how to identify all the bones in the human body and to dissect a frog.

3.   **a.** If I won the lottery I would use the money to go to Europe or buying a new house.
    b. If I won the lottery I would use the money to go to Europe or to buy a new house.

NOTE: A discussion of this exercise can be found on pages 413–414.

EXERCISE 20A-2 _____

Compare the following pairs of sentences. Decide which is more effective and why.

1. a. After dinner, we had coffee, brandy, and sat by the fire.
    b. After dinner, we had coffee, brandy, and chocolate mints.

2. a. There were grains of rice in my hair, in my clothes, and they got into my ears.
    b. There were grains of rice in my hair, in my clothes, and in my ears.

3. a. On the roller coaster, the children laughed, screamed, and they shouted to each other.
    b. On the roller coaster, the children laughed, screamed, and shouted to each other.

4. a. The clerk asked us what we wanted, she directed us to the correct section, and explained the sale prices.
    b. The clerk asked us what we wanted, she directed us to the correct section, and she explained the sale prices.

NOTE: A discussion of this exercise can be found on pages 414–415.

 EXERCISE 20A-3 _____

Proofread the following sentences and correct any errors. All errors will involve faulty parallelism.

1. My participation in sports has taught me to value teamwork, to follow directions, and self-discipline.

2. Uncle Russell was an older man with flashing blue eyes, a ready smile, and always in good spirits.

3. Most of the students in my class had read the chapter, worked the problems, and completed the mimeographed handout.

4. Some years ago that statement would have been considered un-American, disloyal, and probably labeled communistic.

5. Lying will cause you to be unhappy and eventually the destruction of your marriage.

6. I explained to the real estate agent that the house was too small and the price was too high.

7. The students in Tom's class learned how to develop film, the enlarging of negatives, and the steps in printing pictures.

8. I learned to lie, to cheat, and the techniques of stealing.

9. My favorite meals are salads, sandwiches, or making a casserole.

10. I like my coffee black and my whiskey straight.

EXERCISE 20A-4

Sometimes the items in a series cannot be made parallel, and a different way must be found to correct the faulty parallelism. Study the following examples to see how their faulty parallelism is corrected.

1. Awkward: An unwanted child is likely to grow up in an environment that is devoid of love, deficient in supervision, and receiving minimal education.

   Better: An unwanted child is likely to grow up in an environment that is devoid of love and deficient in supervision. He or she is also likely to receive minimal education.

2. Awkward: It would be interesting to see what would happen if the models in cigarette ads were old, wrinkled, and sat in rocking chairs.

   Better: It would be interesting to see what would happen if the models in cigarette ads were old and wrinkled and if they were photographed in rocking chairs.

3. Awkward: Jackson's paper was badly organized, illogically argued, and should have been typed.

   Better: Jackson's paper was badly organized and illogically argued. In addition, it should have been typed.

NOTE: A discussion of this exercise can be found on page 415.

EXERCISE 20A-5

Proofread the following sentences and correct any errors. All errors will involve faulty parallelism.

1. Through the ages the family has remained strong as a matter of survival and providing a bond of affection.

2. These signs are used to remind the men not to be late, don't waste time, and clean up your area.

3. My work experience includes being a mother, a nurse, cleaning houses, and student teaching.

4. My group knew how to work together on a project and how to enjoy a Saturday afternoon.

5. Carmen is a baseball player with great promise and who can already hit as well as most boys her age.

6. In this discussion of Aldous Huxley and B. F. Skinner, I will compare their writing styles, the issues they raise, and point out the similarities in their conclusions.

7. The committee's proposal is based on the belief that competition encourages excellence, faith in the human sense of fairness, and that rules can govern human behavior.

8. I believe in watering plants no more than twice a week and in repotting them every spring.

9. Children in infancy and even older need nurturing.

10. Fitzgerald was a writer with only one story to tell and who told it with a growing sense of desperation.

EXERCISE 20A-6

This exercise illustrates another way that sentences can have faulty parallelism. In each group, figure out which sentence is not parallel and why.

1. a. In her purse, she had a lipstick, mirror, and a comb.
   b. In her purse she had a lipstick, a mirror, and a comb.
   c. In her purse, she had a lipstick, mirror, and comb.

2. a. Casey looked for her cat in the basement, in the bedroom, and the back yard.
   b. Casey looked for her cat in the basement, in the bedroom, and in the back yard.
   c. Casey looked for her cat in the basement, the bedroom, and the back yard.

3. a. Mr. Washington told the children there would be no yelling, fighting, and no crying while their mother was asleep.
   b. Mr. Washington told the children there would be no yelling, no fighting, and no crying while their mother was asleep.
   c. Mr. Washington told the children there would be no yelling, fighting, or crying while their mother was asleep.

NOTE: A discussion of this exercise can be found on pages 415–416.

EXERCISE 20A-7

This exercise illustrates a final way that sentences can have faulty parallelism. In each group, figure out which sentence is not parallel and why.

1. a. Students are losing confidence and respect for Dr. Boele.
   b. Students are losing confidence in and respect for Dr. Boele.
   c. Because students are losing confidence in Dr. Boele, they are also losing respect for him.

2. a. George expected and planned on getting promoted.
   b. George expected to be promoted and made plans based on that expectation.

3. a. Being fired has and will continue having a devastating effect on Margie.
   b. Being fired has had a devastating effect on Margie, and that effect will continue for a long time.

NOTE: A discussion of this exercise can be found on pages 416–417.

EXERCISE 20A-8

Proofread the following sentences and correct any errors. All errors will involve faulty parallelism.

1. Gertrude's mother expected to drive to our house, ring the bell, and to be invited to dinner.

2. On this trip we will do some snorkeling, some dancing, and even a symphony or two.

3. When I discoverd that my dog was missing, I looked all over the neighborhood, called the police, and I wrote the SPCA.

4. Julian intended to write, proofread, and to have his paper typed before the spring break.

5. When I got my paper back, it had marks in the margins, a note at the end, and he had written a big, red C+ at the top.

6. People are losing faith and respect for their government.

7. Inflation has and will continue to put a strain on the family.

8. Having run a travel agency of her own and she had been a C.P.A., so she would not be interested in the job we advertised.

9. The locusts came out that spring, they were everywhere for ten days, and then they disappeared again.

10. Sue has studied the trees, fungi, and the mosses in the Everglades.

DISCUSSION OF INDUCTIVE EXERCISES

EXERCISE 20A-1

In all three pairs, the a versions are awkward, and the b versions are more effective. To see why, let's look at the differences between the two versions of each sentence.

The phrases in brackets are the ones that need to be parallel.

1. a. To start my research for a term paper, I like [to browse] around in a number of books and [making] notes as I go.
   b. To start my research for a term paper, I like [to browse] around in a number of books and [to make] notes as I go.

2. a. The final exam in biology will require that we know how [to identify] all the bones in the human body and [dissecting] a frog.
   b. The final exam in biology will require that we know how [to identify] all the bones in the human body and [to dissect] a frog.

3. a. If I won the lottery I would use the money [to go] to Europe or [buying] a new house.

b. If I won the lottery I would use the money [to go] to Europe or [to buy] a new house.

In the a versions, the awkwardness comes from the fact that the two phrases joined by the "and" or "or" are not similar in form. In sentence 1, they are "to browse" and "making." To improve number 1, as we did in the b version, all we did was to make the form of the two items similar; we changed the word "making" to "to make." Each of the other examples was corrected in the same way.

The technical term for making the two phrases alike, as we did in these sentences, is to make them "parallel." The awkwardness in the a versions is caused by "faulty parallelism."

Notice that in these sentences the two phrases are joined by "and" or "or." In fact, when phrases are joined by any of the seven coordinating conjunctions that you learned in Chapter 8 (and, but, or, for, so, yet, and nor), you must ensure that the phrases are parallel.

EXERCISE 20A-2

As in the first exercise, the problem with the a versions is that they are not parallel. The difference is that in these sentences *three* items are joined by the conjunctions. In number 1a, for example, the three items are the following:

> coffee
> brandy
> sat by the fire.

The third item, "sat by the fire," is not parallel with the other two. The first two are nouns and the third is a verb phrase. In the b version, the verb phrase "sat by the fire" has been changed to the noun "chocolate mints," and the sentence is parallel:

> coffee
> brandy
> chocolate mints

In 2a, the three items are not parallel:

> in my hair
> in my clothes
> they got into my ears

The first two are prepositional phrases, but the third is an independent clause. In the b version, the independent clause is changed to the prepositional phrase "in my ears," and the sentence is parallel:

> in my hair
> in my clothes
> in my ears

In 3a, the three items also are not parallel:

> laughed
> screamed
> they shouted to each other

The first two are verbs, and the third is an independent clause, so they are not parallel. In 3b, the independent clause is changed to a verb phrase, and the resulting sentence is parallel:

laughed
screamed
shouted to each other

In 4a, the three items are not parallel:

The clerk asked us what we wanted
she directed us to the correct section
explained the sale prices

The first two items are independent clauses; however, the third is merely a verb phrase. Therefore, the sentence has faulty parallelism. In 4b, the third item has been changed to an independent clause and the parallelism is fine:

The clerk asked us what we wanted
she directed us to the correct section
she explained the sale prices

Now you know that parallelism is necessary whether the coordinating conjunction joins two items or a series of three or more. You also know that the items being joined may be verbals, nouns, verbs, prepositional phrases, and even independent clauses. In fact, just about any grammatical structure can be joined by coordinating conjunctions, as long as the structures joined are parallel.

EXERCISE 20A-4

In each of these items, there was no way to correct the faulty parallelism, so the sentence was rewritten with one of the items removed from the series.
In sentence 1, for example, the items in the series were the following:

devoid of love
deficient in supervision
receiving minimal education

Since there was no way to make the third item parallel with the first two, the sentence was rewritten so that only the first two were joined by "and":

devoid of love
deficient in supervision

The third item was moved to a separate sentence:

He or she is also likely to receive minimal education.

The other two examples are corrected in a similar fashion.

EXERCISE 20A-6

Let's look in some detail at the first set of sentences. The three items being joined by the "and" in these sentences are the following:

1A	1B	1C
a lipstick	a lipstick	lipstick
mirror	a mirror	mirror
a comb	a comb	comb

From these examples it is easy to see that to make the list parallel either the word "a" must be repeated in front of each item or it must be placed in front of the first one only. The following sentences demonstrate the same thing using brackets:

1. a. In her purse, she had [a lipstick], [mirror], and [a comb].
    b. In her purse, she had [a lipstick], [a mirror], and [a comb].
    c. In her purse, she had a [lipstick], [mirror], and [comb].

In other words, each item in the series must "connect" smoothly with the rest of the sentence.

The items in 1a won't connect smoothly, as the following sentences demonstrate:

1. a. In her purse, she had [a lipstick].
        In her purse, she had [mirror].
        In her purse, she had [a comb].

But the items in 1b and 1c connect just fine:

1. b. In her purse, she had [a lipstick].
        In her purse, she had [a mirror].
        In her purse, she had [a comb].

1. c. In her purse, she had a [lipstick].
        In her purse, she had a [mirror].
        In her purse, she had a [comb].

The other sentences in this exercise are similar, as you can see:

2. a. Casey looked for her cat [in the basement], [in the bedroom], and [the back yard].
    b. Casey looked for her cat [in the basement], [in the bedroom], and [in the back yard].
    c. Casey looked for her cat in [the basement], [the bedroom], and [the back yard].

3. a. Mr. Washington told the children there would be [no yelling], [fighting], and [no crying] while their mother was asleep.
    b. Mr. Washington told the children there would be [no yelling], [no fighting], and [no crying] while their mother was asleep.
    c. Mr. Washington told the children there would be no [yelling], [fighting], or [crying] while their mother was asleep.

EXERCISE 20A-7

As in the previous exercise, the problem in these sentences is with the way the items being joined with an "and" connect with the rest of the sentence. The difference is that these problems are with the way the phrases connect with what comes after them rather than what comes before. This can be seen clearly in the first one:

1. a. Students are losing [confidence] and [respect] for Dr. Boele.

        Students are losing [confidence] for Dr. Boele.
        Students are losing [respect] for Dr. Boele.

Sentence 1b is an improvement over 1a:

1. b. Students are losing [confidence in] and [respect for] Dr. Boele.

        Students are losing [confidence in] Dr. Boele.
        Students are losing [respect for] Dr. Boele.

Here the "confidence in" connects smoothly, but the way the preposition "in" is left hanging is a little troublesome. The best way to correct this one is to completely rewrite it, eliminating the parallel construction.

  1. **c.** Because students are losing confidence in Dr. Boele, they are also losing respect for him.

      The other two examples in this exercise are also corrected by rewriting the sentence to eliminate the parallel construction.

Part B · Misplaced Modifiers

In this part, you will learn about a second cause of awkwardness in sentences, modifiers that are placed in the sentence so that they are confusing or ambiguous.

EXERCISE 20B-1

In each of the following pairs, decide which is more effective and why.

  1. **a.** I saw a rabbit cross the road in my rearview mirror.
      b. In my rearview mirror, I saw a rabbit cross the road.

  2. **a.** I was served a chocolate mint by a waiter wrapped in gold foil.
      b. A waiter served me a chocolate mint wrapped in gold foil.

  3. **a.** I bought a jacket at the Hecht Company that was on sale.
      b. At the Hecht Company, I bought a jacket that was on sale.

NOTE: A discussion of this exercise can be found on page 420.

EXERCISE 20B-2

Proofread the following sentences and correct any errors. All errors will involve misplaced modifiers.

  1. I found out that my brother had been in an accident in the morning paper.

  2. I placed the daisies in a vase that I picked in Donna's garden.

  3. Loaded with gravy, I didn't eat any of the potatoes.

  4. My daughter is the one who handed you a pair of scissors in a purple blouse.

  5. The fruit that I bought at the Safeway gave me a stomachache that is located on Belair Road.

  6. I found the book that my instructor told me about in the library.

  7. All the sunflower seeds were eaten by a squirrel that I put in the bird feeder this morning.

  8. Debbie told me about the man who won two thousand dollars playing the lottery on the telephone.

9.   We bought the sunglasses for twenty-five dollars that had once belonged to Jacqueline Kennedy Onassis.

10.   I learned about the dangers of taking Valium in a sociology class.

EXERCISE 20B-3

The following sentences illustrate a slightly different kind of problem with misplaced modifiers. In each, a modifying phrase has been underlined. Draw an arrow from the underlined modifier to the word it modifies.

1.   <u>Loading the trunk of the car</u>, I crushed my hat.

2.   <u>Holding a garage sale</u>, we made almost two hundred dollars.

3.   <u>After leaving Memorial Stadium</u>, we discovered our wallets were missing.

Notice that in each sentence, the modifying phrase is at the beginning of the sentence, and the word modified is the subject of the sentence.

In the next group, the modifying phrases have been underlined. Again, draw an arrow from the modifier to the word modified.

4.   <u>Loading the trunk of the car</u>, my hat got crushed.

5.   <u>Holding a garage sale</u>, our house was burglarized.

6.   <u>After leaving Memorial Stadium</u>, the tarps were rolled over the infield.

NOTE: This exercise is discussed on pages 420–421.

EXERCISE 20B-4

Proofread the following sentences and correct any errors. All errors will involve misplaced modifiers.

1.   Having my tax return prepared by an accountant, the bill was eighty-five dollars.

2.   Walking past the lake, spring finally made its appearance.

3.   Hoping the rain would stop, we went ahead with the picnic.

4.   Arriving early at my office, the door was locked.

5.   Whistling quietly, she was getting on everyone's nerves.

6.   To read in a car, the road must be very smooth.

7.   Driving a motorcycle for the first time, my dog ran right in front of me.

8.   Running in the marathon, Melia sprained her ankle.

9.   Cowering under my car, I spotted the missing cat.

10.   Clawing through her purse, Monique begged the bus driver to wait a minute.

EXERCISE 20B-5

The misplaced modifiers in the following sentences are not easy to spot. Study each group of sentences to decide which one in the group has a misplaced modifier and what it is.

1. a. The police officer told me carefully to turn off my ignition.
    b. The police officer carefully told me to turn off my ignition.
    c. The police officer told me to turn off my ignition carefully.

2. a. When we put her to bed, the baby almost cried for an hour.
    b. When we put her to bed, the baby cried for almost an hour.

3. a. Ms. Liang's husband asks her weekly to take a vacation in Hawaii.
    b. Weekly, Ms. Liang's husband asks her to take a vacation in Hawaii.

NOTE: A discussion of this exercise can be found on page 421.

EXERCISE 20B-6

This exercise reviews everything you have learned about misplaced modifiers. Proofread the following sentences and correct any errors.

1. Sonny's dog had almost eaten half the turkey.

2. To keep from getting in trouble, Alison told the teacher that her name was Emily.

3. My cat almost fell off the top of the bookcase.

4. Ms. Lopez told me softly to walk into the kitchen where the baby was taking a nap.

5. Remembering my father, I almost cried for ten minutes.

6. To park a car, the space must be very large.

7. The teacher promised at the end of class to return our papers.

8. The baby nearly screamed until he was hoarse.

9. Driving home in the rain last night, my windshield wipers stopped working.

10. I gave the woman an umbrella who interviewed for the position.

11. Calling my dog's name, I walked through the neighborhood.

12. The coach told Marilyn frequently to point her toes when she was diving.

13. Not understanding Spanish, the man's comments didn't make any sense to me.

14. Marie's parents have hardly lent her any money despite the difficulties she has had.

15. I placed the bunch of irises in the refrigerator that I bought for the center of the table at the party tonight.

16. I asked her nicely to pay me the money.

17. She paid hardly any attention when he explained how to lock up the store at night.

18. Riding his bicycle, Carol was spotted by Vince as she and her mother weeded the garden.

19. Opening the door, a strange cat ran through my legs.

20. After clearing his throat, his voice sounded much better.

DISCUSSION OF INDUCTIVE EXERCISES

EXERCISE 20B-1

In each of the a versions of these sentences, a phrase is placed in the sentence at a location that leads to confusion. In number 1a, for example, the phrase "in my rearview mirror" modifies the verb "saw"; it tells where I did the seeing. It is located, however, at the end of the sentence after the noun "rabbit" and the verb "cross." From this position, it seems that the *rabbit* was actually located inside the mirror.

   1. **a.** I saw a rabbit cross the road in my rearview mirror.

       In 1b, the prepositional phrase has been moved to the beginning of the sentence, near the verb "saw," and there is no confusion about what it modifies.

   1. **b.** In my rearview mirror, I saw a rabbit cross the road.

       In each of the other two sentences, the a version is confusing because of a modifying phrase that has been misplaced.

       In English, there is considerable flexibility about the location of modifying words or phrases; however, that flexibility is not so great as to allow modifiers to be located anywhere. They must be placed so that there is no confusion about what word they are modifying.

EXERCISE 20B-3

You probably indicated modifiers as we have below:

   4. Loading the trunk of the car, my hat got crushed.

   5. Holding a garage sale, our house was burglarized.

   6. After leaving Memorial Stadium, the tarps were rolled over the infield.

A closer examination reveals, however, that the indicated nouns are not really the words these phrases are modifying. In number 4, for example, it is clear that it was not the hat that was "loading the car," and therefore "loading the car" cannot be modifying the noun "hat." But what is it modifying? Common sense suggests that the word modified must be "I." It was "I," the person writing this sentence, who was loading the car. But the word "I" doesn't appear in the sentence, so grammatically it seems like the hat was loading the car. To fix this problem, we need to return to sentence 1:

1. Loading the trunk of the car, I crushed my hat.

In this sentence, the word "I" does appear, and it is the subject of the sentence. That is why number 1 is an effective sentence while number 4 is not.

What you should remember from all this is that, when you place a modifying phrase at the beginning of the sentence, you must make sure that you intend that phrase to modify the subject of the sentence. If you don't, you will create flawed sentences like number 4. The term "dangling modifier" is sometimes used for this kind of a misplaced modifier.

Sentences 5 and 6 have similar problems. In number 5, it sounds like the house was having a garage sale, and in number 6, it sounds like the tarps left Memorial Stadium.

EXERCISE 20B-5

The problem in these sentences also involves the placement of a modifier. The modifier is placed so that it could be modifying either one of two different words. This makes the sentences confusing.

Take a closer look at sentence 1:

1. a. The police officer told me carefully to turn off my ignition.

As the arrows indicate, the modifier "carefully" could be describing either how the police officer spoke to me or how he wanted me to turn off the ignition. In the b and c versions, the word "carefully" has been placed so that it is clear which verb it is modifying:

b. The police officer carefully told me to turn off my ignition.

c. The police officer told me to turn off my ignition carefully.

Sentence 2a has a similar problem:

2. a. When we put her to bed, the baby almost cried for an hour.

The modifier "almost" seems to be describing the verb "cried," but think about it. Did that baby really "almost cry"? Or was it that the baby cried for *almost* an hour. Of course, it is the latter, so sentence 2b is correct:

b. When we put her to bed, the baby cried for almost an hour.

Sentence 3a is similar:

3. a. Ms. Liang's husband asks her weekly to take a vacation in Hawaii.

The way it is written, the sentence may mean he asks her once a week or it may mean that he suggests that she should fly each week to Hawaii. Sentence 3b resolves this ambiguity:

b. Weekly, Ms. Liang's husband asks her to take a vacation in Hawaii.

R E V I E W

EXERCISE 20-REVIEW-1

The following sentences contain errors involving both kinds of awkwardness that you learned about in this chapter—faulty parallelism and misplaced modifiers. Read each sentence and correct any errors. Each sentence may contain no errors, one error, or more than one error.

1. My job requires skill in budget preparation, motivation, and supervision of people.

2. After reading the article, the students expressed disbelief and disgust for polygamy.

3. The dentist told him frequently to floss his teeth.

4. We scarcely got three nibbles in a whole day of fishing.

5. Female students outnumber male students, making up 59 percent of the campus.

6. My family endured my hectic schedule out of love and support of my effort to be successful.

7. Until her death, my mother was a woman with considerable talents and who knew what she wanted in life.

8. Craig would not agree to take care of my dog who lives in a one-room apartment.

9. Neither the rise in inflation nor what the administration is doing in Washington will have any effect on my plans.

10. We must look at what is happening objectively.

11. At her wedding, Nancy served a delicious Chinese dinner to each of her guests on paper plates.

12. When I told her the news about her father, my daughter seemed upset and in a depressed mood.

13. To taste really tangy, you should use some lemon in the sauce.

14. I thought about going to Mexico, Canada, or staying home for my two weeks of vacation.

15. I had trouble locating and deciphering my tax records for 1984.

16. Mark warned his sister firmly to close the door.

17. The responses to his speech were what you would expect: some people loved it, some anger, and some indifference.

18. This haircut only cost five dollars.

19. Waving his hat in the air, I could see him in the window of the train.

20. We hired a woman who has an A.A. degree, two years of data-processing experience, and is an excellent manager.

 ## EXERCISE 20-REVIEW-2 _____

The following sentences contain errors involving both of the kinds of awkwardness that you learned about in this chapter—faulty parallelism and misplaced modifiers. Read each sentence and correct any errors. Each sentence may contain no errors, one error, or more than one error.

1. Ted insisted on taking the tie back to the shop that he had bought.

2. I want a dog with a good disposition and that will bark if anyone enters the house.

3. Involvement with student government, working on the newspaper, and volunteering as a tutor are very rewarding activities.

4. To understand Taoism, a two-hour lecture is just not enough time.

5. The basic purpose of this drug is sedation or even to eliminate aggressive impulses.

6. My brother loves things like jumping out of airplanes or to go scuba diving.

7. I asked the driver slowly to take me to the airport.

8. Eleanor Roosevelt was a woman with great talents and who always had compassion for others.

9. I had barely opened the door when a bat flew into the kitchen.

10. My dog sniffed under the table, behind the door, and in the trash can, but he couldn't find the new kitten.

11. I went for a ride on my bike with wet hair.

12. I plan to go to a community college, get an A.A. degree, and then to transfer to the state university.

13. Listening to the president's speech, I had the feeling that I had heard it all before.

14. My daughter is a child with a mind of her own and who isn't afraid to express it.

15. In my psych class, the instructor said that we would be conducting original research, putting our data in the computer, and we would submit a written summary of the results.

16. This is a cat with a perfect disposition and which will keep your feet warm at night.

17. The man collecting tickets in green pants is my brother.

18. Margie is the kind of woman who will do anything for you and who will not expect anything in return.

19. Patti only ran one mile today.

20. Because this is the last one of these sentences, I'm going to kick off my shoes and dance like crazy.

 EXERCISE 20-REVIEW-3 _____

The following letter contains awkward sentences caused by faulty parallelism and misplaced modifiers. Proofread the letter and correct any errors.

Dear Mr. Kroc:

I'm writing because I know how hard you have worked to make McDonald's into the national success it has become. And, McDonald's is also a success with me personally. A Big Mac tastes better to me with a tomato, lettuce, and lots of catsup, than a fancy steak dinner. I've also watched over the years as you have made various improvements in your restaurants. I appreciated each new item you added to the menu. Adding breakfast to your offerings, I sometimes found myself coming to McDonald's twice a day. Most of the time, however, I only eat at McDonald's once a day. Also, I love the new decor with its attractive wooden tables, artistic murals, and plenty of plants. What all these improvements have said to me is that your company is genuinely interested in making McDonald's a pleasant place for your customers. You are obviously willing to invest money so that we will enjoy eating in your restaurants. This leads me to my reason for writing you this letter.

If you are willing to spend money on the furniture, murals, and the plants, why have you not worried about the one thing that makes your restaurants unpleasant places to eat in? This one thing, if you haven't guessed, is noise. Why do you think that pleasant surroundings are important to the eye but not to the ear? Why don't you realize that ugly noise can be just as detrimental to an enjoyable meal as ugly surroundings?

Let me be more specific. Your company has installed loudspeakers to amplify the orders to the kitchen. What this means is that the customers eating their Big Macs, their Egg McMuffins, or drinking their thick milk shakes have to listen to every order as it is sent to the kitchen. Is this really necessary? In this age of electronics, using some kind of video equipment, the orders could be sent to the kitchen without blasting out the customers.

Then there are the French fry machines. Every few minutes, one of them has to announce that an order of French fries is done. This announcement is made by the most piercing beeping sound I have ever heard. Couldn't some system be developed that would spare the customers the periodic torture of the French fry alarm? Eating my Big Mac a few nights ago, the French fry beeper went off six times before I could finish!

In between the French fry beepers and the amplified orders to the kitchen, the customers are subjected to the most boring music anyone could come up with. I know that McDonald's could do better than this. Once you get rid of the noisy distractions, why not play some music that would really be enjoyable? Why not become the only fast food chain that plays classical music? There is plenty of classical music with a universal appeal. How about some Chopin piano sonatas, Schubert impromptus, or some Vivaldi concertos? These are pieces that everyone could enjoy, that would offend no one, and might make your restaurants really distinctive.

If you think the classical music idea is not realistic, at least you could get rid of the French fry beeper and the loudspeaker to the kitchen.

21

Spelling

Part A   Correct Spelling as a State of Mind
Part B   Some Spelling Rules

Part A · Correct Spelling as a State of Mind

Just like errors in grammar, punctuation, and capitalization, spelling errors can greatly detract from an otherwise well-written paper. It is important that you do all you can to reduce the number of spelling errors in your writing. But like the other errors, spelling is something you should not focus on until the major parts of your paper are the way you want them. In other words, spelling is something you should work on, primarily, in your final draft.

The most important factor in reducing spelling errors is your state of mind. As when someone is trying to lose weight or quit smoking, the crucial ingredient is desire. If you are determined to improve your spelling, this chapter can help you do it.

The most important tool to improving spelling is a dictionary. If you are going to improve your spelling, you need to own a dictionary and keep it within arm's reach when you are proofreading. This is important. If your dictionary is downstairs or across the hall from where you are proofreading, you are much more likely to just guess at the spelling of words you're not sure of. Keep a dictionary *within arm's reach* when proofreading.

"Okay," you may be saying. "I've got my dictionary within arm's reach, but what good will it do me when I don't know how to spell the word?" A good question. Actually, however, you are about to learn that some strategies allow you to find a word in the dictionary even if you don't know how to spell it.

To start with, you usually will have some idea how to spell the word. Write down the two or more ways that you think it might be spelled; then, look each possibility up. Chances are, one of them will be correct.

You may not be sure whether the correct spelling is *restaurant* or *restaraunt,* for example, but you know it starts with *rest.* That's enough to find it in the dictionary. You will find that all the words in English that start with *rest* fit on a page or two (depending on the size of your dictionary). Once you've found the *rest* page you can look up the two spellings you're trying to choose between. In this case, you would find that *restaurant* is the correct spelling.

So, the first strategy is the following:

1. Write down the possible spellings and look each of them up.

Maybe you're thinking that *restaurant* was too easy an example. After all, you had a fairly good idea how it was spelled. Let's take a look at a harder one, a word that you have almost no idea how to spell.

Suppose you want to say that a particular proposal is not realistic or possible with the budget that has been allocated. But you know there is a better word than *realistic* or *possible.* The word you want is something like *feesable,* but you know it's not spelled like that. Let's try to find that word in the dictionary.

The place to start is with the first letter. It seems to be an *f.* Is there any other possibility? Well, sometimes a *ph* is used for an *f* sound, but you're fairly certain this word starts with an *f.* How about the second letter? That's where you run into trouble because it's a vowel sound. (The vowels are *a, e, i, o, u,* and *y* when it makes an *ee* sound as in *happy* or an *i* sound as in *sky.*) The vowels are hard letters to figure out because often more than one vowel and even several combinations of vowels can represent the same sound. In the word we're working on, the second letter is something that creates an *ee* sound. In English, this sound can be represented by the following letters:

e as in *complete*
ee as in *feet*
ea as in *heat*
ei as in *receive*
ie as in *piece*
y as in *happy*

The third sound in the word is almost certainly an *s,* although it also could be a *z.* The word, then, starts with one of the following sets of letters:

fes			
fees			
feas			
feis			
fies			
fys			
			able
or	and ends with one of these		abel
			ible
fez			ibel
feez			
feaz			
feiz			
fiez			
fyz			

Since *s* as the third sound seems more likely, you start with that set of possibilities. Since all but two of these have *e* as the second letter, it makes sense to start by looking up the *fe* options. You look up *fes* and find no word that could be the one you want. Next you try *fees* and again find no word that looks like the one you want. Then you try *feas* and find *feasible*. To make sure you have the right word, you check the definition and find "capable of being accomplished; practicable; possible." *Feasible,* then, is the word you want.

This second strategy can be summarized as follows:

2. Focus on the first three to five letters of the word. Figure out as many options for spelling those sounds as you can think of. Then, look each of them up to see if it is, in fact, a word. If it is, check its definition to see if it means the same thing as the word you want. Continue until you have located the word you are seeking.

As you sound the word out, trying to think of possible ways it could be spelled, pay particular attention to the vowel sounds; that is where there are usually the most possibilities. Also, watch for the following alternatives:

1. *c* and *sc* as well as *s* can represent the *ss* sound (for example, bi*c*ycle and *sc*ience)
2. *ch* and *ss* as well as *sh* can represent the *sh* sound (for example, *ch*auffeur and ti*ss*ue)
3. *k, ck, qu,* and *ch* as well as *c* can represent the *k* sound (for example, *k*ill, li*ck*, li*qu*or, and s*ch*ool)
4. *s* and *ss* as well as *z* can represent the *zz* sound (for example, hi*s* and *s*cissors)
5. *ph* and *gh* as well as *f* can represent the *ff* sound (for example, *ph*one and rou*gh*)
6. double letters may sound like one (as in a*ll*oy, gi*dd*y, or in*n*ing)

There are many more alternative spellings in English, but this list will help you with the most common ones.

EXERCISE 21A-1

The following are misspellings of actual but unusual words; the spellings do indicate how the word sounds. We are using such unusual words to show you that it is possible to find most words in the dictionary, even ones you have never seen before. For each word, list as many possible spellings as you can. Then refer to a dictionary to find the correct spelling.

1. kartoosh—an oval figure containing ancient Egyptian writing

    possible spellings: _____   _____

    _____   _____

    _____   _____

    _____   _____

    _____   _____

    _____   _____

    actual spelling: _____

2.   sentila—a very small amount of something

    possible spellings: _____ _____

                           _____ _____

                           _____ _____

                           _____ _____

                           _____ _____

    actual spelling: _____

3.   krizm—a mixture of oil and balsam used in religious ceremonies

    possible spellings: _____ _____

                             _____ _____

                           _____ _____

                           _____ _____

                           _____ _____

    actual spelling: _____

4.   fraetrie—a clan or subdivision of a Greek or Hellenistic tribe

    possible spellings: _____ _____

                             _____ _____

                           _____ _____

                           _____ _____

                           _____ _____

    actual spelling: _____

5.   ihlaeshun—the act of drawing conclusions

    possible spellings: _____ _____

                             _____ _____

                           _____ _____

                           _____ _____

                           _____ _____

    actual spelling: _____

    Now you should be able to find most words in the dictionary. If you are still having trouble, however, there is still hope. You need to buy a special kind of dictionary known as a "bad speller's dictionary." In these, words are listed according to the way they are usually misspelled as well as by the correct spelling. If you look a word up under the wrong spelling, it will tell you what the correct spelling is.

Having mastered the dictionary, you must undertake another project if you want to improve your spelling. Remember that good spelling is a "state of mind"; if you want to improve, you will have to be ready to put some effort into it.

You must start a collection of the words you have trouble with. Every time you have to look a word up, put it on your list. Every time you get a paper back from your instructor with misspelled words on it, add those words to your list. When you write words on your list, enter both the misspelling and the correct spelling. If you misspell or have to look up a word that was already on your list, list it again so you have a record of which words you have had trouble with more than once. Later, your list will be much easier to analyze if you enter the words on three-by-five cards, rather than on sheets of paper.

After your list grows to fifty words or so, you are ready to spend some time analyzing it. First, arrange the words in alphabetical order and identify the ones you misspelled more than once. You may want to clip duplicates together with a paper clip. Next, look at each word and write a brief description of the error on the card. If you spelled *occurred* as *occured* by mistake, for example, you would list the error as "r/rr" meaning that you wrote an *r* where you should have written an *rr*.

Next, using these short descriptions of your errors, group similar patterns together. You may, for example, find a number of errors involving double consonants (these would be listed as "c/cc," "mm/m," or the like). Once you have figured out the patterns of your spelling problems, you can begin to work on solutions. You may need to work on some of the rules in Part B of this chapter, or you may just need to memorize a list of words that have a certain ending.

The point is that your spelling problems *are* manageable. Until you make a list and analyze it, it may just seem that you are a "terrible speller" who makes a million different spelling errors and who has no hope of correcting them. But once you have studied your spelling problems, you may find that most of them can be eliminated if you will just memorize a few words and learn a few rules.

One student who thought of herself as a terrible speller found that, using this system, she could eliminate about 75 percent of her errors by memorizing the spelling of eight words and learning two of the rules in Part B. She had been making between fifteen and twenty errors in a five-hundred-word paper. After working on spelling for about two months, she reduced her rate to about four errors per paper.

To help you understand how to analyze your spelling list, let's take a look at a typical list of spelling problems. The following are all the words misspelled during a one-month period by a fictitious student whom we will call Larry.

MISSPELLING	CORRECT SPELLING	MISSPELLING	CORRECT SPELLING
tommorrow	tomorrow	annonymously	anonymously
innoculated	inoculated	innaccuracies	inaccuracies
controling	controlling	briming	brimming
occured	occurred	innacurately	inaccurately
fiercly	fiercely	relavence	relevance

MISSPELLING	CORRECT SPELLING	MISSPELLING	CORRECT SPELLING
innaccurate	inaccurate	ammendment	amendment
enterred	entered	ommision	omission
occured	occurred	tommorrow	tomorrow
excitment	excitement	begining	beginning
accidently	accidentally	personel	personnel
licence	license	chosing	choosing
seperate	separate	enterred	entered
speaches	speeches	seperate	separate
existance	existence	licence	license
ommission	omission	seperate	separate
insistance	insistence	speach	speech
begining	beginning	existance	existence
chosing	choosing	licence	license
tendancies	tendencies	chosing	choosing
consistant	consistent	occuring	occurring
equivalant	equivalent	accidently	accidentally
existance	existence	refered	referred

It is impossible to make much sense out of this list as it is, so the first thing Larry did was rearrange it in alphabetical order. This is where the three-by-five cards come in handy. Larry also entered a brief description of each error on its card. In the first entry, for example, the error was that he spelled *accidentally* with an *ly* ending instead of an *ally* ending. His third error was that he used an *mm* where he should have used just an *m* in *amendment*.

MISSPELLING	CORRECT SPELLING	DESCRIPTION OF ERROR
accidently	accidentally	ly/ally
accidently	accidentally	ly/ally
ammendment	amendment	mm/m
annonymously	anonymously	nn/n
begining	beginning	final consonant
begining	beginning	final consonant
briming	brimming	final consonant
chosing	choosing	o/oo
chosing	choosing	o/oo
chosing	choosing	o/oo
consistant	consistent	a/e
controling	controlling	final consonant
enterred	entered	final consonant
enterred	entered	final consonant
equivalant	equivalent	a/e
excitment	excitement	final e
existance	existence	a/e
existance	existence	a/e
existance	existence	a/e
fiercly	fiercely	final e
innaccuracies	inaccuracies	nn/n
innaccurate	inaccurate	nn/n
innacurately	inaccurately	nn/n

MISSPELLING	CORRECT SPELLING	DESCRIPTION OF ERROR
innoculated	inoculated	nn/n
insistance	insistence	a/e
licence	license	c/s
lisense	license	s/c
occured	occurred	final consonant
occured	occurred	final consonant
occuring	occurring	final consonant
ommision	omission	mm/m; s/ss
ommission	omission	mm/m
personel	personnel	final consonant
refered	referred	final consonant
relavence	relevance	a/e; e/a
seperate	separate	e/a
seperate	separate	e/a
seperate	separate	e/a
speach	speech	ea/ee
speaches	speeches	ea/ee
tendancies	tendencies	a/e
tommorrow	tomorrow	mm/m
tommorrow	tomorrow	mm/m

Next Larry grouped the words on his list according to the kinds of errors and decided on a strategy for avoiding each kind of error:

MISSPELLING	CORRECT SPELLING	DESCRIPTION OF ERROR	
ammendment	amendment	mm/m	
ommision	omission	mm/m; s/ss	
ommission	omission	mm/m	
tommorrow	tomorrow	mm/m	
tommorrow	tomorrow	mm/m	*study these as a group*
annonymously	anonymously	nn/n	
innaccuracies	inaccuracies	nn/n	
innaccurate	inaccurate	nn/n	
innaccurately	inaccurately	nn/n	
innoculated	inoculated	nn/n	
consistant	consistent	a/e	
equivalant	equivalent	a/e	
existance	existence	a/e	
existance	existence	a/e	
existance	existence	a/e	
insistance	insistence	a/e	
tendancies	tendencies	a/e	*study these as a group*
relavence	relevance	a/e; e/a	
seperate	separate	e/a	
seperate	separate	e/a	
seperate	separate	e/a	

MISSPELLING	CORRECT SPELLING	DESCRIPTION OF ERROR	
begining	beginning	final consonant	
begining	beginning	final consonant	
briming	brimming	final consonant	
controling	controlling	final consonant	
enterred	entered	final consonant	*study Rule 2 in Part B*
enterred	entered	final consonant	
occured	occurred	final consonant	
occured	occurred	final consonant	
occuring	occurring	final consonant	
personel	personnel	final consonant	
refered	referred	final consonant	
excitment	excitement	final e	*study Rule 3 in Part B*
fiercly	fiercely	final e	
(2) accidently	accidentally	ly/ally	
(3) licence	license	c/s	*memorize these troublesome words*
(2) speach	speech	ea/ee	
(3) chosing	choosing	o/oo	

You can see from all this that analyzing your spelling list is not the sort of thing you want to do every day. For people who are weak spellers, however, it's the only way to figure out a strategy for reducing the number of spelling errors. We recommend that you do it once you have a list of fifty or so words and that you do it again periodically to check your progress.

Now that you have analyzed your list of spelling errors, what next? How do you actually learn to spell these words?

First, this also is going to take some time and effort. This is where that "spelling is a state of mind" business comes in again. You have to be willing to invest some effort to overcome your weaknesses.

Assuming you are willing, there are three basic strategies to use. Each of these strategies works with different spelling problems.

1. If some of the mistakes are accounted for by one of the rules in Part B of this chapter, you can learn that rule and thereby learn to spell those words. (On Larry's list, the words with errors involving the final consonant or the final e when a suffix is added are in this category.)
2. Other groups of words don't follow a rule but involve a similar problem. These just require some memorizing on your part, but they are more easily mastered if you work on them in groups. (On Larry's list, the words that have errors involving the doubling of the letters m and n are in this group.)
3. Finally, the mistakes in some words have little to do with any other mistakes in any other words. These you just have to learn one at a time. There are two approaches to doing this:
   a. Just memorize the spelling.
   b. Develop a trick to help you remember.

For example, I used to have trouble remembering whether the correct spelling is *restaurant* or *restaraunt.* One evening, I lost my temper and ranted at the waiter in a restaurant. I made a fool of myself, but from that night on, I knew how to spell *restaurant* because I remembered that *restaurant* has a *rant* in it.

A friend of mine always remembers the two *a*'s in *separate* because they are "separated" by an *r*.

If either of these tricks helps you, fine. But for most words you'll have to make up your own tricks to help you remember. By the way, the technical term for this kind of trick is *mnemonic*.

Once you've got your problem words learned, or even partly learned, by any combination of the three strategies, there are some other techniques to help you reinforce them.

If you have a patient friend, you can ask him or her to read your words out loud while you write them down. Later you can check the spelling. If you repeat this process enough times, gradually eliminating from the list the words that you have mastered, you will eventually learn the entire list.

This practice, however, is a little hard on friendships. Few friends are willing to read words out loud as often as we need them. A more reliable but less sociable technique is to read the words on your list into a tape recorder. Then you can play the tape back as many times as necessary. As you learn words, you can erase them from the tape, or you can keep track on your three-by-five cards and periodically remake the tape including only the words you still don't know.

In the last few years, word processors have become more and more common in schools and in the workplace. For most word processing programs, there is also a program called a "spelling checker." After you have finished a draft of a paper or other writing on a word processor, you just run it through the "spelling checker." This program shows you each word that may be misspelled and gives you a chance to change it. You decide whether it is or is not spelled the way you want it. The machine doesn't correct the spelling; it just shows you any "suspect" words. These programs can be a real blessing for people who are weak spellers. If your office or your school has any word processors, ask about spelling checkers. They are not even very expensive.

One last comment about spelling checkers. They can be an excellent tool for improving your spelling skill. Each time you check the spelling of a document, the computer asks you if you want a list of the words you corrected. Tell the computer "yes." Then save the printouts it gives you, and you will have a list of the words you have trouble spelling.

Finally, here is a list of words whose spelling gives many people trouble; sometimes these are known as "spelling demons." You may want to use a friend or a tape recorder and test yourself on all of these. Then add the ones you don't know to your spelling list.

absence	deceive	inoculate	religion
accidentally	definite	intelligent	religious
accommodate	dependent	interest	repetition
actually	desert	interruption	rhythm
adequately	desperate	jewelry	ridicule
adolescence	dessert	judgment	ridiculous
amateur	develop	knowledge	roommate
among	development	laboratory	sandwich
analyze	dilemma	leisure	schedule
annually	dining room	length	seize

answer	disappoint	library	separate
appreciate	disastrous	license	similar
apologize	discussion	losing	sincerely
applying	disease	luxury	skiing
appropriate	eighth	lying	sophomore
argument	eligible	marriage	speech
assassination	embarrass	mathematics	studying
athlete	environment	medicine	succeed
attendance	exaggerate	necessary	sufficient
available	excitable	nickel	surprise
beautiful	exercise	ninety	swimming
becoming	familiar	nuclear	technique
beginning	fascinate	nuisance	temperature
behavior	favorite	omission	thoroughly
believe	February	oppressed	though
benefited	finally	parallel	thought
bureaucracy	financially	paralyze	together
business	foreign	personnel	tragedy
calendar	forty	persuade	transferred
category	fulfill	possess	truly
changeable	genius	preferred	twelfth
cigarette	government	prejudice	unnecessary
coming	grammar	privilege	until
committee	guarantee	probably	usually
completely	guidance	proceed	vacuum
conscience	happened	professor	valuable
condemn	height	psychology	villain
conscientious	heroes	pursue	visibility
controlled	hoping	quarrel	vitamin
convenience	humorous	receipt	Wednesday
courtesy	illogical	receive	weather
criticize	immediately	recommend	writing
cruel	independence	recommendation	written

Part B · Some Spelling Rules

There are several rules which are of some help in spelling. The only problem with these rules is that, because English spelling is so irregular, there are a number of exceptions to each rule. Nevertheless, in this part you will learn the most useful of these spelling rules and the most common exceptions to each one.

Rule 1: *i* Before *e*

This is probably the best-known spelling rule. Almost everyone has heard the basic rule before, and some people even remember the exceptions included in lines three and four:

- RULE 1: *i* before *e*
  except after *c*
  or when sounded like *ay*
  as in *neighbor* or *weigh*

Perhaps a few examples will make clear exactly how this rule works:

believe	the *i* comes before the *e*
niece	the *i* comes before the *e*
receive	the *e* comes before the *i* because they come after *c*
deceive	the *e* comes before the *i* because they come after *c*
eight	the *e* comes before the *i* because they sound like *ay*
vein	the *e* comes before the *i* because they sound like *ay*

The preceding examples all follow the rule; however, even this fairly complicated rule doesn't cover all the cases in English. There are several exceptions that just have to be memorized:

either	leisure	seize
foreign	neither	their
height	protein	weird

Rule 2: Adding Suffixes to Words Ending with Consonants

- RULE 2:   When a suffix (ending) that begins with a vowel (like *er*, *est*, *ed*, or *ing*) is added to a word, the consonant is doubled if *all* of the following are true:
  1. the word ends in a single consonant
  2. the final consonant is preceded by a single vowel
  3. the accent (stress) is on the last syllable (or the word has only one syllable)

Let's look at how this rule applies to some specific cases:

occur   This word ends in a single consonant (*r*). This consonant is preceded by a single vowel (*u*). The accent is on the final syllable (ocCUR, not OCcur). Since all the conditions under rule 2 are met, the final consonant must be doubled when a suffix beginning with a vowel is added: *occurred*.

run   This word ends in a single consonant (*n*). The consonant is preceded by a single vowel (*u*). The word has only one syllable. Again, all the conditions for rule 2 are met, so the final consonant must be doubled: *running*.

listen   This word ends in a single consonant (*n*) preceded by a single vowel (*e*). However, the accent is not on the final syllable (the word is pronounced LISTen, not listEN). Since one of the three conditions of rule 2 is not met, the final consonant is not doubled: *listener*.

fight   This word does not end in a single consonant (it ends in three consonants—*ght*), so the final consonant is not doubled: *fighting*.

meet   This word ends in a single consonant (*t*) that is not preceded by a single vowel (it is preceded by two vowels—*ee*), so the final consonant is not doubled: *meeting*.

Rule 3: Adding Suffixes to Words Ending in Silent *e*

- RULE 3:   When words end in a silent *e*, the *e* is dropped before adding a suffix that begins with a vowel. The *e* is retained before a suffix that begins with a consonant.

Let's apply this rule to a few examples:

SUFFIXES BEGINNING WITH VOWELS	SUFFIXES BEGINNING WITH CONSONANTS
move + ing = moving	move + ment = movement
close + ed = closed	close + ly = closely
love + ing = loving	love + less = loveless
lone + er = loner	lone + ly = lonely

This rule is fairly straightforward; however, it is complicated by a number of exceptions, which can only be memorized:

argue	+ ment	= argument
canoe	+ ing	= canoeing
change	+ able	= changeable
courage	+ ous	= courageous
judge	+ ment	= judgment
manage	+ able	= manageable
mile	+ age	= mileage
notice	+ able	= noticeable
true	+ ly	= truly

Rule 4: Changing the Final *y* to *i*

- RULE 4: When adding a suffix to a word ending in *y*, change the *y* to an *i* if both of the following conditions are met:
   1. the letter preceding the *y* is a consonant
   2. the suffix is not *ing*

Let's look at some examples:

happier   *Happy* ends in a *y* and the preceding letter (*p*) is a consonant. The suffix (*er*) is not *ing*, so the *y* is changed to an *i*.

happiness   *Happy* ends in a *y* and the preceding letter (*p*) is a consonant. The suffix (*ness*) is not *ing*, so the *y* is changed to an *i*.

delayed   *Delay* ends in a *y*, but the preceding letter (*a*) is not a consonant, so the *y* is retained.

worrying   *Worry* ends in a *y*, and the preceding letter (*r*) is a consonant. The suffix begins with a vowel, but, since the suffix is *ing*, the *y* is retained.

This rule too has exceptions:

said
paid
laid
daily

These four spelling rules are the primary ones that you need to know to improve your spelling. A number of spelling problems, however, were covered under other topics in earlier chapters. If you have spelling trouble related to any of these, you may want to refer to the appropriate chapter.

1. Confusion between contractions and possessives (for example, *its* vs. *it's*): Chapter 17, Part D (pages 376–377).

2. Difficulty forming plurals of nouns (for example, *two wives*): Chapter 13, Parts A and B (pages 282–289).

3. Confusing similar words (for example, *then* vs. *than* or *effect* vs. *affect*): Chapter 18 (pages 382–399).

Index

A/an/and, 389–393
Accept/except, 388
Adverbial conjunctions. *See* Conjunctive adverbs
Affect/effect, 386
Agreement, pronouns. *See* Pronouns, agreement
Agreement, subject-verb. *See* Subject-verb agreement
All right/alright, 393
A lot/alot, 393
Also, 193
And, 131, 185
Antecedents, 338–339
Apostrophes, 362–379
As a result, 193
Assertions, 248–262
Audience, 13–15
Awkwardness, 409–421

Backward outlines, 169–172, 216–226
Brainstorming, 7–8, 162–163, 206–215
Break/brake, 383
But, 131, 185

Capitalization, 289–296
Choice of words, 382–397
Clauses, dependent
  distinguished from independent clauses, 125–126, 131
  punctuating, 234–238

Clauses, independent
  commas and coordinating conjunctions, 179–185
  commas with, 173–185
  identifying, 120–131
  punctuating, 173–197
  semicolons with, 191–197
Clauses, subordinate. *See* Clauses, dependent
Coherence, 267–272
Commands, 50, 54
Comma splices, 175–176, 179
Commas
  with conjunctive adverbs, 192, 197
  with coordinating conjunction, 179–185
  with dates, 357–358
  with dependent clauses, 234–238
  with independent clauses, 179–185
  with introductory clauses, 234–238
  with introductory elements, 227–238
  with introductory phrases, 227–234
  with places, 356–357
  with series, 354–356
Complex sentences, 62–63
Compound sentences, 61–62, 64
Concise language. *See* Wordiness
Concrete details, 110–119
Confusing words, 382–397
Conjunctions. *See* Coordinating conjunctions

Conjunctive adverbs, 191–197
Consequently, 193
Consistency
  of point of view, 272–275
  of tense, 275–281
Contractions, 374–375
Contractions/possessives, 375–378, 395–397
Coordinating conjunctions
  defined, 131, 185
  punctuation with, 179–185
Could have/could of, 394
Course/coarse, 387

Dangling modifiers, 418, 420–421
Dates, commas with, 357–358
Definition, 216
Demonstrative pronouns, 334, 338
Dependent clauses. *See* Clauses, dependent
Dessert/desert, 387
Development, 248–266. *See also* Concrete details
Diction, 382–397
Dictionary entries for irregular verbs, 317–318, 321–322, 326
Dictionary, locating words, 427–430

Effect/affect, 386
Evidence, 248–266
Except/accept, 388

False humility, 403–404
Finally, 193
Fine/find, 385
For, 131, 185
For example, 193
Fragments
  correcting, 135–151
  identifying, 131–134
Freewriting, 8
Furthermore, 193
Future perfect tense, 305, 312–314

Generalizations, 248–262
Gerunds. *See* Verbals

Here/hear, 382–383
Homophones, 382–385
However, 192–193, 197

Imperative sentences, 50, 54
In addition, 193
Indeed, 193
Indefinite pronouns, 331–333, 337, 368, 372
Independent clauses. *See* Clauses, independent
In fact, 193
Infinitive phrases, punctuating, 227–230, 233–234
Infinitives. *See* Verbals
Instead, 193
Interrogative pronouns, 333–334, 337–338

Introductory elements, punctuating, 227–238
Irregular verbs, 314–326
Items in a series, 354–356
Its/it's, 376–377, 378–379, 395–397

Knew/new, 383
Know/no, 383

Linking verbs, 31–32, 41–42
List making, 206–215
Lose/loose, 386

Meanwhile, 193
Mine/mind, 385–386
Modifiers
  dangling, 418, 420–421
  misplaced, 417–421
  squinting, 419, 421

Nevertheless, 193
New/knew, 383
No/know, 383
Nor, 131, 185
Nouns
  capitalization of, 289–296
  irregular, 285–289
  possessives of, 362–374
  singular and plural, 282–289

Of course, 193
Opinion, 403–404
Or, 131, 185
Organization, 205–226
Outline, backward, 169–172
Outlines, 205–206

Paragraphs, 68–80
  unity, 76–79
Parallelism, 409–417
Participial phrases, punctuating, 227–229, 233
Participles. *See* verbals
Past/passed, 383
Past perfect tense, 304–305, 309–312
Past tense, 314–321, 325–326
Patience/patients, 384
Perfect tenses
  future, 305, 312–314
  past, 304–305, 309–312
  present, 302–304, 306–309
Periods, 134
Personal pronouns, 330–331, 336
Personnel/personal, 384
Planning, 3–19, 112, 157–167, 205–216
Plural of nouns, 282–289
Point of view, 272–275
Possessive pronouns, 331, 336–337
Possessives, 362–374
  forming, 367–374
  recognizing, 362–367
Possessives/contractions, 375–378, 395–397

Prepositional phrases, 47–48, 52–53, 100–101, 105–106
    punctuating, 227–228, 230–231, 233
Present perfect tense, 302–304, 306–309
Present tense, 81–82, 88–89
Prewriting. *See* planning
Pronoun agreement, 342–350
    with compound antecedents, 343–344, 348–349
    with indefinite pronoun antecedents, 344–346, 349–350
Pronouns, 330–350
    demonstrative, 334, 338
    identifying, 330–338
    identifying antecedents, 338–339
    indefinite, 331–333, 337, 368, 372
    interrogative, 333–334, 337–338
    person of, 272–275
    personal, 330–331, 336
    possessive, 331, 336–337
    reference, 339–342
    reflexive, 334–335, 338
    relative, 333–334, 337–338
    wh- words, 333–334, 337–338
Proofreading, 19, 26
Punctuation. *See* Commas, Semicolons, Periods
Purpose, 16–19

Questions, 35–36, 43
Quit/quite/quiet, 387

Reference of pronouns, 339–342
Reflexive pronouns, 334–335, 338
Relative pronouns, 333–334, 337–338
Revising, 19–26, 76–78, 112–114, 167–172, 216–226
Run-on sentences, 173–175, 178

Semicolons
    to join independent clauses, 185–197
    with conjunctive adverbs, 191–197
Sentence fragments, 131–151
Sentences
    complex, 62–63, 125–126, 131
    compound, 61–62, 64, 124–125, 131
Series, items in, 354–356
Sexist language, 347–348
Should have/should of, 393
So, 131, 185
Spelling, 426–438
Squinting modifiers, 419, 421
Still, 193
Subject of an essay. *See* Topic
Subject of paragraph, 69–70
Subject-verb agreement, 81–106
    with compound subjects, 102–103, 106
    with *do* and *does,* 94–95, 99
    with *have* and *has,* 92–93, 99
    with helping verbs, 95–97, 99–100
    simple, 81–90

    with intervening prepositional phrases, 100–101, 105–106
    with inverted word order, 101, 106
    with irregular verbs, 90–100
    with *is, are,* and *am,* 90–91, 99
    with *was* and *were,* 314–321, 325–326
Subjects of sentences
    in commands, 50, 54
    compound, 48–49, 53
    in imperative sentences, 50, 54
    with intervening prepositional phrases, 47–48, 52–53
    with inverted word order, 49, 53–54
    with more than one clause, 61–64
    in simple sentences, 43–54
    with verbals, 54–61
    with verbals as subjects, 57, 61
    you understood, 50, 54
Subordinate clauses. *See* Clauses, dependent
Support, 248–266
Supposed to/suppose to, 393

Telling details, 116–119
Tense, 300–327
    consistency, 275–281
    future, 300–302
    future perfect, 305, 312–314
    past, 314–321, 325–326
    past perfect, 304–305, 309–312
    perfect, 302–314
    present, 81–82, 88–89
    present perfect, 302–304, 306–309
Their/they're, 376–377, 378–379, 395–397
Then, 193
Then/than, 386
Therefore, 193
Thesis, 157–172
Thus, 193
Topic, 6–13
    narrowing, 11–12
    sentence, 68–76
To/too, 384
Transitions, 267–272
Try to/try and, 393

Unity, 76–79, 167–172, 223–225
Used to/use to, 393

Vague language. *See* Concrete details
Verbals, 54–61
Verbs
    action, 27–31, 39–40
    auxiliary, 33, 42
    future perfect tense, 305, 312–314
    future tense, 300–302
    helping, 33, 42
    irregular, 314–326
    linking, 31–32, 41–42
    past perfect tense, 304–305, 309–312
    past tense, 314–321, 325–326
    perfect tenses, 302–314
    present perfect tense, 302–304, 306–309

Verbs (*cont.*)
    present tense, 81–82, 88–89
    tense, 275–281, 300–327

Was, 314–316, 325–326
Weather/whether, 386
Were, 314–316, 325–326
Were/we're/wear/where, 387
Whose/who's, 395–397
Wh- words, 333–334, 337–338

Word choice, 382–397
Wordiness, 400–404
Would have/would of, 393
Writing process, 3–6

Yet, 131, 185
Your/you're, 376–377, 378–379, 395–397
You understood, 50, 54